Indian Roots

of American Democracy

Edited and with Introduction by
José Barreiro

AKWE:KON PRESS
Cornell University
Ithaca, New York

Designed and edited by Susan R. Dixon
Production editing by Jennifer Bedell

Akwe:kon Press, Cornell University
Ithaca, NY 14853

First Edition published by the *Northeast Indian Quarterly*, Cornell
University, 1988.

Library of Congress Cataloging in Publication Data

Indian Roots of American Democracy / edited and with
    introduction by José Barreiro
        p.   cm.
    ISBN 1-881178-00-5
        1. Iroquois Indians--Philosophy. 2. Iroquois Indians--
Politics and government. 3. United States--Politics and
government--1775-1783   I. Barreiro, José
E99.I7I385   1992
323.1 ' 1975--dc20   92-25144

Contents

The Law Is in the Seed

Alex Jacobs/Karoniaktatie

The Law is in the Corn
the people of the southwest say this...
to be there with the morning star in that sacred time...
to talk to the corn, to hear it talk in the wind
in the language of movement...what to do.
Out here at the Eastern Door, we say, it is
the Original Instructions,
but also that a sacred thing happened when we were
given the Great Law for we had forgotten
the Original Instructions...
when crooked men arise and become dictators,
murderers, thiefs, cannibals...
The people would take the seed and move
to plant their Corn in a new place,
once again under the shelter of the Tree of Peace,
This is called Democracy,
it is in the land, it is in the seed.

The Law Is In The Corn
The Law Is In The Seed.

Inspired by two films: *HOPI: Songs of the Fourth World* and
ONENHAKRENA: White Seed (Corn and Culture Among the Mohawk)

Foreword

The Honorable Daniel K. Inouye (D-Hawaii) is chairman of the Senate Select Committee on Indian Affairs and a distinguished senior lawmaker. He has been an advocate for the recognition of the American Indian contribution to American democracy. On September 16, 1987, four days following the Cornell Conference, "The Iroquois Great Law of Peace and the United States Constitution," Senator Inouye introduced Senate Concurrent Resolution S. 76 to commemorate the Iroquois' early advice to the American founding fathers and to reaffirm the government-to-government relationship. On December 2, the Indian Committee hosted several Indian affairs scholars, including Onondaga Chief Oren Lyons, Lakota author Vine DeLoria, Jr., Lumbee attorney Arlinda Locklear and professors Donald Grinde and Gregory Schaaf, to testify on the bill. The following excerpts are from Senator Inouye's remarks at both events and in conversation with *Northeast Indian Quarterly* editors.

Senator Inouye:

If one studies the early history of United States-Indian relations, one finds that in the early days, 200 years ago, the United States Congress considered the relationship to be extremely important. Congress had a standing committee made up of many of its most important members. They had special debates in the constitutional conventions on Indian relations. Even in the White House, they had men who were conversant on Indian problems. The relationship was obviously equal. No question as to sovereignty.

With the passage of time, this relationship of respect changed. And, of course, one can see the reason. In the early days, Indians were found to be necessary to maintain the well-being of the United States. Would they be allies or enemies of the United States? This was a crucial question. They provided food and resources important to the very existence of Americans. But when the non-Indians began to organize and to outnumber and to intimidate, the importance of Indians became less and less. The treatment of the Indian became terrible.

I think that as we celebrate the Constitution bicentennial, we should realize that our Constitution came into being, in many ways, because of Indian contributions. George Washington and Benjamin Franklin, in several papers, spoke with great admiration, great awe, over the skill with which the leaders of the Iroquois nations were able to maintain the sovereignty of each nation, but yet were able to form a confederacy and serve as a unit. This gave our Founding Fathers the idea of the federal-state relationship.

Now we must also speak of our trust relationship, the ongoing government-to-government relationship that we have with Indian nations and tribes throughout this land. Many of my colleagues join me in introducing S. 76 to commemorate the bicentennial of the drafting and signing of the United States Constitution, and to acknowledge the great contribution made to our nation by the ancestors of the Iroquois.

Introduction:

The Persistence of Culture

José Barreiro

The cultural and spiritual beliefs of the Haudenosaunee (the Onondaga, Seneca, Mohawk, Cayuga, Oneida, and Tuscarora) signal deep concepts and systems of knowledge on everything from ecology to governance. By maintaining their ancient traditions, the Haudenosaunee have been a model for other Native peoples, who are faced with the desire to retain their ancient cultures and yet to adapt, survive, even thrive, in a world shaped by Eurocentric expansions. The need to synthesize, to assimilate the trappings of the European model and yet not lose one's own identity and culture, is the reality of the Indian world.

The miracle is, to paraphrase Mohawk spokesman Tom Porter, a contributor to this volume, that for all the destruction (and self-destruction) caused by Eurocentric impositions, core families and clans of Indian culture and thinking have persisted in putting forth studied perception, remembered history and cosmological worldview. Generation after generation, in small doses, Native elders and spokespeople have carried these messages to the non-Indian population of North America and Europe.

Truly remarkable about the Iroquois has been the consistency of their message, which asserts the continued existence of a base of governance and nationality that predates contact with Europe. This most powerful system of perception and symbol is embodied in the comprehensive oral tradition known as the Great Law of Peace (*Kayanesha 'Kowa* in Mohawk), which informs the workings of the Iroquois clanmothers and their councils of chiefs. Its teaching of the White Roots of Peace has been the basis of efforts by Iroquois statesmen to educate Europeans and other peoples. Thus, in 1921, at the League of Nations, a traditional Iroquois chief, Deskaheh, delivers a message from his Cayuga nation, underscoring the right of small nations of the world to exist and be respected. Thus, in 1924, the Iroquois Grand Council refuses the offer of United States citizenship; in 1934, it refuses the Indian Reorganization Act; in 1950, it is represented at the founding of the United Nations, and; through the 1960s and 1970s, it sends delegations to intellectual and international political forums (United Nations), again, to reassert the right of Native traditional peoples to represent themselves among the nations of the world. The persistence of their activities have gained for the Iroquois contemporary Grand Council recognition as a spearhead for the establishment of the U.N. Permanent Working Group on Indigenous Populations, a precursor to the development of an international covenant on the protections and rights of Indigenous populations. This is no small achievement. Asserts Onondaga elder Oren Lyons, another contributor, "We have faced off with the white man for three hundred years and right from the beginning he has learned much from us. He just doesn't want to admit it."

A memory that has been told and retold among Haudenosaunee traditionals holds that in the formative days of the American republic, statesmen from the still powerful Iroquois Confederacy informed prominent colonists, including some of the Founding Fathers, on Indian concepts of democracy as embodied in their Great Law of Peace. In recent years, a number of historians have pointed out that the Iroquois, as the most powerful Native nation to confront the incoming European powers, engaged in countless councils with colonists. They contend, as do the Iroquois elders, that in these councils, Indians tried to teach American colonists how to behave in this new land and that they transferred some of their own culture's most cherished values to the newcomers.

Among the historians, Drs. Donald Grinde and Bruce Johansen have published important histories on the subject. Others, such as professor and novelist Bruce Burton, historian Dr. Robert Venables and attorney Robert Coulter, have conducted exhaustive research into specific questions about the colonial period while working on projects in their own fields. On the Indian side, it has been John Mohawk, as well as Iroquois spokesman Oren Lyons, Mohawk chiefs Jake Swamp and Tom Porter, Onondaga clanmother Audrey Shenandoah and the Iroquois Tadodaho, Chief Leon Shenandoah, who have been most prominent this decade in posing the question of Indian influence. Lyons, who has been profiled by Bill Moyers and in the *National Geographic* and the *New York Times Magazine,* has said, "It has been a difficult question to raise, but I think we are starting to get through."

CORNELL CONFERENCE

In the fall of 1987, on the occasion of the celebration of the Bicentennial of the United States Constitution, Cornell University's American Indian Program and its journal, *Akwe:kon (Northeast Indian Quarterly)* sought to explore the historical reality of that Indian oral memory. In light of the Iroquois assertions that during treaty meetings in the 1700s their chiefs admonished colonists to unite, particularly around the events of the 1754 Plan of Albany, we invited here a number of scholars working on the topic. As 1987 marked the Bicentennial of the United States Constitution, and as the 1754 Albany Plan of Union is historically accepted as a precedent to the writing of the United States Constitution, it seemed proper to pursue their findings. The question posed: What has been the legacy and influence of the Iroquois Great Law of Peace and other genuine Indian constructs on the United States system of government and on the general philosophy of democracy in America?

That conference, "The Iroquois Great Law of Peace and the United States Constitution," results of which were published in the first edition of *Indian Roots of American Democracy,* touched off an ongoing debate on the historiography of northeastern Indian peoples and on the question of whether there is, in fact, a basis for the contention of influence by American Indians on the formative processes of the American government.

The discussion has traveled to a number of other professional conferences, to the pages of Native studies journals, newspapers and radio and into several books. Long sessions were devoted to it in Philadelphia, on the occasion of the Constitution Bicentennial, at the annual Ethnohistory Conference, held in Chicago, November 1988 and at the Iroquoian scholars meeting, held in Rensselaer in October 1989. The debate has been the focus of articles in publications as varied as the *Philadelphia Inquirer,* the *Syracuse Post Standard,* the *National Enquirer,* the *National Geographic, Ethnohistory,* the *American Indian Culture and Research Journal* (UCLA) and the *New Republic.* Two books, one of essays from several noted scholars of Indian history and law, *Exiled in The*

Land of the Free: Democracy, Indian Nations and the U.S. Constitution, edited by John Mohawk and Oren Lyons (SUNY-Buffalo) and another one written by Drs. Bruce Johansen and Donald Grinde, titled *Exemplar of Liberty: Native America and the Evolution of American Democracy,* have since been published on the subject.

The 1987 forum also touched a nerve in the Native communities. Many Indian tribal organizations responded. The conference itself drew some 400 participants, including a hundred Indian people and many academics. There were registrants from Maryland, Massachusetts, Quebec, Texas and California. Later, several other college programs and student clubs sponsored similar programs. The United States Senate's Committee on Indian Affairs, chaired by Senator Daniel K. Inouye (D-Hawaii), held hearings on the event.

ORAL TRADITION

An important related question had to do with the validity of oral tradition, its accuracy and dependability, and how it compared to the written tradition of the West. At one session, Steve Fadden (Mohawk), an instructor in the Department of Communication, framed the question for the three dozen early participants during an informal discussion. Fadden pointed out the difference between pen and paper as tools to record agreements and the use of wampum belts as mnemonic devices by the oral tradition, "where people are trained to remember what they hear." Fadden described a common communications exercise, called "the Gossip Game," that supposedly demonstrates the eroding accuracy of information as it transfers orally through successive retellings. This exercise is frequently used in academia as an argument against the strength of the oral tradition.

Billy Two Rivers, a Mohawk spokesman from Kanawake Reserve near Montreal, Canada, asked to speak. Having been raised in an oral tradition, he said he had to disagree with the "gossip" idea of oral tradition. "When you are handed down an oral tradition," he said, "it's coming from your family, parents and grandparents. There is a feeling of legitimacy and truth in what is being passed down to you."

This is an Indian perspective, Two Rivers said, so the opposite viewpoint of the validity of the written tradition is held. "In the early writings about Indians, there were many distortions. And there was no one to correct them. The people who came from a generation or two afterward took that as the truth, and consequently the written word that we get to this day comes through a counterfeit or distorted route." Two Rivers stressed that many factual items can still be verified "to this day, through Indian nations where the oral tradition is still alive."

Charlotte Heth, Cherokee ethnomusicologist, spoke about studying Indian songs recorded as early as 1883. Where the particular Indian tradition was still current, she said, "you will find that the songs fundamentally don't change—you may find one maybe a little bit faster or a couple of words dropped out—something of that nature, but basically they do not change. Singers have incredible memories. If you go back and compare their songs to the early recordings, they are near to exactly like they were. I think those of you that grew up in the oral tradition know that the things that you remember in your own head stick with you longer than the things you read on paper."

In a similar vein, Elwood Green, Mohawk artist and director of The Turtle—Native American Center for the Living Arts in Niagara Falls, spoke about the need to understand why oral tradition is a formalized way of passing on cultural knowledge. "It should not be confused with gossip, at least not the way our traditional people utilize this. The analogy about someone telling a story, then the story being told again and again so that by the time it gets to a dozen people it is totally changed—that really cannot happen among a traditional use of the oral memory. The reason for this is because there is a built-in framework in the culture; it is not told as loose gossip." Green contrasted that to the level of imagination used in written history, where the historian or researcher cannot possibly know all the facts. "Historians," he said, "put together as much as they can of a story and then have to try and fill in what is probable. The Indian oral tradition, on the other hand, is very exacting."

Green pointed to passages in the work of colonial historian Francis Parkman, where Parkman mentions the words to the "chiefs' roll call," where the fixed titles of the fifty Haudenosaunee *royaner* are written. The ways of speaking in that 100 year old text can still be heard, exactly, in the Longhouse protocol. He also cited an 1825 book written by a Tuscarora, Nicholas Cusick. "Many of the terminologies he uses are still in use today. A non-traditional historian may miss something like that.

"Whether or not an oral tradition is valid as a written tradition would depend on who does the oral tradition. If it is done in a manner such as the Iroquois have done it for hundreds and thousands of years, then yes, it is accurate. That is proven out by the continuity of our ceremonies, that existed then and today. In our language, there is only one way to say something. You can't give an ambiguous statement. So, it would have to be accurate."

Another question of interest for the audience was on the denial of Indian cultural validity. "Why," one man asked, "has there not been more major research done about Indian influence?" Longhouse traditional chief Ron LaFrance answered this way: "They—

anthropologists, archaeologists, historians—have always viewed our societies and our systems as being very simplistic," LaFrance said, explaining the intricacy of the ceremonial life of the Iroquois: "Just the condolence ceremony, when they put up the new chiefs, requires many cultural technicians, so that it is done accordingly."

To wrap up the session, Fadden asked John Mohawk to speak on the traditions behind the use of wampum as memory devices. On ten seconds notice, Mohawk, who is uniquely positioned as a scholar raised in the Longhouse tradition, provided a distinctive example of extemporaneous Iroquois oratory. As the discussion ended, the group called for more Indian efforts at producing curricula and for more projects geared to educating the national society about Indian realities.

CONTROVERSY

The contention of influence, based on the record of proximity and substantive contact by colonists and their Indian neighbors, as well as on actual references by various founding fathers to the forms of American Indian society, has been challenged by several scholars who have argued that the record does not show a cause and effect, or causal link, proving definitively an influence on the framers of the United States Constitution by the Iroquois sachems and their Great Law of Peace.

Most prominent among critics of the proposition of influence are Drs. William Starna (SUNY-Oneonta) and William Axtell (William and Mary), anthropologist and historian respectively, and Dr. Elisabeth Tooker (Temple University), a senior anthropologist and author of the "Iroquois Ceremonial of Midwinter." Tooker's review of the idea can be found in "United States Constitution and the Iroquois League," *Ethnohistory*, XXXV, 4 (Fall 1988). Starna and Axtell have communicated their disagreements more through radio and newspaper reporters and Starna in a letter opposing the inclusion of the position in a curriculum guide currently in preparation at the New York State Education Department. Tooker concedes that there was cognizance of the confederation by the colonists, but not enough knowledge about the workings of the League to have real influence.

Axtell stresses the lack of a causal link in the pro-influence evidence. He argues that the colonists "did not emulate the Indians so much as form our character against them, by fighting them as enemies...." In an interview with radio producer Catherine Stifter, Axtell says: "The Americans needed to cultivate these people [Indians], bring them to Philadelphia, talk in the treaty language of the day, the diplomatic metaphors, talk about friendship and brotherhood and so on. It doesn't mean they are emulating the Iroquois constitution. On the contrary, they are trying to build a very European style civilization in this neck of the woods and they want to essentially get rid of Indians eventually."

Axtell, author of *The Invasion Within: The Contest of Cultures in Colonial North America*, also questions the validity of comparing the United States Constitution to a version of the Iroquois Great Law of Peace codified in the late 1800s, an approach advocated by Professor Greg Schaaf and published by the Mohawk newspaper, *Akwesasne Notes*. The codification of the Iroquois Constitution in itself, according to Axtell, was a result of influence from the United States Constitution. "Just the opposite has happened," he tells Ms. Stifter. "The Iroquois Constitution has taken many elements from the United States Constitution.... The influence worked almost exactly the opposite from the way that these people are arguing."

Starna echoes some of both Tooker and Axtell's arguments. There is a big question as to whether the Iroquois system was "well enough known so that it could then be applied to the precepts of the American Constitution," he states, pointing to Dr. William Fenton's comment that the Iroquois system of government was not well discerned prior to Lewis Henry Morgan in the 1850s. Starna compares the assertion of Iroquois influence to the story of George Washington chopping down the cherry tree. He calls the notion an "obscure" academic issue and is unconvinced by references to the Iroquois' "Covenant Chain," which, he feels, "has nothing to do with the Iroquois Constitution." Finally, it is historian Axtell who closes in with the argument that the whole notion of influence is "reinvented history," an attempt by contemporary Iroquois to "hoodwink" politicians into granting them more political recognition and clout. Axtell's is an interesting perception, identifying the Indian representation in the present and joining historical arguments to current political camps.

CONTINUITY

A contemporary people with a living culture, the Iroquois maintain not only the assertion of influence, but, as professor Richard Hill, Tuscarora, points out, they assert a continuity of government and assume the legal validity of aboriginal jurisprudence, a serious and transcendental position. As has been pointed out, in the company of Hopi, Lakota and other traditional peoples, Iroquois spokespeople continue to be prominent in the international arena, holding seats, for instance, at the Global Forum of Parliamentary and Spiritual Leaders and at the United States Working Group on Indigenous Affairs. Iroquois spokespeople are often chosen at Native people's gatherings to represent the Indigenous positions to the family of nations. The reasons for such positioning by this small nation of Native people with little economic base and no standing army include a remarkable oratorical tradition and a clear cultural mandate to pursue international goals. Iroquois worldview, its attendant ideology and rhetoric, has significantly elevated and impacted the hemispheric and international discussion on Indigenous and natural world rights.

The present volume, a second edition, does not attempt to cover the material in contrapuntal form. Rather it focuses on the presentations at the 1987 conference and includes further research by the conference presenters and other scholars on the nature and record of influence by the Iroquois and other eastern Native nations upon various aspects of American life. Among the new contributors, lawyer Paul Williams details oral and written traditions surrounding the wampum belts, professor and novelist Bruce Burton reviews Squanto and the origins of the New England Town Meeting and South Dakota historian, Dr. Sally Roesch Wagner, reviews the record of contact and influence of women's leadership in Iroquois political custom on the 19th century founders of the women's rights movement. Twentieth century continuity is provided by Tuscarora scholar Richard Hill's article on the consistency of operations and statements emanating from the League up to the present, the presence in the volume of several statements by contemporary Haudenosaunee speakers and my own piece on the return of Haudenosaunee wampum belts to the Onondaga traditional council in 1989, after some ninety years of keeping by New York State. As before, many of the presentations in the volume are edited from recordings and transcriptions of talks, by both community people and academics, prepared and impromptu, bringing to the subject that "overlapping of edges" or reiteration that is the hallmark of oral tradition.

INFLUENCE

The formation of the world's most formidable nation-state and its largest democracy is necessarily a most important topic. What ideas, principles and perceptions informed the process and what precedent they all might have set is likely to encompass the accessible range of creative thinking in the search for solutions to many of today's pressing problems.

Along with many other Indigenous peoples, the Iroquois continue to hold other ethical yet pragmatic concepts within their traditions that could yet improve upon Western civilized life. One potential teaching that merits reflection is the message of the Great Law of Peace itself, that marvelous Indian document of representative democracy among kinship nations. The Great Law of Peace of the Iroquois is one of the fundamental messages of humankind. Dr. Tooker makes a good point in her article of rebuttal to the contention of influence when she says that the Great Law stands on its own and need not be compared with the United States institutions to be of interest. Certainly the pursuit of American Indian to Euroamerican influence should not overshadow an equally important focus: the Indigenous cultures of the Western Hemisphere, whose respectful exploration could yet yield a bold and transcending new paradigm for human activity on Earth.

Words That Come before All Else

Jacob Thomas

As is customary in Iroquois gatherings, the Cornell "Great Law of Peace and the United States Constitution" conference was begun with a recital of the Thanksgiving Address. This address, which can take several hours to recite, is an acknowledgement of the full circle of Creation. It is a central prayer among the Iroquois and considered a foundation to everything in the human life, including the Great Law of Peace. An ancient custom, the address is given to help human beings living in society to achieve what the Iroquois call "one-mindedness." From the basis of that perception, in the traditional Indian view, a human gathering can be set to work consensually toward unanimity. Iroquois elder and chief Jacob Thomas gave the address in the Cayuga language. Ron LaFrance, Mohawk Longhouse chief, briefly explained the message.

At our gatherings among the Iroquois people this salutation, or opening address, is always given and, in a way, is our preamble to our way of life, our society. The Thanksgiving Address acknowledges the whole universe.

We begin by acknowledging the people. We ask that we come together with peaceful thoughts, that we have not heard any words of any bad calamity or sudden deaths, and that we acknowledge each other as human beings. We ask that we come here with peace in our minds and good thoughts and that we extend greetings to each other. If you can look in your mind's eye, the address acknowledges the whole universe.

The next part deals with our Mother the Earth. It normally takes anywhere from a half hour to an hour and forty-five minutes if it is said in its entirety because everything is mentioned in there: all of the gifts that have been given to us by the Creator. As we go through it, we put all these acknowledgments in a bundle; all of the things that our Mother the Earth has given to us to sustain us, to make us strong through our daily lives.

After each passage there is a phrase that he says, and maybe some of the Iroquois folks sitting next to you sort of grunt, which means, "yes, I agree with what you are saying." It says that we are all in agreement, we still acknowledge all of the things that were given to us. We acknowledge each other as human beings; we acknowledge our Mother the Earth—all of the things that she has given us.

We talk about the beings above our heads: the birds, the Four Winds that still continue in their duties, the Thunderers, our grandfathers that bring the rain. We appreciate that they still hold a balance, they freshen the waters, and they sustain us again, so that each cycle that the Creator has created for us has continued on and those are things that we acknowledge.

Towards the end, Mr. Thomas spoke about a man that delivered what we call the Third Message to the Iroquois. His name was Handsome Lake and we acknowledge the message he brought us, so that this activity, this preaching, still goes on. Next week there will be a meeting in Tonawanda, as there has been every fall for about the last 100 years, when they send the speakers out to the different Indian communities to talk about the message that Handsome Lake received. This is to sustain our people, because we are going through difficult times.

The last part thanks the Creator. In many of our nations we say that all the Creator wants is for us to acknowledge creation, that we try to remain peaceful not only between ourselves and among ourselves, but also in our minds and that we help the creation, that we protect it and that we nourish it. At the end Mr. Thomas reminds us that he was asked by the people to speak on our behalf, to deliver these words.

For many years I have heard, and many people here have heard, the same words by other speakers as they give the opening address. We start all of our functions this way and it sets a tone of agreement, not on every specific thing, but at least for peace in our minds, for keeping an open mind. We acknowledge the universe and each other and then we all agree to that.

Men Who Are of the Good Mind

Tom Porter

The word *chief* in our language means a position or office. We call it *royaner* and if there are many of them we call them *rotiianison*. If we take that word apart, what does it mean? It is coming from the root word *ioianere* which means, in English, nice or good. Then, when you put *io* at the beginning it means it is masculine or a man who is of the nice or of the good. And so that is literally, when translated into English, what Iroquois people think of their leaders—those men who are of the good.

In the history books, in the television shows, and in the documents that have been recorded, the intellectuals who have observed our people throughout the years, studied us and tried to communicate to the outside world what we are and how we think, were successful maybe fifty percent of the time but the other fifty percent of the time they were way off track. So, when you say anthropologist, archaeologist, or somebody who studied Iroquois, what we think, right away is, "Oh no! Not another one."

I know that it is supposed to be a high professional matter to have a Ph.D. with doctor this and doctor that, but to an Iroquois when you say those words, it doesn't mean that at all, it just means, "Oh no!" I don't make these remarks in any means to be degrading but merely to tell you, in fact, how an Iroquois thinks. So my apologies to anyone who has a Ph.D.

I would like to make, I guess, another clarification. Before I talk about leaders, *rotiianison*, which in English translates into chief, maybe we ought to expound upon that just a bit further. The word "chief" kind of makes you think of a fire chief or a kind of big man, but it is not at all what an Iroquois leader is. Perhaps that might be one of the first things attempted by the intellectual people of the world—that is to translate properly from one culture to another culture exactly what is meant and then there would be more grounds, and easier means by which peace could be achieved.

It is a wonder—I was thinking as I was sitting there and I was looking at all of you people, elder people, younger people, I think that it is a wonder—and I say this statement in the strongest of terms—that it is a wonder that of all of the things that have occurred in history, to the Iroquois people, it is a miracle that there are any people left in the Iroquois today—it is a miracle.

If any other people in this world had to go through what we have to go through, my grandfathers, myself and my children, and what is going to happen to my grandchildren if they come and that probably won't be too long, it is going to be a miracle again if we can still say "I am an Iroquois, a Mohawk, a Seneca, an Onondaga, a Cayuga, a Tuscarora, or an Oneida."

So, that is the first Mount Everest that we must recognize, just to be thankful that the Iroquois are still here and to be thankful of their great efforts over the years to retain their culture, to retain that language, to retain those clans, to retain those midwinters and the whole spiritual year of the Iroquois people. To give hope to their children when the outside world is such a big ocean of influence that every day makes waves that are as tall as the Empire State Building and we stand at its first floor door—it is a miracle.

And so it is in that way that I want to begin to speak to you today, this evening about the Iroquois. I do not proclaim in any way, to you or to anyone, that I know lots of things about the Iroquois, about the Mohawk. I am not a doctor, I am not a lawyer, I am not an engineer, I am none of those things. All I am is a young man who has children, who had a mother, a father just like you all did, a grandmother, and a grandfather, and uncles and aunts. I can remember and I can share the stories that I heard—the interpretations that I heard Grandma talking about, the stories that my Grandfather talked about, the stories and the histories that were carried by old chief Alec Grey, old faithkeeper Paul David who are now in the spirit world, who used to talk to us when we were just little kids in our longhouses.

I remember not too many people listened to them, really. I mean everybody paid respect and there was a command of obedience by everybody being quiet, but when I say not many really listened, I mean that it went in one ear and went out the other to many, many people. But, I remember in our longhouse, years ago, when I was just a kid—because Paul David was my grandfather and all of those old chiefs that are passed on, those leaders, those faithkeepers, they were always telling us, all our clans as we sat in those midwinter ceremonies, maple festivals, strawberry ceremonies, green corn ceremonies, harvest ceremonies—they used to tell us, we want you young people, my nephews and grandchildren, to pay attention every day to what's going on, we want you to listen when the faithkeepers are talking, we want you to listen when the chiefs are talking and making council.

We want you to pay attention, and put away in your body, what clan you belong to. We want you always to speak your language because all these ceremonies have to be spoken in our language, not English, French or German, or Yiddish, or any other language. It's got to be done in Mohawk, Cayuga, Seneca, Onondaga or whatever, because there are many things in this world that the English do not know or have a word for it—only Mohawks do because we have our own world that the Creator gave to us.

So those old guys taught us: you young people listen, when those singers come to sing, dance the feather dance or drum dance, or all the different ceremony dances or spiritual dances, we want you to listen to them when they are singing because one day it is going to come, and it will come very quickly. We who are speaking to you today, we'll be leaving this world, we will have ripened our humanity, and we will become old and it will be time for us to leave as it is the nature to do that way and then when we leave, it is up to you guys, you ladies to become the next ones to sit in those chairs. You will be the next ones who will sing the spiritual song for our people to the Creator.

It will be you young guys and girls who will be marrying the young men and women. It will be you people who will have to name the babies and bury the dead, and all those speeches that go with marriage, that go with burying of your dead, or to perform the different rituals of sickness through the different societies, all involve long speeches, very long speeches presented in organized fashion. The old people said, you must know what you are talking about in order that someone should get well, or if someone is going to get married. You must know what you are talking about so that their marriage will prevail and persevere for many years.

We just had, two weeks ago, in our longhouse in Akwesasne, our green corn dance and as we were sitting there in our longhouse, the people came there dressed up in their clothes, in the Mohawk clothes, moccasins, to give thanks to the green corn which will sustain us throughout the winter. As we sat there, that is what I thought about. I looked right over there in the north end of our longhouse and I saw, actually sitting there, those old chiefs that are passed on. And I looked to this east side and I saw the certain clan leaders and faith keepers still sitting there at our green corn and a great sadness came over and I remembered what they used to tell us as kids, and by golly, there we are singing those songs now, marrying those people so babies can come to the world and burying those of us, our people that have passed on and barely being able to do it the right way, and there we are.

And so it was very true what those old faithkeepers and old leaders told us and so I want you to know that too. When you talk, I'm going to tell you too, that I am not a chief. There are laws, very strict laws that our ancestors were given by the Creator. A great messiah was born, hundreds of years ago, that brought the Law of Peace to the Iroquois nations and that prophet, the messiah, performed wondrous miracles in his name to show the Iroquois nations that he, indeed, was a spiritual power. He had to do this because the Iroquois were a very stubborn people, as yet today it is still the same case. Maybe that is why we are still here.

But, at any rate, sometimes a man like myself will sit in Council for an old chief. The chief that I was sitting for, he passed away a year ago last February; he was ninety-seven years old. He sat as a chief in the Mohawk nation for over fifty-five years and he passed away. Before he passed away, for about sixteen years or seventeen years, I was sitting in his position on our Council in our nation in Akwesasne, because he was getting hard of hearing. Our Constitution of the Confederacy says that a leader must have full hearing, must have full eyesight, must have full physical ability of the body, must have his full faculties in order because they have a big responsibility and they need all those to meet that responsibility.

So he passed away a year ago February, probably one of the finest men that was ever born in this world. He was just a little man, but he was always kind no matter when you went there, he always fed you, he always made tea for you, and he always talked for a couple of hours and joked. But now, as he is no longer in that position, he has been buried, so there is no more subchief for him because there is no more there, he is dead. And so I was free of that position a year ago in February which I did hold for about sixteen to seventeen years. Then my clan put me back in there which, according to the Law, is not really supposed to be.

Audrey suggested a while ago that today in modern times we try to do whatever we can do to keep the ship afloat and sometimes what we want to do that isn't always what keeps it afloat. It sometimes sinks it. So I just wanted to make that clear that all I am today is an interpreter and helper to our chiefs in the Akwesasne Council. That's all I am is a helper.

But, let me now talk about what my grandmother told me about chiefs, what my grandfather told me, my uncles told me, what I heard Jake Thomas over the years talk about, what I heard old chiefs who are no longer here talk about to me. But I am going to tell you the honest truth that I am forty-three years old and I never heard our Great Law in my life from beginning to end and that's the truth, I never did. I did, however, hear from my Grandma some parts and interpretation of sections of it, and I heard my uncle say other sections of it, and I heard those old chiefs say other sections of it all through my life. And so maybe you might say that I probably heard the whole thing but not in order from a to z, but sometimes b to t back to b, but it all went through my head at some time or another in interpretations.

So let me tell you what Grandma talked about, and Audrey too, what she talked about. I am married to a Choctaw Indian from Philadelphia, Mississippi. I know that many of you here have a United States world and it's hard to understand and see beyond geographical boundaries of the United States of America. I know that the Iroquois are in the geographical boundary, too, but yet the world is different for us. But my marriage was matched up by my grandmother through spiritual means, and I've been told that ever since for many years, my grandmother did that through medicine—found my wife for me, through spiritual means. In order to understand Iroquois you've got to talk about Grandma too, and you've got to talk about all the old people that you knew. Otherwise, you are not telling about Iroquois because Iroquois means old grandmothers, old grandfathers, uncles and aunts, cousins, brothers and sisters and little kids running around. When you say Iroquois, it means all that.

So, Grandma, she used to wear an apron all the time, she had eleven kids, strong worker, wasn't afraid of nothing, a neat, neat woman. She spoke nothing but Mohawk, not a word of English, and she used to always smoke a pipe. Any time something happened, a problem or a little bit of confusion in the family or in our community, she would grab her pipe and she would grab her tobacco bag, and I am not talking about regular tobacco, I'm talking about special tobacco that the Iroquois nations all have, which we call our sacred tobacco or our ceremonial tobacco and she puts it in that pipe, and she used to sit on her rocking chair with her apron on and her pipe with that sacred tobacco, and the whole house would get full with smoke and she would, what you would say in English, pray. She would request from the powers of the Creator's world a help to get us through this calamity or this problem whatever it was and that's how I remember Grandma. You couldn't keep a secret from her, I don't care what you did.

Well, anyway, this is what she said. She found my wife for me and we have four kids now and she is a really good woman. I think my own thinking and I don't care if anybody agrees with me. It doesn't matter, but this is the way I think. I wrote an article not too long ago about it because they asked me to at home, about men and women, about marriages, this so-called fifty-fifty proposition—I think it's a bunch of baloney! It always was, and it always will be; there's no such thing as a fifty-fifty proposition. I am going to tell it's my opinion as a Mohawk man that a woman, in marriage or otherwise, pulls at least eighty percent of the work and the responsibilities on this earth, twenty percent maybe to the men, if they are lucky. So women anywhere in this world, I will honor them. I will be the most grateful to the women of this world because I know that is a fact, and how do I know that? Because I am married to a wonderful woman and my mother was a wonderful woman, and my aunts were wonderful women and I knew them for many years and I know what they do. No man can match their stamina and their endurance and their kindness. So to the women all here, I give you my honor and when you leave here tonight and you rejoin your families, extend these greetings to those women who are at home.

Now, this is what grandma said. A chief, a *royaner*, what does this mean? He who is of the good mind is this. You must look when the kids are small. You start to look at them, she said, when they are little ones, even just little babies. Is that baby mean? Does he have a mean streak in him like an outburst, impatient, does he get angry fast? Is he possessive in his infancy? Does he pull his toys or whatever he has away from others? The women leaders look at that when they are going to choose men leaders when they grow up. So, they start when they are little kids, to start to read if that human being is, indeed, going to grow up to be a full-fledged leader, so they start when they are little boys and they watch them carefully.

And then, over the years as they are growing up they watch their behavior too. How do they interact with others growing up? How do they interact with their old people? Then they grow up. Do they like to go to the ceremonies at the longhouse? Do they like to do the midwinter game there? Do they belong to this kind of society or whatever? What do they do, are they spiritually connected to this world? That's all taken into consideration; that's what my grandmother said.

Then, when that young man becomes a man, if he's going to become a leader, my grandmother said, the old law says he has to have a clan which you get from your mother and your father has a clan, a different kind of clan and then that's when you're born you have two clans, one from your mother and one from your father's side. There's a term in our language we call for that, but you have to have two: one is your mother's side, one is your father's side, and they have got to be different clans. Then that makes a good candidate to become a leader because it means his bloodline is free from incest or inbreeding.

Then she said that a chief, he has to be married. Before he is a leader he has got to be married first and have children; then he has some qualifications to become a leader. He must be a man who never likes to fight, or to hurt somebody, that is the kind of man who has to be a leader. The reason he has to be married and have children is because that is where the natural kindness of one's heart is exposed or shown to the world or to the community or to the nation. When he has children a natural love occurs. But if a man were to be chosen to become a leader who was not married or did not have children how is he going to love his country? How is he going to love his people? He will not know how to do it, it's too risky.

She said that this man, he must never have killed anyone, never have been a killer; whether it was a war or anything, he cannot have been involved with that. And then when he is to become a leader, there is no such thing as nine to five in that leader's life. Our leaders are considered to be the same as the King of England, the same as the prime minister of any country, the same as the president of any country, or whatever leadership title you want to put on him, regardless of what kind of society, our leaders are considered like that.

So, any time any of the people, my grandma said, needs the advice of the leaders, even if it was two o'clock in the morning and something critical happened to them, that person can go to that chief's house. Two o'clock-three o'clock in the morning, they're all sleeping [he makes the sound of someone knocking on the door] and that chief, a real chief is going to get up, he's going to open that door, and he's going to see that person who has a problem and who is in trouble, and then that chief is going to open that door. Then he'll make some tea or coffee, or something to give to them and then he'll say *Ta sa ta we iat*, come in. That means it must be a very important issue what brings you here, or what you're bringing here. Have a chair over here, let us talk. Then he is going to talk to that person even if it is three o'clock in the morning. That's a real leader, that's a real president, that's a real head of nation of people, and that's part of Iroquois leadership.

An Iroquois leader must know how to speak, and not be bashful. He has to be able to speak loud and clear so everybody can hear. He has to know how to talk about the marriage, about the midwinter, about the spiritual things. And if he has to talk to the President of the United States or the Prime Minister of Canada, or I don't know what Russia calls their leader, but Mr. Gorbachev, the leader has to be able to do those things, political and spiritual. Because in the Iroquois world there is no such thing as political leaders and over here you have your spiritual leaders, no such thing. Everything is together—spiritual and political—because when the Creator, whoever the Creator is, made this world, he touched the world all together, and it automatically became spiritual and everything that comes from that world is spiritual and so that's what leaders are, they are both the spiritual mentors and the political mentors of the people.

And those leaders are just that, what it says, *rotiianison*, those men who are *of the good*. That is the best that I can summarize to you, and it is true, no matter when anybody has a problem they are going to go see the leaders, day or night. No matter how small the problem, you never say, come back another day, I got a headache. No, they are first. That's why they say when leaders are put up then they start to carry the biggest load in the world on their shoulders. And they are the ones, my grandmother said, who are the real leaders.

She used to say—I like to remember the way she used to talk about it—she said if you were to recall in the old, old people's telling of the chiefs or leaders, those leaders are the most humble ones. They are the poorest people of all of the nation because they are always giving, always giving, always giving—materially, psychologically, spiritually, and politically of themselves to all the people of the nation. They are always giving.

And so consequently, when you go into a community, you will know where the chiefs live because they will have the smallest, the most humble house of any in the whole nation, and that is how you will know where there is a leader. I don't want to continue much longer; time is going on and there are many great speakers here, but I want to thank you for affording me this short time to tell you how proud I am about my grandmother, my wife, the old faithkeepers, and the old leaders of our clans who are not here anymore. I just hope we have the guts to go on. Thank you.

The Indian Way Is a
Thinking Tradition

John Mohawk

As this evening got under way, it dawned on me that something happened this evening that for twenty years I have studiously avoided and that is following Tom Porter.

I want to underline something that he was saying—I think it is very important. Sometimes when I go out and talk, I am introduced as a faithkeeper or something. I'm not; I don't have any title, and when Tom was talking, he was reminding me how lucky I am that I don't, because the people beat up on the chiefs and the clanmothers.

I think it takes lots and lots of courage and determination to hold one of those positions, because in the Iroquois traditions when he talks about carrying a load, the chiefs are supposed to have skin seven thumbs thick, and I don't think it means the width of the thumb, it means the length of the thumb because the chiefs really have to withstand a great deal of criticism and an awful lot of pressure from the people. And we know, not everyone can do that. It takes a great deal of determination and an awful lot of understanding to carry out the rules that the traditional leaders are required to. It is fortunate that our world still has people who are willing to do that kind of a job.

I want to talk a little bit this evening about how our worlds got to be the way they are. To do that we have to have some little inkling of how our worlds once were.

I believe that we are living in a world that is a product of a confluence of two other worlds, and we share that reality. We live in a variety of situations and perspectives on our contemporary reality, and people who live in the Iroquois reality have their own understanding of it. And even from community to community, people's realities are a little bit different. But, generally speaking, our population of North America lives in a world which is a result of a confluence of two worlds, and we seem to know so little about the previous worlds. We know so little about what this world is really about, what its roots are. I want to spend a little bit of time talking about that because I think tomorrow they are going to spend some time talking about the specifics. I want to spend some time talking about generalities. So, I am going to talk about each world separately for a couple of minutes and then we'll talk about the confluence.

Back during the medieval times, there was once a great debate that arose in Europe; some of you might have heard about it. It was a debate that sought to answer the question of how many teeth are to be found in a horse's mouth. This debate lasted for years. The great scholars of the great universities of Europe met and discussed it and papers were passed, and I am sure Ph.D.s were earned. The discussion went on and on while the scholars sought the body of knowledge that held the answer to all of humanity's questions. They searched the writings of the Greek and Roman scholars of antiquity, the philosophers, and then they searched the holy scriptures. They were the legitimate sources for understanding the world in the 14th and 15th centuries and this is where people went to look for the answers. After a considerable and vigorous search they concluded that it was not possible to discover the number of teeth in a horse's mouth because it had never been placed in the body of information that stood as human knowledge.

Then, we all know, in 1492 Columbus sailed the ocean blue and he discovered, they heard, Indians. But, we all know he didn't reach India—we all know that, and we know that his effort to find a new world was not the first effort. At least we *should* all know that. In fact, there is some evidence that there were a number of people prior to him that had gone across the ocean and had reached land. But Christopher Columbus was really special because he was on an official voyage, and he made an official report when he got back. He reported that the people he encountered were Indians.

For a number of years nobody dared counter it. People who were mathematicians know that he was about 3,000 miles short of where he said he was going when he reached land, and people who had been to

India before and heard his description pretty much knew it wasn't India. Rumors started going around that it was not India, but it took a long time for anybody to say so.

The reason it took so long to say so was because the world that existed at the end of the 15th century had a rather narrow scope of liberalism when it came to people who suggested that there might be things in the world that deviated from their sense of propriety. They burned you if you suggested that all of the world's information might not have been in the writings of the Greek and Roman philosophers or in the holy scriptures. The information that people and continents existed that were not included in the Bible or the writings of the ancients not only suggested that those writings were incomplete, it challenged the basic premise that all the information that God intended humans beings to know about the universe was contained in the scriptures.

That raised the question of what else was not contained in the scriptures. It brought on a crisis of faith among the European peoples of the 16th century who then sought to find out for themselves what was contained in the holy writings. They set forth a revolution that divided the European spiritual world. Just that alone, just the fact that there was a world that people knew nothing about, that they called the New World, changed the Europeans' ways of coming to knowledge.

One time I remember hearing people talk about how much the Indians have contributed to the material culture of the present time by looking at things that Indian technology created that we, today, benefit from. The list is long. It includes corn, potatoes, peanuts, peppers, tomatoes and all kinds of food products. It has different kinds of things like snowshoes. But the real contribution of the Indians to the modern world was that the Indians, by their existence and by their thinking, transformed the Europeans of the 15th century into the Euroamericans of the 20th century.

Things have changed. They have changed irreversibly. They have changed in such a way that the Europeans, the Euroamericans and the Americans today, are as different from their 15th century ancestors as their ancestors were from the Indians they saw standing on the sands of the islands of the Caribbean in 1492. The smallest evidence of this is that no one today would hesitate for a minute to count the teeth in a horse's mouth; that's just how we do it.

For those people standing on the shore watching those ships come across the ocean, it was a different kind of process. It is hard to imagine how they could have been more different, or how people of the same species could arrive at the same place at the same time with such extraordinarily different versions of reality, different experiences of the world—as those Indians who were inhabiting the North American forests and those Europeans who found their way across the Atlantic Ocean.

From what we know—and I think it's extremely important that we know, that we understand the significance and the importance of this— the Indians had a tradition of law and the Iroquois are our surviving example of it. The Iroquois possessed a tradition of law, and that tradition of law is what has created them as a people. That part is definitely true, but the Iroquois tradition of law is not a tradition of law, exactly. The Iroquois tradition of law is a tradition of responsible thinking. It is not something written in paragraphs and lines because it doesn't matter whether the letter of the thing is right. The questions that have to be put before the people are *what is the thinking? Is the thinking right?*

At any rate, standing on the shore were a people who had suffered through a period of catastrophe, a social catastrophe and a chaos which I suggest to you is quite different from anarchy. They had suffered a period of chaos in which their systems of negotiated settlement had broken down to the point where they no longer had those systems. When people tell the story of the coming of what they would call the "Law," they talk about a period when people killed one another in revenge feuds. Then one person arose who put forth a very interesting argument, one which would have found its way comfortably in the Athens of Plato, because it began with an almost Greek philosophical point. He said human beings have the capability of thinking, human beings can reach the conclusion that peace is a more appropriate state of being than war, and that all human beings who are capable of thinking will want to find ways to reach peace and the absence of violence. He said that peace is not only the absence of violence. He said peace is arrived at through the conscious and energetic struggle by human beings to use their intelligence to negotiate a place in which all injustice has been spoken to, and all persons feel that they have been treated fairly. When we create that reality, a reality in which all people can say that no one in their society is abused, we will have reached a state of peace. Then our job would be to extend that ideal to all the peoples of the world and there would be peace among nations and peace among clans and peace among families and peace between individuals. There would be peace across the earth.

It is an interesting idea, resident on the shores of America when the ships of Columbus were sailing across the Atlantic. Consider that on that boat the thoughts were of how to have war. On the boat were a people who had just experienced several hundreds of years of thinking about how to re-establish their religion in what they believed to be their holy land. They had carried banners of recognition of their religion with them on crusade after crusade, had organized under a spiritual upheaval and had moved large armies across land and water and had invaded foreign lands again and again and again. They were crossing the largest body of water that they had yet crossed but they carried with them the thinking of the Crusaders because the first question even in Christopher Columbus's own journals was, "What is there here that is of value to the crown?" The first answer was slaves. Their second question was how to conquer this land. And the answer was by the law of the crusader, "just" warfare.

So, the history of North America, and all of the Americas would become the history of that invasion and of its explanation of how that invasion was right. It was right because these were heathens; it was right because these were savages; it was right because The Word must be brought in; it was right because they were the conquerors; it was right because they had might. That mentality also said that as they went into Mexico, Florida, into the Inca country, Nicaragua, and a thousand other places, they had to explain their behavior in a way that shed light on them properly. They had to look good in doing it.

So they burned the manuscripts of the great libraries of the Aztec and Maya, burning and maybe forever destroying the scholarship that those people had done, and called the Aztec and the Maya barbarians and savages. They moved and marched on the villages of the Caribbean, carrying before them a man with a scroll who read in Latin in the village squares of dirt floor, thatched hut buildings: *We implore all of you to come forth with all your worldly goods into the service of Spain or we will put you to the sword and to the torch.* But no one understood Latin and when no one came forward with their gold and their bone necklaces and whatever they had to offer the King of Spain, the Conquistadors attacked them and butchered them.

It is said that the Conquistadors spilled more blood than any group of people ever spilled up to that time, and that would be quite a contest if you know the history before that time. That mentality also said that they had to dehumanize the victims of the conquest. Two things were born of that. One was racism. Even modern scholars identify the period of the conquest as the birth of racism in the modern world. It was the first time that arguments were seriously put forward in courts of Spain, especially at Valladolid, arguing that the Indians were biologically inferior human beings, that they were not even human beings at all that they were really beasts of burden, that they were subhumans and therefore subject to the treatment of subhumans as you would treat a burro or as you would treat a monkey. Some of the same things are still being argued in the Western hemisphere: whether peoples of different physical characteristics are fully human and have full human rights and have full civil rights. All those arguments still go on, certainly in places like Guatemala and Peru and Mexico where the conquest, I say, is not ended.

In the process of conquest it was necessary also to convince their own people that there were no intellectuals or philosophers among these barbarians. You will notice that, in the high schools and colleges and universities of the United States, the great philosophers of the West are celebrated, which I say is right to do. They are celebrated. Hardly anyone can name a great philosopher who is not a Western philosopher. You have to be in your fourth year of graduate school in philosophy before you can pick one out. It is almost as though there were no great thinkers except the thinkers of the West. This denial of thinking among peoples other than Europeans was so great that when these two worlds came together, the people who wrote the history wrote the Indian thinking right out of the history because by the theories of the conquistador, the Indian could not think, a burro cannot think.

So the very idea that Indians could have helped thinking among Europeans has been negated. There are still people who will swear to you that there were never any Indians who ever did any thinking that contributed in any concrete way to any of the institutions of the West. But, I say this, when the Europeans landed on the shores of New England, had there been no Indians standing there—if Squanto had gone on vacation that month—the first Puritans would have starved to death in their tracks. They had to find him and they had to get him to show them where the corn was. In my high school, that first Thanksgiving was always presented to us that the Puritans came ashore and they had all this food to eat and they invited the Indians over for Thanksgiving. I protest! It was the Indians who invited the Puritans over for Thanksgiving; it was an Indian celebration.

The Indian celebration of the harvest is your Thanksgiving and it's the *smallest* gift the Indians gave to the Americans. As they were standing on the shore watching these people come ashore, the Indians carried with them a tradition of meeting and democracy, of free speech, of free thinking, of tolerance for each other's differences of religion, of all those things which got attached to the Bill of Rights. All those things that we say are truly American were born on *this* soil generations before Columbus ever set sail.

If the Indians hadn't been on that shore, if there had been no one living in the woods, do you really believe that all those ideas would have found birth among a people who had spent a millennium butchering other people because of intolerance over questions of religion, killing people who suggested that the earth was not the center of the universe, burning people who said that the sun was only one little thing in a whole bunch of stars, killing people who said they did not want to send their taxes to Rome? Do you think that that tradition would have found its way, by itself? I think not.

The first thing the European new settlers saw when they landed in the country was the Indians, meeting, and it wasn't long before the Europeans who were there were meeting like the Indians did. And, in fact, that tradition still stands in parts of New England. There is still participatory democracy in the United States in some small enclaves even yet. Beyond that, the Indian had two other traditions that I think need to be mentioned as we talk about how wonderful it is to have the freedoms that North Americans tell the world they represent. The first was the idea of the dignity and rights of the individual and the rights of the individual against the powers of the state. In Europe anyone who said anything the king didn't like ended up in the basement of the palace. In this country, if people who spoke out against the policies of the state were put in jail, it would have ruined, and would still ruin to this day, the whole idea of a democratic society. Democracy is built on the idea that you have to be able to have the opposite point of view (any Indians here can correct me if I'm wrong).

The next thing is the most important thing, while we're sitting here talking about the Constitution of the United States. You know everyone's saying, *Wow! This is a great document!* And it really is just a document. But the idea of the Constitution of the United States is much bigger than the document, is it not? What we think the Constitution of the United States is, especially if we don't read it carefully, is our compact with the government of the United States. We think it's our compact that guarantees our rights and liberties. But what it really is, is a part of a tradition that found its way into the American people of the 20th century that says that the rule of law is sacred. The arbitrary thoughts of a dictator or somebody else are not sacred, and a people have said they will die unless they can be ruled by a rule of law based on a principle of fairness. They have insisted, from the time of the first signing of the United States Constitution until today, that they increase and hone and develop and make grow that idea of fairness.

It's the idea of fairness which is harder to institutionalize than it looks and we found that out. There are many questions where it's very difficult to tell what is fair and there are always people who are willing to diminish other people's rights; always, just as it's true among Indian peoples.

There are always people who want more control, who want to run everything for themselves, and we have seen that in the United States. But the principle that law should rule was not born in the courts of Europe, was it? The principle that law is sacred was not born in Greece or Rome. The principle that law should determine our agreement among ourselves to act in a way that brings safety and freedom to us all was argued between Indians and European explorers in the 16th, 17th and 18th centuries. It was argued between the Indians and the people that the Jesuits sent into the Indian country. It was carried over to France by writers and by voyagers. It was argued in France and it found its way back to America when the Americans heard it from the French.

The idea of that law goes back to a tradition, still alive among the people of the Six Nations, that tells of a philosopher who came across Lake Ontario and journeyed among the Mohawks and went from man to man among the leadership of the Mohawks and argued with them that reason can bring us peace. He argued that we can create a world in which people look to thinking instead of violence and created the council of the Five Nations as a place that sits under a tree, protected by the law, and around the idea that the chiefs hold their hands together to do clear thinking about the welfare of the coming generations, of the people of this earth.

I've heard in the last ten years everywhere, people saying we have to think about the faces of the coming generations, we have to think about the ideas of the Mother Earth. Those are part of the language now, part of the language of America, trying to rethink what it means to live on this planet, trying to rethink our group responsibilities to future peoples, trying to rethink what humans are and their relationship to the natural world, using language that finds its way back to that prehistoric moment, all the way back into the North American forest to those people who could have been standing on the shore when Columbus found his way across the ocean.

We as a people living in the 20th century must have a clear understanding that our roots come from those two places. We must understand that from the one place came the technologies and the abilities to move into the kinds of philosophical knowledge that finds its way into the hard sciences and also to work on building institutions around the issues that we call the social sciences and the arts and humanities. But the other confluence of this talks about the need to think about our responsibilities as human beings to one another, our responsibilities to the people of the future, and our responsibilities as human beings when we create institutions to remember those institutions must respect and must reflect on the rights and the sacredness of the individual.

So now we're here in the 20th century and when we want to know how many teeth there are in a horse's mouth we count them. And when we want to devise some kind of government, we think about some kind of way other than dictatorship. When we want to think about how to create institutions we try to have some responsibility in the world. And we now face, as every generation has faced, a tremendously difficult time. In some ways I wonder if this generation of people, as they think about the 200th anniversary of the institutions that led to this world as we know it, can think a little bit about what it means when the United States, for example, borrows money that it knows its grandchildren must pay back. It's an idea that I know would not find its way through the powerful thinking of a council of chiefs that had to consider the welfare of its generations yet unborn.

Another thing comes to my mind. Until very recently, if I may be permitted to castigate America a little bit, until very recently, America has told the world we represent a democracy. We believe in it. That's what we are, what we're fighting for—the free world. And yet in my lifetime the United States has armed and moved to back some of the most hideous dictators with the most rapacious kinds of personalities, and the most vicious kinds of policies that existed in the world at the time. Dictators in Central America, dictators in South America, dictators in Asia and Africa, the scum of the earth, and the United States sends those people guns and bullets and says it is protecting democracy. And too often when there is a rise of a democratic center, our government has closed its eyes to it and walked away from it and disowned the democratic center.

Our government has consistently, over a whole generation, embraced the extreme right. Now in the last few years they've stopped a couple of times. I know they did it for pragmatic, not ideological purposes. I'm aware that it was not the goodness of their heart, it's just the fear the communists will take over in the Philippines. But we should encourage that because in a way it fits some of the thinking. It actually uses thinking for a change instead of sending guns. Without thinking, without a tradition that says that we have to do the best job that we can do, the whole tradition is meaningless. It has no meaning.

Anyway, the Indians are one of those peoples who are, at this hour, I say, a foundation point of American democracy, of world democracy. The thinking that arose out of the northeastern forest finds its way into the institutions of the 20th century. I think it's undeniable. I think if you study what was talked about then, you'll know that we've inherited a very great deal of the spirit of what those Indians were talking about when the Peacemaker walked the earth. The Indians of today face the same problem, the "I want, I want." There are enough Indians here that I do not need to mention this. The Indians of today still face the problems of maintaining fairness, of maintaining the idea that no one is abused, of maintaining that very high ideal, that peace will be reached when we come to do our best thinking about what's the best for everybody, and also that very high ideal that says that law prevails, not might.

Law prevails. That was what our law was about. In our world the law came about when the people who had the weapons said, we put our weapons away in order to sit and do thinking. And I'm hoping that tradition will catch on a little more. I've sometimes thought, when I was a little boy, that the old people used to say all the time that the Indian taught the world about these ideas. But the world hasn't got enough of it to survive with it yet, and I think that, as I get older, I understand more and more what they mean.

But I'd like to say that once in awhile when we gather like this, in a year when the very institutions that created the United States world, and the parallel institutions that created the Iroquois world, can come together in an institution like this one, and share ideas, that reflects very well that the two families of peoples have gone on a path for a long time parallel to one another and have come across that path fairly well. There are good feelings among people that are able to do this.

Land of the Free, Home of the Brave

Oren Lyons

I am going to discuss early history, prior to the coming of the white man to this continent. This time receives little attention in the history books of the country, but it was in these early times that the development of democratic processes came about on this land. I would like to give you our history, a very short history, of course, but it will deal with those times. So, I shall begin.

Upon the continent of North America prior to the landfall of the white man, a great league of peace was formed, the inspiration of a prophet called the Peacemaker. He was a spiritual being, fulfilling the mission of organizing warring nations into a confederation under the Great Law of Peace. The principles of the law are peace, equity, justice, and the power of the good minds.

With the help and support of a like-minded man called Ayonwatha, whom some people now call Hiawatha, an Onondaga by birth and a Mohawk by adoption, he set about the great work of establishing a union of peace under the immutable natural laws of the universe. He came to our Iroquois lands in our darkest hour, when the good message of how to live had been cast aside and naked power ruled, fueled by vengeance and blood lust. A great war of attrition engulfed the lands, and women and children cowered in fear of their own men. The leaders were fierce and merciless. They were fighting in a blind rage. Nations, homes, and families were destroyed, and the people were scattered. It was a dismal world of dark disasters where there seemed to be no hope. It was a raging proof of what inhumanity man is capable of when the laws and principles of life are thrown away.

The Peacemaker came to our lands, bringing the message of peace, supported by Ayonwatha. He began the great work of healing the twisted minds of men. This is a long history, too long to recount today in this forum. Suffice it to say it is a great epic that culminated on the shores of the lake now called Onondaga where, after many years of hard work—some say perhaps even 100 years—he gathered the leaders, who had now become transformed into rational human beings, into a Grand Council, and he began the instructions of how the Great Law of Peace would work.

The Peacemaker set up the families into clans, and then he set up the leaders of the clans. He established that the League of Peace would be matriarchal and that each clan would have a clanmother. Thus, he established in law the equal rights of women.

He raised the leaders of each clan—two men, one the principal leader and the second his partner. They worked together for the good of the people. He called these two men *royaner*, or *the good minds*, the peacemakers, and they were to represent the clans in council. Thus, he established the principles of representation of people in government.

Henceforth, he said, these men will be chosen by the clanmother, freely using her insight and wisdom. Her choice must first be ratified by the consensus of the clan. If they agree, then her choice must be ratified by full consensus of the Chiefs' Council of their nation. Then her choice must be ratified and given over to the Council of Chiefs who then call the Grand Council of the Great League of Peace, and they will gather at the nation that is raising the leader, and they would work together in ceremony.

He made two houses in each nation. One he called the Long House and the other he called the Mud House. They would work together in ceremony and council establishing the inner source of vitality and dynamics necessary for community.

He made two houses in the Grand Council, one called the Younger Brothers, consisting of the Oneida and the Cayuga Nations and later enlarging to include the Tuscarora. The other was the Elder Brothers, consisting of the Mohawks with the title Keepers of the Eastern Door, the Onondaga, whom he made the Firekeepers, and the Senecas, who were the Keepers of the Western Door. Now, he made the house, and the rafters of the house were the laws that he laid down, and he called us Haudenosaunee, the people of the Longhouse.

Now, the candidate for the clan title is brought before the Grand Council to be judged on his merits, and they have the right of veto. If they agree, then he may take his place in Grand Council. But before that, he is turned back to the people, and they are asked if they know a reason why this man should not be a leader and hold title. Thus, the process is full circle back to the people. Thus, the Peacemaker established the process of raising leaders for governance, and, by this process, a leader cannot be self-proclaimed. He is given his title and his duties, and his authority is derived from the people, and the people have the right to remove him for malfeasance of office.

He established the power of recall in the clanmother, and it is her duty to speak to him if he is receiving complaints from the people concerning his conduct. The clanmother shall speak to him three times, giving sufficient time between warnings for him to change his ways. She shall have a witness each time. The first will be her niece, in other words, a woman. The second shall be the partner of the chief in council or the principal leader, as the case may be. And the third and final warning comes with a man who holds no title, and he is coming for the chief's wampum and for the chief's emblem of authority, the antlers of a deer. Thus he established the power of recall vested in the people.

The leader must be free from any crime against woman or a child. He cannot have killed anybody and cannot have blood on his hands. He must believe in the ways of the Longhouse. His heart must yearn for the welfare of the people. He must have great compassion for his people. He must have great tolerance, and his skin must be seven spans thick to withstand the accusations, slander, and insults of the people as he goes about his duties for the people. He has no authority but what the people give him in respect. He has no force of arms to demand the people obey his orders. He shall lead by example, and his family shall not influence his judgment. He carries his title for life or until he is relieved of it by bad conduct or ill health. He now belongs to the people.

At the first council, there were fifty original leaders, and their names became offices to be filled by each succeeding generation. So, it continues up to this very day. The Great Peacemaker had established a government of absolute democracy, the constitution of the great law intertwined with the spiritual law.

We then became a nation of laws. The people came of their own free will to participate in the decision-making of the national council and the Grand Council. Thus, the Peacemaker instilled in the nations the inherent rights of the individual with the process to protect and exercise these rights.

Sovereignty, then, began with the individual, and all people were recognized to be free, from the very youngest to the eldest. It was recognized and provided for in the Great Law of Peace that liberty and equality demanded great moral fortitude, and it was the nature of free men to defend freedom.

Thus, freedom begat freedom and great societies of peace prevailed, guided by the leaders, the good minds. The men were restrained by moral conduct, and the family with the woman at its heart was the center of Indian societies and nations.

Now, the Peacemaker said the symbol of the Haudenosaunee shall be the great white pine with four white roots of truth extending to the four cardinal directions, and those people who have no place to go shall follow these roots back to the tree and seek shelter under the long leaves of the white pine that we shall call the great tree of peace. I shall place an eagle atop the tree to be ever-vigilant against those who shall harm this tree, and the eagle shall scream his warnings to our chiefs whose duty it is to nurture and protect this tree.

Now that this is done, the chiefs, clanmothers, and faithkeepers being raised and the Great Law being firmly established in place, he said, *I now uproot this tree and command you to throw all of your weapons of war into this chasm to be carried by the undercurrent of water to the furthest depths of the earth, and now I place this tree back over this chasm, throwing away forever war between us, and peace shall prevail.*

This is what prevailed upon this great Turtle Island at the first landfall of the white man. They found here in full flower, free nations guided by democratic principles, all under the authority of the natural law, the ultimate spiritual law of the universe. This was then the land of the free and the home of the brave.

Sovereigns and sovereignty as understood by the Europeans related to the power of kings and queens, of royalty to rule men as they saw fit, to enslave human beings and control in total the lives and property of their subjects. Strange indeed it must have been for these immigrants to find a land with nothing but free people and free nations. The impact has reverberated down through history to this time. As Felix Cohen put it, "the Indian people had 'Americanized' the white man."

The first treaty between the Indians and the white man took place where the pines begin (it is now called Albany, New York) in 1613 or thereabouts. It was a treaty that was the grandfather of all treaties, and it was called the Guswenta or Two Row Wampum.

That treaty established our equal rights in this land and our separate and equal coexistence on this land between our two peoples, the canoe of the Indian and the boat of the white man going down the river of life in peace and friendship forever. The last three principles were memorialized in the great silver covenant chain with the three binding us together forever—peace and friendship forever. As long as the grass grows green, as long as the water runs downhill, and as long as the sun rises in the east and sets in the west shall we hold this treaty.

It is this treaty that I brought today. It is this belt I speak of. This is our canoe, the Indian people, their government, and their religions. This is our brother the white man's boat, his religions, his government, and his people. Together, side by side, we go down the river of life in peace and friendship and mutual coexistence. As you note, we never come together. We are equal.

Benjamin Franklin observed these differences in government in 1770, "The care and labor of providing for artificial and fashionable wants, the sight of so many rich wallowing in superfluous plenty, whereby so many are kept poor and distressed for want, the insolence of office, and the restraints of custom all contrive to disgust the Indians with what we call civil society."

So, we now come to the process of this transference of democratic ideas and ideals from the Indian to the white man. It was a process of associations, of years of meetings, discussions, wars, and peace. Treaties became a process of relationships. Early America was steeped in Indian lore and social and political associations.

There were longstanding interrelationships between the colonies and the Indian nations that surrounded them. It was our grandfathers who took your grandfathers by the hand at the Treaty of Lancaster in 1774, and urged them to form a union such as ours so that they may prosper. It was Benjamin Franklin who took notes at that treaty and became inspired to such a union. It was your grandfathers who said to our chiefs at German Flats in 1775 that they would now take our advice and form such a union and plant a tree of peace in Philadelphia where all could seek shelter.

Finally, it was our chiefs and leaders who first acknowledged you as a new and separate nation, independent and free, with these words, "Brothers, the whole Six Nations take this opportunity to thank you that you have acquainted us with your determination in so public a manner and we shall for the future consider you as thirteen independent states." And they gave a white belt, a row of wampum, to commemorate this great occasion. This recognition was stated Friday, August 9, 1776, at the German Flats Treaty.

This was the culmination of the long history and association with the Haudenosaunee and the immigrants who became Americans. Your people went on to develop the Constitution of the United States encompassing the symbols of our constitution, the bundle of arrows symbolizing the new thirteen states, the leaves of the pine tree, and the eagle that we place upon the tree of peace. This and more we share as common history.

Brothers, we now turn our faces toward the future and continue to wish you well in your endeavors as a nation. Perhaps it would be well for you to look back again at our principles of peace, justice and equality, to grasp firmly our hand in recognition of our long association and heed the treaties that were made so long ago that these treaties may continue to thrive for our posterity as we continue down the long journey to eternity and we continue our association as government to government.

With this statement, I close the message from the Haudenosaunee, and I thank you very much for your kind attention.

Everything Has To Be in Balance

Audrey Shenandoah

Being born as humans to this earth is a very sacred trust. We have a sacred responsibility because of the special gift that we have, which is beyond the fine gifts of the plant life, the fish, the woodlands, the birds, and all the other living things on earth. We are able to take care of them. We are able to see, if we live right and follow our own instructions, that they might have a good earth, have good air, good water, a good life, just as we would have if we would follow the instruction of our Creator.

Humans have a sacred trust—men and women. The women within our own society have a special place, a special place of honor. We have the ability to bring forth life to this earth. We are given, further, the sacred responsibility of nurturing that life from the beginning, from the most necessary and important time in a human's life: from the time that they are infants and learning their first things about living, the first ways that they must treat one another as humans, the first ways that they are to survive.

In the days past, a long, long time ago, we have all read how the women had such a big responsibility of taking care of the gardens. They did the gardening, they did all that is called hard work, what actually was an honor. The women of the village taught the children, everybody's children, all the things they had to know in order to survive on this earth. They taught them how to look after one another, they taught them from a very young age what kinds of food were good for them to eat, what kinds of foods were not good for them, and they taught them medicine from a very early age. The children up to an age of, let's say, eight or nine years were in the trust, the responsibility, of the women.

The gardening was not specifically labeled women's work by our people. There were always men and male children around who helped and did the harder work, because there were always some men who did not go on the hunts, some men who stayed behind to help the women, and taking care of the gardening was not the big chore that some people believe it to be. Today, women still do much of the gardening around people's homes for those who plant.

So when the children became of an age that they went out into mixed society and began to learn whatever their natural talents led them to—some people became singers, some speakers, some dancers, some workers—they just seemed to know how to do all kinds of things. For a while they went about learning these things and practicing them from either men or women, whoever could see what this person was designated to become. And then when it came time to learn the man things—the hunting, and all of those things that took them away from their home, away from the village—they were prepared to meet life in the wilderness. The women taught them all the things they needed to know about preparing food, taking care of each other and all of the things that I mentioned before.

When it came time for a young man or a young woman to be married, to join with another, and to lead a life of their own and make their own family, again it was the women's responsibility; it still is the women's responsibility to give them the instruction. The women were the ones, in the old days, who chose a mate for their young people and still, today, it is the mothers who must give their consent when a young couple are joined together, to lead a life together—marriage they call it in English, making a home and a life together and taking care of one another is what we call it in our language. As time goes on and little children come into the family, again the grandmothers, the aunts, have the responsibility.

Taking care of little children is not a job or a chore; it is something people enjoy doing. There is a special bond between the grandchildren and the grandparents or aunts, anyone who has grandchildren knows this. And as life goes on, and now the young people reach an age themselves when they are going to leave this earth, again they are prepared by the women. So, all through a person's life, from the time they are conceived, from the time they are born, until the time they leave this earth, their care is truly in the hands of the women, the mothers of our nations, and that is a sacred trust.

We, the Haudenosaunee, have a matrilineal system among our nations. When they have a family, the mother's clan determines the clan of her children, and so we have a clanmother. Before assimilation took so many of our people from us and into another world, it used to be that the eldest woman in the clan was the clanmother. She must perpetuate the ways of our people; she must be able to teach the ways of our people to the young people. She must be able to look out for large numbers of people because now, all of the clan people are one family. And so, because of the changing of the times, in these days we don't necessarily have the eldest women being the clanmother of certain clans, but the eldest eligible woman. We cannot have someone teaching our children our traditional ways who does not follow the traditional ways themselves and cannot perpetuate this way. Some have followed a foreign way, maybe they have become Christianized, or maybe they are following, let's say the government of another country, the United States. They cannot be truly one of our people because once a person begins following another way of thinking, their thoughts can become divided, their thoughts cannot be pure and clean anymore, totally for the people, for the good of perpetuating the traditions which are so important among our people.

The ways of our people are important because these are the ways that have sustained our people from the time of contact until today. Among our ancestors, the traditionals were the strong ones, the ones who kept to the ways of our people. They were the ones who did battle—not necessarily only physically. Our leaders are still doing battle today. They are not armed to the teeth with weapons of war, because of the message of peace that came to our people so many years ago. We know that they were the strong ones, these are the strong ones here today. They are younger maybe, but they know the ways, they have followed the way of our elders, and so these have to be the people that are going to hold our people together. These have to be the kinds of people who are going to be able to sustain, to survive and to teach our young people to survive. So, a woman who is designated to be leader of a clan must have these feelings and they have got to be intact, otherwise the clan and the nation are in danger.

The clanmother's duties have to do with the community affairs, the nation affairs, but they also have another role and that has to do with the spiritual side. I have already said that they must perpetuate the ways of the Ongwehonwe but they must also set ceremonial times and be able to watch the moon for our people. We don't have many people any longer in this time who can communicate with the stars and the moon in the ways that they did when they were still pure and strong. We watch the printed calendar like you do now, but we still have those people who must watch the phases of the moon, who know when it is time to call the faithkeepers and the women together to sit, and to set the time for the ceremonies which are held at various times throughout the year. So this becomes another duty of the clanmother—she must watch these times and always be ready to call the people together when it is time for a ceremony. She must be ready to call her clan people together if a person from another clan has suffered sickness, some kind of tragedy or emergency. Any time a family needs help the duty of the clanmother is to tell her people now this family over here has had some trouble come upon them, sickness or whatever, a death in the family. She must designate people in her clan to go over and help that family, for it is our way that we do not leave a family alone in time of trouble, we must be there to help them. And so, that becomes another duty of the clanmother.

The names within all of our clans are handed down from generation to generation. The clanmother also has that duty. In our language they say she has a bag of names by her side. When a new baby comes to her clan she must reach into that bag and pull out a name. So the clanmothers also have the privilege and responsibility of naming the young babies, the young people in their clans.

In these days, we have many young people who were not born into our traditional way, but after they have the ability to make decisions of their own, when they become mature enough to make their decisions about what kind of a life they want to lead, they come to our longhouses, all through our territories, and have this name given. When they are grown up, mature young adults, they come with a desire to have a name within their clan and this is given because we never turn people away from our longhouse or from our way. Those of our people who wish to come back to that way, who find something lacking in the inner self, because they have missed the things the grandfathers could have taught them, are all welcome to come back. They come and get their names, they learn about the ceremonies, and they begin taking part.

The clanmothers also have a duty of watching out for the young people. I said when the young people are married, it is up to the mothers to give their consent. The mothers are the ones who bring them with their basket to what is today a marriage ceremony and so if this young couple runs into problems, as everybody does, differences of opinion, many reasons that they would need help and support, the clanmother has the duty again of being there to support these young people who have found themselves in need of help.

Each clan has a clanmother who has the duty to select the leadership of our nations. In English they call them chiefs; these are the leaders of our nations. Each clan has its own leader and the clanmother is, again, responsible for selecting a candidate to lead her people. To be a person worthy of that trust, I believe, to be a person who is given all of this responsibility is a very honorable position within our society.

Sometimes our young people become confused. In the last few years it has become a trend for women to feel that they need to do something to become more than a woman, or more than what a woman's responsibilities are. But this is something that we have always had within our society. Women have always been able to do anything that they are physically able to do. There have been, as I mentioned before, no labels to say that this is women's work, and this is man's work among our people. It has always been a balance, a cooperation, and so when I say that the women, the clanmothers have the responsibility of selecting a candidate to lead our people, selecting the leadership of our nations, that is a very honorable position. But, it does not mean that she is now going to be the one who is going to tell him what to do. She must work with him; a balance has to be there. She must work with him and they, together, work for the will of the people. Whatever the people want is what they must work to do, for the good of the people.

There are many duties, probably some that I have not mentioned here. For the cooking of the food at ceremony time, the clanmother has a faithkeeper who stands beside her. She has the duty of preparing food so that her chiefs and her people will always have food, the children will always have food. Some people, I have read many times in magazines, have dared to write that preparing food and looking after food is looked on as some kind of a lowly position. Taking care of the children and keeping house can be looked at by some people as a lowly kind of a position, a lowly kind of a job, not very important. In our way of life, it is very important, one of the most important jobs that a person can have.

Now, I don't mean to sound as if they exclude the fathers altogether. I don't mean to sound as if the men are, let's say, put into a position where they are not as important. Everything has to be in a balance, just like the thanksgiving that was given at the beginning of this meeting here, this gathering. The balance of everything in creation is what allows us to continue to be. The balance is what allows us to continue to live. We breathe the air, we use the water, we share the space and the balance must be looked at very carefully. We must try to keep that balance.

Within our society we maintain a balance between the responsibilities of the women, the responsibilities of the men, of the chiefs, of the faithkeepers. All the people in between have a special job to do to help to keep this balance so that at no time do we come to a place within our society where anyone has more power than any of the rest, for our leadership all have equal power. They must be able to listen to one another.

Speaking and listening are two fine arts that are much forgotten in today's society. We do not know how to listen to one another anymore. We don't know how to listen and hear the people who have the good things to tell us. All of these things have to be kept in the balance—the listening and the speaking, the male and the female, the clanmother and the chiefs, and all of the people in between. And so, as a woman within my own society, I have never had the desire or the feelings to join these great big congregations, conclaves of women who are trying to get what I guess they call equal power. They all have the power; they only need to assert themselves. You do not need permission from anyone to do what it is your inner person tells you that you must do. The only thing that people leave out is the spiritual side. That is the guideline that our people must use to choose the leaders, to choose the faithkeepers, to choose the clanmother who is going to look after the clan family. She, in turn, will choose a candidate for leadership, a chief to look after his nation. The spiritual side of these responsibilities that I have mentioned tonight is the most important part. It's the very foundation of everything that would allow this system to work peacefully.

I was asked, I don't even remember how many years ago, if I would sit in for awhile and take notes for our Grand Council when they meet. I have a large family and at that time my children were very young, and I didn't have the time to do the many things, the many trips and the outside work that it would take for a person to do justice to the job. But the man who had been the former secretary became sick and could not do the job anymore. Because I had attended meetings as much as I could ever since I was fifteen, I attended our Grand Council. The old ones knew me and those coming up knew me, and I was asked if I would take their notes and become the Recording Secretary for the Council.

I was raised by my grandmother. She was very old when I came to her. I was an infant, nine months old, and she was fifty-six years old when I came to her. She did not speak English at all and all of her friends, of course, spoke in our own language when they visited. All of her friends were old people and I think that I am very fortunate that I was able to grow up in that kind of environment. They talked about the old things; they talked in our own language all the time. My grandfather was Mohawk. His family used to come down and visit, and stay all winter. People used to do that a long time ago, do a lot more visiting than we are able to do nowadays. And so I learned Mohawk that way.

My grandmother's father was a Seneca so she had many relatives from the Seneca Nation who came also and visited for long periods of time. I consider myself very fortunate that I was able to grow among people who spoke nothing but our own native languages in our house. And so, because of that I have been able to work as Recording Secretary for the Grand Council of the Haudenosaunee and I am thankful that I can be helpful in any way.

When Council is held we use our own language. But we have many people who come to listen to the Council who cannot understand our language. So, from time to time today we use the English language so that people can understand exactly what is going on. However, the leadership, the chiefs, as they sit in Council, use our own languages as they speak and send the messages across the fire.

I think it is good that young people can get together like this in these learning institutions and bring this knowledge to other young people who are out to learn about other people. I think people learning about other people is one of the most important things that can be happening today because it seems, as I talk to many, many different kinds of people that everybody wants to live in a peaceful world. Everybody wants to look for a way that we might live in peace together. People learning to know other people, to know other people's ways, is one of the ways that can bring that time closer and closer to us, so that maybe our children and our grandchildren can have a realization of people working together and communicating in a peaceful way.

The Great Law Takes a Long Time To Understand

Jacob Thomas

I remember when I was a kid, I would sit to listen. I never, never interfered in anybody's speaking. They always said, "You listen, you sit down and all you do is listen." So there was a few of us who grew up about the same age and we all sat and listened. A lot of times old people used to come to our home, as my grandfather was very knowledgeable. My father was very knowledgeable coming as the third generation from my great-grandfather to my grandfather to my father. My grandfather's name was Chief David Sky and he's one of the knowledgeable chiefs. He was a chief who passed away in 1931, and I missed quite a lot from there, but all the things that I've learned from there, I learned from my father.

I don't claim myself to know everything, because I am not that age yet to know everything or I'll never reach that age. Native culture is something that you keep on learning, you may become knowledgeable but still you are learning everyday, it never stops, right 'till you die. So I learned, from the time when I was a boy, to listen. I never, ever forgot what I was taught and I also kept learning.

There is a sequence. I have heard some speakers say you have to make it in a sequence in order to understand your culture and you have to have the language, that the language is a way of life.

Now we're taking about the Great Law. I've heard so much about it since I've been here, about the Great Law. A lot of people helped me study the Great Law of Peace. So as I say, it goes a long way for oral traditions once you learn it. It's true when you only hear it once, you can forget. But there's many nights and many days that I have spent with my elders sitting and listening. I get so fed up sometimes, listening because it's the same thing over and over and over. And I often wonder but I never say anything. I don't want to hurt the elders.

Now a lot of people here were very anxious to hear the Great Law but I'm very sorry to say to you I would not be able to do all that in what very little time we have. You don't realize how much time it takes to recite the Great Law in my native tongue and it would be easier to recite it in my native tongue.

I went recently to the Lake of the Two Mountains to preach. I taught the Great Law for six days and still we didn't finish. I figured it would take about eight days, and that was four hours a day—reciting in the morning and then in the afternoon elaborating what the Great Law meant. So it took the whole day. It takes a long time for a person to understand because there is a lot, not only knowing the right words to say about the Great Law, but what it means, the symbolism.

The Peacemaker took the structure of the longhouse from the east to the west when he made the Great Law. It stretched from the east to the west to the western nations. It was symbolic, everything was symbolic. They used symbols for the clans they belonged to: wolf, bear, hawk, eel, beaver, snipe, sandpiper. I happen to be one of the Cayuga chiefs of the Confederacy, condoled in 1973, and I belong to the Sandpiper Clan of the Cayuga Nation.

When the Peacemaker made the League of the Five Nations, when he planted the Great White Roots of Peace, the great long leaves, he said, "Here. Now we have elevated all the five nations, all the fifty sachems. Now we will all join hands and that will show the covenant. When we join hands, all of our people will be inside of the circle. All our people and also our culture will be inside of that circle. Our language will be inside of that circle. Our traditions will be inside of that circle. And so it all belongs to Iroquois, names and everything. That means that there is strength in power of the longhouse of one family."

As I said, they used a lot of these symbols. Symbols mean a lot, if you study what the symbols are used for. So when they planted the Great White Root of Peace, the Peacemaker said, "Now we will get the wisest bird there is, the eagle, which will sit on the top of the Great White Pine and will watch over all nations." I have been told the reason they used the eagle. It is a very wise bird that can see very far. It can notice anything that is coming from the distance, and it will squeal if there is any trouble coming, that would invade a nation.

Now a lot of people ask questions about different things. "What is the meaning of the eagle?" Well, the meaning of the eagle is that the chiefs who are surrounding the tree will take on the nature of that bird. That's the way it is made for the Confederacy chiefs. They shall be very knowledgeable and sharp-eyed so they can see anything approaching.

But since the time of the American Revolution the tree has fallen. Today, it lies across the arms of the Confederacy as they're holding hands. There are some links that have been broken, but they're still trying to hold that tree up. It's not up; it's almost down. That's the struggle we face today. We are trying to understand how we're going to bring that tree back up.

Royaner is similar to what we call the Creator. *Royaner* is only acting on behalf of the Creator. That's the message, the prophecy, that was brought to the chiefs so that they would work for the Creator. And they would work for many generations to come, even the coming faces yet unborn. Today we look back at our ancestors. The clanmothers and the chiefs at that time were looking out for us. We were the coming faces at that time.

It was the Creator who sent the Peacemaker to Earth to work through him. The Peacemaker was the one who organized and brought peace. He was the one responsible to bring all nations together. He worked with a man named Ayonwatha. The name, Ayonwatha, means that he's always awake, always alert. Ayonwatha was the first one who was also given power by the Peacemaker, and they worked together to organize great peace and also the Great Law. And Ayonwatha was the first to be crowned by the deer antlers. The Peacemaker told him, "This is the kind of animal that you should eat, not humans. This is what the Creator provided for you to eat but not to go and destroy humankind." So then from there Ayonwatha began to understand and he began to grasp the Great Peace. And he was crowned by the Peacemaker who said, "You will become Ayonwatha."

There is a symbol, the deer, which they even use for clans. The Iroquois use different kinds of animals like a deer and beaver. And the deer antlers have a great significance. This goes back again to a time in the Iroquois cosmology, of the battle between the left-handed twin and the right-handed twin. The good twin used the antler to gain power and drive away his brother who did evil.

I've been at Trent University for a good many years now, and I've learned a lot too. I learned from other professors about different things that coincided with the different things that I knew. I met this professor at Trent University who talked in class about animals, about nutrition. And then, he got talking about the deer and all the animals that have antlers—moose and even little bugs that roam the ground. They have all kinds of antennas like the deer. When the deer is wandering in the bush it stops and it looks around. The professor said, "You know why? 'Cause that animal is a clean animal. It only eats twigs and other things like that. It's clean when it eats." And that, I believe, is the reason why that kind of meat is helpful to gain knowledge, to gain wisdom. I was really amazed at what he told me, and I learned this only a year ago. He said, "You know the way it is with an animal, with a deer. They have found through research, why they have these antlers." He said, "There is a power going between the antlers that tells them what's coming. That's their reporter. And it feeds in there and that's why they're always alert, always looking. That's what tells them. Same way with the little bugs. If you try to touch one, it runs away because it's some kind of a feeling there. It's sort of radiation, I guess you might call it, some energy going through there. But we don't see it. So that's the way it is with this deer and also moose. The closest points between the antlers, there is power going through there. And that is why it could tell something's coming, how it could protect its little ones. And that's how they're used."

This amazed me how good it is that I knew this, because that is the reason why the Peacemaker used the antlers, so that the chief can get all of this knowledge coming in. He described it. It's the same as when you put rabbit ears on a television set. He says that's what happens to the deer. It's coming through his antenna. So that's why he knows. All animals know. And now I said I was glad to know that because it coincides with the things that I know about why the Peacemaker used the deer antlers.

We should not only learn about the Great Law, we should know also the meanings, the symbols. They even used beaver in the Great Law. It says that all the Iroquois nations will come together, and they will sit, and they will eat this beaver tail. That will also give them wisdom.

PART II

Iroquoian Political Concept and the Genesis of American Government

Donald A. Grinde, Jr.

T here is ample scholarly opinion and factual data to conclude that the Founding Fathers respected and used American Indian ideas as the American government evolved. Recently, a few anthropologists and ethnohistorians, unfamiliar with the interpretive and documentary evidence, have concluded that there is no evidence to support the notion that the Iroquois and other Native American confederacies had an influence on the evolution of American government. Such sweeping generalizations are facile and dated in light of the interpretive and documentary evidence that has emerged in the last two generations.

Much of the scholarship that ignores the importance of Native American ideas in American history also marginalizes the role of American Indians in our history. The process of marginalization has gone so far that it is difficult for some scholars to believe that Iroquois sachems were present at the debates surrounding the Declaration of Independence. As the debates on independence took place, Benjamin Franklin proposed his revised Albany Plan of Union as the new form of government. The Iroquois visit to Congress in 1776 was no casual affair.

In August of 1775, they had been invited to view the workings of the "Grand Council Fire" in Philadelphia. In reality, scholars have painted the Iroquois out of the historical picture that portrays the road to American independence and self-government.

Three hundred years ago, the ideas and political systems of the Iroquois and other confederations were so appealing that William Penn would describe Indian government in complimentary terms:

> Every King hath his council, and that consists of all the old and wise men of his nation...nothing is undertaken, be it war, peace, the selling of land or traffick, without advising with them; and which is more, with the young men also...The kings move by the breath of their people. It is the Indian custom to deliberate...I have never seen more natural sagacity.[2]

Penn described the Native confederacies of Eastern America as political societies with sachemships inherited through the female side. Penn was also familiar with the Condolence ceremony of the Iroquois which was crucial for an understanding of their confederacy. He stated that when someone kills a "woman they pay double [the wampum]" since "...she breeds children which men cannot...."[3] After exposure to American Indian forms of government and unity, William Penn proposed a "Plan for a Union of the Colonies in America." Although it was just an outline, Penn seemed inspired by his observations of American Indian polities.[4]

A couple of generations later another Pennsylvanian, Benjamin Franklin, would formulate another plan of colonial union that would more closely reflect Iroquois influences. Franklin, familiar with the ways of the Iroquois, published a series of Indian treaties. He attended a Condolence ceremony in 1753, less than a year before his authorship of the Albany Plan of Union. Franklin recognized the enormous appeal of American Indian ways in 1753 as well. He wrote in 1753 that American Indian children reared in white society returned to their people when they took but "...one ramble with them." Furthermore, Franklin asserted that when

> white persons of either sex have been taken prisoners young by Indians, and lived a while among them, tho' ransomed by their friends [they] take the first good opportunity of escaping again into the woods, from whence there is no reclaiming them...."[5]

While discussing the attractions of American Indian society, Franklin wrote of the "Great Council" at "Onondago" and how the Six Nations educated their men in "...what was the best manner."[6]

Just nine months before the Albany Congress of 1754, Franklin attended a treaty council at Carlisle, Pennsylvania in October, 1753. During this treaty with the Iroquois and the Ohio Indians, Franklin saw the rich imagery and ideas of the Iroquois at close hand. On October 1,

1753, he watched the Oneida chief, Scarrooyady, and a Mohawk, Cayanguileguoa, condole the Ohio Indians for their losses against the French. Franklin listened while Scarrooyady spoke of the origins of the Iroquois Great Law to the Ohio Indians.

> We must let you know, that there was friendship established by our and your Grandfathers, and a mutual Council fire was kindled. In this friendship all those then under the ground, who had not obtained eyes or faces (that is, those unborn) were included; and it was then mutually promised to tell the same to their children and children's children.[7]

The following day, Franklin and the other Treaty Commissioners echoed earlier statements of the Iroquois when they said:

> We would therefore hereby place before you the necessity of preserving your faith entire to one another, as well as to this government. Do not separate; Do not part on any score. Let no differences nor jealousies subsist a moment between Nation and Nation, but join together as one man....[8]

In replying to these remarks, Scarrooyady took for granted the knowledge that the Treaty Commissioners had of the structure of the Iroquois Confederacy when he requested that "...you will please to lay all our present transactions before the council at Onondago, that they may know we do nothing in the dark."[9]

Thus on the eve of the Albany Congress, Franklin had a great deal of exposure to the imagery and political ideas of the Iroquois both from first hand experience and from his reading of Cadwallader Colden's *History of the Five Nations*.[10]

At the Albany Congress the next year, the Mohawk sachem Hendrick challenged the Americans to use Iroquois style unity and to bring "...as many into this covenant chain as you possibly can."[11] With this admonition and his previous knowledge of the imagery and concepts of the Iroquois Great Law, Franklin met with both colonial and Iroquois delegates to create a plan of unity that was, in part, derived from some of the tenets of the Great Law of the Iroquois. In fact, Franklin admitted that the debates over the Albany Plan "...went on daily with the Indian business."[12] During the discussions, Hendrick openly criticized the colonists and hinted that the Iroquois would not ally with the English colonies unless a suitable form of unity was established among them. Hendrick asserted on July 9, 1754, that "(w)e wish this fire [tree] of friendship may grow up to a great height and then we shall be a powerful people."[13]

James DeLancey, Acting Governor of New York, replied to Hendrick's speech in this manner: "I hope that by this present Union, we shall grow up to a great height and then we shall be as powerful and famous as you were of old."[14]

The next day, Franklin formally proposed his plan of union before the Congress. It had a "Grand Council," a "Speaker" and called for a "general government... under which...each colony may retain its present constitution."[15] In 1943 after editing Franklin's Indian treaties, Julian P. Boyd stated that Benjamin Franklin in 1754 "proposed a plan for union of the colonies and he found his materials in the great confederacy of the Iroquois." Boyd also believed that the ability of the Iroquois to unite peoples over a large geographic expanse made their form of government "...worthy of copying."[16] As Americans grew more restive under the autocracy of British rule, they turned to Native American ideas for alternatives. The Iroquois also provided the rebellious colonists with an alternative identity.

During the Stamp Act crisis, the New York City Sons of Liberty sent wampum belts to the Iroquois asking them to intercept British troops moving down the Hudson to occupy New York City. After this appeal, the Sons of Liberty put up a "pine post...called...the Tree of Liberty" where they conducted their daily exercises.[17] In 1772, the "Constitutional Sons of St. Tammany" (which grew out of the Sons of Liberty) claimed that they wished to preserve their "Constitutional American Liberties." Tammany was a respected Delaware chief who American patriots sainted. The New York City Sons of Tammany traced their roots to the Sons of Liberty.[18] Indeed, Benjamin Franklin was a member of the Tammany society, and after his death the society continued to tell Indian "Anecdotes of Franklin" at its meetings.[19]

As the American Revolution drew nearer, the American colonists turned to American Indian ideas and images to assert their desire for freedom and autonomy. In 1773, the Sons of Liberty in Boston dressed as "Mohawks" to dump tea in Boston harbor.[20] In August of 1775, members of the Continental Congress met with the Iroquois and recalled Iroquois admonitions of unity and said we have taught "our children to follow it." The Americans also invited the Iroquois to visit and observe our "Great Council Fire at Philadelphia...."[21] In January of 1776, George Washington introduced John Adams as a member of "the Grand Council Fire at Philadelphia."[22] In May and June of 1776, chiefs from "4 tribes of the Six Nations" were at Independence Hall.[23] In fact, the meeting with the Iroquois sachems was so important that the Continental Congress ordered George Washington to leave his post in New York City and come to Philadelphia to review Pennsylvania troops in late May 1776.[24]

On June 11, 1776 during the debates on independence, an Onondaga chief gave President John Hancock the name, "Karanduawn, or the Great Tree."[25] On the same day, plans for a confederation based on Franklin's 1754 Albany Plan of Union were reported to a committee of the Continental Congress that later drafted the Articles of Confederation.[26] After the Iroquois sachems left in late June and as Franklin's revised Albany Plan was in committee, James Wilson, delegate from Pennsylvania and future author of the first draft of the United States Constitution, argued forcefully for a confederation similar to the Iroquois League. On July 26, 1776, Wilson asserted that "Indians know the striking benefits of confederation..." and we "...have an example of it in the Union of the Six Nations." Wilson recalled his diplomatic mission to the Iroquois in 1775 when he stated that the "...idea of the union of the colonies struck [the Iroquois] forcibly last year."[27] In essence, Wilson, a friend of Franklin, believed that a strong confederation like the Iroquois Confederacy was crucial not only to the development of the new nation but also to the maintenance of friendly relations with the Iroquois.

In 1777, the Continental Congress published propaganda using an Iroquois prophecy that emphasized the synthesis of European and Iroquois ways in North America. The pamphlet, *Apocalypse de Chiokoyhekoy, Chiefs des Iroquois* (1777) asked the French to side with the Americans and implied that America was developing a government that reflected some Iroquois ways. Using a diplomatic idiom (a newscarrier bird, Tskleleli), the pamphlet proclaimed that an Iroquois prophecy was coming to pass and that if the French allied with the Americans it would be a "great victory for humanity."[28]

As the revolution unfolded, the Iroquois example of strength through unity gained a powerful hold on the American people. At Valley Forge, the Continental Army staged an elaborate St. Tammany Society ceremony on April 30 and May 1 of 1778. Washington's men marched past "May poles" and clasped bundles of thirteen arrows to demonstrate American unity in the style of the Iroquois. On the evening of May 1, 1778, the officers had a "song and dance in honor of King Tammany."[29]

After the American Revolution, three Virginia politicians and future presidents (James Madison, Thomas Jefferson, and James Monroe), decided to visit the Iroquois. The first to go was James Madison in 1784. Observing that Virginia and other states were unwilling to give powers to a central government, Madison decided to accompany the Marquis de Lafayette and his entourage on a trip to Iroquois country (the trip was to Fort Stanwix, near Rome, New York). What Madison witnessed was startling. Ostensibly, western expansion was Madison's main concern for the trip. Also, he must have been thinking about a government that would unite diverse peoples across a great geographic area when he thought of westward expansion. Perhaps this is the reason he consulted with his old friend Grasshopper, an Oneida sachem, when he got to Iroquois country.[30] However, the Oneidas gave Madison and his French companions some lessons about the virtues of Iroquois life before he got to Fort Stanwix. Several days into their journey up the Mohawk River, an Oneida scout accompanying Madison identified himself, in excellent French, as Nicolas Jordan from a village near Amiens. The Oneidas had captured Jordan during the French and Indian War, and he had married a chief's daughter. Jordan admitted to missing France initially but quickly said that "my age, ...my children, fix me here, forever." Jordan told Madison that as soon as the Oneidas adopted him, he experienced "...great humanity from them." Such a revelation surprised Lafayette and Madison.[31]

Even more surprising was the discovery of a white woman with strong opinions about the advantages of Iroquois life living among the Oneidas. On their trip up the Mohawk River to Fort Stanwix, Madison and his companions noticed a woman who was fairer than the other Oneidas. The woman admitted to being white and told them that she had been a servant girl in a New York manor house and had fled to the Iroquois in adolescence. The Oneidas freely welcomed her into their society, and she lived happily among them. She told the puzzled Frenchman and Madison that

> (t)he whites treated me harshly. I saw them take rest while they made me work without a break. I ran the risk of being beaten, or dying of hunger, if through fatigue or laziness I refused to do what I was told. Here, I have no master, I am the equal of all the women in the tribe, I do what I please without anyone's saying anything about it. I work only for myself,—I shall marry if I wish and be unmarried again when I wish. Is there a single woman as independent as I in your cities?[32]

These remarkable experiences had an impact on Madison as he was seeking to forge a new government in the next few years. While at Fort Stanwix, Madison renewed his friendship with the Oneida sachem, Grasshopper, who had visited Philadelphia several years earlier. Madison was exposed first hand to the ideas and political concepts of the Iroquois.[33]

Although Thomas Jefferson had wanted to visit the Iroquois with James Monroe in 1784, his appointment as French Ambassador forced him to abandon his plans to go to Iroquois country. However, James Monroe did go without Jefferson.[34] Jefferson was very emphatic about his lifelong interest in American Indians. In a letter to John Adams, Jefferson pointed out that, as a child and as a student, he was in continual contact with Native Americans. He explained this contact in these terms:

> ...concerning Indians, ...in the early part of my life, I was very familiar, and acquired impressions of attachment and commiseration for them which have never been obliterated. Before the Revolution, they were in the habit of

coming often and in great numbers to the seat of government, where *I was very much with them* [emphasis added]. I knew much the great Ontassete, the warrior and orator of the Cherokees; he was always the guest of my father, on his journeys to and from Williamsburg....[35]

John Adams responded to Jefferson's experiences with American Indians in this manner:

I have also felt an interest in the Indians, and a commiseration for them with my childhood. Aaron Pomham and Moses Pomham...of the Punkapang and Neponset tribes were frequent visitors at my father's house...and I, in my boyish rambles, used to call at their wigwam....[36]

Both Jefferson and Adams felt that their experiences with American Indians were important. Adams, like Jefferson, was skeptical of European ideas. Indeed, Adams felt "...weary of Philosophers, Theologians, Politicians, and Historians. They are an immense mass of absurdities and lies."[37]

In this intellectual environment, the innovative minds of the period easily turned to American Indian ideas. Franklin, Madison, Jefferson, and Adams were pragmatic enough to know that many of the concepts of American Indian liberty and freedom could not be transferred rapidly to Euroamerican forms of government. A few months before the Constitutional Convention, Jefferson wrote Madison about the virtues of American Indian government: "Societies...as among our Indians...[may be]... best. But I believe [them]... inconsistent with any great degree of population."[38]

Although most scholars are aware of the knowledge that Jefferson, Madison, and Franklin had of the Iroquois, few have noticed that Adams discussed American Indian governments in his works of American and world governments.

Sensing the need for an analysis of American and world governments, Adams wrote his *Defence of the Constitutions...of the United States* in 1786, and published it in 1787 on the eve of the Constitutional Convention. The *Defence* had been called "...the finest fruit of the American Enlightenment...."[39] Adams saw two conflicting views on the nature of government in America on the eve of the Constitutional Convention. He recognized in Franklin's admonitions of a unicameral legislature (as in the Pennsylvania Constitution of 1776) a sense of serenity of character, since the Pennsylvania Constitution placed a great deal of faith in one house as the best way to express the will of the people. However, Adams believed in a kind of intellectual perpetual motion where balancing the interests of the aristocracy and the common people through a divided or "complex" government seemed the best course to avoid anarchy and tyranny. Adams pointed out that the French *Philosophes* were on Franklin's side. Documentary evidence indicates that Franklin talked a great deal about the Iroquois and their customs in the French salons during the American Revolution. French physician and Philosophe Pierre Jean George Cabanis observed that while discussing concepts of liberty and government, Franklin "...loved to cite and practice faithfully the proverb of his friends the American Indians, 'Keep the chain of friendship bright and shining.'"[40]

Rather than believing, as Franklin did, in the voice of the people, Adams held a more pessimistic view of human nature and all orders of society in his *Defence*. He felt that a separation of powers in government was crucial to maintain a Republic.[41] With these ideas in mind, one can see how American Indian governments, and more specifically, the Iroquois League, were factored into the intellectual discourses on government at the time of the Constitutional Convention.

Drawing on his knowledge and experience with American Indians, Adams's *Defence* urged the Founding Fathers at the Constitutional Convention to investigate "the government of...modern Indians" because the separation of powers in their three branches of government "...is marked with a precision that excludes all controversy."[42] In creating a new constitution, Adams believed that the study of "the legislation of the Indians...would be well worth the pains."[43] In making these statements Adams recognized that some of the "great philosophers...of the age...," such as Benjamin Franklin and Turgot, were arguing in part for the establishment of "governments [like]...modern Indians."[44] Adams implied that the Iroquois style of government had "...fifty families governed by all authority in one centre." He believed that people like Franklin, advocating such unicameral governments, ran the risk of setting up governments that would develop the "individual independence of the Mohawks."[45] Adams knew the basic political structure of Native American confederacies since he described them in this manner:

> Every nation in North America has a king, a senate, and a people. The royal office is elective, but it is for life; his sachems are his ordinary council, where all national affairs are deliberated and resolved in the first instance; but in the greatest of all, which is declaring war, the king and sachems call a national assembly round a great council fire, communicate to the people their resolution, and sacrifice an animal. Those of the people who approve the war partake of the sacrifice; throw the hatchet into a tree, after the example of the king; and join in the subsequent war songs and dances. Those who disapprove, take no part of the sacrifice, but retire.[46]

When the men at the Constitutional Convention embraced the two house concept of John Adams, they were not enacting a copy of the English Houses of Lords and Commons. Rather they were trying to balance the parts of government one from another.[47] Obviously, Adams saw the wisdom of balance and separation of powers in American Indian governments and urged that their examples be examined and copied, in part.

Adams's admonitions to study Indian governments were not the only ones. During the Constitutional Convention, an editorial addressed "...to the Federal Constitution" used the bundle of arrows imagery (Section 57 of the Iroquois Constitution) and urged the drafters of the Constitution to incorporate the idea of "UNITE OR DIE" into their deliberations.[48] During the ratification period of the United States Constitution, Matthew Carey in consultation with Benjamin Franklin, asserted in a major Philadelphia magazine that Franklin's Albany Plan of Union (1754) had a strong "resemblance to the present system." Carey believed that an examination of the similarities of the Constitution and the Albany Plan will "convince the wavering, the new constitution is not the fabrication of the moment."[49] In reflecting on the process of drafting the constitution, Charles Pinckney (delegate from South Carolina) observed that "from the European world no precedents are to be drawn for a people who think they are capable of governing themselves."[50]

During the debates in South Carolina after the ratification of the Constitution, the Tammany Society toasted the constitution as our "tree of peace [that will] shelter us with its branches of union."[51] The Tammany Society (which had added "Or Columbian Order" to its name in the 1780s) believed that the United States was a synthesis of European and American Indian ideas. This notion persisted in the history of the Tammany society well into the 20th century.[52]

The interpretive and documentary data demonstrate that Native American/Iroquois ideas were used in American political discourse during the latter part of the 18th century. Moreover, American Indian notions of confederation, federalism, separation of powers, and uniting vast geographic expanses under a non-colonial government were important alternative concepts that the Founding Fathers used when they found portions of the British system lacking or repugnant (i.e., the monarchy, hereditary nobility, the lack of enumeration of human rights). In essence, America is not a complete transplantation of European society and the revolutionary generation rejoiced in that fact. Although there are a few scholars of the American Indian that oppose the notion that the ideas of the Iroquois and/or other Native American peoples were a factor in the evolution of American government, there is a body of interpretive and documentary evidence that provides a strong basis for a debate over the degree of American Indian (and more specifically the Iroquois) influence on the evolution of American government. Many colonists and some contemporary scholars may have wanted to assume that Euroamericans evolved a discrete transplanted European culture without American Indian influences, but the behavioral controls to facilitate such a policy were not present 200 years ago, and it is doubtful that they effectively exist today. Why is it so difficult to understand that when Europeans left Europe, they encountered non-Caucasians and thus were forced to function in a multi-cultural, multi-racial environment? We know that through slavery, segregation, theories of environmental decay, and scientific racism, Europeans and Euroamericans sought valiantly to create genetic and cultural extensions of Europe. However, North America was not and never would be Europe. Educational, religious and social institutions were not present to replicate the European order. Moreover, the Euroamericans needed more institutional control to perpetuate European ways than did the Europeans because the Euroamerican people had viable alternatives to European ways at their doorstep. Colonial governments in America recognized the difficulties in maintaining European ways. In 1747, George Clinton, Royal Governor of New York, believed that most American democratic leaders "...were ignorant, illiterate people of republican principle who have no knowledge of the English Constitution or love of their country."[53]

Postscript: A Critique of Responses

Ignoring the processes whereby Euroamericans created a new culture out of the American experience impoverishes everyone. As the American people become increasingly de-Europeanized culturally and genetically, it appears that some scholars are seeking to stop the process of de-Europeanizing American history. Such attempts in the 21st century will be seen as last ditch efforts to maintain an Anglo cultural veneer that sought to dominate new scholarship in a rapidly changing intellectual and social environment. This Eurocentric approach with its "gatekeepers," etc. is playing to the subliminal motivations that are present in the contemporary political situation.

In her criticism of the notion that the Iroquois influenced American democracy, Temple University anthropologist Dr. Elisabeth Tooker asserts that the Iroquois and other American Indian governmental ideas figure "not at all in the standard histories of the Constitution, nor in the documents on which they rest."[54] She asserts that it is a "myth" that the Iroquois and, by implication, other Native American confederacies had any influence on the evolution of the United States government. Tooker states that the Iroquois League and the United States Constitution are so structurally dissimilar that there is no relationship at all between the two documents. She argues that the matrilineal political nature of the Iroquois League is not reflected in the United States Constitution since it seems unlikely that the delegates would have opted for a "system under which each legislator was chosen by a close female relative of the previous holder of the office."[55] According to such logic, a student of history would be forced to assert that the American form of government drew nothing from the British model since England had a hereditary chief that was chosen by virtue of his or her patrilineal birth order. The fact is that the Founding Fathers embraced neither a matrilineal nor a patrilineal system, but chose an elective system for their executive and legislative branches.

Tooker also states "And should John Locke be demoted as honorary founding father of the United States and Deganawida and Hiawatha, legendary founders of the Iroquois League, be promoted in his place?" James Axtell, a scholar of Colonial American Indians and John Locke, believes that you cannot argue that John Locke was important in the creation of American government since "he wasn't very influential in either the revolution or the Constitution."[56]

Tooker also asserts that the Iroquois influence on American government "figures not at all in the standard histories." However, after editing Franklin's Indian treaties two generations ago, Julian P. Boyd (President of the American Historical Association, 1964) concluded that Franklin in 1754 "...proposed a plan for the union of the colonies and he found his materials in the great confederacy of the Iroquois."[57] In 1980, Arrell H. Gibson also concluded that the "Colonists...copied [Iroquois] democratic procedures and models."[58] Finally in a book published a year after Tooker's article, Robert D. Marcus and David Burner state that "Franklin was...so impressed with the structure of the Iroquois Confederacy that he recommended its government as a model for the colonies to join separate sovereign states into a powerful nation."[59]

Tooker discourses extensively on the work of Daniel K. Richter (an editor of *Ethnohistory* and Associate Professor of History at Dickinson College). Richter believes that the Iroquois "Grand Council was not designed to make policy decisions or to provide a central government for the villages of the Five Nations." Indeed, Richter states that the colonial documents "tell a different tale."[60] But if the League did not make policy decisions, then why did the Continental Congress deal with it and assume that it had such powers? In 1778, James Duane (delegate from New York) wrote Henry Laurens of South Carolina that "We expect daily the Resolution of the Indian council at Onondago. Much depends on it, and I wait here to receive it...."[61]

Tooker assumes that the factual data pertaining to the debate of the Iroquois influence on American government ends in 1775.[62] Yet many Iroquois sachems were present at the debates over independence in June of 1776 and they named the President (John Hancock) "The Great Tree."[63] She also ignores John Adams's *Defence of the Constitutions of the*

Governments of the United States,[64] which discussed a variety of American Indian polities, and on page 511 discussed American Indian governments and specifically mentioned the independence of the "Mohawks" and implied that the Iroquois government was composed of "...fifty families governed by all authority in one centre...."[65] Although Adams declined to attend the Constitutional Convention, he had his *Defence* published in Philadelphia in March of 1787 so that it could be used as a resource at the convention. Adams's *Defence* is recognized as one of the foremost works of political theory in late 18th century America.[66] Tooker also states that there is a "...lack of resemblance between the forms of government contained in the Albany Plan of Union...and in the Articles of Confederation...." Yet, Paul Smith, editor of the *Letters of the Delegates to Congress*, [67] observed that on June 11, 1776, plans to form a confederation based on Franklin's 1754 Albany Plan of Union were formulated in a committee of congress and that the "...4th, 7th, 8th and 12th of Franklin's Thirteen Articles are conspicuously incorporated into the committee's work." June 11, 1776 is also the same day that the Iroquois Sachems name the President of Congress, "the Great Tree." Tooker fails to consider the "Albany Papers" that were published in consultation with Benjamin Franklin in the *American Museum*,[68] in which it was stated that the Albany Plan bore a strong "resemblance...to the present system [U.S. Constitution]."

In apparent haste to debunk the myth of Iroquois influence on American government, Tooker routinely minimizes the historical data and then turns to an examination of the "ethnographic evidence," where she is more comfortable as an anthropologist. After a description of the Iroquois League, she then turns to an analysis of the "Development of the Myth" concerning the Iroquois and the development of American government. American Indian scholars in the past and today are her main culprits. She argues that Seneca scholar Arthur C. Parker gave the myth legitimacy in the early 20th century. But according to Tooker, the main source of the "myth" is a press release based on statements by the long dead Tuscarora anthropologist, J. N. B. Hewitt. Tooker concludes (after asserting earlier in her article that there was no scholarly opinion supporting the contention) that a host of scholarly opinion including the work of Ruth M. Underhill, A. Irving Hallowell, G. Elmore Reaman, Allan W. Eckert, and Peter Farb was derived from a press release[69] issued under the auspices of J. N. B. Hewitt (Tuscarora anthropologist at the Smithsonian Institution). Tooker offers no concrete evidence that these scholars had even read this press release and were thus misguided by Indian scholars Arthur C. Parker and J. N. B. Hewitt.

At the beginning of Tooker's article in *Ethnohistory*, the reader is told that there is no scholarly opinion on the issue of Iroquois influence, but then we find out at the end that there is significant scholarly opinion on the question. However, Tooker discounts all of this newfound scholarly opinion by saying it is all derived from a press release in 1936 issued at the behest of an American Indian scholar (it is significant that none of the above scholars allegedly led astray by Hewitt cite the press release).

Tooker's article has spawned even more misinterpretation. James Clifton believes that the American Indian claims about roots of the U. S. Constitution being in the Iroquois League during the Constitutional Bicentennial are part of a larger "Indian conspiracy." He states that:

> ...this was a skillfully staged media event, one of many organized in this period to support the lobbying effort to persuade Congress to swallow and support the political myth about the Iroquois, and that...instead of retelling traditional stories that their grandfathers had told them, were reading or quoting from the same press release issued elsewhere.[70]

Clifton accuses American Indians of manipulating the press for political purposes and his documentation on this allegation is Elisabeth Tooker's article in *Ethnohistory*. [71] However, Tooker's article contains only the obscure 1936 press release by the Tuscarora anthropologist, J. N. B. Hewitt, and she cannot prove that anthropologists of the last generation were influenced by it, let alone American Indians of the current generation.[72] The article does not mention any conscious press release carrying contemporary American Indians. With no documentation, can such accusations by Clifton be considered as scholarship?

In a similar vein, James Axtell (History) of William and Mary believes that there is no Iroquois connection to American government. He believes that the idea is "logically and historically fallacious."[73] Axtell thinks that as more and more American Indian scholars enter history and anthropology, there will be an "Indian threat" to history. He has observed the same debates in the political and scholarly arenas and stated:

> Frankly, some of us poor little white academics sitting in our little ivory towers are jealous of the access that some of the Onondaga leaders and some of these so-called Pro-Indian historians have had...The Indians are visible and have such legitimacy as Indians, of course you would expect them to know their history.[74]

Axtell fears that people will accept the "genetic fallacy" that American Indians are the only people capable of understanding their own history (has Axtell pondered the Anglo-American threat to the study of the Founding Fathers?).[75] In Axtell's statement below, one can see the state of ethnohistorical methodology at the end of the 20th century.

> ...I have a better shot at getting at the truth about this constitutional issue because I'm neither a descendant of a founding father, [and] I'm certainly not descended from the Iroquois, although I'm an Iroquoianist and love that as a subject, as I do all people in Eastern America.[76]

Also, the debate over the Iroquois influence on American government has caused William A. Starna (Anthropology) of SUNY, College at Oneonta to conclude that I write "...awful history, but it's political." In attacking me, Starna believes that in history "...like any scientific inquiry, you are dealing with empirical evidence." Then in a turn of logic, Starna's critique asserts that people can "...see the fallacy of what Grinde is doing without even having to know the information, without even having to look at the documents." Starna, like many anthropologists, believes that the issue of the Iroquois and the evolution of American government is linked to a larger "agenda." He believes that

> ...issues like the constitution, wampum, human burials, and a number of others have been very strong symbolic political elements for the [Iroquois] Grand Council. The Grand Council has been very effective in using these elements to...consolidate its own power base among the other Iroquois in New York State and also to promote itself as the government that the state and federal government should talk to.... There are a series of land claims in New York State, large land claims, and in fact, the Iroquois Grand Council...has intervened in one of those cases, although that isn't entirely clear because they would have to appear in some sort of a court setting to substantiate their intervention.[77]

Starna accuses me of being political and not using empirical evidence and then freely speculates on the behavior of the Iroquois Grand Council with hearsay evidence. He also believes that people have some *a priori* insight into the evolution of American government without even having to "look at the documents."

America is a synthesis of many peoples and cultures and that synthesis began when Europeans and Native Americans first met. Virginia's first native-born historian, Robert Beverly, saw America as the cradle of natural liberty and he believed Europe to be the symbol of authority. Beverly deliberately sided with the notion of natural liberty and American Indians, when he stated "I am an Indian."[78] Thus, the founding fathers who utilized American Indian governmental examples were engaging in a time-honored colonial intellectual tradition. After all, they had the advantage of observing Eastern American Indian governments in their full flower. In the final analysis, a balanced interpretation of the role of American Indian ideas in American history will yield a richer and more diverse history for us all.

Notes

This article was originally published in the *Northeast Indian Quarterly*, Volume VI, Number 4 (Winter 1989).

1. Julian P. Boyd, ed., *The Papers of Thomas Jefferson* (Princeton: Princeton University Press, 1950-) XI: 92-93. Note that Jefferson is writing Madison a few months before the Constitutional Convention. Both Madison and Jefferson had a great deal of experience with American Indian people and polities.
2. "William Penn to the Society of Free Traders, August 16, 1683," in Richard S. and Mary M. Dunn, eds., *The Papers of William Penn* (Philadelphia: University of Pennsylvania Press, 1982) II: 452-453.
3. Dunn, ed.: 454.
4. "Mr. Penn's Plan for a Union of the Colonies in America," February 8, 1697, O'Callaghan, ed. IV: 296-297.
5. Leonard W. Larabee and Whitfield J. Bell, Jr., eds., *The Papers of Benjamin Franklin* (New Haven: Yale University Press, 1962-) IV: 481.
6. Larabee and Bell IV: 482.
7. Carl Van Doren and Julian P. Boyd, eds., *Indian Treaties Printed by Benjamin Franklin, 1736-1762* (Philadelphia: Historical Society of Pennsylvania, 1938) 197-199. This reference is to the imagery of the Great Law of the Iroquois (see Arthur C. Parker, *Constitution of the Five Nations* (Albany: State Museum, 1916), Section 28. In using Parker's version of the Iroquois Great Law, the author recognizes that it is essentially a 19th century version. However, the salient rhetoric and imagery in the Great Law can be traced historically to the 17th century.
8. Van Doren and Boyd, eds. 131. Here the Pennsylvania Commissioners are reiterating the counsel of the Iroquois Sachem, Canassateego, a decade earlier, see Van Doren and Boyd 75. Once again, the "join together as one man" phrase is derived from Section 59 of the Iroquois Great Law, see Parker, Section 59.
9. Van Doren and Boyd, eds. 131.
10. Larabee, ed. V: 80-81. Indeed after returning from the Carlisle treaty, Franklin wrote Colden that he would send him a copy of the treaty, and Franklin also told Colden he had a copy of his book.
11. O'Callaghan, ed. VI: 869.
12. John Bigelow, ed., *Autobiography of Benjamin Franklin* (Philadelphia: J. B. Lippincott, 1868) 295.
13. O'Callaghan, ed.VI: 869-884.
14. O'Callaghan, ed. VI: 884.
15. Larabee, ed. V: 387-392. The term "speaker" is used in Section 14 of the Great Law. See Parker, *Constitution*.
16. Boyd, "Dr. Franklin: Friend of the Indians," in Roy N. Lokken, ed., *Meet Dr. Franklin*, (Philadelphia: The Franklin Institute, 1981) 239, 246. Arrell M. Gibson, in *The American Indian* (Lexington: D.C. Heath, 1980) 580-581 concurs in this analysis as does Vine Deloria, Jr. and Clifford Lytle in *American Indians, American Justice* (Austin: University of Texas, 1984) 122 that "American Indians...provided the empirical model for [Jefferson's] political vision."
17. See "Journals of Captain John Montresor, 1757-1778," April 4, 1766, *Collections of the New York Historical Society* (New York: Printed for the Society,

1868-1949, 2nd Set), XIV: 357 & 367-368. The White Pine or "Great Tree" is a symbol of the Great Law of the Iroquois Confederacy.

18. *Pennsylvania Chronicle*, May 4, 1772. Tammany was a respected Delaware chief who American patriots canonized. The New York City Sons of Tammany traced their roots to the Sons of Liberty. See "Preface to the Constitution," in "Constitution and Roll of Members of the St. Tammany Society, 1789-1916," MSS Div., New York Public Library.

19. *Pennsylvania Herald*, May 4, 1786. See also "Anecdotes of Franklin recited," in "Society of St. Tammany or Columbian Order, 1792-1916," in MSS Div., New York Public Library.

20. See John Adams to Hezekiah Niles, May 10, 1819 in *Niles Register*, XVI: 226.

21. "Proceedings of the Commissioners...to Negotiate a Treaty with the Six Nations, 1775," Papers of the Continental Congress (M247, roll 144, Item #134). The Iroquois expressed concern about the nature of the executive of the Continental Congress. No doubt, this concern resulted in the naming of John Hancock, "The Great Tree" in 1776. In the 19th century, Lewis Henry Morgan stated in *Houses and House-Life of the Aborigines* (Chicago: University of Chicago, 1965) 32 that the "Iroquois commended to our forefathers a union of the colonies similar to their own..."

22. Lyman H. Butterfield, ed., *Diary and Autobiography of John Adams* (Cambridge: Harvard University Press, 1961) II: 226.

23. Caesar Rodney to Thomas Rodney, May 28, 1776 in Smith, ed., *Letters of Delegates* IV: 99 & 281.

24. *Pennsylvania Gazette*, May 29, 1776.

25. Paul L. Ford, ed. *The Works of Thomas Jefferson* (New York: Putnam, 1904-1905) V: 430.

26. See Charles Thomson's "History of the Articles of Confederation," in Papers of the Continental Congress, National Archives (M247, Roll 22, Item #9). According to an editorial note in Smith, ed., *Letters of Delegates* IV: 252 "...the 4th, 7th, 8th and 12th of Franklin's Thirteen Articles are conspicuously incorporated into the committee's work."

27. Ford, ed., VI: 1078.

28. See *Apocalypse de Chiokoyhekoy, Chief des Iroquois (1777)*, Library Company of Philadelphia, and Dwight W. Hoover, *The Red and the Black* (Chicago: Rand McNally, 1976) 56-57. The prophet bird, Tskleleli or newscarrier, was an image used in the rhetoric of Iroquois diplomacy (especially with the French). See Peter Force, ed., *American Archives* (Washington: Government Printing Office, 1837-1853), 4th Series, vol. 3: 479, 491 for examples of how this image was used by the American commissioners and the Iroquois at the Albany Conference of 1775. Perhaps Benjamin Franklin, Arthur Lee, and Silas Deane as American Commissioners to France, worked on this pamphlet since they were all familiar with Iroquois ideas and imagery (see Ford, ed. II: 186). In 1776 while debating independence, it was asserted that Spain and France might be jealous of the United States since it might "...one day...strip them of all their American possessions" (see Ford, ed. VI: 1088). This pamphlet was a combination of ideas and images to alleviate Spanish, French, and Dutch fears about American independence. It also appeals to the "noble savage" sentiments so ardently advanced by French philosophers like Jean Jacques Rousseau. In the 19th

century, the Tuscarora anthropologist, J. N. B. Hewitt recorded a Tuscarora story, "The Prophet Bird-like Being" that could foresee events important to the survival of the tribe (see J. N. B. Hewitt Collection, MSS # 422, Nation Anthropological Archives, Smithsonian Institution). For a contemporary version of a similar apocalyptic prophecy, see Wallace (Mad Bear) Anderson (Tuscarora), "The Lost Brother: An Iroquois Prophecy of Serpents," in Shirley Hill Witt and Stan Steiner, eds., *The Way: An Anthology of American Indian Literature* (New York: Vintage, 1972) 243-247.

29. See John C. Fitzpatrick, ed., *The Writings of George Washington* (Washington: Government Printing Office, 1931-44) XI: 342. The Oneidas had brought corn to the Continental Army during the winter. See Cara Richards, *The Oneida People* (Phoenix: Indian Tribal Series, 1974) 53-54.

30. James Madison to Thomas Jefferson, August 20 & September 15, 1784 in William C. Rives and Philip R. Fendall, eds., *Letters and Other Writings of James Madison* (Philadelphia: J.B. Lippincott, 1865), I: 101. Madison was quite clear about the conditions of the time. He observed: "It required but little time...in the house of delegates in May 1784 to discover that...the Confederacy...retained the aversion of its predecessors to transfers of power from the state to the government of the union..." from Gaillard Hunt and James B. Scott, eds., *Debates in Federal Convention* (New York: Oxford, 1920) 6.

31. Eugene B. Chase ed., *Our Revolutionary Forefathers: The Letters of Francois, Marquis de Barbe-Marbois* (Freeport, New York: Books for Libraries Press, 1969) 191-193, and Irving Brant, James Madison (Indianapolis: Bobbs-Merrill, 1941) I: 330-331. It should be noted that Thomas Jefferson wrote *Notes on Virginia* at Barbois's request. Charles Thomson (adopted Delaware and Secretary to Congress, 1774-1789) would write a description of American Indian confederacies (including the Iroquois) in Jefferson's Notes (see Ford, ed., III: 314-315 & 499-504).

32. Chase ed. 211-212.

33. For a lengthier account of this affair, see Brant I, Chapter XXI. It should be noted that Madison was skeptical of the British Constitution also. In "The Federalist No. 53," Madison denounced the "dangerous practices" of Parliament and its damages to the British Constitution demonstrated by the Septennial Act of 1716. As a consequence, Madison abhorred the British Constitution's ability to change "by legislative acts, some of the most fundamental articles of government." In contrast, Madison advocated a "...constitution paramount to the government" or a written constitution (see Jacob E. Cooke, ed., *The Federalist* (New York: Meridian books, 1961) 576-578. For Thomas Paine, the Septennial Act of 1716 was proof that "...there is no constitution in England" (see Thomas Paine's "The Rights of Man," in Charles H. McIlwain, ed., *Constitutionalism: Ancient and Modern* (Ithaca: Cornell University Press, 1947) 2.

34. Stuart G. Brown, *The Autobiography of James Monroe* (Syracuse: Syracuse University Press, 1965) 38-39.

35. Thomas Jefferson to John Adams, Monticello, June 11, 1812 in Albert E. Bergh, ed., *The Writings of Thomas Jefferson* (Washington: Jefferson Memorial Association, 1903-1904) XI: 160. During this reconciliation correspondence with Jefferson and Adams, Benjamin Rush had written that he hoped

...the chain which now connects Quincy with Monticello continues to brighten with

every post (see Benjamin Rush to John Adams, February 12, 1812 in Lyman H. Butterfield, ed., *The Papers of Benjamin Rush* (Princeton: Princeton University Press, 1951) II: 1124.

In subsequent correspondence with Adams, Rush referred to "Scotch Sachem," (Dr. John Witherspoon of New Jersey), in Butterfield, ed. II: 1134, and he referred to Isaac Norris of Pennsylvania as "Quaker Sachem," see Butterfield II: 1167.

36. John Adams to Thomas Jefferson, Quincy, June 28, 1813, in Bergh, ed. XI: 288.

37. Bergh. In their reconciliation correspondence, Adams and Jefferson lamented the fact that Americans on the east coast by the War of 1812 were not being exposed to American Indian people and their ideas.

38. Thomas Jefferson to James Madison, January 30, 1787, in Julian P. Boyd, ed., *The Papers of Thomas Jefferson* (Princeton: Princeton University Press, 1950-) XI: 92-93. In discussing American Indian governments, the term "Indian" was often used to explain eastern Native American confederacies and tribal ways. When observers in the 18th century used the term it often implied "Iroquois" since they were the archetypal Indians of the 18th century in the American mind in much the same way that the Lakota or Sioux people are considered the "generic" Indian of the 20th century.

39. Gordon S. Wood, *The Creation of the American Republic* (Chapel Hill: University of North Carolina, 1969) 568.

40. Pierre Jean George Cabanis, *Oeuvres Posthumes de Cabanis* (Paris: Firmin Didot, Pere et fils, 1825) V: 256. Franklin is using the rhetoric and imagery of the Iroquois in the "Covenant Chain" quotation. Cabanis notes that Turgot, Helvetius, La Rochefoucault and other Enlightenment thinkers were in these discussions. This was probably why Adams levelled some of his criticism of unicameral governments at Turgot in his *Defence* as well. See Adams, ed., *Works,* IV: 299-302, 401-415, and for a copy of the 1776 Pennsylvania Constitution, see Francis N. Thorpe, ed., *The Federal and State Constitutions: Colonial Charters and Other Organic Laws* (Washington: Government Printing Office, 1909) V: 3084-3092.

41. Adams, ed. IV: 390. Having two legislatures, according to Franklin, resembled the practice of moving heavy laden wagons down hills by hitching teams of oxen at each end of the wagon to insure a slow, safe descent. See Charles Francis Adams, ed., *Works of John Adams* (Boston: Little, Brown, 1851) IV: 389-391.

42. Adams, ed. IV: 296.

43. Adams, ed. IV: 296-297.

44. Adams, IV: 296. See also 273-274, 279 and 391-393 for how Adams perceives the arguments of Franklin and Turgot. It should be mentioned that Franklin mentioned the Iroquois constantly in the salons that he attended in Paris from 1777-1784 (see Cabanis V: 256). Americans tend to forget that Franklin was styled the "Philosopher as Savage" in France during this period. See Peter Gay "Enlightenment Thought and the American Revolution," in John Howe, Jr., ed., *The Role of Ideology in the American Revolution* (Melbourne, Florida: Krieger, 1976) 48.

45. Adams, ed. IV: 511. In Jack P. Greene *The Intellectual Heritage of the Constitutional Era* (Philadelphia: The Library Company, 1986) 54. Adams's Defence is termed one of the "most significant works [in] the discussion of the

problem of forming new constitutions." Green also characterized Adams's Defence as "massive and learned."

46. Adams, IV: 566-567. Adams is obviously describing the Iroquois Confederacy here. His reference to animal sacrifice is probably the "White Dog Ceremony" of the Iroquois and his references to the sachem office being "elective" and the process of going to war come from the Great Law of the Iroquois, see Parker, ed., *Constitution of the Five Nations*, Sections 36-41 and 79-91 and for interesting eyewitness portrayal of the "White Dog Sacrifice," see "The Onondagan Indians," *Harper's Weekly*, February 17, 1872.

47. Wood 571, and Adams, ed. VI: 93.

48. *The American Museum*, II (August, 1787) 201. For the pertinent part of the Iroquois Great Law, see Section 57 in *White Roots of Peace, The Great Law of Peace of the Iroquois People* (Rooseveltown, New York: White Roots of Peace, 1971). James Wilson, delegate to the constitutional Convention from Pennsylvania, used this same "UNITE OR DIE" phrase when discussing at the Pennsylvania ratification convention how the delegates overcame some of the problems of unity and federalism (see Max Farrand, ed., *The Records of the Federal Convention of 1787* (New Haven: Yale University Press, 1911) III: 411. This phrase was also frequently used by the Tammany Society.

49. *American Museum*, V (February, 1789) 190.

50. *Charleston Columbian Herald*, June 9, 1788.

51. *New York Journal*, August 10, 1790.

52. *New York Journal*, August 10, 1790 and "Preface to Constitution" in "Constitution...of the Tammany Society, 1789-1916," in New York Public Library.

53. E. B. O'Callaghan, ed., *Documents Relative to the Colonial History of New York* (Albany: Weed, Parsons, 1853-1887) 670-671.

54. Tooker 306.

55. Tooker 313.

56. James Axtell radio interview with Catherine Stifter, October 14, 1989.

57. Julian P. Boyd, "Meet Dr. Franklin: Friend of the Indians," in Roy N. Lokken, ed., *Meet Dr. Franklin* (Philadelphia: The Franklin Institute, 1981) 239.

58. Arrell H. Gibson, *The American Indian* (Lexington, Massachusetts: D.C. Heath, 1980) 580.

59. Robert D. Marcus and David Burner in *America Firsthand* (New York: St. Martin's Press, 1989) 9.

60. Daniel K. Richter, "Ordeals of the Longhouse," in Daniel K. Richter and James H. Merrell, eds., *Beyond the Covenant Chain* (Syracuse: Syracuse University Press, 1987) 18, 12.

61. see James Duane to Henry Laurens, Albany, New York, April 24, 1778, Paul H. Smith, ed., *Letters of the Delegates to Congress* (Washington: Library of Congress, 1976-) 476.

62. Tooker 306-310.

63. Worthington C. Ford, ed., *Journals of the Continental Congress* (Washington: Government Printing Office, 1904-1937) IV: 430.

64. Charles Francis Adams, ed., *Works of John Adams* (Boston: Little, Brown, 1851) IV: 292, 298, 398, 566-67.

65. Adams 511.

66. Jack P. Greene, *The Intellectual Heritage of the Constitutional Era* (Philadelphia:

The Library Company, 1986) 54.

67. Paul Smith, *Letters of the Delegates to Congress*, IV: 99 & 281.

68. *American Museum*, V (February 1789) 190.

69. Tooker 325-329.

70. James Clifton *Being and Becoming Indian*, Chicago: Dorsey Press, 1989, 9.

71. Clifton 35.

72. Tooker 325-329.

73. James Axtell, *After Columbus* (New York: Oxford University Press, 1988) 252.

74. James Axtell radio interview with Catherine Stifter, October 14, 1989.

75. James Axtell to William Fenton, September 10, 1975, in William N. Fenton Papers, MSS collection #20, Correspondence Box 1979-1982 in the American Philosophical Society.

76. Axtell radio interview with Catherine Stifter, October 14, 1989.

77. William Starna radio interview with Catherine Stifter, October 14, 1989.

78. Robert Beverley, *The History and Present State of Virginia* (Chapel Hill: University of North Carolina Press, 1947) 9.

The Founding Fathers:
Choosing to be the Romans

Robert W. Venables

I n forming a new government for the United States in 1787, the Founding Fathers drew upon many philosophical traditions without replicating any. The Constitution was shaped by many different eras, peoples, and philosophies, and each of these influences made a unique contribution to the Constitution's cultural context and political content. Yet retrospectives of the Constitution refer to the medieval Magna Carta and other European precedents, but not to the Iroquois and other American Indian influences.[1] The Magna Carta certainly influenced the course of English events which, slowly over the centuries, evolved in English history to include more modern liberties. But of course the United States Constitution is not a replication of the feudal pact made between King John and his nobles in 1215 A.D. The Haudenosaunee influence on the Founding Fathers should be considered by using the same standard applied to the Magna Carta: replication is not a prerequisite for demonstrating influence.

When discussing property, for example, the Founding Fathers of the newly independent United States clearly drew upon variations of

European political structures and theories, primarily because the American Indian focus on property rights, especially with regard to land, was usually communal. A communal definition of property was antithetical to the Founding Fathers' faith in individually-owned property. However, when the colonists wanted to emphasize "liberty"— especially liberty from European tradition—they called upon images of American Indians to provide "noble" examples.

American Indians, and specifically the Haudenosaunee, influenced more than the concept of "liberty." As trading partners and military allies of the English, the Haudenosaunee played a primary role in encouraging colonial efforts to achieve inter-colonial coordination and unity. These Haudenosaunee efforts promoting colonial unity were important precedents to the unity finally achieved in the United States Constitution.

Since "replication" is not required in order to sanctify a European idea as having influenced the Constitution, Haudenosaunee influences belong in the history books alongside influences such as the Magna Carta. All are parts of the synthesis which led to the American Constitution. Alternatively, if one leaves out the Haudenosaunee influence, one should also leave out the Magna Carta.

A SUMMARY OF THE MAJOR INFLUENCES

The Haudenosaunee both directly and indirectly influenced the generation of the Founding Fathers and their various efforts to achieve unity. The summary listed below outlines the major influences which evolved from the historical events and philosophies discussed in this essay.

• The Haudenosaunee were major players on the political and economic stage, in what came to be known after 1677 as the Covenant Chain. In addition to being a counterbalance to French interests in Canada, the Haudenosaunee were important economic allies. The foundation of seventeenth century economic prosperity in New York was primarily the Haudenosaunee fur trade, and this fur trade remained an important element of the New York economy throughout the eighteenth century. Economic prosperity for New York also depended upon continuing a relatively peaceful (if frequently fraudulent) expansion onto eastern Haudenosaunee lands by white colonial land speculators and farmers. Thus Haudenosaunee political, economic, and military concerns were taken seriously by the colonists.

• Because of their importance to colonial English survival and prosperity, the Haudenosaunee often used councils that renewed the Covenant Chain to encourage the English to unite. Haudenosaunee admonitions for colonial coordination were a significant factor in broader colonial efforts at unity, and thus the Haudenosaunee contributed toward the precedents that culminated at Philadelphia in

1787 when the Founding Fathers drafted the United States Constitution.

• The Haudenosaunee were political examples for the colonists. The Haudenosaunee did not simply streak across the political sky once like a shooting star, only to disappear like so many coastal Indian nations had done. The example of the Haudenosaunee political structure could not be easily ignored—success against the odds always attracts attention. The colonial discussion of Haudenosaunee confederate unity was not simplistic: the colonists were interested in discerning both the strengths and the weaknesses of the Haudenosaunee "confederate" system compared to centralized systems from their European traditions.

• Haudenosaunee spokesmen (such as Canasatego in 1744) deliberately projected their Confederacy's goals as well as self-image into the cultures and politics of Europe and the colonies. The Haudenosaunee manipulation of the colonial and European media was considerable. Because the Haudenosaunee leadership realized that their society played serious economic and political roles, they also responded by "playing" their roles as American Indian chiefs to the hilt. Their use of wampum in their protocol and their dramatic oratory, for example, projected positive and assertive images to the Europeans and colonists who encountered them or, more often, read about them in newspapers, pamphlets, or books. Not incidentally, Haudenosaunee success at impressing the English colonists added to their own confidence and self-image.

• Indirectly, images of the Iroquois were philosophical and aesthetic symbols. The Europeans and colonists perceived these symbols through the prisms of their own European-oriented philosophies and expectations. The Haudenosaunee represented admirable political and social qualities, and thus the Haudenosaunee became symbols within the colonial culture of widely held ideals such as "liberty." The colonists' cultural perspective of the Haudenosaunee and other American Indians came into special focus with the philosophies of the European Enlightenment.

As a consequence of all of the above, the United States Constitution reflected the influence of the Haudenosaunee (and other American Indians) in the following ways:

• The Haudenosaunee and other American Indians were an influence on the Preamble, especially in the Preamble's poetic evocation declaring how and why the authority of "we the people" would be asserted in the Constitution. The concept "we the people" had long been symbolized during the colonial era by the images of American Indians. The concept was emphasized in the late seventeenth century philosophy of John Locke, who used American Indian examples among his primary arguments. In the decades just prior to the Revolution, that concept had often been personified by an Iroquois, especially a Mohawk. For the

Founding Fathers' generation, the concept "we the people" meant that the basic foundation for government came from people of European descent born in America. These American-born people had interests which were separate from those of Europeans. Ultimate power resided in these people. The political foundation was not the Divine Right of monarchs or royal lineage. It did not depend upon popes or archbishops, nor did it emanate from the nobility or from economic elites, or even from local or regional political powers such as "states."

• The Haudenosaunee and other American Indian nations influenced two specific provisions of the Constitution relating to Indians.

Article I, Section 2, Clause 3 ("Representatives and direct Taxes shall be apportioned among the several States...according to their respective Numbers...excluding Indians not taxed"). The Haudenosaunee were among the Native Americans defined as "Indians not taxed"—that is, not under the internal jurisdictional powers of the United States. Had the Haudenosaunee and other American Indian nations such as the Cherokees and the Creeks not successfully maintained their sovereignty during the colonial period, it is unlikely that the first provision would have been necessary. This provision is a significant recognition of the unique sovereignty of American Indian nations.

Article I, Section 8, Clause 3 ("The Congress shall have Power...To regulate Commerce...with the Indian Tribes"). This was an attempt to resolve an old grievance frequently raised by the Haudenosaunee and many other Indian nations and directed at corrupt colonial trading practices. Specifically, this Constitutional provision was in part a direct carryover from the trade and trade-related diplomatic issues raised by the Haudenosaunee both before and during the Albany Congress of 1754.

• By implication in five places, the Constitution reflects the impact of the Haudenosaunee and other Indian nations who continually urged that the colonists should coordinate Indian negotiations and policies through a central authority:

a) Article I, Section 10 prohibiting states from entering into treaties

b) Article II, Section 2, which also prohibits states from entering into treaties

c) Article II, Section 2, Clause 2, defining the treaty process

d) Article VI, Section 2, defining treaties as the supreme law of the land

e) Article III, Section 2, the power of federal courts over U.S. citizens who violate treaties

• The Haudenosaunee and other Indian nations were referred to euphemistically by the Founding Fathers during the Philadelphia convention, and these euphemisms survive in the Constitution (as do euphemisms for African-Americans such as "three-fifths of all other persons"). All references to "western" territories, "western" lands, and "new states" are in fact references to Indians and their lands. Rather than frankly affirm that the United States intended to take most of these Indian homelands, the delegates at the Philadelphia convention euphemistically referred to these Indian homelands as "western" lands, "western" territories, and as colonial and revolutionary claims and grants. In this guise, Article III, Section 2, clause 1 of the Constitution includes Indian homelands within the provision of lands claimed "under Grants." Article IV, Section 3, clauses 1 and 2 include Indian homelands within the terms "New States," "the Territory or other Property belonging to the United States," and "any Claims of the United States, or of any particular State."

By 1787, ironies had appeared in the long history of Haudenosaunee influence on English North America. One reason the Haudenosaunee were vital to English colonial policy makers was that they were allies against England's rivals in Canada, the French. The American Revolution which finally forged colonial unity reversed historic roles. The French, once fearful of English colonial unity, became allies of the American rebels. The Haudenosaunee, once so eager to promote English colonial unity, found that the American Revolution severely challenged their own confederate unity. Their warriors fought on both sides, just as their English colonial neighbors fought on both sides in that colonial civil war. Furthermore, the unity which the Haudenosaunee encouraged their colonial neighbors to implement was finally hammered out in the 1787 Philadelphia convention and secured in the Constitution. But because the Revolution destroyed the Covenant Chain, interdependence with Native Americans was no longer a goal of the united former colonies. The centralized powers of the Constitution, once urged upon the colonists by the Haudenosaunee, ironically enabled the united ex-colonists to seize most of the Haudenosaunee homeland.

PURSUING GOALS OF UNITY

The Haudenosaunee influenced both the political history which led to the Constitution and the philosophy upon which it was based. Any discussion of efforts by the colonists to unite is in part a discussion of Haudenosaunee influence.

In the seventeenth century, the Haudenosaunee had to deal with seven major and often revolutionary changes in the whites' colonial government along the Hudson. The Dutch were "in" until 1664. The English replaced them from 1664 until 1673, but the Dutch reoccupied the Hudson from 1673 to 1674. The English replaced the Dutch government again in 1674, but constant political shuffling marked the English colonial government on the Hudson until a dramatically new order, the Dominion of New England, was implemented along the

Hudson in 1688. This "Dominion" was overthrown by colonial revolutionaries in 1689, but these revolutionaries were in turn defeated during an English counterrevolution in 1691. During the eighteenth century, the various political factions struggling to dominate New York politics often created conflicting policies with regard to the fur trade, the acquisition of Haudenosaunee lands, and other Indian policies. No wonder the Haudenosaunee were eager to have the colonists stabilize their New York government.[2]

The inter-colonial context was equally stormy. The Haudenosaunee had to deal with New England colonies to their east and English colonies to their south which were rivals of the Dutch. After an English government replaced the Dutch in 1664, all the Haudenosaunee white neighbors except the French in Canada were now under English rule from London. But throughout the seventeenth and eighteenth centuries, New York, the New England colonies, and the English colonies to the south of the Haudenosaunee did little to exhibit the coordination implied by their being "subjects" of the same London government. The Haudenosaunee reaction to this continuing inter-colonial confusion was to urge virtually each colonial generation to unite. [3]

A major readjustment for the Haudenosaunee occurred between 1664 and 1677, when the Haudenosaunee and other northeastern Indian nations contended with complications arising from the 1664 English conquest of the Dutch colony of New Netherlands. Although the Dutch government was replaced by an English one, the Dutch colonists stayed. As one Mahican summarized this situation, "the English and the Dutch are now one and the Dutch are now English."[4] The English occupation of the Hudson Valley also meant that the Haudenosaunee had to cooperate with former English rivals in New England, Maryland, and Virginia—a problem further compounded when the Dutch reoccupied New York from 1673 to 1674.

Finally, at Albany in the summer of 1677, various Haudenosaunee spokesmen such as Carachkondie and Cannondacgoo joined with English officials from New York, Maryland, and Virginia in stipulating just how a unified colonial policy would be reciprocated by the Haudenosaunee. Thus nearly a century prior to the American Revolution, the Haudenosaunee encouraged English colonial unity and the coordination of policies. [5]

Of course, throughout the colonial period the Haudenosaunee experienced internal shifts of power as well. These would have occurred as part of the normal political evolution of any society. These political shifts were also influenced by factors such as smallpox epidemics and wars with the French in Canada and with rival American Indian nations to the north, south, east, and west. But internal Haudenosaunee debate was accentuated by the lack of English colonial unity. Each member nation of the Haudenosaunee Confederacy (from east to west: Mohawks, Oneidas, Onondagas, Cayugas, and Senecas) had to contend with different and often conflicting English colonial interests on each of their immediate borders.[6]

By encouraging the English colonials to coordinate their policies, the Haudenosaunee believed that their own trade and other relations with the English would be improved. The Haudenosaunee were often openly allied with the English militarily, and their trade was consistently dominated by ties to the English, despite French efforts to the contrary. The English trade link remained strong even when—and in many ways because—the Haudenosaunee pursued their own policy of armed neutrality between 1700-1701 and 1744. This armed neutrality played the English off against the French economically, in the fur trade, after it became clear in 1697 that the English lacked the will to defeat the French in Canada.[7]

Haudenosaunee armed neutrality, which began in 1700-1701, should be viewed within the wider historical context of eastern North America. From the end of King William's War in 1697 until 1744, France and England went to war only once—during Queen Anne's War between 1702 and 1713. During Queen Anne's War, the Haudenosaunee shifted from armed neutrality to openly aiding the English. Armed neutrality was a necessity for most of the period. Otherwise the Haudenosaunee were in danger of being politically dominated by the English and absorbed—already the fate of many of the coastal Indian nations. Armed neutrality meant that if the English were not careful in their trading relations, the Haudenosaunee could shift to a French military alliance. This in turn had the effect of keeping the English traders from creating an English trade monopoly, a real danger during the extended detente of the early 1700s when the English did not immediately need Iroquois military aid. During this period, the Covenant Chain provided a premise for improved trade relations and for attempted resolutions of Haudenosaunee-English issues such as the frequent crimes of colonial frontiersmen and corrupt colonial land transactions. In this context, if English policies were better unified, the member nations of the Haudenosaunee Confederacy would also be subject to fewer competing pressures from the various English colonies, and this in turn would decrease the needs of each Haudenosaunee nation to respond at a national level rather than at a confederacy level. The efforts of Haudenosaunee diplomats at encouraging greater English colonial coordination and unity was therefore a vital part of their own foreign policy. At the same time, by speaking out in favor of greater English colonial unity, Haudenosaunee speakers could reinforce the need to maintain their own confederate unity.

From the north to the south, virtually every effort English colonial leaders made to improve colonial unity had some kind of American Indian issue connected to it. Not all had Haudenosaunee influence—for example, the 1643 Confederation of New England was intended to unite the New England colonies for their next war with the local Algonquin Indians, so that the colonies would have more land to settle for their own people. But one of the goals of the Dominion of New England (1686-1689, implemented in New York during 1688) was a better coordination of trade relations and military alliance with the Haudenosaunee—a coordination the Haudenosaunee had called for since 1677. More significantly, as will be discussed below, the Haudenosaunee were the major reason the 1754 Albany Congress was convened and a major factor in the Albany Congress's Plan of Union.[8]

The colonists' premise for virtually all these efforts was that any improved coordination or unification would take place within Britain's larger political/imperial system. "Independence" was not a premise of colonial unification efforts. Unification for the purpose of independence was not even a goal at the beginning of the American Revolution. From April 1775 when the war began until July 1776, more than a year later, the goals of the revolutionaries were premised on securing "the rights of Englishmen" within the English empire.[9] Therefore, Haudenosaunee encouragement of colonial unity was also on the premise that the London government would be intricately involved. Moreover, except for the period during which the Puritan Revolutionaries dominated England (1649-1660), the premise included the point that any colonial unity would be under the authority of the Crown.

The fact that the premise for all colonial and the early Revolutionary efforts at unification included a political tie to London does not negate these efforts as being precedents for the unity sought under the United States Constitution. To separate all efforts at unity according to whether or not they occurred before or after the July 1776 Declaration of Independence is artificial. The issue of independence evolved from the issue of unity. Furthermore, it is important to note that the concept of unity—especially how much unity—was continually debated throughout the colonial period. There was no single, rigid definition of the idea of unity (a colonial tradition continued in the Constitution's considerable flexibility between federal and the "united" states rights). The Founding Fathers did not forget or ignore the range of attempts to achieve unity prior to 1776. Thus Haudenosaunee influences on colonial unity, which began in 1677, should be regarded as contributions towards the eventual Patriot unity at the beginning of the Revolution (1775-1776), the Declaration of Independence in July 1776, the Articles of Confederation (debated 1776-1781 and officially in effect 1781-1789) and the United States Constitution (1787-1789). One of the greatest ironies which emerged from all of these unification efforts is the fact that the Founding Fathers' Constitution established some of the same centralizing forces which many colonial governors—in part as a response to admonitions from the Haudenosaunee—had tried unsuccessfully to secure for more than a century.[10]

An appreciation of the "London Connection" in the efforts to achieve colonial unity is especially important in understanding the writings of a preeminent colonial leader and advocate of a more coordinated empire, New York's Cadwallader Colden. Colden provides an example of how the Haudenosaunee's persistent appeal to the colonies to unite could be made to work in tandem with similar appeals being voiced by many colonial leaders. Leaders who sought greater colonial unity often publicized the Iroquois' advice to forward their own arguments. Thus Cadwallader Colden's *The History of the Five Nations Depending Upon the Province of New York in America* (Part I, 1727 and Part II, 1747) reviewed Haudenosaunee history and quoted many Haudenosaunee speeches. Colden abhorred local factions such as that controlling Albany. He advocated a more centralized coordination of the British North American empire and desired a greater coordination of colonial policy, including colonial Indian policy. In 1747, Cadwallader Colden noted that Part I of his *History of the Five Indian Nations*—which included all of the speeches quoted above from 1693 and 1694—had been read in England as well as in the colonies after its publication in 1727. This is an indication that the influence of Haudenosaunee history was not simply being recognized among the colonists, but that it was an influence in England as well. Colden's publication in 1747 of Part II of his *History of the Five Nations* appeared during another period of significant interaction between the Haudenosaunee and the English colonists, precipitated by King George's War between France and England, 1744-1748.[11]

In 1727, Colden began Part I of his *History of the Five Nations* with an explanation of why he wrote it. In this explanation, Colden incorporated his belief that the Haudenosaunee illustrated an important premise of philosopher John Locke (1690): that American Indians governed themselves in ways which reflected the origins of government among all peoples.

> This Collection will, at least, be useful to any Person of more Capacity, who shall afterwards undertake this Task. When a History of these [Haudenosaunee] Nations shall be well wrote [sic], it will be of great use to all the British Colonies in North America; for it may enable them to learn Experience at the Expence of others [in eighteenth century usage, by carefully weighing the examples set by others]; and if I can contribute anything to so good a Purpose, I shall not think my Labour lost.
>
> ...We are fond of searching into Remote Antiquity, to know the Manners of

76

our Earliest Progenitors: if I be not mistaken, the Indians are living Images of them.

My Design in the Second was, That thereby the Genius of the Indians might better appear....

As I am fond to think, that the present state of the Indian Nations exactly shows the most Ancient and Original Condition of almost every Nation; so I believe, here we may with more certainty see the Original Form of all Government, than in the most curious Speculations of the Learned; and that the Patriarchal, and other Schemes in Politicks are no better than Hypotheses in Philosophy, and as prejudicial to real Knowledge.[12]

COLONIAL UNIFICATION AND THE COVENANT CHAIN

Because the Haudenosaunee and the English were so interdependent politically and economically, the Haudenosaunee admonitions to the English to unite often overlapped with Haudenosaunee declarations of alliance with these same colonists. This political and economic alliance was known from at least 1677 onwards as the Covenant Chain. How clearly the Covenant Chain was interrelated with Haudenosaunee calls for colonial unity is seen during a 1693 council at Albany, as recorded by none other than Cadwallader Colden in Part II (1747) of his *History of the Five Indian Nations*. At the time of this council, Governor Benjamin Fletcher of New York was also governor of Pennsylvania—an attempt by London at furthering colonial unity during a time Pennsylvania's proprietor, William Penn, was out of favor in London. Colden states that Fletcher "renewed the Covenant for all the English Colonies."[13]

A Haudenosaunee spokesman then replied to Governor Benjamin Fletcher in a speech quoted by Cadwallader Colden:

We are glad that our Brother Cayenguirago [Governor Fletcher] renews the Chain, not only between us and this Government [i.e. New York], but likewise with New-England, Virginia, Maryland and Pensilvania; it shall be kept inviolable by us the Five Nations, as long as the Sun Shines. We pray our Brother Cayenguirago to have a watchful Eye, that none of the other Colonies keep any Correspondence with the Enemy [the French and their Indian allies], but use their Endeavours to destroy them.[14]

A year later, in 1694, an Onondaga speaker, Sadakanahtie, also addressed Governor Fletcher. Sadakanahtie's speech clearly reveals that within the context of the Covenant Chain, Haudenosaunee concerns for their alliance with the English overlapped with Haudenosaunee concerns for increased English colonial coordination and unity. In his address, quoted by Cadwallader Colden in his *History*, the Haudenosaunee spokesman began by proclaiming trade and military unity with the English: "We assure you we will never separate from you, we still have one Head, one Blood, one Soul, and one Heart with you."[15]

Because this was a mutual obligation, however, Sadakanahtie noted that he was confident that the Governor would not make a separate peace with some of the enemies of the Haudenosaunee:

> As to [the Haudenosaunees' enemies] the Dewagunhas and Shawonons, we are confident Cayenguirago [Governor Fletcher] will not admit them into his Government, till they have made Peace with us, which we shall willingly grant. [16]

Sadakanahtie then reviewed how the Covenant Chain was connected to another Haudenosaunee symbol, the pine tree of peace:

> When the Christians first arrived in this Country, we received them kindly. When they were but a small People, we entered into a League with them, to guard them from all Enemies whatsoever. We were so fond of their Society, that we tied the great Canoe which brought them, not with a Rope made of Bark to a Tree, but with a strong iron Chain fastened to a great Mountain. Now before the Christians arrived, the General Council of the Five Nations was held at Onondaga, where there has, from the Beginning, a continual Fire been kept burning; it is made of two great Logs, whose Fire never extinguishes. As soon as the Hatchet-makers (their general Name for Christians) arrived, this General Council at Onondaga planted this [pine] Tree [of peace] at Albany, whose Roots and Branches have since spread as far as New-England, Connecticut, Pensilvania [sic], Maryland and Virginia; and under the Shade of this Tree all these English Colonies have frequently been sheltered. Then (giving seven Fathom of Wampum) he renewed the Chain, and promised, as they likewise expected, mutual Assistance, in Case of any Attack from any Enemy.[17]

Finally, having reviewed how the Haudenosaunee and the various colonies were united in the Covenant Chain and under the pine tree of peace, Sadakanahtie told the New York governor that if the English colonies were not going to assist the Haudenosaunee, the Haudenosaunee would have to make a separate peace with the French:

> Brother Cayenguirago [Governor Benjamin Fletcher], speak from your Heart, are you resolved to prosecute the War vigorously against the French, and are your Neighbours of Virginia, Maryland, Pensilvania, Connecticut and New-England, resolved to assist us?...if our Neighbours [the colonies] will not assist, we must make Peace. [18]

Despite continual setbacks, the Iroquois and the English spent much of the eighteenth century polishing this Covenant Chain. The Covenant Chain was a clear recognition by both sides that their political systems would remain separate even as their system of trade and alliance linked them together. If the Iroquois had not been a separate, independent people, the English would not have had to continually request their assistance, but would have simply required it.

During the year 1744, two Haudenosaunee emissaries, Hendrick and Canasatego, demonstrated how the Haudenosaunee implemented the Covenant Chain. That July, Canasatego spoke to an inter-colonial council at Lancaster, Pennsylvania while Hendrick addressed Algonquin Indians in Boston. In their speeches, both orators evoked the imagery of the Covenant Chain.

Hendrick, a Mohawk, was one of the most dominant Iroquois spokesmen during the colonial period. The Haudenosaunee had sent him, along with three other ambassadors, to the court of England's Queen Anne in 1710, and his influence ended only with his death in battle, on behalf of the English, in 1755. On July 24, 1744, in Boston, he warned Algonquins along the northern border of Massachusetts not to forget their role within the Iroquois-English Covenant Chain. The role for these Algonquins was subordinate. It was not unlike the roles expected from Indian nations to the north, west, and south of the Haudenosaunee who, during various wars, had been brought into the Covenant Chain either through negotiations or by being defeated—if not entirely conquered—by the Haudenosaunee. The Haudenosaunee and the English saw their mutual interests increased by evoking the common Covenant Chain to incorporate other Indian nations into the Haudenosaunee-English trade network. Neither the Haudenosaunee nor the English were as coordinated or as powerful as they each claimed to be, but empires of all ages and races have successfully bluffed their way across the stage of history because at least they were more coordinated and stronger than the opposition. Furthermore, as Hendrick's speech and the Algonquins' reaction to it demonstrates, subordinates fear the consequences of challenging the imperial authority. Hendrick's speech was recorded by a physician, Dr. Alexander Hamilton (no relation to the future Founding Father of the same name). Dr. Hamilton, a Scot, had settled in Maryland and was on an extensive tour of the colonies when he recorded Hendrick's address to a gathering of Algonquins in Boston, on July 24, 1744.

> We, the Mohooks...are your fathers, and you, our children. If you are dutifull and obedient, if you brighten the chain with the English, our friends, and take up the hatchet against the French, our enimies, we will defend and protect you; but otherwise, if you are dissobedient and rebell, you shall dye, every man, woman, and child of you, and that by our hands. We will cut you off from the earth as an ox licketh up the grass.[19]

However ambiguous the theoretical and political structure of the Haudenosaunee-English Covenant Chain may have been, the risk of challenging it was cruelly unambiguous. Thus an Algonquin spokesman replied:

> It is true you are our fathers, and our lives depend upon you. We will always be dutifull, as we have hitherto been, for we have cleared a road all

the way to Albany [the traditional site for Covenant Chain meetings] betwixt us and you, having cut away every tree and bush that there might be no obstruction. You, our fathers, are like a porcupine full of prickles to wound such as offend you; we, your children, are like little babes whom you have put into cradles and rocked asleep.[20]

However cruel Hendrick's ultimatum was, it incorporates an even harsher reality of colonial life. It was, after all, made on behalf of the Haudenosaunee-English Covenant Chain. Threats such as Hendrick's were one reason future Founding Fathers such as John Adams (b. 1735) and John Hancock (b. 1736/37) would be able to spend their teenage years in Massachusetts speaking English instead of French. Ironically, Hendrick's threats to insubordinate Algonquins outlived him. Four years after his death, in 1759, the English ordered Major Robert Rogers and his Rangers—including some Mohegan Stockbridges who were directly part of the Covenant Chain—to destroy the Abenaki village of St. Francis—inhabited by some of the relatives of the Indians Hendrick had warned in 1744. [21]

Hendrick's 1744 speech starkly represents one aspect of how the Covenant Chain functioned. As noted above, however, Hendrick's was not the only significant Haudenosaunee speech of 1744. Precisely how the Covenant Chain originally evolved between the Haudenosaunee and the English was explained in 1744 at Lancaster, Pennsylvania, by Canasatego, an Onondaga chief representing all of the Haudenosaunee. Canasatego's speech was to have a far wider impact on colonial history than Hendrick's.

Canasatego's speech on June 26, 1744, was translated by the interpreter Conrad Weiser. Canasatego eloquently reviewed how the Covenant Chain had its historic roots in trade—in a rope securing a Dutch trading ship to the Hudson River's northern shore. He went on to use imagery very similar to that used fifty years before by Sadakanahtie. Canasatego also refuted Maryland's claim to lands the Iroquois called their own, and in so doing outlined a stirring analysis regarding the place of Iroquois history and the history of the recent arrivals, the colonists. It is clearly the speech of the representative of an independent people who did not consider themselves to be subjects of the English Crown. Quite to the contrary, the Iroquois regarded themselves as the "elder brethren" of the English, at one with them in spirit, upon the same land. Canasatego's sense of history was dramatic, perhaps because he had been born in the 1680s and was about sixty years old—tall, strong, vigorous, and broad-chested—when he gave his Lancaster speech.

Brother, the Governor of Maryland,

WHEN you mentioned the Affair of the Land Yesterday, you went back to old Times, and told us, you had been in Possession of the Province of

Maryland above One Hundred Years; but what is One Hundred Years in Comparison of the Length of Time since our Claim began? since we came out of this Ground? For we must tell you, that long before One Hundred Years our Ancestors came out of this very Ground, and their Children have remained here ever since. You came out of the Ground in a Country that lies beyond the Seas, there you may have a just Claim, but here you must allow us to be your elder Brethren, and the Lands to belong to us long before you knew any thing of them. It is true, that above One Hundred Years ago the Dutch came here in a Ship, and brought with them several Goods;...and...we were so well pleased with them, that we tied their Ship to the Bushes on the Shore; and afterwards, liking them still better the longer they staid with us, and thinking the Bushes too slender, we removed the Rope, and tied it to the Trees; and as the Trees were liable to be blown down by high Winds, or to decay of themselves, we, from the Affection we bore them, again removed the Rope, and tied it to a strong and big Rock [here the Interpreter said, They mean the Oneido Country] and not content with this, for its further Security we removed the Rope to the big Mountain [here the Interpreter says they mean the Onondago Country] and there we tied it very fast, and rowll'd Wampum about it; and, to make it still more secure, we stood upon the Wampum, and sat down upon it, to defend it, and to prevent any Hurt coming to it, and did our best Endeavours that it might remain uninjured for ever. During all this Time the New-comers, the Dutch, acknowledged our Right to the Lands, and sollicited us, from Time to Time, to grant them Parts of our Country, and to enter into League and Covenant with us, and to become one People with us.

AFTER this the English came into the Country, and, as we were told, became one People with the Dutch. About two Years after the Arrival of the English, an English Governor came to Albany, and finding what great Friendship subsisted between us and the Dutch, he approved it mightily, and desired to make as strong a League, and to be upon as good Terms with us as the Dutch were, with whom he was united, and to become one People with us: And...he found that the Rope which tied the Ship to the great Mountain was only fastened with Wampum, which was liable to break and rot, and to perish in a Course of Years; he therefore told us, he would give us a Silver Chain, which would be much stronger, and would last for ever. This we accepted, and fastened the Ship with it, and it has lasted ever since.[22]

Several days later, Canasatego gave his concluding remarks to the English colonial subjects of King George II, urging them to consider the example of the Haudenosaunee:

We heartily recommend Union and a good Agreement between you our Brethren. Never disagree, but preserve a strict Friendship for one another, and thereby you, as well as we, will become stronger.

OUR wise Forefathers established Union and Amity between the Five Nations; this has made us formidable; this has given us great Weight and Authority with our neighboring Nations.

WE are a powerful Confederacy; and, by your observing the same Methods our wise Forefathers have taken, you will acquire fresh Strength and Power; therefore whatever befals you, never fall out one with another.[23]

Coincidentally, the date in 1744 on which Canasatego spoke the words quoted above was the fourth of July.

Unfortunately, Canasatego's advice was offered to the English colonies whose unbridled diversity would continue unchecked by colonial administrators. This was due to rivalries among the colonies, each of which continued to be jealous of its own particular economies, land claims, lifestyles, and forms of government. They even quarreled over which of the many Christian religions, if any, each colony would follow. But among the many colonists who attempted to use Canasatego's advice to further their own interests in colonial unity was Benjamin Franklin.

Benjamin Franklin printed Canasatego's speech as part of the full record of the 1744 Lancaster negotiations. Franklin sent three hundred copies to London to sell. Thus, in addition to the speech's availability in the colonies, Canasatego's words were read in London as well. The treaty's publicity served two purposes: it was news, but it was also literature, to be read as current affairs or as literary recreation—or both. Clearly, however, the lack of unity among the colonists was disturbing to political thinkers like Franklin. It is therefore not surprising that Franklin echoed Canasatego's sentiments when he wrote to James Parker on March 20, 1750/51, irritated that the colonists had yet to accomplish a union comparable to that of the Iroquois.

> It would be a very strange Thing, if six Nations of ignorant Savages should be capable of forming a Scheme for such an Union, and be able to execute it in such a Manner, as that it has subsisted Ages, and appears indissoluble; and yet that a like Union should be impracticable for ten or a Dozen English Colonies, to whom it is more necessary, and must be more advantageous; and who cannot be supposed to want an equal Understanding of their Interests.

> Were there a general Council form'd by all the Colonies, and a general Governor appointed by the Crown to preside in that Council, or in some Manner to concur with and confirm their Acts, and take Care of the Execution; every Thing relating to Indian Affairs and the Defence of the Colonies, might be properly put under their Management.[24]

In the above quote, note that Franklin immediately follows his analogy to Iroquois unity—the use of the Iroquois as a symbol—with the fact that the coordination of Indian affairs is a primary reason for seeking colonial unity. Thus symbol and political reality are cited simultaneously by Franklin, further proof of how direct influences upon the colonists by the Haudenosaunee were more than just philosophical.

Far from simply remaining the view of a private citizen, Franklin's statement became a topic of public discussion when it was published anonymously in New York in 1751 as part of a larger work on Indian-white relations (also written anonymously, by Archibald Kennedy)–*The Importance of Gaining and Preserving the Friendship of the Indians to the British Interest*. In 1752, this work was reprinted in London. Thus Franklin's reference to the Iroquois became a matter of public discussion on both sides of the Atlantic—at a time when people had already been stimulated by Franklin's publication of Canasatego's 1744 speech and by the 1747 publication of Part II of Cadwallader Colden's *History of the Five Nations*.[25]

By encouraging the English to unite, the Haudenosaunee hoped to make the English a stronger part of the Covenant Chain. Because the Covenant Chain was a vital part of English colonial prosperity, Haudenosaunee advice was not received by colonial leaders such as Franklin as simply theoretical or rhetorical. Thus in 1753 the Mohawk spokesman Hendrick forced the colonists to consider greater unity when he appeared before the colonial council of Governor George Clinton in New York City and complained about corrupt trade practices and fraudulent land transactions. Angrily, he declared that the Covenant Chain had been broken. Comparable complaints were being made by other Indian nations in the south. The colonists—and their imperial masters in London—responded, and the Albany Congress of 1754 was convened. Virginia did not send delegates, but New York, Pennsylvania, Maryland, Connecticut, Rhode Island, Massachusetts, and New Hampshire did. Although the proposed Albany Plan of Union, authored primarily by Benjamin Franklin, was not implemented, it became a precedent. During the American Revolution, Franklin authored another plan of unity, one version of which would evolve into the Articles of Confederation. Finally, Franklin would become the gray eminence at the Philadelphia Convention in 1787.[26]

The Haudenosaunee admonished the English colonists to unite because the Iroquois wanted English policies and actions to be coordinated and consistent. That is, the Haudenosaunee advice was based on self-interest. It was not altruistic, and it was not theoretical in its foundation. It was aimed at securing the English as economic and military allies so that the Haudenosaunee and their culture would survive.

Of course Haudenosaunee philosophy was only one among many influences on those colonists who were attempting to secure greater colonial unity. Colonists pursuing that goal drew on their own heritage and history. They discussed ancient Greece, ancient Rome, medieval Europe, and contemporary political unions such as those of Switzerland and The Netherlands. They also drew upon the examples (good and bad) of seventeenth century attempts to unite the colonies: for example, the 1643 Confederation of New England and the 1686 Dominion of New England. They were also very aware of various plans of unity continually proposed and discussed by English government officials in London. In reading history and philosophy, however, the colonists saw all the examples they could draw upon as worthy of comparisons and contrasts. Haudenosaunee influences should therefore be viewed in a comparative context, rather than in isolation. For example, Cadwallader Colden, quoted earlier, compared the Haudenosaunee people with the earliest Greeks and the earliest Romans, and he also compared the Haudenosaunee Confederacy with The Netherlands.[27]

NOBLE SAVAGE, NECESSARY ALLY

For the Founding Fathers, the Philadelphia convention of 1787 was a final step along a path which had begun for their generation in 1754 at the Albany Congress. In contrast, United States citizens today tend to see the Constitution as a beginning, not an end—as the term "Founding Fathers" proclaims. Similarly, different perspectives of Native Americans are found in the eighteenth and twentieth centuries.

The Founding Fathers' perception of Indians in general, and the Haudenosaunee in particular, was based in part on the recent conflict of American Revolution which found whites and Indians fighting on both sides. But the foundation of the Founding Fathers' views of the Iroquois and other Indians was a cultural accumulation of three centuries of Indian-white interaction and interdependence.

Regarding American Indians, the Founding Fathers' chronological frame of reference was 1492 to 1787. Between 1492 and 1787, Indian issues were far more interdependent with white political and economic survival. Following the 1787 Philadelphia convention and the implementation of the Constitution in 1789, the United States' political and economic survival was no longer based on interdependence with Indians. Instead, national prosperity increasingly depended upon subjugating them. This subjugation often included war, but it could also be carried out through removal to other geographic locations and concerted, government-sponsored efforts at forced assimilation. Ultimately, subjugation is still carried out in Congress and in the federal courts, often through the unilateral imposition of United States claims to sovereignty.[28]

The colonial image of Native Americans was, at best, that of "noble savages." Today's popular image of Native Americans among non-Indians continues to include a part of this idealistic vision. But it has also been broadly shaped by the nineteenth century, when the United States or its citizens were constantly at war with one Indian nation or another. At best, the nineteenth century created a new image of the American

Indian as a kind of "noble opponent"—none more noble than the Plains Indian warriors with their flowing feathered headdresses.

In contrast, all the Founding Fathers grew up in a world where Haudenosaunee traders and diplomats regularly frequented colonial capitals and other towns. The Haudenosaunee were regarded as valued trading partners and essential military allies in the long struggle with the French in Canada. In fact, if the Haudenosaunee had not been allies, it is probable that the Founding Fathers would have spent their childhoods learning French, not English. This fact of colonial life, that the Haudenosaunee were friends and not enemies, needs to be emphasized in analyzing the impact the Haudenosaunee would have on the Founding Fathers.

Of course some American Indians were enemies of the English colonists. These enemies were often the Indian allies of the French or Spanish, but sometimes they were enemies simply because they were defending their homelands. This negative image, however, was more than counterbalanced by a significant colonial reality: the constant interaction and interdependence with Indian nations such as the Haudenosaunee, the Creeks, and the Cherokees. Most of the Indians the colonists encountered for most of their lives were friends, not enemies. Part of the tragedy of the American Revolution is that in less than a decade the Revolution obliterated a century and a half of Indian-white cooperation.

Noble Mohawks: Haudenosaunee Symbol of "America"

Because of the Haudenosaunee's political, economic, and military importance, the Haudenosaunee in turn exerted an important influence on colonial culture. The image of an Iroquois, especially that of a Mohawk male, played an important and ubiquitous role as a symbol in the culture of the Founding Fathers.

The symbolic image of a Haudenosaunee, especially a Mohawk, can perhaps be appreciated through an analogy. A common Indian image today is the "stereotype" of the Plains Indian warrior wearing a feathered headdress. By comparison, during the one hundred years before the American Revolution, the image of a Mohawk had become as ubiquitous. The difference was, of course, that the Mohawk was, in all but the last decade of the colonial era, a "friend"—whereas at best the Plains Indian was a "noble opponent."

On maps, in fine arts such as sculpture and painting, on fine porcelain, in political cartoons, and even on wall murals and wall coverings, the figure of a noble Mohawk came to represent the essence of "Indian." This image was in turn a cultural extension of earlier images of other Indians—of Caribs, Aztecs, and various other North and South American Indians. During the sixteenth and seventeenth century, these

Indians' physical characteristics and costumes had come to symbolize the essence of the Western Hemisphere or "America."[29] The image of a noble Haudenosaunee, especially a Mohawk, gradually became synonymous with this broader symbol of "America."

What do positive symbols reveal? To be effective and widely used—which the symbol of the "Mohawk" was—a positive symbol must already be widely recognized by the people who use it. A positive symbol must also provide a kind of shorthand, compacting qualities which are admired by the people who use the symbol.

Of course, the positive symbols of the Haudenosaunee, and of the Mohawks in particular, were not necessarily complete portrayals. But both symbols and influences frequently come from what is believed, complete or not.

Many colonists were thoroughly familiar with the Haudenosaunee. Colonial officials such as Sir William Johnson actually observed and to a certain extent participated in the complex inner workings of the Haudenosaunee political system. Johnson reported directly to the British commander-in-chief for all of North America, General Thomas Gage, who in turn relayed Johnson's reports to London.[30] Even colonists who did not fully understand the internal mechanisms of the Haudenosaunee Confederacy or League appreciated its successes: in trade, in war, and in its diplomatic balancing of its formidable English and French neighbors.

The rich tapestry which interwove Haudenosaunee and colonial experiences included a major linguistic twist in the visual symbol of an American Indian representing "America." The Founding Fathers and other Patriots of the American Revolutionary era used the word "American" to identify themselves as a unique people, born in America, and not simply a people who were colonial extensions or expatriates of the societies of Britain and the rest of Europe. But "American" was originally synonymous with the word "Indian." In the seventeenth century, had anyone asked Captain John Smith at Jamestown or Miles Standish at Plymouth how the "Americans" were faring, both would have reported on the local Indian nations. Smith and Standish were, after all, "Englishmen." But after the middle of the eighteenth century, the English colonists co-opted the word "American" just as they had the land. By the time the American Revolution began, the English colonists were regularly calling themselves–and becoming known in Europe—as the "Americans."[31]

To be an "American" was to be separate and different from a European. After the Declaration of Independence, "American" also meant "independent." As mentioned above, American Indians symbolized this separateness, difference, and independence. American

Indians were seen as free from the feudal heritage of Europe, where monarchs still ruled and where hereditary nobles dominated society.

Europeans and European colonists had often perceived American Indians, even those of Mesoamerica, as living at an earlier stage of human development, a stage which the ancestors of the Europeans had also once experienced. Indians north of Mexico were also often stereotyped as people of the woods, in French "sauvage" and in English "savage." When Europeans were originally observing what they believed to be the true nature of the American Indians, the term "savage" by itself did not imply cruelty. "Savages" could be either "noble savages" or "brutal savages."[32]

An important element on the "noble" side of the noble/brutal equation might best be characterized as the "common cause." The "common cause" was an attempt to bridge the European and American Indian cultures by defining universals which transcended racial and cultural differences. Finding a "common cause" was not illogical, because the analogy between American Indians and European tribal people prior to the Roman conquest was already widespread in England during the age of Shakespeare. In 1590, an illustrated edition of Thomas Hariot's 1588 *A briefe and true report of the new found land of Virginia* included engravings of American Indians as well as the ancient Picts of pre-Roman Britain. All were drawn by John White and engraved by Theodore de Bry. The caption accompanying one of these ancient Picts stated [with spelling modernized]: "In times past the Picts, habitants of one part of great Britain, which is now named England, were Savages...."[33]

The poet John Dryden first used the term "noble savage" in 1670 to describe primitive Europeans (in *The Conquest of Granada*).[34] The term "noble savage" was eventually extended to include American Indians and other Indigenous people like the Hottentots of South Africa. In seeking to identify common links among all of humanity, many Europeans believed or hoped that American Indians shared universals, and—whatever their political, social, technological, and economic differences—an inherent human equality. The philosopher John Locke used this concept as a major premise for concluding that power originated in the people and not in Divine Right of monarchs. The concept of all humans as originally "noble savages" and Locke's concept of power in the people combined to become a part of the premise for Thomas Jefferson's eloquent declaration that "all men are created equal."

In the eighteenth century, the Haudenosaunee were perceived by many colonists such as Benjamin Franklin to have admirable traits that the colonists would do well to imitate and learn from. In this sense, the Haudenosaunee were perceived as noble savages with whom the colonists had "common cause." This perception fostered an interaction based on respect, and flawed as it was, it served as a precursor to twentieth century pluralism and ethical relativism. At the same time, however, a self-serving aspect of this belief in a common cause allowed Europeans to believe it would not be impossible—and in fact it would be logical—to "convert" the Indians to the whites' allegedly "advanced" or "civilized" approach to religion, economics, and politics.

CULTURAL CONTRASTS

Because Europeans so frequently related American Indian examples to their own needs and viewpoints, Europeans developed an ethnocentric appreciation of Indian cultures. The Europeans probably could not have done otherwise, for they devotedly believed in a single God who had created a single universe. At the same time, the Haudenosaunee dealt with the European colonists from their own Iroquois perspective. This Haudenosaunee worldview included a perspective that the environment was teeming with a variety of life forms, all of whom possessed spiritual essences ("souls") which were spiritually equal to each other. This was in marked contrast to the Europeans' view of the natural world as inferior. The Europeans believed that humans held the premier position atop a hierarchy defined by Genesis and ordained by their God. Given these basic differences in world view, cultural influences and interactions were uneven and partial.[35]

The fact of major cultural differences between Indians and European colonists has a vital implication in understanding the Haudenosaunee impact on the Founding Fathers and the Constitution. Because of the cultural contrasts, the replication of one culture's system by another was impossible. Because there could be no replication, influence is all that can be expected. To expect the replication of a Haudenosaunee concept by the Founding Fathers is to deny the vast cultural differences which kept the Haudenosaunee and the generation of the Founding Fathers apart, and in a positive sense made each of them distinct peoples.

The details of one encounter particularly suggest the contrast of Haudenosaunee and European politics and cultures. In 1710, a delegation of four Mohawk Iroquois (including at least one who was actually an adopted Mahican) visited London and the court of Queen Anne. The Mohawks' experiences on their diplomatic journey reveal examples of the cultural abyss which existed between European and Haudenosaunee but simultaneously suggests some insights into what might have been potential cultural bridges as well. This encounter is also perhaps the most famous diplomatic visit to Europe by any Indian group. Called by their hosts the "Four Kings" (one more than the Magi), these Haudenosaunee were in fact simply the ambassadors of their people. They brought with them a great purple/black and white wampum belt of sacred beads to a monarch whom they considered to be an ally, a friend, and—most importantly—their equal. Their leader was Te Ye Neen Ho Ga Prow of the Wolf Clan. Known primarily by his English name Hendrick, he would later befriend William Johnson on the frontier of colonial New York and, as an old man (about seventy years old), die in 1755 during a furious battle with the French at Lake George. Equally impressive among the delegates was Saga Yean Qua Prab Ton, known as Brant. Brant was beautifully tattooed upon his face and chest. His grandson, Joseph Brant, Thayendanegea, would visit London in 1775 and later fight during the American Revolution as an ally of the British.[36]

Hendrick and Brant, together with Oh Nee Yeath Ton No Prow (John) and Elow Ob Koam (the Mahican, known as Nicholas), presented the wampum to Queen Anne at St. James Palace on April 19, 1710, and spoke to her through a translator:

GREAT QUEEN!

WE have undertaken a long and tedious Voyage, which none of our Predecessors [among the Iroquois] could ever be prevail'd upon to undertake. The Motive that induc'd us was, that we might see our GREAT QUEEN, and relate to Her those things we thought absolutely necessary for the Good of HER and us Her Allies, on the other side of the Great Water.

We doubt not but our Great Queen, has been acquainted with our long and tedious War, in Conjunction with Her Children (meaning Subjects) against Her Enemies the French; and that we have been as a strong Wall for their Security, even to the loss of our best Men....[37]

They then admonished the Queen to fight the French by better coordinating efforts with her colonies—a trans-Atlantic version of the now-traditional call by the Haudenosaunee for the English to unite.

We were mightily rejoiced when we heard...that our Great Queen had resolved to send an Army to reduce Canada...and in Token of our Friendship, we hung up the Kettle, and took up the Hatchet.... But at last we were told, that our Great Queen, by some important Affair, was prevented in Her Design for that Season. This made us extream Sorrowful....

We need not urge to our Great Queen, more than the necessity we really labour under obliges us, that in Case our Great Queen should not be mindful of us, we must, with our Families, forsake our Country and seek other Habitations, or stand Neuter; either of which will be much against our Inclinations.[38]

In addition to being a warning that the Haudenosaunee could return to their 1701 policy of armed neutrality, the threat of standing neutral also demonstrated that the Haudenosaunee saw themselves as independent, for no true "subject" of a European monarch would have the power to declare neutrality.

Those Englishmen who could not crowd around the Haudenosaunee diplomats in person could read about them in the *Spectator*. Indeed, so popular was the image of the Mohawks that a group of young gentlemen formed a club called the "Mohocks." They soon became famous for wrecking taverns, rioting in brothels, and in general wreaking havoc around London, with the result that the word "Mohawk" took on a connotation in England of lawlessness. This was an "influence" the Haudenosaunee diplomats could not have anticipated.[39]

"THE MOHAWKS ARE COME!"

Sixty years later, different gangs again took on the disguise of Mohawks. On November 27, 1773, a broadside appeared in New York City protesting a British tax on tea and promising trouble to any merchant who stored the detested tea in his warehouse. The broadside was signed "The Mohawks."[40] Then, a month later, a Boston gang of "Mohawk" Sons of Liberty dumped tea into the harbor to protest British taxation. Shouting "The Mohawks are come!" and other rebellious slogans such as "Boston harbor a tea pot tonight!"[41] thousands of demonstrators surged out of Boston's Old South Meeting House just as the sun set on December 16, 1773. As the mob surged toward the waterfront, the Sons of Liberty took the lead—all disguised as Mohawks. The crowd punctuated their enthusiasm with war-whoops. Among the protesting colonists, one couldn't be more "American" than to be "Mohawk." (Much to the dismay of conservative scholars two hundred years later, these Mohawk Sons of Liberty did not march to the Boston Tea Party chanting "Mag-na Car-ta! Mag-na Car-ta!")

At the same time the image of the "Mohawk" symbolized the determination of colonial political protest, the Mohawk image and that of other Iroquois were significant in the aesthetic world of the Founding Fathers. Of all the paintings and portrayals of American Indians, no work is more famous than a canvas executed in 1770 by Benjamin West, "The Death of General Wolfe," commemorating the death in battle of British General James Wolfe as his troops defeated the French in 1759 at Quebec. Benjamin West, born in Pennsylvania but painting in England, placed an Iroquois warrior—almost undoubtedly a Mohawk— prominently in the left foreground of the painting.[42]

"The Death of Wolfe" was so popular that West duplicated his dramatic canvas at least seven more times for his wealthy admirers. Beginning in 1776, an engraving of the painting by William Woollett began to be sold in England, America, and France. This engraving became, according to art scholars Helmut von Erffa and Allen Staley, "one of the most commercially successful prints ever published."[43]

Clearly, by the beginning of the American Revolution, Europeans and their colonial kin had built up a complex—and often contradictory—impression of the Haudenosaunee (and of all American Indians), a rich tapestry involving all the arts and literature and intertwined with nearly every aspect of eighteenth century life.

BENJAMIN FRANKLIN AND THE HAUDENOSAUNEE

The man who singularly bridged European philosophical ideas with the reality of American life was Benjamin Franklin. Born in 1706, he would be eighty-one when the Philadelphia Convention was convened. Franklin understood the complexities of Indian-white relations. During his lifetime, he had lived through several wars between the French and the English during which each side had its Indian allies.

In 1783, while in France as the Patriots' ambassador, Benjamin Franklin focused many of his previous impressions of the Iroquois into one essay. In the tradition of Montaigne, whom Franklin admired, Franklin's succinct "Remarks Concerning the Savages of North-America" remains a classic of both literature and history. Of all the Enlightenment thinkers on either side of the Atlantic, Franklin comes the closest to the cultural relativism and pluralism which was missing in the vast majority of Enlightenment thinkers. Franklin's major examples are drawn primarily from his understanding of the Iroquois Confederacy, although he draws upon events involving the Susquehannas and the Delawares as well. Franklin's clear admiration for the Haudenosaunee and the other Northeastern Indian peoples begins with a paragraph in the spirit of Montaigne and continues in the spirit of philosophers John Locke and Jean-Jacques Rousseau:

> Savages we call them, because their manners differ from ours, which we think the Perfection of Civility; they think the same of theirs....
> Our laborious manner of Life compared with theirs, they esteem slavish and base; and the Learning on which we value ourselves; they regard as frivolous and useless. An Instance of this occurred at the Treaty of Lancaster in Pennsylvania, Anno 1744, between the Government of Virginia & the Six Nations. After the principal Business was settled, the Commissioners from Virginia acquainted the Indians by a Speech, that there was at Williamsburg a College with a Fund for Educating Indian Youth, and that if the Chiefs of the Six-Nations would send down half a dozen of their Sons to that College, the Government would take Care that they should be well provided for, and instructed in all the Learning of the white People. It is one of the Indian Rules of Politeness not to answer a public Proposition the same day that it is made; they think it would be treating it as a light Matter; and that they show it Respect by taking time to consider it, as of a Matter important. They therefore deferred their Answer

till the day following; when their Speaker began by expressing their deep Sense of the Kindness of the Virginia Government, in making them that Offer; for we know, says he, that you highly esteem the kind of Learning taught in those Colleges, and that the Maintenance of our Young Men while with you, would be very expensive to you. We are convinced therefore that you mean to do us good by your Proposal, and we thank you heartily. But you who are wise must know, that different Nations have different Conceptions of things; and you will therefore not take it amiss, if our Ideas of this Kind of Education happen not to be the same with yours. We have had some Experience of it: Several of our Young People were formerly brought up at the Colleges of the Northern Provinces; they were instructed in all your Sciences; but when they came back to us, they were bad Runners, ignorant of every means of living in the Woods, unable to bear either Cold or Hunger, knew neither how to build a Cabin, take a Deer, or kill an Enemy, spoke our Language imperfectly; were therefore neither fit for Hunters, Warriors, or Counsellors; they were totally good for nothing. We are however not the less obliged by your kind Offer, tho' we decline accepting it; and to show our grateful Sense of it, if the Gentlemen of Virginia will send us a dozen of their Sons, we will take great Care of their Education, instruct them in all we know, and make Men of them.[44]

Four years after Franklin wrote the following observations on Haudenosaunee government, he became the sage of the 1787 Philadelphia Convention.

The Indian Men, when young, are Hunters and Warriors; when old, Counsellors; for all their Government is by the Counsel or Advice of the Sages; there is no Force, there are no Prisons, no Officers to compel Obedience, or inflict Punishment. Hence they generally study Oratory; the best Speaker having the most influence. The Indian Women till the Ground, dress the Food, nurse and bring up the Children, and preserve and hand down to Posterity the Memory of Public Transactions....
Having frequent Occasions to hold public Councils, they have acquired great Order and Decency in conducting them. The old Men sit in the foremost Ranks, the Warriors in the next, and the Women and Children in the hindmost. The Business of the Women is to take exact notice of what passes, imprint it in their Memories, for they have no Writing, and communicate it to their Children. They are the Records of the Council, and they preserve Tradition of the Stipulations in Treaties a hundred Years back, which when we compare with our Writings we always find exact. He that would speak, rises. The rest observe a profound Silence. When he has finished and sits down, they leave him five or six Minutes to recollect, that if he has omitted any thing he intended to say, or has any thing to add, he may rise again and deliver it. To interrupt another, even in common Conversation, is reckoned highly indecent. How different it is from the Conduct of a polite British House of Commons, where scarce a Day passes without some Confusion that makes the Speaker hoarse in calling to order; and how different from the mode of Conversation in many polite Companies of Europe, where if you do not deliver your Sentence with great

Rapidity, you are cut off in the middle of it by the impatient Loquacity of those you converse with, & never suffer'd to finish it.[45]

Another of Franklin's essays centered around the white lynch mob which murdered innocent Conestoga Indians in 1764. However, "A Narrative of the Late Massacres, in Lancaster County, of a Number of Indians, Friends of this Province, by Persons Unknown," also included observations on how the Iroquois scrupulously honored both their treaties and the free passage of peace delegations:

> the Six Nations, as a Body, have kept Faith with the English ever since we knew them, now near an Hundred Years; and the governing Part of those People have had Notions of Honour.... As a Proof of that Honour, I shall only mention one well-known recent Fact. When six Catawba Deputies, under the Care of Colonel Bull, of Charlestown, went by Permission into the Mohawks Country, to sue for and treat of Peace for their Nation, they soon found the Six Nations highly exasperated, and the Peace at that Time impracticable: They were therefore in Fear for their own Persons, and apprehended that they should be killed in their Way back to New-York; which being made known to the Mohawk Chiefs, by Colonel Bull, one of them, by Order of the Council, made this Speech to the Catawbas: –

> "Strangers and Enemies,

> "While you are in this Country, blow away all Fear out of your Breasts; change the black Streak of Paint on your Cheek for a red One, and let your Faces shine with Bear's-Grease; You are safer here than if you were at home. The Six Nations will not defile their own Land with the Blood of Men that come unarmed to ask for Peace. We shall send a Guard with you, to see you safe out of our Territories. So far you shall have Peace, but no farther. Get home to your own Country, and there take Care of yourselves, for there we intend to come and kill you."

> The Catawbas came away unhurt accordingly.[46]

PHILOSOPHY AT THE PHILADELPHIA CONVENTION

Much of the Founding Fathers' debate at the Philadelphia convention would be based on what they wanted to avoid as well as what they wanted to emulate. Throughout the colonial period, the Haudenosaunee had provided examples of both. The Haudenosaunee had sustained their confederacy through a century and a half of constant crisis, an admirable quality to leaders such as Benjamin Franklin.

However, by 1787 it was also clear to the Founding Fathers that their own confederacy—that formed under the Articles of Confederacy—was too decentralized to meet political and economic challenges from within and from Europe. They also noted that the Haudenosaunee Confederacy and other Indian confederacies were crisis-ridden. Thus while the Founding Fathers could admire the positive images and the accomplishments of the Haudenosaunee confederate system, they could at the same time seek to avoid what the Founding Fathers perceived to be the weaknesses of decentralization among all confederacies they referred to—red and white, ancient and contemporary, and of course their own Articles of Confederation.

During the Philadelphia Convention, a speech by Gouvenor Morris on July 5, 1787, appears in the notes of two different Founding Fathers, James Madison and Rufus King. While neither is an exact "transcript," each version conveys the Founding Fathers' sense of how life and liberty were juxtaposed to another ideal of the Founding Fathers: the protection of "property." Gouvenor Morris, July 5, 1787, was thus recorded as saying:

[Madison:] The savage State was more favorable to liberty than the Civilized; and sufficiently so to life.
[King:] Men don't unite for liberty or Life, they possess both in the savage state in the highest perfection[.] they unite for the protection of property[.][47]

Morris's speech is a significant reminder that, in addition to "life and liberty," the colonists had fought their War of Independence against Britain for the protection of their private property. By the time the Philadelphia Convention was convened in 1787, many citizens in the newly independent United States felt that life, liberty, and property required a reorganized and centralized government. Of all the conflicting interests represented at Philadelphia, from the maritime northeast to the plantation south, the greatest conflict was how to balance life and liberty, so well represented by "the savage state," with property. Too great an emphasis on property would have smacked of the corruption which had ossified the European societies and against which the colonists had rebelled. Yet property also had its positive aspect: it was seen as the foundation of political, social, and economic stability. In the chaotic 1780s, such stability seemed very attractive to the new United States.

Given the conflicting impulses of life and liberty on the one hand and property on the other, it is not surprising that at one moment the Founding Fathers could extol the virtues of the savage state—life and liberty—and at the next moment move to establish an executive branch; checks; balances; and separations of powers which would insure the survival of property—prosperity.

The complete context of the partial quote of Gouvenor Morris given above is revealing. When Morris spoke these words, he was addressing the very specific issue of how the United States could expect settlers who moved west of the Appalachian Mountains to unite with the eastern states, joining the older states within one government. Since the Founding Fathers correctly assumed that the western states would eventually have a greater population than the east, the problem was how to protect the east's property. Morris's answer reflects the clear competition of the ideas of life and liberty on the one hand and property on the other:

when the Western Country is settled...We must take care that we don't establish a Rule wh. will enable the poor but numerous Inhabs. of the western Country to destroy the Atlantic States—Men don't unite for liberty or Life, they possess both in the savage state in the highest perfection [.] they unite for the protection of property.[48]

In addition to separating the issue of protecting "property" from the requirements of protecting liberty and life, Morris's speech also reveals one of the many euphemistic references to American Indians during the Philadelphia convention. After all, whose "Western Country" was it? The Founding Fathers could not bring themselves to use frank wording such as "when we conquer the Indians and seize their homeland." Instead, phrases such as "when the Western Country is settled" skipped over the nasty part of imperialism and addressed the issue of post-imperial government.

The Haudenosaunee political system had been observed and studied by colonists such as the French Jesuits in Canada, Robert Livingston, James Logan, Cadwallader Colden, Conrad Weiser, Benjamin Franklin, John Stuart, and Sir William Johnson, as well as English historian William Robertson, who were the exceptions rather than the rule. Often, as was especially the case with the Jesuits and Robertson, even thorough investigators exhibited blinding biases which clouded their work. In general, although European and colonial cultures absorbed American Indian philosophies, motifs, words, and even foods, it was remarkable that after three centuries of contact relatively little factual information had been systematically compiled and carefully studied by the Europeans about American Indian political systems. Thus John Adams (serving in London as ambassador to Britain during the Philadelphia convention) wrote in 1787: "To collect together the legislation of the Indians, would take up much room, but would be well worth the pains."[49]

In any event, major cultural differences made the utilization of specific details from Indian forms of government unlikely. For example, the political power of Indian women within many Indian nations (including the Haudenosaunee) and American Indian concepts of communal property would not translate readily into the system of the Founding Fathers.

However, specific details of Indian governments were not what was important to the Founding Fathers. What was important to the generation of the Founding Fathers were the broad concepts and symbols which Native Americans represented. These ideas had long been catalysts which inspired philosophical insights. None of these broad concepts were as important to the Founding Fathers as those described by the English philosopher John Locke in 1690.

Locke recorded that he had spoken with American Indians when they visited England, but the names of individuals and the specific Indian nations which they represented are not known. Even with this contact with American Indians, Locke's views were primarily based on reports other whites had written. Indeed, Locke is very much in the "noble savage" camp. (Locke helped author a highly structured "Fundamental Constitution" for the Carolina colony in 1668-1669, a document quite different in spirit from his later writings. Since Locke was dealing with the Carolinas, however, it is possible that the Indians he met in England may have been Creeks or their neighbors.)[50]

Locke's philosophy, expressed in his *Two Treatises of Government* in 1690, included an idea which would become a foundation for many of the Patriots' protests during the '60s and '70s: for example, in the Declaration of Independence; the Virginia Constitution; the Articles of Confederation; and the Preamble to the United States Constitution: that political power originally and ultimately resided in the people, not in a monarch. Although there were European examples of this concept, none of these could be demonstrated "scientifically" with contemporary evidence. Ancient and religious examples depended either upon the historical record or upon faith. But Locke and his followers believed that the Indians north of Mexico had continued to live according to many of the social and political standards of the Europeans' ancestors. Indian governments were still founded on the principle that power came from the people.[51]

John Locke, in his *Two Treatises of Government* (1690) states:

To understand political power aright, and derive it from its original, we must consider what estate all men are naturally in, and that is, a state of perfect freedom to order their actions, and dispose of their possessions and persons as they think fit, within the bounds of the law of Nature, without asking leave or depending upon the will of any other man.[52]

Locke also theorized that once one human made a compact or contract with another human, they were beginning to add their own human laws to the laws of nature. This in turn initiated the process of evolving away from the "the state of Nature."[53] In this context, Locke viewed American Indians as having the fewest contractual and governmental controls over them. Locke therefore concluded that Indian leaders, whom he called "kings," had power to "command absolutely in war, yet at home, and in time of peace, they exercise very little dominion, and have but a very moderate sovereignty, the resolutions of peace and war being ordinarily either in the people or in a council."[54]

In this context, Locke believed that

America...is still a pattern of the first ages in Asia and Europe, whilst the inhabitants were too few for the country, and want of people and money gave men no temptation to enlarge their possessions of land or contest for wider extent of ground.[55]

John Locke's perceptions of American Indians were examples which the Founding Fathers drew upon when they declared in the Preamble that the authority of the Constitution was ordained and established directly by "we the people." This concept did not exist simply as an abstract philosophy in 1787. "We the People" was a familiar concept which came directly from the philosophical premises of the Founding Fathers' culture. This culture in turn did not separate the Haudenosaunee (or other American Indians) from the reality or the philosophy of eighteenth century life. For example, when authors such as Cadwallader Colden (*The History of the Five Nations*) and Benjamin Franklin were read by other colonists, they were not read simply as descriptions of the Haudenosaunee. Both Colden and Franklin had, after all, written about the Haudenosaunee in part to verify the validity of Locke's premises. Colden and Franklin were read within the context and spirit of an English and colonial culture which depended upon Locke as a philosophical and political benchmark. In fact, any writing about, or encounter with, the Haudenosaunee occurred within a colonial cultural context attuned to the importance of John Locke. The Haudenosaunee (and other American Indians) were living reminders of the premises of John Locke's philosophy. An awareness of the Haudenosaunee (and all American Indians) was interwoven within the colonial culture's philosophical frames of reference. The philosophy of John Locke was seen by the colonists within a cultural context which included the Iroquois and other American Indians, and the Iroquois and other American Indians were perceived by the colonists within the context of John Locke's philosophy.

As the leaders of an emerging imperial power, however, the Founding Fathers were increasingly inclined to admire the Scottish Enlightenment philosopher David Hume. Hume accepted the influence and importance of "the savage state" philosophically. But Hume made a strong case against trying to replicate that system as a practical government to deal with the challenges of a complex world. By accepting the influence of the past while rejecting the idea of replicating the past, Hume qualified Locke's relevance to eighteenth century European reality. Hume wrote in 1752 that so-called "savages" did not have "a state of civil government" because:

> the chieftain, who had probably acquired his influence during the continuance of war, ruled more by persuasion than command; and till he could employ force to reduce the refractory and disobedient, the society could scarcely be said to have attained a state of civil government. No compact or agreement, it is evident, was expressly formed for general submission; an idea far beyond the comprehension of savages.[56]

Hume thus wrote off "savages" as not having governments worthy of the name. In doing so, Hume cautioned against relying upon John Locke's theory that the origins of government were contracts among humans who were equal. Hume admitted that these original contracts may have been "founded on consent and a voluntary compact"[57] among American Indians and even among early Europeans. But Hume believed that too much history separated that early stage of human history from the present. Thus Locke was not so much wrong philosophically as he was irrelevant in a practical sense—in facing the challenges of the real world of the eighteenth century.

Hume believed that the governments which ruled in his own era had evolved through "a thousand changes." Hume then made telling and revealing points which challenged Locke and any pretense of attempting to protect liberty by reestablishing the simpler governments of the past:

> Almost all the governments which exist at present, or of which there remains any record in story, have been founded originally, either on usurpation or conquest, or both, without any pretense of a fair consent of voluntary subjection of the people....
>
> The face of the earth is continually changing, by the increase of small kingdoms into great empires, by the dissolution of great empires into smaller kingdoms, by the planting of colonies, by the migration of tribes. Is there any thing discoverable in all these events but force and violence?...
>
> It is vain to say, that all governments are, or should be, at first, founded on popular consent.... conquest or usurpation, that is, in plain terms, force, by dissolving the ancient governments, is the origin of almost all the new ones which were ever established in the world....
>
> My intention here is not to exclude the consent of the people from being one just foundation of government where it has place. It is surely the best and most sacred of any.[58]

INDIANS, ROMANS, AND COUNTRYMEN!

In the Constitution, only the Preamble evokes John Locke's original contract theory of "we the people," the concept which Locke had believed had dominated tribal Europe before the Roman conquest and which Locke believed was still present, when he published his views in 1690, among American Indians. The rest of the Constitution establishes rules of government which were hammered out by compromise and were based on the premise that humans act from self-interest. There was no consensus among the Founding Fathers about what to do about differences between northern and southern states, or large and small states, for example. Thus the Constitution represents pragmatic compromises to unite a variety of states each of whose individual needs would have been best served under a confederacy but whose collective survival depended upon government centralization. If there was a single philosophy, it was that there would always be competing philosophies.

When the Founding Fathers turned toward David Hume, they turned towards a more realistic (or pessimistic) view of their fellow citizens, and away from Locke's admiration of the original liberties of the so-called savage state. In doing so, the Founding Fathers increasingly embraced the example of Rome and not the European tribes of northern Europe. The last point is significant. The Founding Fathers were not simply rejecting the political heritage of the Native Americans, they were learning from it. They were consciously aware of a stark lesson they could observe being repeated among the North American Indian nations around them. It was a lesson they compared with ancient European history: their own northern European ancestral tribes had all been conquered by the armies of a more centralized government: that of ancient Rome. Furthermore, Saxon England, also very much admired by the Founding Fathers, had been conquered in 1066 by the more centralized power of the Normans.

The analogy is complex. For example, John Adams admired the Saxons. But he felt that the history of the German tribes had, after the fall of Rome, culminated in the rise of turbulent monarchies. Thus Adams, in his 1787 *Defence of the Constitutions*, reasoned that tribal institutions might over time degenerate into the worse tyranny of monarchies. Adams was specifically suspicious of any clan system, in which chiefs were appointed from a limited pool of men—those within a specific clan—rather than from among all the mature men in a nation. Adams thought this smacked of hereditary rule.[59]

Eleven years earlier, John Adams had had a more enthusiastic view of his ancient heritage. In a letter to his wife Abigail, August 14, 1776, Adams described how Thomas Jefferson's proposal for a national seal included the figures of "Hengist and Horsa, the Saxon Chiefs, from whom We claim the Honour of being descended and whose Political Principles and Form of Government We have assumed."[60]

By 1787, however, John Adams believed that widespread advice to reconstitute the tribal heritage of his ancestors and that of American Indians would not meet the political needs of his generation, and he wrote: "After having known the history of Europe, and of England in particular, it would be the height of folly to go back to the institutions of Woden and Thor, as they are advised to do."[61]

John Adams also specifically compared the Germans with the American Indians and then rejected both as political models, even though these models were recommended by some Enlightenment philosophers. Adams made this comparison at the very beginning of the first volume in an imaginative passage which poses what might happen if the Romans Cicero and Tacitus returned to earth in 1787. The two Romans are then told that Adams and his fellow Americans were advised by some of the greatest philosophers and politicians of the age to...set up the governments of ancient Goths and modern Indians—what would they say? That the Americans would be...reprehensible...if they should listen to such advice.[62]

In a fascinating psychological choice, the Founding Fathers rejected their own tribal histories and adapted the ways of the Romans and Normans who had conquered their ancestors. No matter how much they admired their ancestors, they had to give the Romans and other conquerors their due, for the ultimate lesson was that societies like Rome won, and that less-centralized peoples, be they Germans, Saxons, or American Indians, lost.

The analogy between the Roman conquest of northern Europe and the white conquest of America was older than the Enlightenment and lay at the very roots of English colonization. Captain John Smith, describing colonial Virginia's 1622 war with the Powhatan Confederacy, observed, "What growing state was there ever in the world which had not the like? Rome grew by oppression, and rose upon the backe of her enemies."[63]

CONCLUSION

This essay has reviewed how, in the colonial culture of the Founding Fathers, the ubiquitous symbol of an American Indian—often a Mohawk—represented liberty. It has also indicated how the Haudenosaunee were directly involved in urging the colonists to unite so that they could better coordinate their trade, military policies, and alliance within the Covenant Chain. In part because of their ancestors's own tribal past, the Founding Fathers could admire individual Indians—for example, in praising their wisdom at councils or their oratory. As readily as they rejected their own "Articles of Confederation," however, they could reject the examples of confederated Native American forms of governments, on the basis that the Romans had conquered the tribes of northern Europe because the Romans possessed a greater unity.

There was substantial Haudenosaunee influence on the historical processes and theories which led to the Constitution as well as Haudenosaunee influence on the philosophical intent and content of the Constitution. This essay began by asserting that any discussion of efforts by the colonists to unite must include a discussion of Haudenosaunee influence. Unity was a pervasive theme at the Philadelphia convention, and the precedents for that unity included colonial efforts which in part were due to the admonitions of the Haudenosaunee. Along with other American Indian confederacies, the Haudenosaunee also provided an example at Philadelphia which was compared with European history. On June 28, 1787, James Madison made a lengthy speech on how a greater unity in the United States was necessary because history demonstrated how the lack of unity had ruined past civilizations. He noted how "Carthage & Rome tore one another to pieces instead of uniting their forces to devour the weaker nations of the Earth."[64]

Madison continued by citing the conflicts between Austria and France; between England and France; among the ancient Greek states of Sparta, Athens, and Thebes; and between Prussia and Austria. Even as Madison was speaking, some of the American Indians north of the Ohio were attempting to unify under a new confederation, called "the United Indian Nations." This new confederacy was unable to convince the oldest northern confederacy, that of the Haudenosaunee, to join it. Nor were the Haudenosaunee able to convince the advocates of the new "United Indian Nations" that older ways, not new confederacies, were superior. In this context, Madison summarized his comparative history lesson on the lack of unity:

> What is ye situation of the weak compared with the strong in those stages of civilization in which the violence of individuals is least controuled by an efficient Government? The Heroic period of Antient Greece[,] the feudal licentiousness of the middle ages of Europe, [and] the existing condition of the American Savages, answer this question.[65]

Sceptics might conclude that American Indians had little role in the framing of the Constitution because the Founding Fathers were far more interested in classical Greece and Rome. To the contrary, it is precisely because the Founding Fathers ultimately saw their own era in the historical perspective of ancient Greece and Rome, especially Rome, that Indians were important.

Nearly two thousand years earlier, Roman legions had rolled over the tribal peoples of Northern Europe. In those Roman wars of conquest, the Founding Fathers' Northern European ancestors had played the role of the Indians.

This time, the Founding Fathers were determined to be the Romans.

Notes

This article was originally published in the *Northeast Indian Quarterly*, Volume VI, Number 4 (Winter 1989). A more complete version appears in *Exiled In the Land of the Free: Democracy, Indian Nations, and the U.S. Constitution*, Oren R. Lyons and John C. Mohawk, eds. (Santa Fe: Clear Light Publishers, 1992)

Some of the notes below refer to "classics" which have many editions. To enable the student and general reader to examine the evidence in its context, I have consciously chosen to cite widely available editions, including authoritative paperbacks, whenever possible. These editions will be found in many public libraries.

1. See, for example, Philip B. Kurland and Ralph Lerner, eds., *The Founders'*

Constitution, 5 vols. (Chicago: University of Chicago Press, 1987) an extensive collection of documents, letters, and other writings bearing on the Constitution which was funded by the National Endowment for the Humanities and several foundations. Various viewpoints regarding the motives and philosophies behind the formation of the Constitution can be found in Richard Beeman, Stephen Botein, and Edward C. Carter II, eds., *Beyond Confederation: Origins of the Constitution and American National Identity* (Chapel Hill, North Carolina: University of North Carolina Press, 1987). The general public's perception was significantly influenced by Warren E. Burger, the former Chief Justice of the U.S. Supreme Court and the Chairman of the Commission on the Bicentennial of the United States Constitution. In his "Foreword" to booklet-length copies of the U.S. Constitution made available free of charge by the Commission and by organizations such as Citicorp, Burger ignored American Indian history, especially Iroquois history, when he stated that "[i]n the last quarter of the 18th century, there was no country in the world that governed with separated and divided powers providing checks and balances on the exercise of authority by those who governed." Burger chose to trace the Constitution only to white European roots— "back to Magna Carta and beyond."

Burger ignored both American Indian history and seventeenth century English revolutions when he maintained that "the work of 55 men at Philadelphia in 1787 marked the beginning of the end of the concept of the divine right of kings." Yet Burger also clearly implied that he had surveyed non-white history as well as white history. His "Foreword" concludes that the Constitution was "the first of its kind in all human history." Absurd or not, this is what the American public was given to read, and undoubtedly took to heart. cf. Warren E. Burger, "Foreword," in *We the People of the United States: Official Commemorative Edition, The Constitution of the United States* (Washington, D.C.: Citicorp/Citibank and the Commission on the Bicentennial of the United States Constitution, c. 1986); and Warren E. Burger, "Foreword," *The Constitution of the United States* (Washington, D.C.: Commission on the Bicentennial of the United States Constitution, c. 1986).

2. Allen W. Trelease, *Indian Affairs in Colonial New York: The Seventeenth Century* (Ithaca, New York: Cornell University Press, 1960); Thomas Eliot Norton, *The Fur Trade in Colonial New York, 1686-1776* (Madison: University of Wisconsin Press, 1974); Robert C. Ritchie, *The Duke's Province: A Study of New York Politics and Society, 1664-1691* (Chapel Hill: University of North Carolina Press, 1977); Stanley Nider Katz, *Newcastle's New York: Anglo-American Politics, 1732-1753* (Cambridge, Massachusetts: Harvard University Press, 1968); Georgiana C. Nammack, *Fraud, Politics, and the Dispossession of the Indians* (Norman, Oklahoma: University of Oklahoma Press, 1969); and Patricia U. Bonomi, *A Factious People: Politics and Society in Colonial New York* (New York: Columbia University Press, 1971) discuss this complexity. Comparable dilemmas for the Iroquois are suggested in Daniel K. Richter and James H. Merrell, eds., *Beyond the Covenant Chain: The Iroquois and Their Neighbors in Indian North America, 1600-1800* (Syracuse, New York: Syracuse University Press, 1987).

3. Jack P. Greene, *Peripheries and Center: Constitutional Development in the Extended Politics of the British Empire and the United States, 1607-1788* (Athens, Georgia: University of Georgia Press, 1986). cf. David S. Lovejoy, *The Glorious Revolution*

in America (1972 ed. with new introduction, (Middletown, Connecticut: Wesleyan University Press, 1987), xxiii-xxvi and *passim*. When the Algonquin Indians of New England fought the New England white colonists, the New York governor, Edmund Andros, launched two ships to invade and occupy a part of Connecticut. The New York governor was turned back without firing a shot only because the Connecticut colonists surprised the governor by being prepared to fight him. Douglas Edward Leach, *Flintlock and Tomahawk: New England in King Philip's War* (1958; New York: W.W.Norton, 1966), 60. Ritchie, *Duke's Province*, 149, notes that even within the colony of New York there was a lack of coordination: in December 1675 the Dutch colonists of New York were accused in Boston of supplying the Algonquin Indians rebelling under King Philip against New England. cf. Stephen Saunders Webb, *The Governors-General: The English Army and the Definition of Empire* (Chapel Hill: University of North Carolina Press, 1979); and Stephen Saunders Webb, *1676: The End of American Independence* (New York: Alfred A. Knopf, 1984).

4. "Proposals by the Chiefs of the Mahikanders," February 14, 1674/75, in Lawrence H. Leder, ed., *The Livingston Indian Records, 1666-1723* (Stanfordville, New York: Earl M. Coleman, 1979) 37.

5. Records of the Summer 1677 council, in Leder 43-48.

6. For the impact of smallpox and other diseases, see Henry F. Dobyns, *Their Number Became Thinned: Native American Population Dynamics in Eastern North America* (Knoxville: University of Tennessee Press, 1983), especially the tables on 15-16, 17, 19, 20, and 315-317. The impact of wars is discussed in Francis Jennings, *The Ambiguous Iroquois Empire: The Covenant Chain Confederation of Indian Tribes with English Colonies* (New York: W.W. Norton, 1984), especially 145-173; in Richard Aquila, *The Iroquois Restoration: Iroquois Diplomacy on the Colonial Frontier, 1701-1754* (Detroit: Wayne State University Press, 1983); and in the classic by Randolph C. Downes, *Council Fires on the Upper Ohio: A Narrative of Indian Affairs in the Upper Ohio Valley until 1795* (Pittsburgh: University of Pittsburgh Press, 1940). The continuing divisions within the ambiguous English empire and the efforts to resolve these divisions are discussed in Greene, *Peripheries and Center*, especially in Chapter Three: "An Ambiguous Accommodation: Liberty, Prerogative, and the Imperial Constitution, 1713-1763."

7. Paul A.W. Wallace, *Indians in Pennsylvania* (Harrisburg: The Pennsylvania Historical and Museum Commission, 1968), 102, reviews what he calls "armed neutrality." cf. Norton, *Fur Trade*, 19-27; Jennings, *Ambiguous Iroquois Empire;* and Daniel K. Richter, "Cultural Brokers and Intercultural Politics: New York-Iroquois Relations, 1664-1701," *Journal of American History* 75, no. 1 (June 1988) 40-67.

8. "The Articles of Confederation between the Plantations under the Government of the Massachusetts, the Plantations under the Government of New Plymouth, the Plantations under the Government of Connecticut, and the Government of New Haven with the Plantations in Combination," 1643, in Henry Steele Commager, ed., *Documents of American History*, 9th ed. (Englewood Cliffs, New Jersey: Prentice-Hall, 1973), 26-28; Lovejoy, *Glorious Revolution*, 104-106, 179, 208, 215 ("A chief purpose of the Dominion was to improve the colonists' defenses against the French in Canada and their Indian allies. Its extension [in 1688] to include New York was part of the scheme, for the added troops and larger revenues would help defend the frontier generally but also the

English fur trade, most of which was channeled through Albany in partnership with the Iroquois Indians," 215).

9. For example, on July 6, 1775, one year before the Declaration of Independence, the Patriots' Continental Congress issued the "Declaration of Causes of Taking Up Arms." This included the statement that "We have not raised armies with ambitious designs of separating from Great Britain, and establishing independent States." Instead, the rebels hoped that "through this great conflict, to dispose our adversaries to reconciliation on reasonable terms." Samuel Eliot Morison, ed., *Sources and Documents Illustrating the American Revolution, 1764-1788, and the Formation of the Federal Constitution,* 2nd ed. (Oxford: Oxford University Press, 1961), 145, 141-145

10. Jack P. Greene's perceptive work, *Peripheries and Center* (1986)—see footnote 6 above—disappointingly chooses not to discuss Indian influences, but his work demonstrates the importance of colonial efforts at unity as precedents for the Constitution. Greene states that he "seeks to trace and analyze the developing structures and theories of constitutional organization in the extended polities of both the early modern British Empire and the revolutionary United States between the founding of Virginia in 1607 and the adoption of the federal Constitution in 1788." Green notes that "this search was a significant and persistent concern for British Americans...and...it provides an underlying unity to early American constitutional history from the colonial through the early national periods." Greene, *Peripheries and Center,* ix and 3. A different interpretation is included in an article by Elisabeth Tooker, "The United States Constitution and the Iroquois League," *Ethnohistory* 35, no. 4 (Fall 1988), 305-336. Tooker states on p. 331, in footnote 3: "Only after the success of the Revolution could the various earlier plans of union be seen as forerunners of the federal union." Tooker's premise affects her interpretation of events such as the 1744 speech of Canasatego and the 1754 Albany Plan of Union, and their affects on the Founding Fathers. Tooker discusses these issues at length on pages 330-331, in footnote 3.

11. Cadwallader Colden, *The History of the Five Nations Depending on the Province of New-York in America (1727 and 1747)* (Ithaca, New York: Cornell University Press, 1958), 78 and Bonomi, *A Factious People,* 152-154 and 233.

12. Colden, *History of the Five Nations,* ix-x and xxi; and John Locke, *Two Treatises of Government* (1690; 1924; reprint ed., London: J.M. Dent & Sons, 1975) 171 and 166-171.

13. Locke 136. The 1677 date for the first known reference to the covenant chain is in "The Onnodagoes Ansr To ye propasitiones [sic] made to ym the 20 of July 1677... In the Court house of Albany ye 21 of July 1677," in Leder, ed., *Livingston Indian Records,* 43. At this conference, Carachkondie, an Onondaga, said "wee...doe make now ane absolut Covenant of peace wch we shall bind wth a chayn."

14. Colden, History of the Five Nations, 137.

15. Colden 149.

16. Colden.

17. Colden 149-150.

18. Colden 150.

19. Alexander Hamilton, *Gentleman's Progress: The Itinerarium of Dr. Alexander*

Hamilton, 1744, edited with an Introduction by Carl Bridenbaugh (Chapel Hill: University of North Carolina Press, 1948) 112-113.

20. Hamilton 113.

21. Francis Parkman, *Montcalm and Wolfe,* with a new Foreword by C. Vann Woodward (1884; New York: Atheneum, 1984), 452-456; and Francis Jennings, *Empire of Fortune: Crowns, Colonies and Tribes in the Seven Years War in America* (New York: W.W. Norton, 1988), 200 and 200 fn. 43. Jennings maintains that Rogers' Rangers "killed indiscriminately."

22. Speech of Canasatego, Lancaster, Pennsylvania, 26 June 1744, in Benjamin Franklin, ed., *Indian Treaties Printed By Benjamin Franklin, 1736-1762,* Introduction by Carl Van Doren and Historical & Bibliographical Notes by Julian P. Boyd (Philadelphia: The Historical Society of Pennsylvania, 1938), xxxvii and 51-52. Canasatego's imagery is an elaboration of similar imagery used by an Onondaga in 1694 (Colden, *History,* 149). cf. Francis Jennings, "Iroquois Alliances in American History," and "Glossary of Figures of Speech in Iroquois Political Rhetoric," both in Francis Jennings, ed., *The History and Culture of Iroquois Diplomacy* (Syracuse, New York: Syracuse University Press, 1985), 38 and 116-117; and Francis Jennings, "The Constitutional Evolution of the Covenant Chain," in *Proceedings of the American Philosophical Society,* Vol. 115 No. 2 (April 1971) 88-96.

23. Speech of Canasatego, Lancaster, Pennsylvania, 4 July 1744, in Franklin, ed., *Indian Treaties,* 78.

24. Benjamin Franklin to James Parker, 20 March 1750/51, in Leonard W. Labaree, ed., *The Papers of Benjamin Franklin,* 26 vols. (New Haven, Connecticut: Yale University Press, 1959-1987) IV, 118-119. The number of copies of Canasatego's 1744 speech which were sent by Franklin to England is discussed in Franklin, ed., *Indian Treaties,* vii and 304.

25. Franklin to Parker, 20 March 1750/51, in Labaree, ed., *Papers of Benjamin Franklin,* IV, 117-119. This letter is also reprinted in J.A. Leo Lemay, ed., *Benjamin Franklin: Writings* (New York: The Library of America, 1987) 442-446.

26. LeMay, ed., *Franklin: Writings,* 375-410. These pages include a collection of Franklin's views of the Albany Plan of Union, and the plan itself. cf. Jennings, *Empire of Fortune,* 71-108; Greene, *Peripheries and Center,* 154; and Nammack, *Fraud, Politics, and the Dispossession of the Indians,* 31-52.

27. Greene, *Peripheries and Center,* 7-18; and Colden, *History of the Five Nations,* xvii. Another excellent review of the major philosophical and cultural issues which influenced the Founding Fathers is Henry Steele Commager, *The Empire of Reason: How Europe Imagined and America Realized the Enlightenment* (New York: Doubleday, 1977). Although Commager discusses the major philosophical themes of the American Revolution and the Constitution primarily in terms of the colonists' European heritage, he often refers to issues raised by European viewpoints of Indians, especially in chapters three and five.

28. All these issues are reviewed in Russel Lawrence Barsh and James Youngblood Henderson, *The Road: Indian Tribes and Political Liberty* (Berkeley: University of California Press, 1980).

29. An excellent review of figures of American Indians as symbolic of "America" is Hugh Honour, *The New Golden Land: European Images of America from the Discoveries to the Present Time* (New York: Pantheon Books, 1975).

30. Clarence Edwin Carter, ed., *The Correspondence of General Thomas Gage with the Secretaries of State, 1763-1775*, 2 vols. (New Haven: Yale University Press, 1931 and 1933), I, x-xi and 8. These two volumes are filled with examples of the information passed by Johnson to Gage and to London.

31. *The Compact Edition of the Oxford English Dictionary: Complete Text Reproduced Micrographically*, 2 vols. (New York: Oxford University Press, 1971) I, 70.

32. *Oxford English Dictionary*, II, 2646; and Honour, *New Golden Land*, 118.

33. Thomas Hariot, *A Briefe and True Report of the New Found Land of Virginia* (1590; n.p.: Readex Microprint Corporation, 1966), at "The true picture of one Picte I."

34. Honour, *New Golden Land*, 118.

35. Christopher Vecsey, "American Indian Environmental Religions," in Christopher Vecsey and Robert W. Venables, eds., *American Indian Environments: Ecological Issues in Native American History* (Syracuse, New York: Syracuse University Press, 1980) 16-20.

36. Richmond P. Bond, *Queen Anne's American Kings* (Oxford: Oxford University Press, 1952), *passim*, and Malvina Bolus, "Four Kings Come to Dinner with Their Honours," in *The Beaver* (Autumn 1973) 4-11.

37. Bond, *Queen Anne's American Kings*, 94.

38. Bond 94-95.

39. Bond 76 and 135-136; and *Oxford English Dictionary*, I, 1830.

40. Thomas Jefferson Wertenbaker, *Father Knickerbocker Rebels: New York City During the Revolution* (New York: Charles Scribner's Sons, 1948) 32.

41. Benjamin Woods Labaree, *The Boston Tea Party* (New York: Oxford University Press, 1964) 141.

42. Helmut von Erffa and Allen Staley, *The Paintings of Benjamin West* (New Haven: Yale University Press, 1986), 54-68, 211-216; and Ann Uhry Abrams, *The Valiant Hero: Benjamin West and the Grand-Style History Painting* (Washington, D.C.: Smithsonian Institution Press, 1985) 176.

43. von Erffa and Staley, West, 213.

44. Benjamin Franklin, "Remarks Concerning the Savages of North-America," in LeMay, ed., *Franklin: Writings*, 969-970.

45. LeMay 969, 970-971.

46. Benjamin Franklin, "Narrative of the Late Massacres, in Lancaster County, of a Number of Indians, Friends of this Province, by Persons Unknown; With Some Observations on the Same," in LeMay, ed., *Franklin: Writings*, 553-554.

47. Max Farrand, ed., *The Records of the Federal Convention of 1787*, 4 vols. (1937; reprint of revised ed.; New Haven, Connecticut: Yale University Press, 1966) I, 533, 536.

48. Farrand 536 [Rufus King version].

49. John Adams, *A Defence of the Constitutions of Government of the United States of America*, 3 vols. (London: C. Dilly, 1787-1788) I,xxvi.

50. John Locke, *An Essay Concerning Human Understanding*, 2 vols. (1947; rev. ed., London: J.M. Dent & Sons, 1974) I, 169.

51. Locke, *Two Treatises*, 166-171.

52. Locke 118.

53. Locke 124.

54. Locke 171.

55. Locke.

56. David Hume, "Of the Original Contract [1748]," in Sir Ernest Barker, ed., *Social Contract: Essays by Locke, Hume, and Rousseau* (1947 reprint; London: Oxford University Press, 1960), 149. Hume's description is in direct contrast to the Haudenosaunee tradition that the Iroquois Confederacy was inspired by the "Peacemaker" and those leaders who followed him by agreeing to organize a confederacy based on consent and consensus.

57. Hume 151.

58. Hume 151-152, 154.

59. Adams, *Defence*, I, xv, xxvi, and 225-226.

60. John Adams to Abigail Adams, 14 August 1776, in L.H. Butterfield, Marc Friedlaender, and Mary-Jo Kline, eds., *The Book of Abigail and John: Selected Letters of the Adams Family, 1762-1784* (Cambridge, Massachusetts: Harvard University Press, 1975) 156.

61. Adams, *Defence*, I, xxv-xxvi.

62. Adams xxii-xxiii, xxvi, 225-226.

63. John Smith, *The General Historie of Virginia by Captain John Smith, 1624; The Fourth Booke*, in Lyon Gardiner Tyler, ed., *Narratives of Early Virginia, 1606-1625* (1907; reprint, New York: Barnes and Noble, 1966) 365.

64. Farrand, *Records*, I, 448.

65. Farrand and "Speech of the United Indian Nations," 28 November and 18 December 1786, in Walter Lowrie and Matthew St. Clair, eds., *American State Papers. Class II. Indian Affairs.* 2 vols. numbered as volumes 7 and 8 of the 38 volume American State Papers issued between 1832 and 1861 (Washington, D.C.: Gales and Seaton, 1832 and 1834) I [also, vol. 7], 8-9.

Squanto's Legacy: The Origin of the Town Meeting

Bruce A. Burton

John Fairfield Sly dates colonial local self-government to March 3, 1635/6, the year the General Court of Massachusetts enacted the New Towne (Cambridge) Ordinance for the regulation of towns. This ordinance authorized each town to dispose "of common property, to order its civil affairs, and to chose its owne 'particular officers.'"[1]

Though Sly dates self-government to 1635/6, he acknowledges that the Massachusetts town originated "in a nucleus of 'old planters'"[2] in an eight year "twilight" between the unpreserved actions of Endicott and his council after the arrival of the company at Salem, and the famous ordinance of March 3, 1635/6 giving an organic law to firmly established communities."[3]

By Sly's count in the Massachusetts Colonial Record, thirteen towns had been established by old planters between 1620 and 1628 which, the ordinance recognized, had developed "community consciousness" beyond "a commercial interest to wide social requirements—a condition less susceptible to formal regulation than voluntary cooperation."[4] (From 1630 to 1640, twenty thousand new settlers came to Massachusetts).

As Sly notes, Salem was one of these thirteen towns. Founded by Roger Conant from Plymouth in 1626, Salem was considered "the first foundation on which the colonies were built."[5] That the New Towne

Ordinance legitimized this town and others, and that these old planters like Conant, whom Endicott met, came from Plymouth, questions whether "Plymouth [itself really] furnished little of importance in the field of political origins"[6] relating to the development of local self-government in Massachusetts.

Since town meeting in Massachusetts did not create the ordinance but legitimized it, its origin must be found in either Salem or Plymouth, more likely Plymouth in part because of Plymouth's very smallness and dominance "of [its] governor and council."[7]

The Pilgrims were lucky when they arrived at Plymouth in March 1621 after a brutal winter on board the Mayflower, for they found themselves living in a recently uninhabited Native town, Pawtuxet, growing Native corn, and surviving by hunting and fishing with the guidance of a Native provider.

Pawtuxet, with its previously cleared fields was no "wilderness." It had been a vital town before the plague of 1615-1617. Almost immediately it was renamed Plymouth. Other Native towns also devastated by plague, Wessagusett (Weymouth 1622), Nantasket (Salem 1626), Mishaum (Charlestown 1628), Shawmut (Boston 1630), and Nattapan (Dorchester 1630), for example, were similarly repopulated by Puritan immigration.

The Pilgrims met Samoset who introduced them to Pawtuxet's lone survivor, Squanto, who had been out of the country during the plague. He had learned English after having been sold into slavery at Malagra in Spain by the deceitful Captain Thomas Hunt in 1605. Somehow, Squanto had slipped his chains in Spain and made his way to England where he lived for two years with John Slany, treasurer of the New Foundland Company. After a visit to Newfoundland, Squanto again returned to England in 1618, returning to New England in 1619 as Captain Thomas Dermer's pilot. It is said that Squanto left Dermer before Dermer reached Cape Cod, and that he made his way to Pawtuxet to find it emptied by disease[8] just prior to the Pilgrims' arrival.

Only a few days after the Pilgrims landed, Samoset and Squanto arranged with Massasoit of the neighboring Wampanoags to include Plymouth in a pre-existing Native confederation, the first English experience in the politics of confederation:

4. If any did unjustly warr against him, they would abide him; if any did warr against them, he should abide them, and 5. He should send to his neighbours confederats, to certifie them of this, that they might not wrong them, but might be likewise comprised in the conditions of peace .[9]

Why did Squanto befriend the Pilgrims? His experience with Englishmen was mixed. Hunt had sold him into slavery and Slany had befriended him. Under the circumstances, having lost his family and community to plague, "befriended" perhaps too mildly describes Squanto's intentions toward the English. Adoption, the Native way of re-populating towns ravaged by war or disease, might better describe the relationship. As Pawtuxet's sole survivor, he considered the town his home and he thought the Pilgrims might re-populate it.

The Pilgrims for their part, in a dreadful state after their voyage, had no means of support and Squanto welcoming them was a sign of God's deliverance as Bradford confirms:

> Squanto continued with them, and was their interpreter, and was a special instrument sent of God for their own good beyond their expectation. He directed them how to set their corne, wher to take fish, and to procure other comodities, and was also their pilott to bring them to unknowne places for their profit, and never left them till he dyed. He was a native of this place, & scarce any left alive besids him selfe.[10]

The Pilgrims intended a Platonic community for Plymouth. Having agreed only their own laws would bind them before disembarking from the Mayflower, they meant to work the land in common.

Towne and Plantation described the Pilgrims's intention to farm. The Dutch origin of the word "tunne"[11] simply designated a garden with a fence around it. And in 1628 the English legalist Coke defined a towne as a village with a church.[12] So the Pilgrims a few years earlier referred to Plymouth as a Plantation or town in the European sense, primarily an agricultural community whose legal and spiritual center was the Church.

Although the Pilgrims intended a community on Plato's model, sowing common land, by the spring of 1621, only a third of the people survived their first winter. Some even lived among the Native people to stay alive.

A bountiful harvest didn't result because people didn't profit from their own labor. This

> communitie (so farr as it was) was found to breed much confusion & discontent, and retard much employment that would have been to their benefite and comforte. For the yongmen that were most able and fitte for labour & service did repine that they should spend their time & strength to worke for other mens wives and children, with out any recompence. The strong, or man of parts, had no more in devission of victails & cloaths, then he that was weake and not able to doe a quarter the other could; this was thought injuestice. The aged and graver men to be ranked and equalized in labours, and victails, cloaths, &c., with the meaner and yonger sorte, thought it some indignite & disrespect unto them. And for mens wives to be commanded to doe servise for other men, as dressing their meate, washing their cloths, &c., they deemed it a kind of slaverie, neither could many husbands well brook it.[13]

As important as it was for Plymouth to assume Pawtuxet's place in a Native confederacy, to grow corn in the Native manner, and to hunt and fish where the friendly Natives knew there was fish and game, Plymouth's response to its disastrous harvest that winter of 1621/2 is what really determined the future of colonial New England towns.

In the spring of 1622

> they begane to thinke how they might raise as much corne as they could, and obtaine a better crope then they had done...At length after much debate of things, the Governor (with the advise of the cheefest amongest them) gave way that they should set corne every man for his owne perticuler...And so assigned to every family a parcell of land, according to the proportion of their number for that end...and ranged all boys & youth under some familie. This had very good success; for it made all hands very industrious, so as much more corne was planted then other waise would have bene...The women now wente willingly into the feild, and tooke their little-ons with them to set corne...whom to have compelled would have bene thought great tiranie and oppression.[14]

So much for "the vanitie of that conceite of Platos & other ancients...that the taking away of propertie, and bringing in communitie into a commone wealth, would make them happy and flourishing; as if they were wiser then God."[15]

After dividing land according to families in the spring of 1622, the Anne and a forty-four ton pinnace with sixty people arrived in July. The old planters, those families given land a few months earlier, feared the ship's provisions would run out before the year ended and that they would have to feed the new arrivals. They, therefore,

> besought [the Governor] that as it was before agreed that they should set corne for their perticular...that they might freely injoye the same...and let the new-comers injoye what they had brought...Their requeste was granted them.[16]

Thus the first town meeting, defined as "the politics of families owning land,"[17] occurred in the summer of 1622 with Bradford acting as moderator, hearing officer, and recording clerk. It was at this meeting between the old planters and the Governor that town meeting and economic free-enterprise sprang up simultaneously in colonial America.

As for the idea of dividing the land according to families, there were no European freehold precedents for such a scheme, Europe's land being feudal manors. But family ownership (or a form of stewardship under tribal law) of land was common practice among the Native people as Roger Williams testifies of the Narragansets who bordered Plymouth. Williams notes the Narraganset term "Nittauke" for "My land,"[18] observing further,

> The Natives are very exact and punctuall in the bound of their Lands belonging to this or that Prince or People, (even to a River, Brooke, &c.) And I have known them make bargaine and sale amongst themselves for a small piece, or quantity of Ground.[19]

Although Bradford doesn't say Squanto suggested the ideas of family land tenure, Squanto witnessed the Pilgrims tilling Pawtuxet land in common without regard to a division of labor. Such a division of labor among surrounding Native people was clearly the practice, however, as Roger Williams further observed of the Narragansets.

> The women set or plant, weede, and hill, Yet sometime the man himselfe, (either out of love to his Wife, or care for his Children, or being an old man) will help the Woman which (by the custom of the Countrey) they are not bound to.[20]

> ...the woman of the family will commonly raise two or three heaps of twelve, fifteene, or twentie bushells a heap...and if she have helpe of her children or friends, much more.[21]

Were the Pilgrims aware that Native women tilled their own plots? Undoubtedly, and the debate likely included the Native manner of family land tenure initiated by Squanto or those who returned to Plymouth after living in Native towns that winter. Plymouth, sited on the grounds of Pawtuxet with its newly created private plots, then came to more closely resemble a Native town.

That Bradford agreed to divide the land seems natural given Squanto's presence and the examples of neighboring Native towns. At first Bradford referred to Native towns as plantations, but in 1622 coinciding with his decision to adopt family land tenure he extends to these Native communities an equal status to his own in referring to them as towns. He speaks of Hobamack and Squanto, for example, of going to "an Indean town called Namassakett 14. miles to the west of this place."[22]

Bradford alloted "places for habitations within the towne"[23] to the newcomers of the Anne and its pinnace with the following conditions: that they "obey the laws for the publick good," that they were "exempt from [the] general employments of the company," that they "pay a bushel of wheat to maintain Government," and that they cannot trade with the Native people until "the time of communialitie be ended,"[24] meaning they discharge their debt of passage.

Shortly thereafter in 1624 Bradford held an election to add Assistants to his Council and increase his authority. This dissatisfied old planters such as Roger Conant and, as landowners grown accustomed to discussing matters of public interest, they left the company.

As these old planters and others after them left Plymouth to establish new towns, they took the family land tenure system with them. It was this condition which Endicott found in Salem in 1628 which the Massachusetts General Court legitimized for all Massachusetts towns six years later in the March 3, 1635/6 New Towne Ordinance regulating towns.

When Endicott became Governor after Roger Conant and others from Plymouth founded Salem, the colony allowed for a council of twelve to hold office for one year: seven named by the company; three chosen by the seven in conjunction with the governor; and two selected by the old planters that they "have no just occasion of exception."[25]

As towns multiplied and the "inconvenience of assembling became increasingly evident, the General Court made provisions for its members to vote through deputies."[26] Local affairs were handled by the townsmen, the company relying on past practice: "from the earliest days the planters took civil affairs into their own hands, each group meeting together to discuss matters of common concern, to decide the proper action, and to appoint men to give such decisions effect."[27]

Besides alloting land to families and the "beating of the drum"[28] to call the town meeting together, these early freeholders also used Native corn or beans to count votes during town meeting,[29] and elected steering committees and officials who had no real authority, authority being retained in the hands of the electorate as it was among the Native people themselves. Add to this that these towns, including Plymouth, were re-inhabited Native towns, subsisting on Native corn, trading this corn with the Native people for furs, and forming alliances with Native nations for their defense, and one appreciates the "state of nature"[30] the Pilgrims found themselves in.

New England communities were no longer referred to as plantations, but towns, 'town' conveying a different understanding of community. Unlike the Dutch garden surrounded by a hedge or Coke's village with a church, 'town' meant according to Palmer, for example, "where a number of people have seated themselves together."[31] A town was where people sat, where land was allotted. A town meeting occurred when the land owners deliberated on matters of joint concern. A town was both a people in council (sitting) and where they met on the land they owned. Native towns were no different.

The term 'plantation' dropped out of usage in New England about 1630: "The first mention of towns collectively occurs in the proceedings of the court of Assistants for March 22, 1630/1."[32] But, as observed, the term 'town' with new meaning was used early in Plymouth in reference to itself and to Native communities which had no churches. An agricultural term originally referring to vineyards and farms, a community under manorial jurisdiction, or a community with no political significance outside of its church came to denote a new political organization in colonial America based on the incorporated landholdings of private citizens—something quite different from the Dutch or Coke, or what the Pilgrims themselves initially intended.

Was William Bradford the father of colonial town meeting since he agreed to the old planters' request to divide land? The answer must be yes, for as a pragmatist he gave in to the idea and land was first privatized among the colonists at Plymouth. But it is of interest to note, also, that though his decision was the beginning of democracy for the colonists, Governor Bradford's very zealousness, in fact, in adding two assistants to his council to increase his own authority prompted old planters to leave Plymouth and to found their own towns.

Though the Plymouth colony adopted the Native model of family land tenure, there was an important difference. The Wampanoags and other inhabitants of Native towns, for example, divided their land among families according to female land tenure which produced gender and material equality. Thus gender equality based on the role of Native women laboring on their plots defined Native democracy.

William Wood gives an illuminating 1630s glimpse of the social harmony Native democracy produced:

> To enter into a serious discourse concerning the natural conditions of thes Indians, might procure admiration from the people of any civilized Nations...these Indians are of affable, courteous, and well disposed natures, ready to communicate the best of their wealth to the mutual good of one another...As he that kills a Deere, sends for his friends, and eates it merrily: So that he that receives a piece of bread from an English hand, parts it equally betweene himself and his comerades, and eates it lovingly. In a word, a friend can command his friend, his house, and whatsoever is his (saving his Wife) and have it freely: And as they are love-linked thus in common courtesie, so are they no way sooner dis-jointed than by ingratitude; accounting an ungratefull person a double robber of a man, not only of his courtesie, but of his thankes which he might receive of another for the same proffered, or received kindnesse.[33]

As to Native domestic harmony, a Sagamore's response to witnessing an English woman scolding her husband testifies that the Sagamore left the house and "went to the next neighbour, where he related the unseemelinesse of her behaviour...I have been amongst diverse of them, yet did I never see any falling out amongst them, not so much as cross words, or reviling speeches."[34] Not knowing what angered this English woman, we nonetheless conclude Native women had little to complain of, or their men of them either.

The Plymouth Pilgrims realized their survival depended upon dividing land. But unlike the Native people they divided it among men as the heads of families, making what every family produced the property of landowning men. This was consistent with European gender inequality of the time, but inconsistent with Europe's cast system of a landed aristocracy which the new system came to reject.

The beginning of democracy in America for the colonists, then, first appears on the local town meeting level among the Pilgrims at Plymouth. In this early beginning, the colonies also took the first step toward representative federalism achieved 169 years later with the

114

adoption of the Bill of Rights and ratification of the Constitution in 1791. Town meeting made this event not only possible, but inevitable— derived as it was from Native freedoms, it fixed democracy's long development in the United States.

Notes

This article was originally published in the *Northeast Indian Quarterly*, Volume VI, Number 4 (Winter 1989).

1. John Fairfield Sly, *Town Government in Massachusetts 1620-1930* (Hamden: Archon Books, 1930, reprinted 1967) 20.
2. Sly 20.
3. Sly 26.
4. Sly 20.
5. Sly 6 (from "Hubbard's Narrative").
6. Sly 22 (from "Hubbard's Narrative").
7. Sly 22 (from "Hubbard's Narrative").
8. Dumas Malone, ed. *Dictionary of American Biography* (vol. 9, part 1. New York: Charles Scribner's Sons, 1964) 487.
9. William Bradford. *Of Plymouth Plantation* (New York: Capricorn Books, 1962) 73.
10. Bradford 73.
11. *Oxford English Dictionary* (Compact Edition, 1979).
12. *Oxford English Dictionary.*
13. Bradford 90.
14. Bradford 90.
15. Bradford 90.
16. Bradford 93-94.
17. Joseph Paige, "Early Land Dealing on Long Island," *Journal of Long Island History* (1967, 7 (1):25+).
18. Roger Williams. *A Key into the Language of America.* John J. Teunissen and Evelyn J. Hinz, eds. (Detroit: Wayne State University Press, 1973) 167.
19. Williams 167.
20. Williams 170.
21. Williams 171.
22. Bradford 78.
23. Bradford 94.
24. Bradford 94.
25. Sly 27-28.
26. Sly 29.
27. Sly 29.
28. Sly 30.
29. Sly 44-45.
30. Sly 53.
31. *Oxford English Dictionary.*
32. Sly 73.
33. *Wood's New England's Prospect* (Boston: Publications of the Prince Society, 1865), 77-78.
34. *Wood's* 82.

The Iroquois Influence on Women's Rights

Sally Roesch Wagner

> ...it behooves us women to question all historians, sacred and profane, who teach by examples or precepts any philosophy that lowers the status of the mothers of the race, or favors the one-man power in government.[1]

These are the words of one of the major theorists of the early women's rights movement, Elizabeth Cady Stanton, written 100 years ago. Stanton, along with Lucretia Mott, called the first women's rights convention in Seneca Falls, New York in 1848, and is generally credited with being the "mother" of early feminism.

Stanton and Matilda Joslyn Gage wrote the major documents of the radical wing of the women's movement, and shared leadership positions in the National Woman Suffrage Association and authorship of the monumental *History of Woman Suffrage* with Susan B. Anthony.

With the growing conservatism of the women's movement after 1890, the name of Matilda Joslyn Gage was literally written out of history by increasingly timid new woman suffragists who had taken charge. A similar attempt to sever historical ties with Elizabeth Cady Stanton was only partially successful.

As feminist historians restore Gage and Stanton to their rightful place in history, we find a new history. This is especially true with the rediscovery of Matilda Joslyn Gage, considered by some Women's Studies scholars today to have been one of the foremost feminist theoreticians, and considered during her time as part of the suffrage "triumvirate" with Stanton and Anthony.

The inclusion of Gage and Stanton causes a rethinking of the origin of the nineteenth century women's movement. Previously, twentieth century historians assumed the story of feminism began with the "discovery" of America by white men, or the political revolution staged by the colonists. The underlying assumption seems to have been that there was no seed of feminism in American soil when the first white settlers arrived. White people imported it.

Certainly there was a European foundation for American feminism. Suffragists documented the influence in the *History of Woman Suffrage,* edited by the "triumvirate" of the women's movement: Matilda Joslyn Gage, Elizabeth Cady Stanton and Susan B. Anthony. Gage, regarded as "one of the most logical, fearless and scientific writers of her day," traced the white Western history of feminism back to the early part of the fourteenth century. In her chapter on "Preceding Causes" in the first volume of the *History of Woman Suffrage,* Gage maintained that European women, along with their male supporters, had waged a four hundred year struggle for women's rights.[2]

She documented calls for women's rights during the Revolution which were ignored, as all the pleas by Western women had been for three hundred years before. The United States revolutionaries, once they had cemented power, placed women into a political subordination more severe even than that of the colonial period.[3] Ironically, these decreased rights for women were a result of basing the new state laws on English law.

The European tradition of church and law placed women in the role of property. Gage quoted Herbert Spencer's "Epitome of English History," from the *Descriptive Sociology of England,* which described the condition of women in this way: "Our laws are based on the all-sufficiency of man's rights, and society exists today for woman only in so far as she is in the keeping of some man."[4]

Abigail Adams feared that English common law, which had recently (1765-69) been drawn together into Blackstone's Code, would be used as the foundation upon which the laws of the new United States would be based. Her fear was realized. Blackstone's code was used as the basis for family law as the states concretized their laws after the revolution. It marked a decided set-back for women. Women's "very being or legal existence was upended during marriage, or at least, incorporated or consolidated into that of the husband, under whose wing, protection and cover, she performs everything," according to Blackstone. The two shall become one and the one is the man, the church proclaimed in canon law, and common law echoed the proclamation. According to woman's rights advocates from Abigail Adams to her 19th century counterparts, marriage under common law was a legal institution that robbed woman of her rights and created conditions that encouraged men to act tyrannically.

Under the European-inspired laws that were adopted by each state after the revolution, a single woman might be economically independent, owning property and earning her living; upon uttering the marriage vows, she lost control of her property and her earnings. She also gave away all rights to children she would bear. They became the "property" of the father who could give them away or grant custody to someone other than the mother, in the event of his death. With the words, "I do," a woman literally gave away her legal identity. The woman lost her name, her right to control her own body, and to live where she chose. A married woman could not make any contracts, sue or be sued; she was dead in the law. Wife-beating was not against the law, neither was marital rape.

Women's rights could not be easily incorporated into Eurocentric thought; rather, feminism challenged the very foundation of Western institutions.[5] Gage wrote:

> As I look backward through history I see the church everywhere stepping upon advancing civilization, hurling woman from the plane of "natural rights" where the fact of her humanity had placed her, and through itself, and its control over the state, in the doctrine of "revealed rights" everywhere teaching an inferiority of sex; a created subordination of woman to man; making her very existence a sin; holding her accountable to a diverse code of morals from man; declaring her possessed of fewer rights in church and in state; her very entrance into heaven made dependent upon some man to come as mediator between her and the Savior it has preached, thus crushing her personal, intellectual and spiritual freedom.[6]

Discontent came to a head for radical women's rights reformers in the late 1880s as their goal of equality in the church, state and family remained unmet. Women had been denied the right to vote by the United States Supreme Court, were still seen as the source of evil by the church because of Eve's "original sin," and were still expected to be the "great unpaid laborers of the world," the virtual slave of the household. These reformers, who had worked for change with little success for forty years, began calling for a radical transformation of the social order.

It was not simply the absence of rights that was the problem, they came to believe. It was the fact that, as Stanton said:

Society is based on this four-fold bondage of woman—Church, State, Capital and Society—making liberty and equality for her antagonistic to every organized institution.[7]

Gage expressed it this way:

During the ages, no rebellion has been of like importance with that of Woman against the tyranny of Church and State; none has had its far reaching effects. We note its beginning; its progress will overthrow every existing form of these institutions; its end will be a regenerated world.[8]

Gage and Stanton, the major theorists of the radical wing of the woman suffrage movement, became increasingly disenchanted with the inability/unwillingness of Western institutions to embrace the liberty not just of women, but of all disenfranchised groups. They looked elsewhere for their vision of the "regenerated world" which Gage predicted. Gage, and to a lesser extent Stanton, found it in Upstate New York. They became students of the Haudenosaunee—the Six Nations of the Iroquois Confederacy—and found a cosmological worldview which they believed to be superior to the patriarchal one of the white nation in which they lived.

What were their sources, how did they know about the Iroquois? They read Lewis Henry Morgan, of course, but he was only one of many Gage cites. For example, in documenting the matrilineal system, Gage says:

Although the principal chief of the confederacy was a man, descent ran through the female line, the sister of the chief possessing the power of nominating his successor.[9] ...The line of descent, feminine, was especially notable in all tribal relations such as the election of Chiefs, and the Council of Matrons, to which all disputed questions were referred for final adjudication.[10] ...Not alone the Iroquois but most Indians of North America trace descent in the female line; among some tribes woman enjoys almost the whole legislative authority and in others a prominent share.[11] Lafitte and other Jesuit missionary writers are corroborated in this statement by Schoolcraft, Catlin, Clark, Hubert Bancroft of the Pacific coast, and many students of Indian life and customs.[12]

Clark, the regional historian that Gage mentioned, wrote that with both marriage and separation, among the Iroquois, there was "no special ceremony, no disgrace, and each keeps their property."[13]

Another local historian read by Gage was C. Smith, who quoted Ephriam Webster, who came as a trader in 1786, lived with the Onondaga and Oneidas for a quarter of a century, and was adopted into the Onondaga nation. Webster said,

The Indians have no altercations, and that in ten years I have not heard any angry expression nor seen any degree of passion. They treated their women with respect, even tenderness. They used no ardent spirits. They settled differences amicably, raised wheat and corn in considerable quantities, and also apples.[14]

Gage also read Horatio Hale, who wrote:

When a chief died or (as sometimes happened) was deposed for incapacity or misconduct, some member of the same family succeeded him. Rank followed the female line; and this successor might be any descendent of the late chief's mother or grandmother—his brother, his cousin or his nephew—but never his son. Among many persons who might thus be eligible, the selection was made in the first instance by a family council. In this council the "chief matron" of the family, a noble dame whose position and right were well defined, had the deciding voice.[15]

Now there is another thing we say, we younger brothers. He who has worked for us has gone afar off; and he also will in time take with him all these—the whole body of warriors and also the whole body of women—they will go with him. But it is still harder when the woman shall die, because with her the line is lost. And also with the grandchildren and the little ones who are running around—these he will take away; and also those that are creeping on the ground, and also those that are on the cradleboards; all these he will take away with him.[16]

"Because with her the line is lost." The same sentiment prevailed among the Hurons. "For a Huron killed by a Huron," writes Father Ragueneau in the letter just quoted, "thirty gifts are commonly deemed a sufficient satisfaction. For a woman forty are required, because, as they say, the women are less able to defend themselves; and moreover, they being the source whence the land is peopled, their lives should be deemed of more value to the commonwealth, and their weakness should have a stronger support in public justice." Such was the reasoning of these heathen barbarians. Enlightened Christendom has hardly yet advanced to the mark of these opinions.[17]

Gage remarked:

So fully to this day is descent reckoned through the mother, that blue-eyed, fair-haired children of white fathers are numbered in the tribe and receive both from state and nation their portion of the yearly dole paid to Indian tribes. The veriest pagan among the Iroquois, the renowned and important Keeper of the Wampum, and present sole interpreter of the Belts which give the most ancient and secret history of this confederation, is Ephriam Webster, descended from a white man, who, a hundred or more years since, became affiliated through marriage with an Indian woman, as a member of the principal nation of the Iroquois, the Onondagas.[18]

Gage read at least some of the many non-Indian women who studied and wrote about the Iroquois during her lifetime. There were professional ethnologists like Alice Fletcher or Erminnie Smith, and "amateur" ethnologists, women like her, who had developed an interest in, and friendships with, members of one of the six Iroquois nations. These women, several dozen of them, wrote often with an astonishing understanding, which would no doubt have been recognized and respected into this century had they been men.[19]

Laura M. Sheldon Wright, wife of a missionary at Cattaraugus, published a *Dictionary of the Seneca Language* around 1835. Harriet Maxwell Converse, the woman who arranged for Gage to be adopted into the Wolf clan of the Mohawk nation, wrote extensively for the New York papers. While her *Myths and Legends* have been criticized for being romanticized, her newspaper articles were straightforward and highly descriptive. They also document her extensive support and lobbying work for the Iroquois. Converse "has ready for the press a volume of lyrics, sonnets and Indian myth songs," Harriet Phillips Eaton wrote Gage in the 1890s. Eaton, who was Gage's cousin, wrote about the Iroquois.

Helen F. Troy, of Syracuse, then Auburn, was adopted by Thomas and Electa Thomas into the Snipe clan of the Onondaga nation in 1894. She was given the name Spirit Dipping into the Silent Waters (Gar-wen-ne-sho). *The New York Herald* announced that "Mrs. Troy is at present at work on and is soon to have published an elaborate translation of the 'Book of the Sacred Wampum,' or the Iroquois Bible, also a dictionary for use in the colleges, of the Onondaga and Mohawk tongues with their equivalent meanings in English," the result of fifteen years of research. The book was to be illustrated by her husband, John H. Troy. The manuscript "is about to be submitted to printers for publication" the paper reported.[20]

In 1880, only six years before her death, Erminnie A. Smith became interested in the Six Nations and was appointed by the Smithsonian Institution to study them. She "lived among the Indians to study their habits and folklore and was so well-liked by the Tuscaroras that she was adopted into the White Bear clan" and given the name of Ka-tie-tio-sta-knost, meaning "Beautiful Flower." At the time of her death she was completing an Iroquois dictionary containing 15,000 classified words; 6,000 of the Tuscaroras, 3,000 of the Onondagas, and a thousand each of Oneidas and Senecas. She was just beginning her work with the Cayugas when she died.[21] J.W.B. Hewitt, of the Bureau of Ethnology, a Tuscarora who was her assistant, completed the dictionary, and called Smith "a superbly gifted scholar."[22] Horatio Hale said Smith "had pursued studies which in ethnology alone would make any man famous." The New York Academy of Sciences, in recognition of her work, elected Mrs. Smith a Fellow of their society, the first time this honor was conferred on a woman. A member of the Association for the Advancement of Science, the English Anthropological Society, and one of the leaders of Sorosis, she contributed largely to various scientific journals.[23] Smith's *Myths of the Iroquois*, originally published in 1883, has been reprinted by Iroquois Reprints.

Mary Elizabeth Beauchamp was the daughter of William M. Beauchamp, who *The Dictionary of American Biography* claims "became, among white men, the greatest authority on the history and institutions of the Iroquois. In a sense he was the successor of Lewis Morgan in this field." Mary Elizabeth was her father's secretary and also wrote on the Iroquois.

William Beauchamp wrote, in *Iroquois Folk Lore*, that he had an "interesting series of Seneca tales from Miss Myra E. Trippe of Salamanca, New York, which I procured for the State Library. Unfortunately they were destroyed, along with the Moravian Journals I sent there at the same time." Whether or not any copies still exist, there is a good chance that Gage read them during her lifetime, as she was a friend of the Beauchamps. While Gage read Morgan, Lafitte, Schoolcraft, Catlin, and Clark on the Iroquois, she knew Beauchamp. There were strong family ties between the two. Beauchamp's father was editor of a local paper and Gage wrote for him. Beauchamp's daughter-in-law wrote a song, "The Battle Hymn of the Suffragists" for Gage.

Identifying how a Fayetteville, New York resident of 1890 knew about the Iroquois is an easy task. In fact, it was hard to pick up a newspaper or magazine in upstate New York in the nineteenth century without reading something about the Iroquois. The local paper Gage read, the Onondaga (Syracuse) *Standard*, reported everything from condolence ceremonies to the lacrosse scores when Onondaga played the Mohawks. When legislation was introduced to break up the Iroquois nations' lands into individual ownership, the protests that came from Onondaga were published in full by the paper, along with the names of all the signatures to the petitions. The level of sophistication of these newspaper stories indicates that the average non-Indian in upstate New York 100 years ago possessed a level of knowledge about the Iroquois that, in the white nation, is held only by a relatively small number of scholars today.[24]

It comes as no surprise then, that when reformers like Matilda Joslyn Gage looked outside of their culture for a model upon which to base their vision of an egalitarian world, they quickly found their well-known Indian neighbors.

Rose Yawger wrote about lineage in her *Good Housekeeping* approved book which was published in Syracuse in 1893:

The children always followed the totemship of the mother, and to this significant fact alone much of the existing confusion in regard to the tribe of certain prominent characters is, in a great measure, due. If a Seneca brave married a Cayuga squaw [sic], the children were not Senecas, as might be supposed, but Cayugas, and even though they were born and brought up among the Senecas, they were aliens to the tribe and had to be adopted in the same ceremonious manner that strangers sometimes were. The Cayuga nation could even call on them to take arms in case of war.[25]

Or Minnie Myrtle, who was published by the popular Appleton press in 1855:

The children are of the tribe of the mother, as are the children's children to the latest generation, and they are also of the same nation. If the mother is a Cayuga, the children are Cayugas; and if a Mohawk, the children are Mohawks. If the marriage proves unhappy, the parties are allowed to separate, and each is at liberty to marry again. But the mother has the sole right to the disposal of the children. She keeps them all if she chooses, and to their father they are ever [mere] strangers.[26]

This issue of lineage had great bearing on the status of women, as these early feminists analyzed it.[27] Gage wrote about the absence of a woman's right to her children in the white nation:

The slave code has always been that children shall follow the condition of the mother; hence, as the present law of marriage makes the wife the irresponsible slave of the husband—robbing her of her name, her earnings, her accountability—it consistently follows that she shall be robbed of her children. Blackstone, the chief exponent of common law, says: "A mother has no legal right or authority over her children; she is only entitled to respect and honor." The United States, governing itself by English law, inherited this with other oppressions, and it to this day holds force in most of the thirty-seven States of the Union. One or two States have by statute law placed the mother on equal basis of legal right with the father...men, calling themselves Christian men, have dared to defy God's law, and to give to the father alone the sole right to the child; have dared make laws which permit the dying father of an unborn child to will it away, and to give any person he pleases to select the right to wait the advent of that child, and when the mother, at the hazard of her own life, has brought it forth, to rob her of it and to do by it as the dead father directed. What an anomaly on Justice is such a law![28]

Gage also wrote about the recognition of the primacy of the mother-child bond among the Haudenosaunee:

If for any cause the Iroquois husband and wife separated, the wife took with her all the property she had brought into the wigwam; the children also accompanied the mother, whose right to them was recognized as supreme.[29]

Matilda Joslyn Gage's public connection with the Iroquois began in the 1870s when, as President of the National Woman Suffrage Association and an amateur ethnologist, she published a series of articles on the Iroquois which were featured prominently in the *New York Evening Post* and reprinted in several other papers in the state.[30] The introduction to the series recognized the significance of this suffrage/Indian connection, stating:

Mrs. Gage has given some attention to the traditions of the aboriginal inhabitants of this country, and we understand that she intends to write a book about them... Mrs. Gage, with an exhibition of ardent devotion to the cause of woman's rights which is very proper in the president of the National Woman Suffrage Association, gives prominence to the fact that in the old days when the glory of the famous confederation of savages was at its height, the power and importance of women were recognized by the allied tribes.[31]

In the ensuing series of articles, Gage contended that "division of power between the sexes in this Indian republic was nearly equal."[32] She noted that:

The family relation among the Iroquois demonstrated woman's superiority in power. When an Indian husband brought the products of the chase to the wigwam, his control over it ceased. In the home, the wife was absolute; the sale of the skins was regulated by her, the price was paid to her.[33]

This information was in marked contrast to the cultural mythology of Indian women as beasts of burden. It was precisely this role in the home that gave a woman her status, Gage contended,

...the women being the chief agriculturists...their method of farming was entirely different from our own. In olden Iroquois tillage there was no turning the sod with a plough to which were harnessed a cow and a woman, as is seen today in Christian Germany, but the ground was literally "tickled with a hoe" and it "laughed with a harvest."[34]

...Three of the five ancient feasts of the Iroquois were agricultural feasts connected with this their great staple...Centuries ago was agriculture thus honored by this ancient people...To themselves the Five Nations were known as the Ongwe Honwe, that is, a people surpassing all others. In Christian Europe during the middle ages the agriculturist was despised; the warrior was the aristocrat of civilization. In publicly honoring agriculture as did the Ongwe Honwe three times a year, they surpassed in wisdom the men of Europe.[35]

There are pretty stories of these Three Sisters, the corns, beans, and pumpkins, [squash] but it is noteworthy that the Indian Thanksgiving day antedated our own. It is more American than we have ever claimed.[36]

Women lost all rights to their property when they married in the white nation, and both Gage and Stanton pointed to the contrast between the property rights of white and Iroquois women.

Alice Fletcher, a noted suffragist, ethnographer, and government agent, described the opposite condition among the Indian women in the numerous tribes and nations she had observed. Gage had helped organize an International Council of Women in 1888; Stanton had sailed back from England to attend. Speaking before this audience, Fletcher touched a nerve sensitive to suffragists, their lack of property rights, as she recounted this personal experience with the Omaha:

> At the present time all property is personal; the man owns his own ponies and other belongings which he has personally acquired; the woman owns her horses, dogs, and all the lodge equipment, children own their own articles, and parents do not control the possessions of their children. There is really no family property, as we use the term. A wife is as independent in the use of her possessions as is the most independent man in our midst. If she chooses to give away or sell all of her property, there is no one to gainsay her...[37]

> When I was living with the Indians, my hostess...one day gave away a very fine horse. I was surprised, for I knew there had been no family talk on the subject, so I asked: "Will your husband like to have you give the horse away?" Her eyes danced, and, breaking into a peal of laughter, she hastened to tell the story to the other women gathered in the tent, and I became the target of many merry eyes. I tried to explain how a white woman would act, but laughter and contempt met my explanation of the white man's hold upon his wife's property.[38]

A similar story came from the pen of a Frenchwoman, Emma Borglum, who married the sculptor Solon Borglum, and spent her honeymoon among the Lakota on the Crow Creek reservation of South Dakota in 1891:

> One day I showed some astonishment at seeing a young Indian woman, in the absence of her husband, give two horses to a friend. She looked at me very coldly and said: "These horses are mine." I excused myself saying that in my country a woman would consult her husband before giving such expensive presents. The woman answered proudly: "I would not be a white woman!"[39]

Minnie Myrtle again:

> In regard to property, too, the wife retains whatever belonged to her before marriage, distinct from her husband, and can dispose of it as she pleases without his consent, and if she separates from him, takes it with her, and at her death, either before or after separation, her children inherit all she possessed.[40]

It was far different for white women under common law which denied property rights to non-Indian women, as suffragist attorney Carrie S. Burnham described:

> By marriage, the husband and wife are one person in law; that is, the legal existence of the woman is "merged in that of her husband." He is her "baron," or "lord," bound to supply her with shelter, food, clothing and medicine and is entitled to her earnings—the use and custody of her person which he may seize wherever he may find it.[41]

In a speech before the National Council of Women in 1891, Elizabeth Cady Stanton called on the memoirs of Ashur Wright, a long-time missionary among the Seneca, whose wife Laura had published a dictionary of the Seneca language. Ashur Wright related:

> Usually the females ruled the house. The stores were in common; but woe to the luckless husband or lover who was too shiftless to do his share of the providing. No matter how many children, or whatever goods he might have in the house, he might at any time be ordered to pick up his blanket and budge; and after such an order it would not be healthful for him to attempt to disobey. The house would be too hot for him; and unless saved by the intercession of some aunt or grandmother he must retreat to his own clan, or go and start a new matrimonial alliance in some other.[42]

Stanton was especially sensitive to this issue of divorce. Among suffragists, she was uniquely courageous in publicly and consistently advocating that the laws be changed to allow women the right to leave disagreeable marriages. For this stand, she was labeled an infidel by organized Christian religion which generally held that marriage was a covenant with God which no woman had a right to break, even if her life was in danger from a violent husband. Again, the situation was very different for Indian women, as Alice Fletcher had explained:

> ...the wife never becomes entirely under the control of her husband. Her kindred have a prior right, and can use that right to separate her from him or to protect her from him, should he maltreat her. The brother who would not rally to the help of his sister would become a by-word among his clan. Not only will he protect her at the risk of his life from insult and injury, but he will seek help for her when she is sick and suffering...

In the *Journal of American Folklore*, Beauchamp related an Iroquois story in which "a man who had beaten his wife cruelly upon earth, struck a red hot statue of woman. The sparks flew with every blow and burned him."[43]

Fletcher was concerned about what would happen to the Indian women when they became citizens and lost their rights, and were treated with the same legal disrespect as white women, as she explained to the International Council of Women in 1888:

Not only does the woman under our [white nation] laws lose her independent hold on her property and herself, but there are offenses and injuries which can befall a woman which would be avenged and punished by the relatives under tribal law, but which have no penalty or recognition under our laws. If the Indian brother should, as of old, defend his sister, he would himself become liable to the law and suffer for his championship.[44]

She was referring, of course, to sexual and physical violence against women. Indian men's intolerance of rape was commented upon by many eighteenth and nineteenth century Indians and non-Indian reporters alike, many of whom contended that rape didn't exist among Indian nations previous to white contact.[45]

Hewitt, for example, quoted "Gen. James Clinton, commanding the New York division of the Sullivan punitive expedition in 1779, with orders to disperse the hostile Iroquois and to destroy their homes, [who] paid his enemies the high tribute of a brave soldier by writing in April, 1779, to his lieutenant, Colonel Van Schaick, then leading his troops against the Onondaga and their villages, the following terse compliment: "Bad as these savages are, they never violate the chastity of any woman, their prisoner." And he added this significant admonition to his colonel, "It would be well to take measures to prevent a stain upon our army."[46]

Also Mary Elizabeth Beauchamp, daughter of the noted Iroquoianist, in a letter to the Skaneateles Democrat, dated 10 April 1883, wrote:

It shows the remarkable security of living on an Indian Reservation, that a solitary woman can walk about for miles, at any hour of the day or night, in perfect safety. Miss R.* often starts off, between eight and nine in the evening, lantern in one hand and alpenstock in the other, and a parcel of supplies strung from her shoulder, to walk for a mile or more up the hillsides. [*Miss Remington, "had long been in charge of the mission house." She was adopted into the snipe clan of the Onondaga in 1886, and given the name "Ki-a-was-say."][47]

The reality of a culture in which rape was not allowed is difficult to comprehend by a European tradition which legalized both marital rape and wife battering. As Carrie S. Burnham, the legal genius of the National Woman Suffrage Association who worked with Gage and Stanton analyzed common law:

The husband being bound to provide for his wife the necessaries of life, and being responsible for "her morals" and the good order of the household, may choose and govern the domicile, choose her associates, separate her from her relatives, restrain her religious and personal freedom, compel her to cohabit with him, correct her faults by mild means and if necessary chastise her with the same moderation as [if] she was his apprentice or child.[48]

The vote was the tool that women could use in the white nation to gain their rights, and suffrage was a right which they believed to be inherently theirs in a republic. The white government believed otherwise. State laws denied women suffrage, and in 1874 the United States Supreme Court ruled that they had the constitutional right to do so. Women did not receive the constitutional right to vote in the United States of America until 1920. Iroquois women had always possessed suffrage, as these early feminists well knew. Stanton, for example, wrote:

> The women were the great power among the clan, as everywhere else. They did not hesitate, when occasion required, "to knock off the horns," as it was technically called, from the head of a chief and send him back to the ranks of the warriors. The original nomination of the chiefs also always rested with the women.[49]

Women suffrage papers regularly carried stories like this one which pointed out the contrast between the political position of women in the white nation and Indian nations:

> It is stated that an Indian Pueblo about fifty miles from the City of Mexico, is governed by a council of twelve, half of whom are elderly women who must have raised large families and proved devoted mothers and kind neighbors. "The venerable mothers," is the title by which they are known, which is certainly an improvement on the "old grannies" which we so often hear.[50]

Minnie Myrtle wrote in 1855:

> The legislative powers of the nation are vested in a Council of eighteen, chosen by the universal suffrages of the nation; but no treaty is to be binding, until it is ratified by three-fourths of all the voters, and *three-fourths of all the mothers of the nation!*[51] So there was peace instead of war, as there would often be if the voice of woman could be heard! And though the Senecas, in revising their laws and customs, have in a measure acceded to the civilized barbarism of treating the opinions of women with contempt, where their interest is equal, they still cannot sign a treaty without the consent of *two thirds of the mothers!*[52]

> The emblem of power worn by the Sachem [chief] was a *deer's antlers*, and if in any instance the women disapproved of the election or acts of a Sachem, they had the power to *remove his horns* and return him to private life. Their officers or runners from council to council were chosen by themselves and denominated *women's men*, and by these their interests were always fully represented. If at any time they wished any subject considered, by means of their runners, they called a council in their clan; if it was a matter of more general interest there was a council of the nation, and if the opinions of the women or Sachems of other nations were necessary, a grand council was called as readily to attend to them as to the interests of men. Thus a way was

provided for them to have *a voice* in the affairs of the nation, without endangering their *womanly reserve* or subjecting them to the masculine reproach of publicity, or a desire to assume the offices and powers of men![53]

The purely democratic nature of Iroquois decision-making was described by Gage in this way:

The common interests of the confederacy were arranged in councils, each sex holding one of its own, although the women took the initiative in suggestion, orators of their own sex presenting their views to the council of men.[54]

One implication of the combination of female political power and female property rights was manifested in the making of treaties, according to Gage:

No sale of lands was valid without consent of the squaws[55] and among the State Archives at Albany, New York, treaties are preserved signed by the "Sachems and Principal women of the Six Nations."[56]

Fletcher also described women's involvement in treaty negotiations:

In olden times the women claimed the land. In the early treaties and negotiations for the sale of land, the women had their voice, and the famous Chief Cornplanter was obliged to retract one of his bargains because the women forbade, they being the land-holders, and not the men. With the century, our custom of ignoring women in public transactions has had its reflex influence upon Indian custom.[57]

Iroquois women also influenced war decisions, according to Gage:

Although it was a confederation of warriors, owing its permanence and its growth to prowess in arms, yet its women exercised controlling power in peace and war, forbidding at will its young braves to enter battle, and often determining its terms of peace.[58] ...Sir William Johnston mentions an instance of Mohawk squaws forbidding the war-path to young braves.[59]

Minnie Myrtle wrote:

In the year 1791, when Washington wished to secure the neutrality of the Six Nations, a deputation was sent to treat with them, but was not favorably received, as many of the young Chiefs were for war and sided with the British. The women, as is usual, preferred peace, and argued that the land was theirs, for they cultivated and took care of it, and, therefore, had a right to speak concerning the use that should be made of its products. They demanded to be heard on this occasion, and addressed the deputation first themselves in the following words: "Brother:—The Great Ruler has spared us until a new day to talk together; for since you came here from General Washington, you and our uncles the Sachems have been counselling together. Moreover, your sisters, the women, have taken the same into great consideration, because you and our Sachems have said so much about it.

Now, that is the reason we have come to say something to you, and to tell you that the Great Ruler hath preserved you, and that you ought to hear and listen to what we, women, shall speak, as well as the Sachems; *for we are the owners of this land,* AND IT IS OURS! It is we that plan it for our and their use. Hear us, therefore, for we speak things that concern us and our children; and you must not think hard of us while our men shall say more to you, for we have told them."

They then designated Red Jacket as their speaker, and he took up the speech of his clients as follows:

"BROTHERS FROM PENNSYLVANIA:—You that are sent from General Washington, and by the thirteen fires; you have been sitting side by side with us every day, and the Great Ruler has appointed us another pleasant day to meet again.

"NOW LISTEN BROTHERS:—You know it has been the request of our head warriors, that we are left to answer for our women, who are to conclude what ought to be done by both Sachems and warriors. So hear what is their conclusion. The business you come on is very troublesome, and we have been a long time considering it; and now the elders of our women have said that our Sachems and warriors must help you, for the good of them and their children, and you tell us the Americans are strong for peace.[60]

William Stone in 1841 wrote:

It is one of the peculiar features of Indian polity that their lands belong to the warriors who defend, and the women who till them, and who, moreover, are the mothers of the warriors. And although the sachems, as civil magistrates, have ordinarily the power of negotiating treaties, yet whenever the question of a sale of land is the subject of a negotiation, if both the warriors and women become dissatisfied with the course the sachems are pursuing, they have the right to interpose and take the subject out of their hands.[61]

The Indian women with whom Fletcher had contact were well aware of their superior rights:

As I have tried to explain our statutes to Indian women, I have met with but one response. They have said: "As an Indian woman I was free. I owned my home, my person, the work of my own hands, and my children could never forget me. I was better as an Indian woman than under white law."[62]

She found a similar response among Indian men:

Men have said: "Your laws show how little your men care for their women. The wife is nothing of herself. She is worth little but to help a man to have one hundred and sixty acres." One day, sitting in the tent of an old chief, famous in war, he said to me: "My young men are to lay aside their weapons; they are to take up the work of the women; they will plow the field and raise the crops; for them I see a future, but my women, they to whom we owe everything, what is there for them to do? I see nothing! You are a woman; have pity on my women when everything is taken from them."[63]

Indian men were not unmindful of the unjust political position of non-Indian women, and supported white suffragists in their struggle for political justice. Gage cited Dr. Peter Wilson, Seneca chief and maternal nephew of Red Jacket, who addressed the New York Historical Society in 1866, encouraging white men to use the occasion of Southern reconstruction to establish universal suffrage, "even of the women, as in his nation," according to newspaper reports.[64]

This support for woman suffrage from an Iroquois chief came at a critical historic moment. The fifteenth amendment, which granted suffrage only to black men, was being ratified by the states. Women, black and white, were being told by abolitionists to wait for suffrage until after black men received it. Gage and Stanton's organization, the National Woman Suffrage Association, refused to take a back seat, and it comes as an amazing historical surprise that they received public support from a well-known and respected Iroquois who admonished white men to treat women as well as they were treated in his nation.

Arthur Parker also supported women's rights, writing at length:

Does the modern American woman [who] is a petitioner before man, pleading for her political rights, ever stop to consider that the red woman that lived in New York state five hundred years ago had far more political rights and enjoyed a much wider liberty than the twentieth century woman of civilization?

...The Iroquois woman was never the drudge that history has sought to picture her. She seldom worked as hard as the modern American woman of the middle class, and still the contrary opinion prevails. An instance comes to mind of a prosperous farmer who was arguing with a young man of Indian descent. Arrayed in his Sunday suit the farmer sat in his parlor. "I tell you," said he, "your poor Injun' women had to suffer while you men took it easy huntin', fishin', and killin' enemies. Them poor squaws had to lug water, dig potatoes, chop wood—aye, slaves they were! Now we white men—" There was a confusion of sounds outside, but the practiced ear of the Indian distinguished the sound of the axe, then the creak of the pump and the tread of feet. The outer door of the kitchen opened and a woman clad in a loose calico gown entered, holding in one arm a load of wood and bearing a pail of water in the other. "Your hired girl?" ventured the Indian. "Wall, no," said the farmer with a shamed faced look, "that's my wife."

This is no exaggeration but a true story of what actually happened and barring the Indian from the scene its like occurs daily everywhere in civilization. Women do men's work while men talk. Of course the reverse frequently happens also, but that's "Woman's Rights."

Parker then went on to talk about the taking of captives and related:

no man by word or deed ever offending the dignity of her sex...Civilized man and woman found in so-called savagery the acme of personal liberty. As late as 1826 several captive white women who had been carried by the Indians beyond Lake Superior were discovered by friends and offered every means of escape to home and kindred, but one by one each rejected the overture. They had shaken off the burdens of artificial life and returned to nature. Never more did they wish to resume the troubles of imperfect civilization.

Parker concludes:

Today as woman stands the advocate and petitioner of her own cause, should she not offer an ablation of gratitude to the memory of the Iroquois Indian, who called the earth his "first mother" and through his savage sense of justice gave to the mothers of his race, their rights, maternal, civil, religious, social and political.[65]

The political support went both ways. In her women's rights paper, Gage editorialized:

That the Indians have been oppressed—are now, is true, but the United States has treaties with them, recognizing them as distinct political communities and duty towards them demands *not an enforced citizenship*, but a faithful living up to its obligations on the part of the government.[66]

While most early women's rights advocates found a similarity between the treatment of slaves and married women, Gage made a rare connection in the 1870s, comparing the government's treatment of Indians with that of white men's treatment of wives. She introduced a resolution into the NWSA in 1879 which read: "That the policy of this government in appointing agents to educate and civilize the Indians, to obtain calico dresses for squaws and aprons for papooses and a comfortable salary for their own pockets out of money justly due the Indian tribes, is in harmony with man's treatment of woman in appropriating her property, talents, time and labors, and using the proceeds as he pleases in the name of protection."

Gage saw through the patriarchal posture of chivalry and benevolence that kept women and Indians in economic subservience. And she saw further. This was during a time when common wisdom agreed:

Pity the poor squaw
Beast of burden, slave;
Chained under female law
from puberty to grave.

Gage, on the other hand, believed that "under [Iroquois] women the science of government reached the highest form known to the world."[67] "But the most notable fact connected with women's participation in governmental affairs among the Iroquois," she wrote, "is the statement of Hon. George Bancroft that the form of government of the United States, was borrowed from that of the Six Nations."[68]

This, according to Gage, was the most important conclusion she drew from her Iroquois study. Male-rule, or the Eurocentric social/government system she labeled the patriarchate, based its institutions on inequality of rights as exemplified in its long history of women's oppression. "Thus to the Matriarchate or Mother-rule," she concludes, "is the modern world indebted for its first conception of inherent rights, natural equality of condition, and the establishment of a civilized government upon this basis."[69]

While the Western theory of feminism came from dissidents who were chastised by the church and arrested by the state for their ideas, the Iroquois, on the other hand, practiced feminism. The idea of women's rights may have been refined in the unsuccessful centuries of struggle to gain it in the white nations. But the world-historic fact was that the behavior of equality was uniquely indigenous to Native people, these suffragists believed. Christianity and Western "civilization," they charged, had been the downfall of women.[70]

Knowledge of their lack of rights under English-inspired law was pervasive among these women, as was awareness of the prestigious position of Native women who lived in matrilineal/matrifocal systems.

For Matilda Joslyn Gage, the Haudenosaunee—the People of the Long House—were an example of the political, economic, gender, religious, social system of gynocracy she called The Matriarchate. "Never was justice more perfect, never civilization higher than under the Matriarchate."[71]

Notes

This article was originally published in the *Akwe:kon Journal (Northeast Indian Quarterly)* Volume IX, Number 1 (Spring 1992).

1. Elizabeth Cady Stanton, "The Matriarchate," *The National Bulletin* I (February 1891) 3.
2. Matilda Joslyn Gage, Elizabeth Cady Stanton and Susan B. Anthony, *History of Woman Suffrage* (Reprint ed., Salem NH: Ayer Company, Publishers, Inc., 1985) I: 29. [Hereafter referred to as HWS]
3. See Sally Roesch Wagner, *A Time of Protest: Suffragists Challenge the Republic, 1870-1887* (Carmichael, CA: Sky Carrier Press, 1988) Chapter 4.
4. Gage, Stanton and Anthony I: 26.
5. For an excellent theoretical analysis of the "Eurocentric notion," see José Barreiro, "Challenging the Eurocentric Notion" in *Indian Roots of American Democracy*. (Ithaca, NY: *Northeast Indian Quarterly*, 1988) xii-xvi.
6. Matilda Joslyn Gage, *Woman, Church and State*. (Chicago: Charles Kerr, 1893. Reprint Edition: Watertown, MA: Persephone Press, 1980) 245.
7. Quoted in Lois Banner, *Elizabeth Cady Stanton: A Radical for Woman's Rights* (Boston: Little Brown and Company, 1980) 145.
8. Gage 246.

9. *New York Evening Post*, 24 September 1875.

10. Gage, 1893: 10.

11. Alexander, *History of Women*, quoted in WCS: 10.

12. Gage, 1893: 10.

13. Joshua V.H. Clark, *Onondaga, or Reminiscences of Earlier and Later Times* (Syracuse: N.P., 1848) 49-50.

14. R.P. Smith, *Historical and Statistical Gazetteer of New York* (Syracuse: N.P., 1860) 69.

15. Horatio Hale, ed., *The Iroquois Book of Rights*, with an Introduction by William N. Fenton, (Philadelphia: D.G. Brinton, 1883; repr., Toronto: University of Toronto Press, 1963) 29.

16. Hale 141, 143.

17. Hale 168.

18. Gage, 1893: 10.

19. These women will be the subject of a future article.

20. *New York Herald*, 5 November 1905.

21. *Onondaga Standard*, 8 January 1946.

22. *Marcellus Observer*, 8 July 1949.

23. Unidentified newspaper clipping, 17 April 1893, Iroquois collection, Onondaga Historical Association, Syracuse, NY.

24. The Iroquois collection in the Onondaga Historical Association in Syracuse, NY, is an extraordinarily rich resource of 100 years of newspaper clippings.

25. Rose N. Yawger, *The Indian and the Pioneer: An Historical Study* 1 (Syracuse, New York: C.W. Bardeen, 1893) 39.

26. Minnie Myrtle, *The Iroquois; or, The Bright Side of Indian Character* (New York: D. Appleton and Company, 1855) 85-6.

27. I'm choosing here to look at status as Ann Eastlack Schafer did in her 1941 MA thesis in Anthropology for the University of Pennsylvania, "The Status of Iroquois Women." Schafer defines status as simply, the "collection of rights and duties" of "all the positions which she occupies," as distinct from the Iroquois women's role: "the dynamic aspect of a status."

28. Matilda Joslyn Gage, "The Mother of his Children," *San Francisco Pioneer*, 9 November 1871.

29. Gage, 1893: 10.

30. In 1893 she was adopted into the wolf clan of the Mohawk nation and given the name Karonienhawi.

31. *The New York Evening Post*, 24 September 1875. Matilda Joslyn Gage scrapbook of writings, Gage collection, Schlesinger Library, Radcliffe College.

32. *The New York Evening Post*, 24 September 1875.

33. Gage, 1893: 10.

34. *New York Evening Post*, 3 November 1875.

35. *New York Evening Post*, 3 November 1875.

36. W.M. Beauchamp, "The New Religion of the Iroquois," *The Journal of American Folk-Lore*. 10 no. 38 (July-Sept. 1897) 177.

37. Alice Fletcher, *Report of the International Council of Women* (Washington, D.C.: Rufus H. Darby, Printer, 1888) 239-240.

38. Fletcher 238.

39. Emma Vignal Borglum, *The Experience at Crow Creek; A Sioux Indian Reservation*

at South Dakota, Collection of the Manuscript Division, Library of Congress.

40. Minnie Myrtle, *The Iroquois; or, The Bright Side of Indian Character* (New York: D. Appleton and Company, 1855) 85-6.

41. Carrie S. Burnham, *Tract No. 5: Common Law* (N.P.: n.d.), Women's Rights Volume 2, Department of Rare Books, Olin Library, Cornell University. When Burnham applied to the University of Pennsylvania to study law, Spencer Miller, who was dean of the law department, said that if women or negroes were admitted, he would resign. Ultimately she won and studied law there.

42. Stanton, 1891: 5.

43. Beauchamp 178.

44. Fletcher 238.

45. For a more complete account, see Sally Roesch Wagner, "The Iroquois Confederacy: a Native American Model for Non-sexist Men," *Changing Men* 19 (Spring/Summer 1988) 32-34.

46. Hewitt 482-3.

47. Gage is likely to have had this information. Beauchamp's daughter-in-law wrote a song, "The Battle Hymn of the Suffragists," dedicated to Matilda Joslyn Gage. Gage also wrote short stories for his father's paper, *The Skaneateles Democrat,* in the 1950s.

48. Burnham.

49. Stanton, "The Matriarchate."

50. *Woman's Tribune,* November 1887: 1.

51. Myrtle 303.

52. Myrtle 162.

53. Myrtle 42.

54. *New York Evening Post,* 24 September 1875.

55. Gage, like most non-Indians of her day, was apparently unaware of the derogatory nature of this term.

56. *Documentary History of New York,* in Gage, 1893: 10.

57. Fletcher, 239.

58. *New York Evening Post,* 24 September 1875.

59. Gage, 1893: 10.

60. Myrtle 161.

61. William L. Stone, *The Life and Times of Red-Jacket or Sa-Go-Ye-Wat-Ha; Being the Sequel to the History of the Six Nations* (New York, Wiley and Putnam, 1841) 155-6.

62. Fletcher 238-239.

63. Fletcher 239.

64. *Syracuse Journal,* 10 January 1866.

65. Unidentified newspaper clipping in the Harriet Maxwell Converse collection, State Museum, Albany, NY.

66. *National Citizen and Ballot Box,* May 1878.

67. Gage, 1893: 10.

68. *History of the United States,* volume I, cited in Gage, 1893: 10.

69. Gage, 1893: 10.

70. Nineteenth-century Eurocentric language defined Indians as "savages," "pagans," etc. *Basic Call to Consciousness* (Mohawk Nation via Rooseveltown, NY: *Akwesasne Notes,* 1978) has a helpful analysis of the terminology.

71. Gage, 1893: 9.

Return of the Wampum

José Barreiro

After a week of rainy fog, the sky opened wide that morning. The day was October 21, 1989, and what made it special was that after ninety-two years and much contention, the State of New York, through its Museum at Albany, was returning a dozen old and revered wampum belts to the Iroquois people. One had the feeling the sign of strong sun and blue sky would not go unnoticed among the Iroquois elders.

Many people from all points of New York State and into Canada journeyed to Onondaga that morning to witness the return. The Onondaga Indian community is capital and central fire of the traditionally-minded Iroquois nations, the League of the Haudenosaunee. Official delegations arrived from several Indian communities, from Governor Cuomo's office, from the State legislature, and, of course, from the State Museum at Albany.

The Iroquois capital is now hard to miss. At the Nedrow exit on Route 81, just south of Syracuse, prominent green signs announce ONONDAGA NATION TERRITORY to all motorists. Individual Indians now own the restaurants, cigarette and souvenir shops on the edge of the reservation.

The longhouse, located in the central valley of Onondaga, was surrounded by parked cars. A long structure made of logs and heated by woodstoves, it is the seat of civil and religious ceremonies. That day the longhouse was crowded, with people even standing in the entranceway. Going in past the door and looking left over the many heads to the men's side, chiefs, clanmothers and visitors sat on wooden benches on three sides of a table. On the table, encased in plexiglass, were twelve belts made of strung wampum, the object of the day's ceremony.

The Onondaga Longhouse is the gathering place of the clan and nation chiefs of the League of the Haudenosaunee. Chiefs who hold titles under the Haudenosaunee roll call for the Seneca, Cayuga, Oneida, Onondaga, Mohawk and Tuscarora nations still meet there to hold Grand Council. The tradition that calls together the clan chiefs from the confederated nations stems from pre-colonial days. Although at various times it was nearly impossible for the Grand Council to meet, particularly through the 1800s, meetings of Longhouse Chiefs representing all six nations in the Confederacy have occurred continually and increasingly so since the turn of this century. The Haudenosaunee Confederacy is grounded in a historical and legal framework, the Great Law of Peace, an oral document (though there are written versions), which is still recounted by elders.

That day the well-attended session was not a Grand Council meeting, but had a similar atmosphere and structure. The hosting chiefs from the Onondaga Nation were represented by Chief Leon Shenandoah, who holds the title of Tadodaho, and officially convenes the council. Chief Shenandoah stood behind the table that displayed the wampum belts, with the Onondaga chiefs and clanmothers behind him. To his left sat the chiefs and clanmothers of the Younger Brothers, the Cayuga, Oneida and Tuscarora; to his right sat the chiefs and clanmothers of the the Mohawk and the Seneca, Elder Brothers, along with the Onondaga.

Among honored visitors was a delegation from the New York State Museum at Albany, including its then-director, Martin Sullivan (who has since moved on to become director of the Heard Museum in Phoenix, Arizona), and Native American specialist, Ray Gonyea, both of whom had much to do with making the day possible. Secretary of State Gail Schaffer represented the governor's office. The twelve hundred or so faces in the longhouse also displayed a contemporary "Who's Who" of Haudenosaunee people, including longhouse and elective chiefs, clanmothers, respected elders, teachers, young professionals and students.

The Indian crowd assembled was significant. Not only were the numbers impressive but many represented quite large families and the atmosphere was genuinely social and friendly. For ninety-two years, the argument made against repatriation of the wampum belts, first by a

New York State court and later by several prominent anthropologists, hinged on the position that the Iroquois were disinterested in their culture and that the Confederacy of the Six Nations no longer exists. According to the theory, the Iroquois Confederacy ceased to exist at the end of the American Revolutionary War. The gathered group, while not representative of absolutely all Indians of Iroquois ancestry, was composed of people from a wide spectrum of nations, communities and clans, and is evidence of continuity and respect for tradition.

The wampum belts in the plexiglass case, part of a larger collection still held in various American and Canadian museums, are an important cultural legacy to the Iroquois, and by historical extension, to all North Americans. Dating from the mid-1600s (some of the specific beads go back to the mid-1400s), their function is to serve as memory aids in oral traditions. In the northeastern Indian tradition, treaty meetings and other important negotiations were not considered complete and binding without the preparation and presentation of wampum belts. Thus the Iroquois belts record some of the earliest governmental transactions in the contact and colonial periods.

Perhaps the most important of the group, the Hiawatha Belt depicts the linkage and unity of the Confederacy's original Five Nations and is considered the founding document of the Haudenosaunee. But all the belts are important, each one signifying a process or a moment in Iroquois history and thus part of the cultural patrimony. Today, the Museum also returned other belts: Washington Covenant, First Pale Faces, Champlain, Caughnawaga, Wing (or Dust Fan), Treaty, Alliance, Remembrance, Tadodaho, Council Summons, and Beauchamp "Path," also called the "Old Peace Belt." Each has its own history and meaning. The collection of Haudenosaunee wampum belts were kept, from the distant past, in a "bag woven of elmbark fibre" and taken out to be "read" to the people by the chiefs at various ceremonial times.[1]

Tadodaho opened the meeting with the Thanksgiving Address that begins all longhouse activities. The opening expresses appreciation for all aspects of the natural world in sections directed at the people, mother earth, the grasses and plants we use for medicine, the fruits, woods, animals, birds, waters, the food we plant (the three sisters), wind, the thunderers, the sun, moon, stars, the four beings, Handsome Lake, and the Creator.

Among the delegates near Tadodaho sat Sub-Chief Jacob Thomas, Cayuga Snipe Clan from Six Nations reserve in Canada. Thomas's presence was important. Not only is he a well-recognized culture-bearer, from among a reduced group who can "read" the belts, but he is an Iroquois sub-chief from "the Canada side." Tadodaho introduced Thomas with these words: "Some of our people, during the colonial war, migrated to Canada and set up a reservation there. But, as with our other Confederacy peoples, we have maintained contact and relations visit often with one another."

The Belts Removed

The American Revolution had a great impact on the history of the wampum belts, documents of the governmental affairs of the Haudenosaunee people. Many Onondaga, Cayuga and Mohawk villages were burned to the ground during and after the war, and their people scattered to various parts. Onondaga families, including the Wampum Keeper with the Confederacy's bag of wampum, sought refuge among the Seneca, who designated a "mile square of land to honor the fire and its guardian" at their reservation on Buffalo Creek.[2]

The wampum stayed at Buffalo Creek for many years, although the Onondaga people returning to the homeland asked for the Confederacy fire to be rekindled at their old village and for their wampum to be brought back. In 1784, about 200 Onondagas, as well as Cayugas and Mohawks, chose to go to Canada, joining Joseph Brant's movement to Ontario and Quebec. The wampum belts of the Onondaga were divided at that time, with the Canada-bound chiefs being given the belts "most likely connected to Canadian or English relations" and the chiefs remaining in the American side, retaining the other half of the belts.[3]

In Canada, migrating groups of the various nation longhouses continued to raise chiefs and created a duplicate Grand Council structure to deal with the Canadian government. At the same time, in 1847, as more Onondaga returned to their Central New York territory, the "American side" wampum bag, then estimated at a capacity of more than a bushel and still containing some twenty-five belts, was brought back to the Onondaga fire.[4]

By the turn of the century, the Onondaga Nation still held wampum belts made in early colonial times. Various Onondaga wampum keepers cared for the nation belts through the second half of the nineteenth century, the last being Chief Thomas Webster. Many of the belts returned on October 1989 first changed hands during Webster's tenure.

The belts, which existed at the time of greatest Iroquois colonial influence and must have been held by some of the great ancestral personalities, are records of significant cultural and political events. Like the winter counts of the Plains Indian nations, or the ancient scrolls of Judeo-Christian traditions, the English Magna Carta, and the American Bill of Rights, they represent ideas and elicit a variety of sentiments. However, at the turn of the nineteenth century, the Indian nations were undergoing tremendous stress. The dominant idea was that Indians were "vanishing Americans," and the mandate to acculturate was powerful.

Over the years, several wampum belts and other cultural objects had disappeared. Private collectors, taking advantage of the weakened position of the Indian communities and particularly of the traditional groups, were pressuring to buy off Indian items. Four of the belts in the present collection were thus sold in 1892 to General Henry B. Carrington, who visited among the Onondaga during that time as U.S. Census taker. These four belts, which became known as the Thacher Collection, were the Hiawatha, George Washington Covenant, First Palefaces, and the Champlain. They were sold to Carrington by Thomas Webster for $75.

Webster's understanding with Carrington was that the U.S. National Museum (Smithsonian) in Washington would preserve the belts. Instead, Carrington, who was not backed in his field purchase by the Smithsonian, resold the belts to a friend, Dr. Oliver Crane, for $350. In 1893, the four belts were sold again to then-mayor of Albany, John Boyd Thacher, for $500. Thacher bought the belts as a private collector but with the purpose of facilitating their display in the New York State exhibit at the World Columbian Exposition in Chicago in 1893. The belts thus traveled to Chicago and were offered as part of the legacy of New York State and the American nation.

Two other belts, Wing and Tadodaho, were purchased on behalf of the Regents by the Rev. William Beauchamp, an Episcopal priest with a congregation at Onondaga, for twenty-five dollars. Beauchamp was to become the first official state archaeologist of the State Museum. He also purchased the Path Belt sometime later.

From the beginning the decision to sell the belts was controversial at Onondaga. Thomas Webster lost his position in the Onondaga Council as a result of the sales and council initiated a lawsuit against Thacher to recover the four belts in his possession. It is clear that the Onondaga chiefs felt at the time that the belts were gradually being lost and were upset about it. The fear of permanently losing all remaining belts, particularly to private collectors, prompted the chiefs to invite the State University to join them as co-plaintiff in a lawsuit against Thacher for recovery of the belts in his possession. The moment not being a good one for Indians to be suing white men, they were "persuaded that it would strengthen their case" if they formally elected the University of the State of New York as "wampum keeper."[5]

Mrs. Harriet Maxwell Converse, an honorary curator of the Native American collection at the State Museum, and an instigator of the lawsuit against Thacher, gathered five more belts at the Onondaga nation. Mrs. Converse fed and led the movement, endorsed ten years earlier by Horatio Hale, to convince the Onondaga chiefs that their remaining belts should be placed in the safekeeping of a museum, in Mrs. Converse's preference, the University of the State of New York. The move to select and entrust the State Museum "was aimed at Mayor Thacher and other white collectors who held some of the finer pieces."[6]

Thacher Lawsuit

The lawsuit to recover the belts held by John Boyd Thacher, brought by the Onondagas on behalf of the League and joined by the State, was dismissed by a New York State judge in 1907. The case hinged on two major questions: 1) was Thomas Webster acting as an official wampum keeper when he sold the belts and 2) did the League of the Haudenosaunee, in fact, exist any longer? Several documents from the time shed light on the wampum and Haudenosaunee history, most notably legislative hearings, transcripts from the court case against John Boyd Thacher and General Carrington's report of his 1890 census among the Six Nations communities.

Defense attorneys attacked Thomas Webster's title to hold the belts as official wampum keeper; attacking as well his cultural knowledge about the belts. Webster, attorneys argued, was simply an Onondaga collector of antiquities and the belts and other relics in his possession were only curiosities to him. Attorneys went around and around with Webster's son and with Onondaga Council President Daniel LaFort about the meanings of the belts to the Onondaga and the Haudenosaunee. It is interesting that the testimony of the Haudenosaunee elders, in the court transcript and other documents, reasserts the continuity of culture and structure of the old Confederacy. However, plaintiff's attorneys ultimately convinced the court that the Onondaga's claim of the existence of a Six Nations Confederacy or League of the Haudenosaunee was invalid.

The case for Webster being simply a private collector and ignorant on the meanings of the belts is weak. The complaint about his ignorance of the wampum belts hinges on his shyness with strangers and his family's unwillingness to speak English. According to Beauchamp as interpreted by Fenton, "Webster certainly gave meanings to suit himself or his visitors, not knowing their (the belts') history." According to Beauchamp, the last wampum keeper to have extensive knowledge about the belts was Abram LaFort, who died in 1848. The Websters "had no training for the office." The supposition was that neither Webster nor anyone else among the Haudenosaunee could any longer "read" the belts. The assertion that no one could "read" the belts supports the related assertion that they could no longer be culturally viable or be culturally owned.

But, did Webster not know, or not care to tell what he knew? And, did he have a sense of private or communal ownership over the belts? As early as 1888, Webster, testifying before a New York State legislative committee investigating the "Indian problem," declined to show them the belts because "the property did not belong to him alone." "It is nothing for a white man" Webster told the committee, "it is all for the Indians."[7] Like many Indian traditionalists, the Webster family did not easily display sacred objects. This attitude, passed on in the form of a discipline, is responsible for what survives of many Native religions.

In any case, other traditionalists, both in Canada and Onondaga, knew the history of the belts and of the Haudenosaunee. Hale confirms this in travels to Grand River Reserve in Canada and, five years later, to Onondaga. Hale visited Onondaga "that Autumn (1875)..., where the chiefs met with him to explain the belts." Hale was impressed with the "minuteness and apparent accuracy" with which they could recall the history of their confederation. He wrote to Major J. Wesley Powell of the Smithsonian,

...after a separation of the tribe for a hundred years, the Canadian record keeper (Onondagas) gave substantially the same narrative as I afterward received from those of the Onondaga Reservation of New York...

Even today it is possible to hear elders who can read many of the great belts and recount the epic of the the Great Law of Peace and the Good Message of Handsome Lake. It stands to reason there would have been, in 1900, that many more such culture-bearing elders among the Haudenosaunee. [8]

Carrington, in his 1890 Census report, calls Webster "wampum keeper." It is only later, during the court case that questions the legality of his purchase and resale to Thacher, that Carrington claims Webster held the belts as an individual collector. Carrington also admits to pestering the "very poor" old man three times before he could convince him to even show the belts. The old man was enticed by Carrington repeatedly with the promise of a horse and buggy and with the pledge of safe repository at the Smithsonian for the valued cultural patrimony. Carrington also wrote in that early report, before his direct involvement with the belts, "Daniel LaForte, who has been chairman or president of the League, and also of the Onondagas...still insists that the wampums, as expounded by Thomas Webster 'are government enough for the Nation, and lay down all the rules of duty that are needed.'"

However, the turn of events caused Webster to lose his position as chief in early 1897, as the other chiefs "removed Webster's antlers of office for betraying a trust." They felt the belts were gradually disappearing. The chiefs then did get five of possibly seven remaining belts, which they conveyed to the university regents one year later. William Beauchamp obtained the remaining two for the State University in the spring of 1898.[9]

The apprehension of the chiefs appears to be about the irretrievable dispersal and ultimate loss of the belts. The best solution to that problem at the time was to appoint the State University as official wampum keeper.

This was part of the process started by Mrs. Harriet Maxwell Converse, when she persuaded the Onondaga chiefs to let the State University join their court case to recover the Thacher belts. It is interesting that underlying the willingness of the State to let itself be appointed by the Onondaga council was an implicit recognition of the continued existence and legal jurisdiction of the League of the Haudenosaunee.

In 1909, the process led to a law, passed by the New York State legislature, securing "custody" over "any wampums which have ever been in the possession of any of the Hodenosaunee, or any preceding wampum keeper, and which are now owned by any of them, and assure the State full power to get possession and safely keep forever all wampums of the Onondaga nation and the Five Nations." The State University thus acquired possession of nearly two dozen wampum belts. When, in 1927, Thacher's widow, Emma Treadwell Thacher donated the four belts purchased by her husband to the New York State Museum, most of the central belts of the Haudenosaunee had entered Albany's jurisdiction and safekeeping.[10]

ACADEMIC CONTROVERSY

What the Onondaga chiefs meant to do, whether to relinquish their right to hold the wampum belts forever or only temporarily to the State, has been in contention ever since. As the Haudenosaunee led the effort by North American Indian nations to hold onto their culture throughout the first half of the twentieth century, the question of the wampum belts, significant to all Iroquois descendants, was bound to resurface.

In the late 1960s, the contemporary council of chiefs at Onondaga, often in consultation with delegations of traditional chiefs from the other five nations of the Haudenosaunee, reasserted its right to secure the wampum belts to their national jurisdiction. The chiefs began to petition and to demand repatriation, a controversial move that is credited (and damned) nationally with opening the more general issue about museum-held property, including human remains, belonging to specific Indian tribes. The effort to recover the belts, finally returned in 1989, and always supported by the councils, met with formidable opposition.

The controversy generated contention between the traditional Indian councils and many prominent anthropologists, archaeologists and historians. As part of his own response, Dr. William Fenton, acclaimed dean of Iroquoianists, took up the gauntlet early and has been, in the words of historian Francis Jennings, "bloodied by the issue." It is hard to present even a short history of the Haudenosaunee wampum belts repatriation issue without perceiving the presence of Fenton both as major scholar and as controversial personality.

Fenton, who traced the lore and history surrounding the belts in copious detail, is credited with stopping 1971 legislation that would have returned twenty-six belts to Onondaga. The law had passed one house before the formidable Dr. Fenton took the floor. He framed the issue fundamentally along the lines of the initial court decision against both the State University Museum and the Onondaga Council, though he added some extra reasoning. In a 1971 article, of characteristically flawless scholarship, Fenton argued against repatriation for the following reasons:

1. Skewed motives. The Iroquois want the belts because "if the present generation of Indians could only recover these objects now in museums, it would raise the power and prestige of the Indian people."

2. No unanimity. "All Indians do not share these views, however, many of them realize there is no escape from the mass culture in which we all participate."

3. Ahistorical thinking. As with the "New Left," Indian militants "regard the documentary records of the past century as irrelevant."

4. No longer a Confederacy. "It cannot be fairly said that Onondaga is anymore the capital of the Six Nations." Fenton uses the phrase "descendants of its former owners" to describe present day Onondaga councilors who sought repatriation.

5. No benefit to anyone. "I do not believe that the descendants of the old Five Nations would be materially advanced by returning to them the wampum belts in the New York State Museum which were acquired by outright purchase, by gift and by deed of trust."

6. Indian claimants are publicity seeking leaders, who "when their [press] notices flag, they discover new causes to attract publicity."

7. No one can read them anymore. The claim here is that the "chain of public recitation," necessary for oral retention, was "broken...early in the nineteenth century with respect to the Onondaga wampum belts." He claimed that among the present generation (1970), the "chance of any Iroquois reading their original intent is nil." Then, ever the social scientist, Fenton suggests an experiment: "to test under controlled conditions, the ability of various Iroquois individuals to recognize and interpret symbols present on Iroquois wampum belts."

Fenton capped his formal public positions on the issue several times in letters to editors of the Indian journal, *Akwesasne Notes,* and to the office of then-New York Governor Nelson A. Rockefeller. His use of unfortunate phrases like "illusion of religiosity" when referring to the Onondaga chiefs' "claim to need [the belts] for religious purposes" ruffled feathers wantonly and unnecessarily. Even Indians inclined to agree with Fenton, following the logic of safekeeping by the State, were taken aback by the hostility of his remarks. Even formal responses from the Grand Council lapsed into anger when addressing the scholar and his argument.[11]

Fenton the scholar is far more appreciable than Fenton the polemicist. In the scholarship, he covers the scope of the material so exactingly that he reveals the groundwork of good Haudenosaunee arguments. It is

Fenton, for instance, who writes that, "Webster produced them (the belts) and made them come to life and reveal the past." Interestingly, he also points out the difference in concept of title between European and Indian. "The Indians could give up public property when the sanctions relaxed and then ask for it back when opinion shifted; while the European concept of title alienated property forever."[12]

The use of the word "forever" in another document from the Thacher lawsuit brought by the Onondaga Council on behalf of the Haudenosaunee is most telling. "Forever" is used twice in Point I of the Plaintiff's Brief presented to the Appellate Division of the Supreme Court of New York, for the Fourth Department, on the appeal to the Thacher lawsuit. In the statement, even in a process of common cause with the State, the Onondagas clearly do not relinquish their longterm title to the custodianship over the belt. Though they have placed the State University in line to "get possession of and safely keep forever..." they have also reassigned to themselves, forever, the right of "official custodians."

> *The wampums are the property of the Haudenosaunee—that is the Six Nations or the Five Nations as it may be. The plaintiff —the Onondaga Nation—is their official custodian, <u>forever</u>; and the plaintiff—the University of the State of New York—having been elected wampum keeper by the Onondaga Nation and directed by a resolution of their governing council "to get possession of and safely keep <u>forever</u> all wampum of the Onondaga Nation and the Five Nations and the Six Nations and each of them" is entitled to their possession.[13]*

Traditional Onondaga chiefs in the present day have claimed that it was never their council's intent to relinquish the right to take back their belts at some future time—a claim partly substantiated by the assertion of custodianship, forever. Both *forevers* are underlined here by this writer, but only the first *forever* is in italics in the original. Anyone searching for the Onondaga Council's intent in joining the State University to their cause of safekeeping the wampum belts might find the above paragraph a point of departure.

Whether the League of the Haudenosaunee continues to exist is a point of contention now and was a central question for the court during the Thacher case. General Carrington's Census Report on the Six Nations communities of 1890 contains some interesting comments in this regard. "The League of the Iroquois is stronger in 1890 than it was in 1660," Carrington wrote, referring to a rise in population from an estimated 11,000 in 1660 to 15,870 in 1890. Carrington mentions that the contention, internally, was the struggle between Pagan (traditional) and Christian Indians. "They are in fact almost nations within a nation," he wrote, adding that, "...among the Indians a self-reliant pagan is preferable to a dependent christian."[14]

Carrington continues:

The conclusion is irresistible that the Six Nations are nations by treaty and law, and have long since been recognized as such by the United States and the State of New York and an enlightened public will surely hesitate before proceeding to divest these people of long-established rights without their consent—rights recognized and confirmed in some cases by the immortal Washington and by more than a hundred years of precedents and legislation.[15]

Testimony in the court case establishes that the Onondaga chiefs, as is the case today, were still selected traditionally in the early 1900s.

For the commemorative event planned at Albany to transfer the wampum keeping office on June 29, 1898, the State invited not only the Onondaga council, chiefs and clanmothers, but also representatives of five of the League's six nations, excluding Tuscarora as a latecomer to the League, but including a Mohawk chief from St. Regis and Seneca chiefs from both the Seneca Nation and the Tonawanda council. Cayugas from Cattaraugus represented that nation, with forty-four Iroquois people in all attending the event. "Formal invitations went out to carefully selected sachems, chiefs and head women to represent the Five Nations at the exercise." Chief Chester Lay, of the Seneca Nation, "spoke of a code centuries old written into the belts that was still observed by the Iroquois."[16]

The position that the Haudenosaunee no longer exist as a confederacy, asserted by the New York court, was also put forward by Fenton in the early 1970s. The basis for the assertion was the scattering of the people to disparate "reservations" and even to Canada since the Revolutionary War. That argument is contested by the people of the traditional Haudenosaunee longhouses who have recognized better times for the Confederacy, but who still overlap religious, cultural and jurisdictional duties of traditional councils in the various Iroquois communities and still point to a remarkable network of meetings, hearings, councils and grand councils continually occurring and taking up Confederacy business *vis à vis* New York State and the federal government. The ceremony on October 21, 1989, welcoming back the wampum belts, was a result of a great many such meetings and a continuity of such efforts. One year earlier, at Grand River in Canada, eleven other belts were returned under similar circumstances and Iroquois from the "American side" were likewise in attendance then. Dr. Fenton was a guest on that day and has spoken approvingly of the repatriation.

In the Onondaga Longhouse, Jacob Thomas began his talk in the Cayuga language. Noting the packed longhouse, the distinguished visitors, the pleasant atmosphere and the weather, he stood before the objects of the day, looking down on the belts in the plexiglass cases. Chief Thomas's face welled up with emotion for a few moments as he stood silent. Then he began a long, passionate, and involved talk about the belts, about the founding of the Confederacy, the oral traditions and some of the famous elders who had always spoken, for several generations, about how such important wampum belts were lost, by sale or confiscation, to the State and how the chiefs of the Confederacy should get them back. He was happy, he said, because the belts had in fact begun to return. Thomas spoke in Cayuga, mainly, and at times in Mohawk and Onondaga, as he addressed parts of his talk to the chiefs and clanmothers of the various nations. What I know of what he said was interpreted for me by Native speakers.

The fact that Thomas spoke in his Indian language irritated a man seated by the door. He claimed to be an anthropologist, and was dressed in a suit and tie, was bulky and somewhat thick-tongued with a slight European accent. As Thomas continued to speak, the man exclaimed in a louder and louder whisper: "Why he do this. Nobody understand him, only the Indians. He goes on too long now, going on and on. He is very impolite."

The Onondagas, Senecas and Mohawks immediately around him chose to ignore him. But as Thomas continued his oratory, the man grew more heated and spoke to anyone around him that would acknowledge him. It didn't occur to the man that Thomas was actually being polite in speaking the language of the community and in addressing some of the older Indian elders in their own languages. Thomas did speak long, but that length of time, the cadence of his words and their starkness as they traveled over the silent, crowded room, all had that enduring attitude that goes with so many of the ceremonies and spiritual doings that often take place in that same longhouse. It was in fact the part of the ceremony that most felt like those long Grand Council meetings and speeches of the most important protocols and messages of the Longhouse.

Then, just as I thought the man would explode with troubled tension, Chief Thomas switched to English. "Someone just whispered behind me," he said. "They told me to hurry, because they're getting hungry." Everyone laughed heartily on that one, and, of course, he didn't hurry. He peppered his long, serious narrative with pointed jokes—aimed at Onondagas, at western Indians and at anthropologists. About anthropologists, he said that his grandfather would see them coming down the road and tell him: "Here comes another of them investigators. Just tell him a bunch of nonsense. Never tell them all you know, only maybe ten percent!" At that moment, everyone near to the anxious anthropologist had to look at him.

In English, Chief Thomas went over all he said in the Indian languages, reminding the public about the great messages in the belts, the Peacemaker stories, how the men only sit in council for the women, how the chiefs must open the way to peace. "This is about something that cannot be bought or sold. What is money worth compared to peace? These belts, this is about peace, and how do you buy peace? No, nobody ever bought peace."

One had to watch the faces of the chiefs sitting on the benches, to a man embroiled in community issues that seem to magnify and loom larger and larger over their peoples. No, peace certainly cannot be bought, though the day was a day of atonement, a kind of peace.

Leon Shenandoah next announced the planting of a Tree of Peace, a ceremony taken to the national and international sphere by Chief Jake Swamp, from the Akwesasne Nation Council. Onondaga Chief Irving Powless, Jr. explained the tradition of the Great Tree of Peace, the one under which all weapons of war are buried and of the White Roots of Peace that spread out from the Great Tree in the four directions. The longhouse emptied then, people milling about, observing the belts in the plexiglass case before gathering outside for tobacco burning and to take turns shoveling earth to plant the small pine tree.

Outside, the tree was planted and the crowd continued to gather about the newer and beautifully log-constructed longhouse; inside the smaller "cookhouse," some two dozen Onondaga women, as they have always done, prepared food for the feast. The cookhouse or mudhouse, as it is called in some reservations, is the real hub of longhouse activity. It is the realm of the women. Men are allowed and are served graciously, but here the women talk. Young men helped their mothers, grandmothers and aunties by hauling food trays and boxes in and trash out. In one corner, a grandmother who is also a clanmother, admired several babies brought to her by new mothers. The talk there was of names for new babies, how they would be given at the upcoming Midwinter ceremonies. The clanmothers hold the names for each of the Iroquois clans. They are said symbolically to have a sack by their sides from which to assign names to new babies in their clans. They also hold the chiefs' titles. Thus not only political appointments but the cultural identity of individuals are in the hands of the elder women. There was a lot of teasing in the conversation. An older woman commented on the many babies: "By rights, we ought to have a baby contest around here." Said another: "One of the chiefs would probably win."

At its best, Iroquois humor bites but does not really wound. The women, in fact, seemed to hold the chiefs' system in good esteem. As they talked several men happened by. None were averse to holding babies and the women immediately welcomed them into their circle. There is a depth of independence and strength among the older women of the longhouse not always discernible among other peoples. For all the teasing, theirs is a strength not based on denying the importance of the men's roles, duties and responsibilities, but rather on the specific right of women to teach and demand those values from the men.

Another clanmother was also there. I don't have permission to use her name but she said something very pretty to the young women. "I like the old speeches that the men memorize," she said. "Our Indian language, how we talked to the world, is very beautiful. Like the welcoming for babies. They will hold the new baby up and say: 'Thank you for coming to our village. We hope you like it here. We hope that you will stay to help us.'"

She paused before continuing. "The important thing about today, what the chiefs did to recover our wampum, is that those babies can't help us unless they learn about the wampum. The way to the 'Good Mind' is in that wampum. Our laws and our history are in that wampum. That's what we have to teach our kids."

The court decision and the argument by prominent anthropologists that the old Iroquois Confederacy died two hundred years ago fails to take into account the cultural traditions through the families and clans, which, like the generations, has never ceased. Too many anthropologists focus on the ceremonial moment and on the icons of culture. They focus on the "chiefs" (a misnomer itself) at the expense of the women's side, the mothers and grandmothers.

Iroquoia today is comprised of some 40,000 people on thirteen New York State, Wisconsin, Ontario and Quebec reservations, at least ten longhouses, twelve major urban neighborhoods, dozens of spread-out family homesteads. It is not any more dead in 1990 than it was in 1900, in 1800 or in 1400. Certainly it is divided, full of issues, discussion, contention and opposing viewpoints. Certainly as important elders pass away they take a tremendous amount of cultural knowledge with them. Certainly the young do not receive enough important instruction, not in their own languages, not in their own history, geography, community rights and responsibilities. Certainly there is a lack of internal fairness (and thus efficiency and effectiveness) to the political process in several reservations that is appalling, and should be corrected. But, it really isn't time to call the old Confederacy dead, not yet—not when you see the League at work in the mudhouse, among the women, not when there are chiefs still active in defending long-standing rights and pressing for the recovery of their cultural health.

Note: This article was originally published in the *Northeast Indian Quarterly*, Volume VII, Number 1 (Spring 1990).

Oral Memory of the Haudenosaunee:

Views of the Two Row Wampum

Richard Hill

The contemporary chiefs of the Haudenosaunee have expressed the belief that the relationship between the original people of this land and the Americans was defined in an early seventeenth century treaty with the Dutch. According to the Iroquois chiefs this treaty is the foundation of the political agreements that were to follow in the centuries of conflict. The agreement, often called the "Silver Covenant Chain" is also referred to by Iroquois oral tradition as the Two Row wampum belt. However, there are at least two different versions of what that agreement says.

Until recently the Two Row wampum was the only evidence of the early agreement that may have been signed in 1613. Oral history of the Haudenosaunee states that a white wampum belt with two parallel purple lines symbolizes the terms of the treaty. This Two Row wampum still plays a definitive role in the current Iroquois Confederacy policy on federal-Indian relations. However, a copy of the Dutch version of the treaty, brought to light in 1968 and of controversial authenticity, is very different from the oral traditions of the Haudenosaunee and raises some important questions about the treaty.

The Dutch had come to North America in search of a new route to China, but became principal players in the establishment of the lucrative fur trade among the Haudenosaunee in the seventeenth century. The year 1609 was significant for the Haudenosaunee. The French, under the direction of Samuel de Champlain, attacked the Mohawk with firearms never seen here before, killing three Mohawk chiefs and wounding many more with their guns. From the south came Henry Hudson in what the Iroquois described as a Half Moon ship, to trade for the Dutch East India Company. Hudson reached the present site of Albany, which would become the Dutch trading center. The Dutch laid claim to the territory, calling it "New Netherland." Dutch expansion into North America began quickly. By 1614, the Dutch allowed "... all and every Inhabitant of this country [Holland]..." to seek out new lands.

Written history is not clear about how the Dutch dealt with the Iroquois Indians that lived in these new lands. The Iroquois believe that a treaty was made that would affect the course of history. The Two Row wampum teaching, current in the oral tradition, is said to originate at those proceedings. Then, in 1968, L. G. Van Loon, an American doctor of Dutch ancestry, asserted possession of a small piece of parchment on which the 1613 treaty was recorded. Van Loon, who reported that his written Dutch version of the treaty was acquired from an Indian Agent at the Mississauqa Reserve in Canada "many years ago," provided the translation that followed:

Here assembled in Tawagonshi, we the undersigned Jacob Eelckens and Hendrick Christiaenssen by letter authorized and we ordain the trade with the savage inhabitants, the owners or rulers of the land hereafter considered, and in so far it will be compatible with what follows hereafter to come to accordance with the Royanners of Rotironghsionni, Garhat Jannie, Caghneghsattakegh, Otswirakerongh, and Tijighswegengh, as well as some lower chiefs of them who certify that all of them accord and that we participate promise:

1) that trade between their nation and ours will be admitted as long as we participants accord also reciprocally etcetera;

2) that we the participants will have the privilege to remove goods from the tradestock as long as any purchase-contract has not yet been concluded etcetera;

3) patches of land may be purchased from us, the savage participants, of the land which we consider to be our own, on condition that this be discussed by individuals and be drawn by reciprocal and suitable contract etcetera;

4) that we participants will keep one another in case of lack of food and if this is not sufficient will help one another to necessaries etcetera;

5) in case of difference of opinion concerning real or imaginary injustices we the participants promise that these will stay as an auspice of better times and that any dispute of whatever nature or origin will be brought before an assembly of commissioners in order to investigate it all.

All the above we participants promise to continue and to maintain as long as the grass will be green and as a proof of honor and affection we exchange a silver chain

to a fathom of sailor's cloth.
In acknowledgement of the truth of all this is signed by the participants on this
21st April 1613.
  Jacob Eelckens
  Hendrick Christiaenssen
  Garhat Jannie sign of
  Caghneghsattakegh "
  Otswirakerongh "
  Tijoghswegengh "

In a 1968 article, "Tawagonshi, Beginning of the Treaty Era," published by *The Indian Historian* (San Francisco, Summer, 1968) Van Loon reported on the original document, acquired from the Iroquois at the Grand River Reserve in Ontario, Canada. Van Loon's claim gave a significant boost at the time to the credibility of the Two Row treaty, tending to corroborate Indian oral tradition. In his article, Van Loon writes:

This document, which appears to be a compact binding the Iroquois with a Dutch Company through its agents, was written upon two pieces of hide. It roughly measures seven and one half inches by thirteen inches, when the two pieces are placed to approximate each other, along the mid-line. The two pieces may have been at one time a single piece, or may have been sewn together along this mid-line at some time.

The two Dutch signators to the treaty were known to be officers in charge of the first trading post in 1614. It is also known that there was a Dutch trading ship sent out in 1620. Several authors have considered the "written 1613 Treaty of Tawagonshi" as plausible. However there is no verifiable record of the Treaty of Tawagonshi in the written documents of the period. The parchment of the early treaty came into the hands of the Haudenosaunee chiefs in 1978, at which time they publicly announced its discovery. Although the chiefs could not pass judgment on the parchment's authenticity, they discussed the matter openly in council and, in 1984, assigned a delegate to carry the document to Holland for further study.

Many historians questioned the parchment's authenticity. In the 1985 publication of the Newberry Library of Chicago, titled *The History and Culture of Iroquois Diplomacy*, the 1613 treaty is mentioned as a possibility, but the "authenticity of the sole document referring to the event is highly questionable." Previous histories do not mention any treaty that early, and Dutch records of the time are inconclusive. George Hunt, in his *Wars of the Iroquois* argues against the existence of any treaty, not 1613, or 1618, as was also suggested. He states that Dutch historians and contemporary records make no mention of the treaty. At least one authoritative article, written by Charles T. Gehring, William A. Starna and William N. Fenton, (*New York History*, October 1987) makes a strong case for Van Loon's "discovery" being a fake.

Many traditional Iroquois, however, consider the oral memory and formal readings of the Two Row Wampum by various elders credible. It is unfortunate that the attacks by some social scientists upon the parchment discovery appear to imply guile on part of the chiefs for bringing the parchment to public attention and attempting to verify it. Whatever the authenticity of Van Loon's parchment document, an examination of its contents relative to the content of the Iroquois oral teaching on the Two Row Wampum, as carried by culture-bearing elders, is nevertheless of interest. The Haudenosaunee oral tradition has implicit validity and is worthy of examination and consideration as a seminal agreement between sovereign nations.

The parchment version of the Two Row Treaty recognizes the Haudenosaunee as an equal nation and as owners of the land. The agreement is a foreign trade deal that includes an option for the Dutch to purchase land. This section appears to assume that individual Indians could sell their lands, and conflicts with today's traditional Indian interpretation of land tenure, arguably based on community ownership of land. Did the seventeenth century Iroquois understand the concept of selling land? Would they have understood the significance of that section? How much private ownership or stewardship of land did individual families or clans have? What agreements did they exercise among each other to trade or assign land use areas? Or was this simply an early hustle by the Dutch to set a precedent for future land sales?

The most confusing part of this Dutch interpretation of the treaty is the "etcetera" at the end of each section. It leaves the terms of the deal open ended, but it is difficult to speculate what was meant by including such a phrase in the treaty. It would be interesting to know just how the Dutch interpreted "etcetera" to the Iroquois during the negotiations.

The "treaty," assuming some veracity to its language and content, (though Van Loon is clearly suspect and the case against him is well made by Gehring, *et. al.*), might nevertheless have been an agreement between individual Dutch traders and the Iroquois as they sought to beat out their competition into Indian lands. While Gehring, Starna and Fenton accuse actual forgery in the Van Loon document, ("... the Tawagonshi treaty is not authentic ... it was not composed in 1613 by two Dutch traders, but many years later by a twentieth-century hand and mind ..."), other experts, including Daniel Richter seem to accept authenticity ("Despite its rather suspicious origins, the document has an authentic ring ... It is difficult to imagine a latter-day forger concocting such a cryptic message.")

Three Dutch traders were ransomed from the Minquaes in 1613. Members of a Dutch trading company, these three had been employed by the Mohawk as traders and were captured by the Andastes. There must have been some kind of agreement that brought those three Dutchmen into the employment of the Mohawk. Capt. Hendrick Christiaenssen and Jacob Eelckens, the Dutch names on the parchment treaty, came up the Hudson River in 1613 to establish a trading post for the Van Tweenhuysen Company. The treaty under discussion, whether indicated by the doubtful Dutch parchment of Van Loon or the absolutely authentic Two Row wampum belts of the Iroquois, could have been their formal mechanism for establishing a trade network in Iroquois country. Certainly, immediate, early meetings took place with the Dutch that were formalized by Haudenosaunee ritual.

The historical record confirms that there was a council with Mohawk and Mahican at Tawasgunshi Hill, near Norman Kill in Albany County, and other meetings with the Mohawk, Delaware and Mahican. The treaty that was concluded at Tawagonshi was referred to by Indian delegates well into the eighteenth century. T.J. Brasser, in his article on the Mahicans in the Smithsonian Institution's *Handbook of North American Indians—Northeast* (1978: 202) calls that treaty the first between Indians and Europeans, but states that the treaty included the Mahican Indians, who gave their permission to build a trading post. As a result, Fort Nassau was established in 1614 on Castle Island.

The Haudenosaunee chiefs point to the Two Row wampum as their evidence of the agreement made with the Dutch at the time of the earliest meetings. There are several wampum belts of a white background with two parallel horizontal lines in purple. One is reported still to exist in Indian hands at the Grand River Reserve in Ontario. Another was recently returned to the chiefs at Grand River from the Museum of the American Indian in New York. A Seneca chief claims that he saw a Two Row wampum belt in the collection of the New York State Museum in Albany, but their records do not confirm this. Other belts of a similar design are in museum collections.

In a 1980 traveling exhibit from the National Museum of Man in Ottawa, *The Covenant Chain: Indian Ceremonial and Trade Silver*, the Covenant Chain is described as a symbol of friendship in the alliances of Indian and European allies. The curators of the exhibit believe that the tradition of the Covenant Chain began with Dutch and "River Indians of the Hudson River" as early as 1618. Although the River Indians, the Mahicans, were in time replaced by the Mohawks and the English displaced the Dutch, the diplomatic customs remained.

The Covenant Chain exhibit did not recognize the 1613 treaty, nor the significance of the Two Row Wampum. In fact, the exhibit presented a different belt, one with two figures connected by the "silver chain of friendship, as the Covenant Chain was sometimes called." There have been several versions of this belt as well.

154

Still current in the oral tradition of several local reservations, the Two Row Wampum belt provides the Iroquois view of the first negotiations with "the white brother," and the final agreement that was concluded with the Dutch as representative. Van Loon describes the Indian imagery that is present in Iroquois Indian history regarding the Two Row Wampum idea as "Covenant of the Silver Chain," "the chain which binds our people together," or the "chain we will keep forever bright." Van Loon wrote that this language is not merely metaphorical but it may be a continuing reference to the last paragraph in the Treaty of Tawagonshi: "And as evidence of the honor and goodwill we exchange a silver chain for a fathom of beadwork." That fathom could have very well been the Two Row Wampum belt. Two symbols of the agreement were exchanged between the parties in this disputed first "treaty," one in the standard form of European tradition, the other in the traditional form of the Haudenosaunee.

What follows is an interpretation of the Two Row as provided by Jacob Thomas, an elder Cayuga sub-chief whose father had been responsible for the belt, and Huron Miller, Onondaga, also a recognized culture-bearer in the oral tradition. Their interpretation provides a much broader view of the treaty, as it becomes a map of political protocol between the two races, and a prophetic vision of things to come:

The Onkwehonweh of the Haudenosaunee made a treaty with the early Dutch when they came to this continent. The Onkwehonweh lived very happy enjoying life the way the Creator intended. The Onkwehonweh was totally dependent on nature until the coming of the Dutch people. The Dutch learned the customs, art work, and how to get along with the Onkwehonweh. They became friends and decided to make a treaty and agreed to continue in friendship. Then the time came when the Dutch said, "We shall pronounce ourselves in friendship."

The Onkwehonweh called the Dutch "white people." The Onkwehonweh held a special council informing the people that the time had come for the white people and the Onkwehonweh to continue as friends so that all people may walk upon this earth in peace and love one another. Both races understood this kind of friendship and agreed that the day had come to make friendship.

The Onkwehonweh said, "We now have an understanding about our friendship." The whiteman replied, "I will put our friendship in writing." The Onkwehonweh replied, "This is good, but one thing we must remember, paper will not last. We must find a way to make sure that the friendship will be passed on to the next generation." They agreed.

The whiteman said, "How is the Onkwehonweh going to describe our friendship?" The Onkwehonweh replied, "We must thank the Creator for all his creations, and greet one another by holding hands to show the Covenant Chain that binds our friendship so that we may walk upon this earth in peace, trust, love and friendship, and we may smoke the sacred tobacco in a pipe which is a symbol of peace."

The whiteman said that he would respect the Onkwehonweh's belief and call him "son." The Onkwehonweh replied, "We respect you, your belief, and what you say. You pronounced yourself as our father and this we do not agree with because the father can tell his son what to do, and can punish his son. We suggest that we call each other brother."

The whiteman said, "The symbol of this Covenant is a three link chain which binds this agreement made by us, and there is nothing that will come between us to break the links of this chain." The Onkwehonweh replied, "The first link shall stand for friendship, the second will stand for our good minds, and the third link shall mean there will always be peace between us. This is confirmed by us." The Onkwehonweh said, "This friendship shall be everlasting and the younger generation will know and the rising faces from Mother Earth will benefit by our agreement."

The whiteman said, "What symbol will you go by?" The Onkwehonweh replied, "When the Creator made Mother Earth, man was created to walk upon the Earth to enjoy all nature's fruits, saying that no one will claim Mother Earth except by rising faces which are to be born. We will go by these symbols:

As long as the sun shines upon this earth, as long as the water still flows, and as long as the grass grows green at a certain time of the year, that is how long our agreement will stand. Now we have symbolized this agreement and it shall be binding forever, as long as Mother Earth is still in motion. We have finished and we understand what we have confirmed and this is what our generation should know and learn not to forget."

The whiteman said, "I confirm what you have said and this we shall always remember. What we do about our own ways of belief, we shall both respect having our own rights and power." The Onkwehonweh replied, "I have a canoe and you have a vessel with sails and this is what we shall do. I will put in my canoe my belief and laws. In your vessel you shall put your belief and laws. All my people will be in my canoe, your people in your vessel. We shall put these boats in the water and they shall always be parallel, as long as there is Mother Earth, this will be everlasting."

The whiteman said, "What will happen if your people will like to go into my vessel?" The Onkwehonweh replied, "If this happens, then they will have to be guided by my canoe." Now the whiteman understands the agreement.

The whiteman said, "What will happen if any of our people may someday want to have one foot in each of the boats that are parallel?" The Onkwehonweh replied, "If this so happens that my people may wish to have their feet in each of the two boats, there will be a high wind and the boats will separate and the person that has his feet in each of the boats shall fall between the boats, and there is no living soul who will be able to bring them back to the right way given by the Creator but only one—the Creator himself."

The Onkwehonweh called the wampum belt "Guswhenta." One of the two paths signifies the whiteman's laws and beliefs, and the other signifies the laws and beliefs of the Onkwehonweh. The white background signifies purity, good minds and peace, and they should not interfere with one another's views.

The whiteman said, "I understand. I confirm what you have said, that this will be everlasting as long as there is Mother Earth. We have confirmed this and our generation to come will never forget what we have agreed. Now it is understood that we shall never interfere with one another's belief or laws for generations to come."

The Onkwehonweh said, "What we agreed upon shall renew this every so often so that the Covenant Chain made between us shall always be clean from dust and rust. We shall renew our agreements and polish the Covenant and when we get together to renew our agreements we shall have interpreters. We will dress the same way as we met so that our people will know who we are. I will put on my buckskin clothing, you will dress the same way you dressed when you first came to our people." They both confirmed this. So they completed the treaty of the two parties.

This version does not mention trade or land sales. Instead it outlines the principles of peace and friendship that are to guide the two nations in dealing with each other. It is also a statement on sharing, an ancient Indian principle. Clearly, the Iroquois that agreed to the treaty offered peace and a place to stay.

The two documents differ greatly. Two different cultures (whether in the hand of early Dutch traders or Van Loon's own) viewed the same event with two different perspectives. The Dutch version, as represented in the still contested parchment, emphasizes trade, contracts, land sales, and dispute resolution. The Iroquois version focuses on friendship, peace, equality, and commitment that future generations will remember the agreement. Both agree to the idea of a Covenant Chain to symbolize the terms of the agreement.

The Iroquois put forth the concept of "separate, but equal" in two ways. First they objected to the father-son relationship and asked to be referred to as "brothers." This becomes an important part of the official council protocol in the future. The chiefs continued to call the Europeans, and later Americans, "brothers" throughout history. Secondly, the image of the two water vessels, each containing the laws and beliefs of the two distinct peoples, creates a visual symbol of the separate nations, equal in respect and rights, traveling in the same direction, but not crossing each other's path. The two rows in the wampum illustrate this clearly.

The Iroquois version also states that they will symbolize this peaceful relationship by "holding hands" which could give credence to other wampums that show two figures holding the Chain between them as further verifications of that original agreement of peace and friendship.

A perplexing issue is why the documents differ so much. Did the two sides truly agree? Did the Iroquois clearly understand what the Dutch agreed to? Did the Dutch trick the Iroquois by getting them to sign a written document that was different from what the chiefs expected? The stipulation in the Iroquois version that interpreters be present in the future indicates that they already had a concern over language. The Dutch talk of land sales, contracts and commissioners indicates that they had their own motives for future expansion. Significantly, the Dutch version does not mention peace, friendship or equality.

Written history provides ample evidence of the Covenant Chain symbolism throughout the eighteenth and nineteenth century. This indigenous metaphor had to start somewhere, and likely was introduced at the earliest of covenants. But the written version of the treaty, if reliable, raises questions about the actual agreement. Possibly, the treaty meant more to the Iroquois than it did to the Dutch. It comes down, orally, to our generation as the first treaty between the Confederacy and a white European nation. Thus it makes sense that it would be an important document in the oral history of the Haudenosaunee. Iroquois traditional elders credit the Two Row Wampum with providing an outline for the future, and a fundamental principle in negotiating with the white nations. It shows the sensitivity of the chiefs to protecting the welfare of future generations. It is logical that they wanted their people to remember that historic moment. The oral history of the Iroquois kept the treaty alive for many generations.

If the written treaty only served one Dutch trading company to lay claim to new territory in the ever-increasing fur trade, it would not be a significant document, nor a Dutch "treaty." But we may never know with certainty what the Dutch thought they were doing until more conclusive evidence on the found "parchment treaty" is submitted for review.

Modern versions of the Two Row Wampum vary as well. Some believe that the Two Row states that neither side will make compulsory laws that would interfere in the internal affairs of the other. This has been used as the basis for resisting the Indian Citizenship Act, the Selective Service Act, and even the Internal Revenue Service. However, the United States disagrees.

In his book *Wampum Belts*, Tehanetorens (Ray Fadden), an ardent sustainer of Iroquois traditional philosophy and history, describes a "Two Road" Wampum that looks similar to the Two Row Wampum. He states that this second belt describes how the Iroquois tried to remain neutral during the Revolutionary War. This belt, according to Tehanetorens, was held by Joseph Brant as he told the Grand Council that each nation should decide for themselves what road to follow—the English or the American colonists.

Some contemporary Iroquois speakers assert that if the Indian people want to enter the whiteman's vessel, as described in the Two Row, then they must leave their native culture and religion behind. Some actually state that Indians lose their birthright as Haudenosaunee if they enter the whiteman's vessel, and would never be allowed back into the Indian canoe. This kind of person, they say, will be called "Split Mind" and will not be able to make good decisions. The most fundamental interpreters believe that the two vessels also carry the spirit of each people's ancestors, so that there are deeply religious and spiritual interpretations why we must not attempt to steer each other's vessels.

The Thomas and Miller version, authoritative to many Iroquois, says that even in the whiteman's vessel, the Indians should be guided by Indian principles. This is a very important point. Many of today's Iroquois people live in the whiteman's vessel. Many traditionalists call them "sellouts" and have turned their backs on these people. Thomas's and Miller's interpretation of the Two Row takes a kinder view of those Indians in the whiteman's vessel—saying in effect that Indians should retain an Indian value system no matter where they go.

There is also some disagreement as to what the three links in the Covenant Chain represent. Many believe that they symbolize "peace, friendship, forever." The interpretation above suggests that the links represent "friendship, good minds, and everlasting peace." This difference could be due to changing English definitions of Iroquoian concepts. The idea of the "good mind" to the Iroquois has now become synonymous with "peace."

Some modern Iroquois speakers also describe the symbolic significance of the actual structure of the Two Row Wampum. The white wampum symbolizes the purity of the agreement. Each of those sections of white beads has three rows apiece that are said to symbolize peace, friendship and respect.

The Two Row Wampum was chosen to illustrate the final report of a Special Committee on Indian Self-Government in Canada. Ojibwa artist Leo Yerxa explains why he chose the symbolism of the Two Row:

> The cover painting is the two-row wampum belt on a landscape. But it is more than the representation of an object. Like the Haudenosaunee artist who made the belt, I am part of a process of carrying an idea through history—the idea symbolized by the two-row wampum. The belt shouldn't be forgotten in a museum, because it expresses an idea, and an idea can't be killed.

Every four years, upon the election of the President of the United States, the Grand Council of Chiefs of the Haudenosaunee sends an invitation to Washington to "polish the Covenant Chain" and renew the treaty agreements. It still means a lot to the modern Iroquois; it doesn't mean much to the United States. For many years, the federal government ignored those treaties altogether, except for one brief moment. During the Ford administration, a representative from the White House came to a Grand Council to learn about the wampums. He specifically asked for an interpretation of the Two Row Wampum.

The assembled chiefs were surprised to see that he even knew of the Two Row. Laid out in front of the White House delegate were replicas of most of the major wampum belts of the Haudenosaunee. At the time the originals were locked up in museum vaults. Two elder speakers approached the Two Row and began to interpret its meaning for the visiting delegate from Washington. They stated that the Two Row was the foundation of their relationship to the United States. They talked for about twenty minutes on that one belt and then laid it back down. Not much came of that meeting, but for a few special moments, the chiefs polished the Covenant Chain, hoping that the renewed brightness would attract the federal government once again to steer their great ship in harmony with Haudenosaunee principles.

The Two Row has become a symbol of the desired relationship of Indian nations and the world—separate, but equal. The belt was used by all Indian speakers at the Fourth Russell Tribunal on the Rights of Indians of the Americas in 1980, in Rotterdam, Holland. A reproduction of the belt was laid across the speaker's podium for all to see as they presented their testimony. A large public in Europe was listening and reacting to the Indian nations's struggle for survival.

I believe the Two Row served and still serves a sacred purpose. It was a reminder that at one time our nations and people coexisted. It was also a symbol of hope that peace and friendship could be restored between the Indigenous people and the western nations, if only we could learn to respect our separate but equal rights to land, to sustenance, to culture, and to the future.

No matter what its origins, the Two Row Wampum has become the most significant symbol of a preferred relationship of Indians to the nations of the world. It reflects contemporary thinking about Indian sovereignty, based upon generations of belief by Indians that the words and values contained in the Two Row are true. The Two Row Wampum deserves a second look. In the concepts and ideas it represents, we may find answers to the centuries-old problem of how Indians and other cultures can interact, as equals and as nations of people.

Note: This article was originally published in the *Northeast Indian Quarterly*, Volume VII, Number 1 (Spring 1990).

Reading Wampum Belts as Living Symbols

Paul Williams

> ...*Accordingly we set out
> and took possession of the land assigned to use, and as
> was the custom of our Forefathers we immediately set
> about making a Belt ... by which our Children would see
> that the lands was to be theirs forever, and as was
> customary with our ancestors, we placed the figure of a
> dog at each end of the Belt to guard our property and to
> give notice when an enemy approached...."*
>
> *...Delivers the large belt of
> twenty-seven rows made on the occasion of the first
> settlement of the Indians at the Lake of Two Mountains.*

These were the words and a description of Agneetha, speaker for the Mohawks at Kanesatake, the Lake of Two Mountains, addressing Sir John Johnson, the Superintendent General of Indian Affairs on February 8, 1788. The words matched with the photograph of a wampum belt that the McCord Museum in Montreal had sent to me in early December, 1989 *(fig. 1)*.

However, the Museum's records showed that it had little idea of the meaning or origin of the belt. Its description of the same belt noted:

Belt, commemorating conversion of nation or tribe. In white on a purple ground, a cross in the centre on a solid base. On each side and touching the cross, a red man followed by a white man and a red man alternately on each side. All participants joining hands. Length 5' 6"; depth: 27 rows of beads. [No tribal association is supplied with this belt.]

Several other aspects of the wampum belt in the McCord Museum also pointed to the Lake of Two Mountains area between 1650 and 1750.

The weave is horizontal: if it were diagonal, the belt would most likely have been Huron. Some Huron belts, woven on the diagonal, end up joined like circles; the few surviving photographs show them worn around the neck, instead of as a sash or belt, Iroquois-style. That may be why early French records have the Indians giving "colliers," or necklaces, instead of belts *(fig. 2)*.

The cross in the centre of the belt indicates a Christian community, and only those communities linked politically with the French used the cross as a symbol of official status.

The seven strips of white worked into each end may be a signature of the "Seven Nations of Canada," the mini-Confederacy promoted by the French in the eighteenth century to act as a buffer and means of communication with the Five Nations Iroquois Confederacy. Other Mohawk belts from the same area bear the same seven strips. So does one of the three Algonquin belts now kept at Maniwaki (the Algonquins and Nipissings shared the Kanesatake lands). But many other belts have similar strips at the ends: do they always indicate the number of settlements or communities that they are speaking for *(fig. 3)*?

There is little doubt that the belt with "no tribal association" now in the McCord Museum is the same as the Kanesatake Mohawk belt that Agneetha said in 1788 commemorated the founding of that community. However, identifying any piece of an incomplete puzzle leads only to a slightly more complete picture: mostly, it leads to other pieces.

On their letterhead, the Mohawk Council of Akwesasne have what they have called the "Akwesasne Wolf Belt." The original is still in the New York State Museum in Albany. It shares with the Kanesatake belt several key aspects: the human figures in the middle holding hands; the animals at each end; the seven strips at each end. Is it not likely that it, too, commemorates the founding of a community of the Iroquois of the "Seven Nations of Canada" (which Akwesasne was, at the time of its founding). The animals would then likely be dogs, not wolves, to guard the edges of the village, and not simply as emblems of the Wolf Clan as had been previously thought. It would not simply be "an Akwesasne belt"—rather, it would be the Akwesasne belt, a fitting symbol of the community on wampum and on paper *(fig. 4)*.

Agneetha in 1788 also said about the Kanesatake belt:

"...and as soon as it was finished, we spread it on the ground and covered it with dirt that no evil minded persons should find it, where it remained undisturbed until about seven years ago when a dispute arose..."

Iroquois council "metaphor" includes several ways that things can be referred to as "buried." The weapons of war were all thrown into the pit under the Tree of Peace, never to be seen again—buried. Once peace is made, the hatchet of war is buried. In the ceremony of condolence, the bones of the dead people (or dead person) are gathered up and buried, so that they will not be seen again to disturb the thoughts and feelings of those who are still living. In dealing with murder, too, the presentation of wampum "buries" the matter.

Were wampum belts like this actually buried to protect the territory in a spiritual and sacred sense? Or were they symbolically buried? The belt Agneetha presented to Sir John Johnson shows none of the deterioration associated with buried wampum.

Joining things with the earth as a means of protection is not an exclusively Iroquois idea. The Welsh Mabinogion cycle tells how the head of Bran the Blessed was buried to protect the Island of Britain from invasion. Legend has it that King Arthur dug it up in an act of bravado that brought on the Saxon invasions he spent his life fighting.

Iroquois people (and many others) strongly object to any disturbance of graves, and consider the things buried with people to be sacred and inviolable as the human remains themselves. "Grave wampum," they say, is intended to stay in the ground. The moral position on wampum that was buried for other specific purposes is less clear: probably, people would say that the wishes of the original users should be respected in any case.

The Kanesatake wampum shows a series of human figures holding hands: eight of them—four "white" and four "red," according to the Museum's records. There are other belts which clearly distinguish between Europeans and North American natives by making the Indians darker: the Covenant Chain belt recently returned to the Confederacy Council at the Grand River is one example *(see illustration, page 24)*.

Other belts which record agreements between Euro-American and Indigenous governments show the "white" man as wearing a hat, or as being fatter—or as having a "black heart." But there does not seem to be any convention: it may be that the Kanesatake belt shows the eight figures in two ways out of aesthetics, or because there were several nations of Indians living at the Lake of Two Mountains, including Algonquins, Nipissings and some Odawas.

However, it is rare that anything was placed on a wampum belt simply for the sake of aesthetics. There is probably a good reason why there are eight human figures on the belt, and why they would be shown in white and purple. Maybe other documents, or the traditions of the people, will explain them.

The way the figures have their hands joined is also significant. It is not the straight line of the covenant Chain, nor the relaxed hold of some other belts. The hands are joined in what looks like the letter "W" from shoulder to shoulder of each human figure. In that, the Kanesatake belt resembles another important Iroquois wampum record. That one shows five human figures (for the original Five Nations) with their hands joined "with their elbows crooked." It signifies the resolve of the nations to join together and the protection of the circle of the Great Law. And it symbolized that part of the law that states that should a Confederacy Lord leave the circle and submit to the laws of a foreign nation, he shall leave his title within the Confederacy to be taken up by another. That is, his title shall catch on the "crooked elbows" like a deer's antlers catch in the bushes, and shall fall within the circle. In the Kanesatake belt, the placing of elbows in the "crooked" manner may indicate a circle of protection of the land (fig. 5).

Documentary corroboration of the meaning and intent of wampum records has rarely been found except for the most important Confederacy constitutional records. Yet it is not impossible. The Iroquois cultural/legal process required that the pledges and principles contained in the belts be read and reaffirmed in public repeatedly over the years. Because the important records would have been read more than once increases their chances of being preserved in writing.

The literature that does exist complements the belts. But this is so only where the belt can be identified. Uses of wampum have been documented with no existing physical counterpart: for example, the Delawares gave the British a large belt with strings hanging from it, like torches to light the way along the path. Or, when the Ohio Valley became the "Indian country" in the latter half of the 18th century, a "moon of wampum" with four strings of wampum hanging from it was placed there by the nations. This signified that the land was like a house for all the nations, from the four directions (a "moon" of wampum was a flat shell disk.) No examples of such wampum remain.

Similarly, there are belts that have no documentary or oral tradition, or at least none that has yet been found. For many wampum records, though, this may simply be because the necessary research has not yet been done. Bringing the paper trail and the oral tradition together with real belts often leads to new conclusions.

Though the Europeans frequently wrote descriptions of the wampum exchanged in council, sometimes stating the number of rows, the length of the belt, or describing the symbols worked onto the belt, there are no pictorial descriptions of the belts with the written records. The few existing pictures show the belts indistinctly, or are quick sketches that impart little information.

Written history is full of Europeans and Indians exchanging wampum belts during formal councils. Hundreds of belts and strings moved back and forth, preserving the words of the speakers and the commitments of their nations. Yet today, in the museums and in the hands of the people, there are probably fewer than two hundred wampum belts left in the world. Where did they all go? Were they buried? Destroyed? Seized and hidden by Euro-American governments intent on destroying the evidence of earlier commitments? Are they kept hidden today?

Part of the answer may lie in an early "recycling" policy. The financial records of New France show a special expenditure for wampum to be used in councils with the Indians—but also "to take apart the belts received from the Indians and to rework them into new belts to give back to the Indians."

Considering the volume of wampum exchanged during the eighteenth century, even when the beads had become more readily available and more easily made, it probably made sense for all but the most important records to be taken apart and reused. The permanent commitments, from the Confederacy's constitutional records to the Two Row Wampum, would be preserved. Wampum belts used only procedurally, or to signify temporary pledges or situations, could be reworked once their usefulness had faded.

The earliest accounts show Indigenous nations giving things other than wampum to Europeans to preserve their words: everything from sticks to furs. This has caused some scholars to suggest that wampum was not particularly "Indian," but that its use blossomed only through relations between natives and Europeans during the colonial era. Yet the early French records show that the "porcelaine" was already in use upon their arrival. It may be that when the Indigenous nations thought the Europeans ready to esteem and understand the significance of wampum, they started using it in council. Also, there was probably so little of it in the early days that it was tightly held, within the nations, not to be used lightly in council with people who seemed satisfied with other pledges.

The coming of metal tools and greater ease of travel and trade from the east coast, the source of the shells, made the wampum more plentiful and therefore increased its use. The written record shows a great increase in international use of wampum in councils in the 1700s. That makes sense, but it is dangerous to conclude that wampum before that time had been insignificant or not used. The rarity of the shell and the difficulty of working it may instead have made it all the more precious.

Three years ago, the majority of the wampum records of the Iroquois Confederacy were held in various museums. Today, the majority of the constitutional and treaty records of the Confederacy are again in Iroquois hands. The return of these powerful symbols of Iroquois law and history has healing and encouraging effects. It also leads to the new challenge of using the wampum records most effectively in a modern context.

If the museums had not been keepers of the wampum for many of the past ninety years, the wampum would have been subjected to political, social and economic pressures. On the Canadian side, federal government authorities would almost certainly have tried to seize it. On both sides, private collectors would have sought to acquire it. It is possible that, but for the museums, it might have been scattered or destroyed.

Museums are not ancient institutions; they are a relatively recent phenomenon. If we tend to think of museums as ancient, that antiquity is perhaps borrowed from the age of the things they keep. As museums redefine their roles and their directions, they have been moving away from being custodians of "artifacts" of dead cultures and becoming supporters of living ones.

Two things have helped the Confederacy in dealing with the wampums: the growing sense in the museum community that there is more to running a museum than holding onto things; and the growing field of museum ethics, which presses the institutions to relinquish material acquired under a moral cloud. Another factor which has smoothed the path has been the realization on the part of the museum staff that perhaps they can learn more about the people and their history and culture through a partnership; that the traditions are as much worth preserving as the symbols embodied in the belts.

Most museums do not know the full meaning of the wampum they hold. Learning the meaning of the wampum can help place it in context, culturally, historically and legally. It can also help with the decision as to where the wampum belongs, where and how it can best be used.

I wrote back to the McCord Museum, sending them Agneetha's speech. I also sent the information to the administration office at Kanesatake. The land disputes of the eighteenth century are continuing there today. Perhaps the wampum belt, with its supporting documentation, may again serve as evidence of the Mohawk understanding of land ownership. If so, it would be fulfilling its original intention. And that would be its highest and best use.

Note: This article was originally published in the *Northeast Indian Quarterly*, Volume VII, Number 1 (Spring 1990).

Continuity of
Haudenosaunee Government

Richad Hill

Shortly after several buffaloes were killed by a non-Indian who was trespassing on the Onondaga Nation, President Reagan received a bill from the Onondaga Council of Chiefs. The letter also explained how the United States was responsible to protect the Six Nations from such transgressions, according to the Fort Stanwix Treaty of 1784. One can only imagine the president's reaction to this assertion of sovereignty from the Onondagas, especially when the letter was addressed to "Honnadahguyuss," the Iroquois name for each president, meaning "Destroyer of Towns."

Town Destroyer Reagan faced something that each president since George Washington has had to deal with: what to do with upstate upstarts known as the Six Nations. The Grand Council of Chiefs of the Iroquois Confederacy have repeatedly committed their political position, based on the sacred wampums, into formal letters of protest and requests for reparations from the United States. Through a series of written communiques on a variety of issues, from land claims to bingo, we can trace the political reality of the Six Nations, we can see just how the Grand Council thinks and works.

Some people will never be able to understand why the Iroquois want to remain Iroquois. Some scholars will insist that the Six Nations no longer exist as a nation. Some government bureaucrats cannot accept the concept of a sovereign nation in their backyard. And some Indians feel that the old ways are in their way as they want to gamble on the future of commerce over culture. However, what is important is to look at how the Council of Chiefs view themselves, as sovereign, as independent, and as caretakers of the welfare of the Haudenosaunee. The role of the clanmothers and the confederate chiefs in the 20th century has been to help the people remember their rights and their duties as defined by two overriding laws—the natural law and the Great Law.

Over the course of Iroquois history agreements and treaties have been made to insure the political reality of the Iroquois people for generations to come. Council decisions were made with the future generations in mind, to protect the rights of those yet to be born. To the Haudenosaunee, history is a living truth, evidence for the continuing concern to maintain an Iroquoian identity and homeplace. The recent statements from the Grand Council of chiefs reaffirm this Iroquois concept of history.

First and foremost, the chiefs have steadfastly held that the Iroquois have their own unique national identity, which is separate from the United States or Canada. During the testimony on Senate bill 1683, the Iroquois stated to Congress:

> Although we are referred to in these bills as Indians of New York State, you will realize that we still exist as a sovereign nation and not part of your body politic nor in any district, county, or state of the United States. (March 10, 1948, Senate Hearings on Bill 1683 and Bill 1687)

In constant legal battles over who has civil jurisdiction on Iroquois territories, the Chiefs have clearly stated that such authority rests solely with the Chief's Council of each nation. Elective governments, on the other hand, have an erratic record of conceding that the county, state, or province may have legal jurisdiction within the boundaries of their community. In a 1975 letter to President Ford, the Grand Council restated its long-held position on Iroquois status:

> Our sovereignty has never been lost by conquest or voluntary submission, nor have our original treaties between our two nations been replaced with a document of equal force. (Council correspondence, March 5, 1975)

Brian Deer of Caughnawaga gave testimony on the Iroquois position during a meeting of the Federal-Provincial Talks on Aboriginal constitution matters in Ottawa that reflects the thinking of the Iroquois Land Rights Committee of the Grand Council:

We have never regarded ourselves as Canadians or American or as
Quebeckers or Ontarians or New Yorkers. We have regarded ourselves as
Haudenosaunee.

This firm belief in being and remaining Haudenosaunee is the central
issue in contemporary Iroquois-White relations. The Six Nations have
fought hard to keep their separate status, as they feel it is key to their
survival. All other issues revolve around the Iroquois concept of
nationhood and the responsibilities it brings to each generation to
defend its nation. The modern Iroquois chiefs still point to the
International treaties as both proof of their separate status and of their
sacred duty to uphold these agreements.

The treaties of peace and friendship between the United States and the
Six Nations are also symbolic of Grand Council's concern for the future
generations to be able to resolve their differences. Documented history as
well as the oral traditions of the Iroquois make numerous references to the
"Silver Covenant Chain" that binds the two nations together. This
imagery was called into place in 1981, when the Grand Council sent a
formal greeting to the newly elected President Ronald Reagan:

Honnahdahguyuss
The Honorable Ronald Reagan,
Greetings Brother,
The Grand Council of the Haudenosaunee, Six Nations, Iroquois confederacy
greets you with the ancient title Honnahdahguyuss bestowed upon George
Washington, the first President of the United States and all succeeding
presidents thereafter. It is our desire to wish you success in your new
position. It is also our desire to meet and polish the Silver Covenant Chain of
Peace made between our two peoples.
This ancient treaty is a symbol of peace and a promise to the future of our
nations. This chain was polished by our people and your leaders in the early
years of your nation. This chain has become tarnished in the late years and
we wish to meet with you to renew our friendship. (Council correspondence,
March 1, 1981)

Are the Iroquois citizens of the United States or Canada? The answer
depends on the individual aspirations of each Iroquois person. The
traditional Iroquois prefer not to be citizens of any foreign nation and
maintain their Iroquois citizenship. Practically all Iroquois state they are
"Six Nations" or "North American Indian" when they cross the United
States-Canada border. In 1924 the United States Congress passed the
Indian Citizenship Act, which unilaterally bestowed United States
citizenship on all Indians born in the United States, much to the
dissatisfaction of the Six Nations. The Council voiced its opposition
many times. Forced citizenship was seen as part of the federal

government's plan to assimilate the Iroquois, and the Chiefs had to make it clear that they wished to remain Haudenosaunee. In 1929, during hearings of the Senate Committee on Indian Affairs, Onondaga Chief George Thomas stated:

> I have always maintained that since we never gave up the right of self-government, it wouldn't be very good policy for us to go and vote for some other government. (New York Indians, Part 12, 71st Congress 2nd Session, p. 5031)

As other Indians rushed to accept American citizenship as a way of gaining status and equal recognition, the Six Nations saw such a move as an almost traitorous act that would result in actual loss of independence. To accept American or Canadian citizenship would also nullify the international treaties. In 1944 House hearings the Six Nations Confederacy presented the following position on United States citizenship:

> 1) That said confederacy has vital existing treaties. The character or construction of them cannot be changed by legislation by Congress.
> 2) That they are not citizens of the United States. The act of Congress of June 2, 1924, did not provide for Indians to apply for citizenship...as required by the constitution.

Four years later the Six Nations made an even stronger refusal by stating: "We still hold that the Act of 1924 was not fairly explicitly affected with the full knowledge of and assent of the Six Nations. As a majority, the Six Nations will assert that we neither sought nor requested an act of this nature..."

The citizenship question has become a major issue in determining the sovereign status of the citizens of the Six Nations. The Council of Chiefs realized that some of the Iroquois wanted to become Americans or Canadians, so they decided that it would be left up to individuals to decide for themselves. The official position, however, would be "Thanks, but no thanks."

When President Carter reinstituted peace-time Selective Service registration, the position of the Grand Council was called to task. Federal education assistance was being denied to Iroquois men who did not register; some were threatened with legal action as well. The Grand Council declared its opposition to forced registration on March 27, 1981, as the Council informed the President:

> Our men and women are citizens of the Haudenosaunee, Six Nations Iroquois Confederacy, with allegiance to the Guyyannahgonah, the Great Law of Peace. They are free and not subject to conscription by our nation or any other nation.... We have informed our young people not to register for the United States military draft. (Council correspondence, March 27, 1981)

Perhaps the most dramatic and successful manifestation of the independence of Six Nations citizenship has been the issuing of a Six Nations passport for travel in foreign lands. The passport states that the document is issued by the Grand Council of the League of Haudenosaunee, and that the "Haudenosaunee continues as a sovereign people on the soil it has occupied on the Turtle Island since time immemorial, and we extend friendship to all who recognize our constitutional government and who desire peaceful relations."

More importantly, the passport also defines the loss of Iroquoian nationality as such, "You may lose your Haudenosaunee nationality by being naturalized in, or taking an oath, or making a declaration of allegiance to, a foreign state; or by accepting employment under the government of a foreign state."

In 1977 the Chiefs issued passports for official Six Nations delegates to a meeting of the United Nations in Switzerland. Since then, over seventeen foreign nations have recognized the Six Nations passport as a legal travel document. These nations have included the United States, Canada, Switzerland, Holland, France, Belgium, West Germany, East Germany, Denmark, Italy, Libya, Australia, Turkey, England, Cuba, New Zealand, Iran, and Columbia. Travel on the Six Nations passport can be quite an adventure, as most countries are unaware of the Six Nations and the Grand Council lacks diplomatic relations with many countries.

However, foreign travel has assisted the Iroquois in gathering political support for their sovereign status. The Grand Council has also been able to carry its concerns to new audiences. When Mohawk people were under siege by vigilantes and New York State troopers in the 1980s over a jurisdictional dispute, the six Nations delivered the following to the United Nations in Geneva:

> We call upon the peoples of the world to demand that the United States cease its lawless conduct and respect the sovereignty of our nation. The most fundamental of human rights is the right to exist as a people. It is our common obligation as members of the human community to defend that right with all our strength. (Council correspondence, 1980)

The European people responded quickly and effectively and inundated the New York governor's office with phone calls and telegrams in support of the Haudenosaunee. The words of caution insured that the situation at Akwesasne was peacefully resolved.

To the Iroquois, international politics must be tempered by commitment to the spiritual ways of life as well. In 1982 the Six Nations addressed the United States Committee on Disarmament: "In our ways, spiritual consciousness is the highest form of politics" for "when people cease to respect and express gratitude for these many things, then all life will be destroyed, and human life on this planet will come to an end. We are the spiritual energy that is thousands of times stronger than nuclear energy. Our energy is the combined will of all people with the spirit of the natural world, to be of one body, one heart, and one mind for peace." (Council correspondence, 1982)

Despite the international involvements, the battle at home is still over land, natural resources, and civil and criminal jurisdiction over people who inhabit Iroquois lands. Of course the Grand Council of Chiefs have long held that only their government has authority over the territory of the Haudenosaunee. In fact, the goals of the Iroquois Confederacy land rights policy are: 1) To protect the political sovereignty of the Grand Council, 2) To restore the territorial integrity as defined by treaty, and 3) To maintain the health, education, and welfare of the people. In order to do this, the Six Nations has stated that "It is the opinion of the Haudenosaunee that mutually agreed and equitably negotiated settlements would be the wiser course of action." In 1978 the Grand Council wrote to then President Jimmy Carter to present a synopsis of their land rights position:

Under terms of the Treaty of Ft. Stanwix, it is the obligation of the United States to protect the Six Nations in full right of our lands.... This would include taking all necessary actions, including court action where required, to recover damages for the wrongful dispossession of the lands, for harm caused to the lands and environment, for resources unlawfully taken from the lands, for the loss of water rights, hunting and fishing rights, and other related interests. (Council correspondence, 1978)

Further, the Grand Council tried to clarify that only they can lay such claims to the United States due to the fact that individuals and separate groups have submitted often conflicting land claims. Council correspondence also records the following:

According to the constitution of the Haudenosaunee, individual nations and persons do not have the authority to sell, barter, trade, give up, relinquish, or concede any lands of the Haudenosaunee. The authority rests solely with the Grand Council of the Haudenosaunee which has the responsibility for protecting the lands of our children and the unborn generations yet to come.

To summarize the Iroquois position on land, the recent testimony on the Land Rights Committee of the Six Nations put the entire issue in perspective:

The very serious questions of our rights to our homelands will not go away with the swipe of a pen. We continue to exist, and the lands that the Creator of life gave to us continue to exist.... We have not disappeared as the government of our people, as some American historians have tried to assert.

No other so-called government that has been forced upon our people has a voice in these affairs. The affairs are between the Haudenosaunee and the United States alone.

Because most Iroquois communities have two opposing governments, many people in Canada and the United States wonder who represents the Iroquois people. Which government, the traditional Council of Chiefs or the elective system, has the right to speak on behalf of the Haudenosaunee? The Grand Council offered a detailed explanation of why they feel that only they can truly represent the interests of the Iroquois, as shown in their letter to then President Gerald Ford in 1976:

The Six Nations in Grand Council at Onondaga, Jan. 3 & 4, 1976, issues the following statement concerning the political relationship of the Six Nations Iroquois Confederacy and the elective government system of the Cattaraugus and Allegany Senecas who incorporated their government with the State of New York in the mid 1800s. By their Constitutional Charter, the people who chose the new elective system of government clearly severed themselves politically from the established form of government of the Haudenosaunee, the ancient Confederacy established centuries before the coming of the white man or the establishment of the United States.

The letter quotes from the 1848 Constitutional Charter of the Seneca to illustrate that the Seneca people accepted the overall authority of New York State and the United States to the point where "they cannot call themselves a nation...." Their letter continues:

By accepting another form of government, these Seneca people have removed themselves from the council fire of the Six Nations and the protection thereof. They also, by this action, alienate themselves from the future and claims of the Six Nations. The space left by these people at the Six Nations fire remains open, awaiting their return. They must reject the elective form of government and again raise their chiefs through the traditional condolence ceremonies....

Therefore, be it known that any and all actions by these constituted people and their representatives do not reflect the position of the Six Nations, nor are they binding in any way upon the government and claims of the Six Nations Iroquois Confederacy. (Council correspondence, January 4, 1976).

The recent Ontario Provincial Police raid on private bingo at the Six Nations Reserve and the New York State Police raid at a Tuscarora smoke shop raises an old question of just who has legal jurisdiction on the territory of the Six Nations people. The opinion of the Grand Council has been based on the aboriginal right to self-government, upholding the sovereign right of the Iroquois nations to total jurisdiction on their territories. The Six Nations has been opposed to the assumption of authority by any state or province, or any other government for that matter. In 1948 the Six Nations wrote to the federal government:

> Until such time as we, the Six Nations, desire to become a part of your body politic, or you are willing to cast aside your sense of justice and avow your intention of abrogating our treaties, amending your constitution and thereby disgracing your honor among nations, shall you not fulfill your treaty obligations by protecting the Six Nations from further molestation from forced citizenship; from jurisdiction of the State of New York, and from disturbance by the political and financial interest of the State of New York. (Council correspondence, 1948)

The Grand Council also feels strongly that it is the duty of each American president to uphold the treaty obligations of the United States. They have resisted any move to change that treaty relationship, as shown in this 1975 letter to President Ford:

> The Haudenosaunee Grand Council has never agreed or consented to the transfer of power from the President of the United States to the Congress of the United States or to the State of New York....
> It is not within the power of the Six Nations to change the laws given to our people hundreds of years ago, and it most certainly does not lie within the power of the Congress of the United States. (Council correspondence, 1975)

The arrest of a Mohawk chief by New York State troopers in 1979 led to an armed confrontation between the traditional government and the elective system. Ironically, what was at issue was a violation of treaty procedure on how to resolve disputes between the United States and the Six Nations, but it escalated to a potentially violent situation as to who had jurisdiction at Akwesasne. Fortunately, the Mohawk forces had a reconciliation, but the Six Nations left no doubt how they felt, as shown in their letter to President Carter:

> Brother, understand us clearly, the arrest of one of our chiefs removes any illusion of protection that our people supposedly enjoy through the imposition of United States law. This action clearly demonstrates the course of United States law to destroy Indian values, Indian governments, and Indian ways of life....
>
> We still exercise jurisdiction over these lands and people who reside there. We seek only Peace and Tranquility for our people through the protections provided by our treaties, and we enjoin you to uphold them. (Council correspondence)

The Six Nations have been involved in a variety of political and legal confrontations that have increased the profile of the sovereign status of the Haudenosaunee. As a result of these actions important statements have been written and published that provide insight into the Haudenosaunee mind of today. During the 1973 battle at Wounded Knee, the Oglala chiefs asked the Six Nations for recognition and support. The Iroquois sent an unarmed delegation into the encampment at Wounded Knee and issued the following statement:

> There must be someone among you who is concerned for us, or if not us, at least for the honor of your country.... When will you cease your violence against our people? ... We ask for justice not from the muzzle of an M-16 rifle. ... We have not asked you to give up your religions and beliefs for ours. We have not asked you to give up your ways of life for ours. We have not asked you to give up your government for ours. We have not asked you to give up your territories to us. Why can you not accord us with the same respect? For your children learn from watching their elders, and if you want your children to do what is right, then it is up to you to set the example. (Council correspondence, 1973)

In April 1985, at the Williamsburg conference on "The Imperial Iroquois," anthropologist William Fenton read from his paper that the Iroquois were "not a true political state" and he also stated that the Iroquois Council fire was but smoke "arising from the burning of old tires on the reservation junkyard." This must have come as quite a surprise to the United States government and the State of New York who were frustrated in their attempts to grab Dennis Banks, a federal fugitive, from the confines of that reservation.

Banks sought protection of the Haudenosaunee, as he felt his life was in jeopardy and no other Indian nation had exerted its sovereignty the way the Six Nations did. Eventually the Grand Council approved of granting Banks political asylum. State and federal officials were not able to enter the independent territory of the Iroquois to arrest Banks. The March 22, 1983, statement of sanctuary for Dennis Banks states the Iroquois position, based upon the treaties:

> ...Dennis Banks and his family now sit under the Long Leaves of the Tree of Peace.... [He] sits in the company of many nations and peoples who have at one time or another found shelter under this Great Tree of Peace.... "Treaties are made between nations, not men...." This is a recent quote from the President of the United States. We believe this and we remind the government and the people of the United States that we, the Haudenosaunee, hold the first Treaty of Peace and Friendship with you as a new nation.... These are documents of commitment and are now the responsibility of this generation. Remembering these commitments, we must put our minds together to insure that this Peace and Friendship continues for our children. (Onondaga correspondence, 1983)

The Iroquois have become a symbol among native nations, a symbol of that supreme power over defining for yourself who you wish to be.

The Iroquois have been called upon to exercise that power to help other Native People find their own voice. The Six Nations have monitored tribal elections at Pine Ridge after Wounded Knee, to assure the democratic process. The Six Nations have acted as a mediator between the Sandinistas and the Miskito Indians, to assure that aboriginal rights be respected. The Six Nations have believed in themselves, since the time of Creation. And they have continued to preserve that right for the future generations of the Haudenosaunee.

Perhaps it is best to conclude with a quote from Oren Lyon's speech given at the 1979 Montreal Conference on Indian Government, in which he gave the Iroquois perspective on political reality:

Sovereignty—it's a political word. It's not a legal word. Sovereignty is the act. Sovereignty is the do. You act. You don't ask. There is no limitation on sovereignty. You are not semi-sovereign. You are not a little sovereign. You either are or you aren't. It's simple.

Note: This article was originally published in the *Northeast Indian Quarterly*, Vol. IV, Number 3 (Autumn 1987).

Under These Viaducts

Roberta Hill Whiteman

Author's Note: "Under These Viaducts" is a work in progress. My uncle, Norbert S. Hill, requested a poem that would express the story of Oneida people from before contact to their move to Wisconsin and the settlement there. Because such history is submerged, I have framed the narrative so that in the poem the girl of the present time finds the history revealed in her dreaming, in her vision of the white birds that once warned Good Peter. The poem stops, for now, at the beginning of the Revolutionary War. Time is not always linear. History, the counterpoint to vision, unfolds with the voices and events the girl discovers in her search.

"II. The Man Who Blessed the Phone Poles," was first published in Jamake Highwater, Words in the Blood: Contemporary Indian Writers of North and South America. New York: New American Library, 1984.

Prologue
In April 1792, John Livingston came to Oneida and suggested that the land, like a loaf of bread, could be cut. He wanted a slice so a great man could manage the whole. After his discussions with Good Peter, he disclosed he wanted the entire territory. When the boundaries of the reservation were mapped, Good Peter said, "After this transaction, the voice of the birds from every quarter cried out, 'You have lost your country. You have lost your country. You have lost your country. You have acted unwisely and have done wrong.' What increased the alarm was—that the birds who made this cry were White Birds."

I. A Dream in Moonlight

Decades later, further west
a girl takes the tracks home.
Corth boys call her foreign dirt,
threaten to leave scars.
She feels her blood rebel,
this changeling from *Talu?ko an.*°

Some other child may still believe
trees bless her when she crawls
deep in the neighbor's lot to hide.
She may believe the houses don't see
how dark she is under the morning sky.

At night boxcars grudge the tracks.
She only hears a wolf wailing in the stones,
while something she lacks
goes flickering
down the avenue of maples.

Forehead waffled by the upstairs screen,
she waits for the moon to climb the railroad tower.
A barge sounds out the Fox River
while through the wooly air,
the Angelus rings a second star.
Warmed by blankets,
she flounders from the earth,
the corner, close,
the sill, her mother's arm.

The full moon wears a double face.
Tonight she'll ride, she'll ride.
Leaning north she brightens clouds
from orange to red then blue. Forms measure
her light by trusting time and cold.

What were the whispers
in her closet? Kneesocks uncoil
by the stair. Blue moonlight floats

° *Place where there are*

on the hardwood floor.
She can't look in the mirror, for the moon's
other face tickles her sleepy ear.

Dreamstilled in that April night
the lilac loses a few more leaves.
Rippling her light over houses,
the moon rides through clouds,
until cloud to bird becoming,
she skirrs, lands on the lilac,
on a branch with new leaves
frost bare.

On her feathered throat,
a crescent of foam.
In her eyes, the fire of coral.
Honoring the lilac, the bird bends low,
catches in the web of the girl's ear
the distant ululu of a train
near its tunnel.

Ululu. The earth deepens with cold
and bayborn fog drifts
like the memory of water
into last summer's cove,
up rust-colored rivers.
Ululu. Her guardian scatters an echo
into the labyrinth of earth, ear and ocean.

Threadbare, let's enter the space
of her sigh where we greet the spirits
that replenish our chaos, where we learn
our truth's tangled with whimsical history.
Over the bay, they pull wing deep rhythms,
sea swallows wrapped in the bones of their crossing.
Stars begin pulling waves into mountains.

Under the last frost,
covering hardwoods outside the palisade,
longhouses whirl around a shimmering stone
that sings while they sleep, and
winks back the moonlight. Inside the lodge,
five fires turn to coal and a girl

begins to wake. "Hush, someone will rise
when blue light is stronger.
Smell cedar, rills of woodsmoke? Let elms
jostle their limbs.
Wrapped in buckskin, or you will stay warm."

"Sisters, we call you." sang one woman, rising.
"Robins are singing elms out of darkness.
Earth breathes its floss on our eyes every dawn.
A tumult of song
brims from the oak once the east wind
has broken that bounty of cloud.
The turtle, the wolf,
the trailing arbutus require us
to keep faith with the world.
We're the earth's daughters, dancing
each day in the shade of this Great Law.
All lives as we live, link over link
for thousands of years.
Cold has a name, darkness, a reason."

"*Kgase,*° we call you." said an old man,
rising. "Wind strokes all things
with sunlight and shadow. Fast, be thankful.
This unmeasured morning in our beloved country,
maple sap rises up from the dark.
What had seemed vanquished,
now in its time, charges the treetops.
See the ground flutter
like hair on a cheek?
See the webs flash yellow and blue
in the rising light? Up from the earth,
elders sustain us."

Sea swallows flit from branch to branch
as old men and women,
their loved ones behind them,
dance to the beach
where waves churn with omens,
dance under stars growing fainter,
yet mild.

°*Cousin*

II.

The Man Who Blessed the Phone Poles

Whispering his riddles, the man came up Christiana.
She cut across the yard; her friends scattered home
to avoid him. He must have walked around the earth.
Exiled from daylight, his coat endured its shadow.
His shoes curl now and forever
from street salt and his kingdom's claim.
When he came, the street grew so much longer
in the winter dusk that where the walks converged
to one bright spot, summer slept
in a cup of emerald trees.

He'd stand beneath the streetlight's halo,
waiting its light to embrace him.
From her stairwell she'd see him
bless each pitted shaft.
His cuffs would move
and as he passed, snow burned bluer
and dusk settled in.

Oh magic country shaped by blood and sighs,
was he the one meant to be free?
Were the elders dispersed to fashion from defeat
blessings for this arc of manmade light?

Her father's shirt smelled of pickles.
As they crossed the tracks, she and sister
bounced in the back
past the drop forge with its desperate
clang, the brick and barbed wire
of Port Forward, smoldering mill dirt downriver,
like a slow motion bomb.

They parked where wind snapped at each plastic flag.
"Bill and Myrna's" hung beneath the Schlitz.
An itch danced down her part as they walked
to the corner near the parrot's cage.
Runnels of laughter flowed over her skin.
Fish fry night. They climbed in the booth.
"Is this the Silver Whale?" her father teased.

"Junior, you're too much. I'll tell my sister
Jonah wants a ride." The waitress got beer,
slipped the girls some chips.
Runnels of laughter. She watched
the big waitress and wondered whether she'd
come to fry them chicken before too long.

The bartender's face caught dim winter light.
His eyes, like spring puddles,
had enough space, for birds to bathe,
and popsicle sticks to unload their cargo
of black ant slaves.
Perhaps such people came riding an albatross
over indigo waves.
Those on shore watched it become
a boat manned by bewildered men,
hugging iron and glass beads.
The rats were all eaten,
their pants, waterworn.
Spiral on spiral, no time is the same.
That moment, men landed
while maple seeds whirled like choppers
in sunlight. One astonished woman
offered them corn.

Woolgathering, the girl smelled tides
break against islands, ripple in pineknots.
How many have died?
Plagues introduced them. Carved from the forest,
the faces kept watch, chafed at the bonepile,
and wished they could blister.

Invitations overlapped like waves in high wind.
The French–The English are at it again.
The Dutch will exchange prisoners,
"Come to our meeting."
The French claim they're sovereign, "Come, let's trade."
"Only Englishmen have wanted peace
in this decade." "Come hear our greeting."
"Come for the bleeding." "Come take these pots
and accept our kind king."

Up from the earth, we stood the same height.
The parrot broods in the smoky light.
What catches in the web of the child's ear?
A blizzard wind from 1650
glutting itself on the weapons of war.
No one has had to endure this before.

Huddled together on St. Joseph's Island,
Hurons moan in frozen dreams.
His knees growing numb, a boy whispers,
"Watch how snow geese fly from my thumb."
Backbones split like cold-blasted trees.
They no longer care,
for winter has gripped these refugees
running, running, running,
refugees running away from those wars.

Warm New Yorkers ask for more corn.
The Lamplighter calls out, "Dusk has come in."

III. Sundays

Moonlight, come to comfort these children
burning with plague. Sweep your cool color
over the floor. Grandmother quiet their flailing
arms, rustle their hair with your breath,
for death whose home's at the rim of the world
has come one hundred and twenty times.
When he comes to blossom and wave,
they break until a change occurs.
The fruit begins. The shorelines change,
yet the Standing Stone remains
while brothers sink in the motions of war.

From death's house at the rim of the world,
dust drifts over canned peaches
kept year after year. We live
by eating gestures of care.
Like grey waves slapping
a concrete wharf
little by little we forget
all the important names for things,
replacing them with steel or glass,

good or bad, profit or loss.
Changeling from *Talu?ko an,* the ducks have flown.
The northern geese wear on their sober chins
the camouflage of one white smile.

In a church where every step echoes,
echoes along the aisles, all the children,
combed and greased, piffled their prayers
and heard answers. Poking her eyes,
she tried to stay still,
so the man on the cross would wag his head
and Mary would sniff the dust from her candle.
But the white bird was real
as it cleaned its wings. She let
her eyes heal and it cleaned its tail.
Up through the windows of aqua and flame,
they flew together.
Over the mint green near St. John's head,
it guided her back
to a chip of sky where a priest had come
just for the evening. He helped
the women whose brothers were gone,
offering beads for a memorized song.
He felt what is common to most of mankind—
fear of the unknown and the sublime.
"These old women are witches.
They cannot remember when to say Jesus
and will not surrender to the good word."

The old women nodded, yes, they knew evil.
It's a dog with strange eyes that bites
without warning.

Working their art, the old women walked
the sunlit woods, knew each plant,
knew dock from mallow. Making magic
of seeds, they spun them round until
the wings carried away pain. One by one,
the sick revived and laughter came,
or the final shudder and more tears.

But now chains of guilt and fear
are hurled across a lovely world

and grandparents stand before the pit,
lean over the pole and are hit
on the head. They fell so deep only earthworms
know where they lay. The worms carry back
wisps of their hair. See it float
on the moonlight when summer is gone?

The sister is angry. She wants answers now.
"Who is the martyr? They pulled out his nails."
The girl can't remember but stares at the clock
and wishes a fog could bury this school.
Fog meeting fog over fences of exile.

IV. Train from Chicago

Between the rows of identically different
houses, she shattered into myriad voices,
each with a pagan history, a pearl
of hurt and animal awareness.
Confronting her face in the window of the train,
she counted oaks gliding through her hair,
as remote from their night ways
as she was from herself.
Streaming through her eyes, she saw
how leaves and light
now and then form a blossom.

Approaching a tunnel, the train picked up speed,
for dark made one attend
to voices in the rails.
Big Mouth reminds the Governor–
"This belt preserves my words..."
Longhouse voices shift the rhythm.
"The white birds bear us witness.
Your deals are wild and wrong.
How can we take beads and brass for something
we can't own? As free people,
we'll remain
in our beloved country."

When Frenchmen turn on England,
Senecas lie curled, their scalps torn off,

sticky blood washing down the Genesee.
Those songs became a wedge.
What else did they do? "Faith of our Fathers,
holy, true 'til death."

Lips cancered by wind,
Petuns, Neutrals, Hurons came
for shelter to the League.
"While France bargained for peace,
In Montreal they burned that man
from Chittenango Creek.
Now rain blusters over hills.
He didn't plead release.
The savage crown declared him
in a class with hyenas.
His red skin licked by flames."

This has never changed.
The best of our blood becomes us.
Anna comes with every snow.
Gone, gone, ash and amber bone.
Can we still greet the silent earth,
or is that a splintered moon we passed,
a field of white at the height of summer?

Grandfather, rising in the clouds of March,
in the dry thunder of your voice,
save us from deceit
and the lies we tell ourselves
confronted as we are
with war and greater war.

Massacres continued
in the name of Anne or George.
Eight hundred Tuscaroras refuse to be enslaved.
They lost the future's music
in that long walk north,
yet for a child to live
this day, she dreamed of those
who bore hunger and disease, the cold coming
again. Did they think, in seven generations,
we might smile?
Will such suffering ever stop?

An Englishman might say,
"Let's go another round,
for some left for Canada,
some went west, not looking back,
But our 'allies' will keep the peace,
although their rival's Pontiac."

The attitude of their history–
What's a tribe or two? Twelve million people
whisper to her through the rails.
Last night as the train approached Oneida,
she heard a woman from 1765.
"The year my husband died,
more whites came to trade.
What a deal they made. For eight pounds
of powder, twenty pound of lead,
one iron pot, my man with mole dark eyes,
my laughing man is dead.
Now let the sun fall.
Let the migratory birds wing us into midnight.
Wolf brother, sing for me,
drowned in multiplicity.
Is rage too kind a word?
For sisters of the stone
nothing else matters
but the wholeness of a vision
sequestered in our blood.
The earth's our common home,
but what ramparts remain in a tangle of snakes?"

Time exists, I can tell you that.
One shift in alliance,
my children grow old,
while deserters, king killers
and outlaws begin
to snuff out their brothers,
their own countrymen
with the strangest of cries,
"Freedom, Freedom."

Meeting in 1888 at Letchworth Park to discuss reunification of the Confederacy. The meeting included descendants of Cornplanter, Ely Parker, and Joseph Brant. Note the man second from left wearing what may be the Two Row Wampum. Photo courtesy of Richard Hill.

Roy Buck, Six Nations, Dr. Theodore Mars, representative of President Ford, and Corbett Sundown holding replica of the Two Row Wampum, 1975. Photo by Richard Hill.

Fig. 1. Woodlands Wampum Belt. Courtesy McCord Museum of Canadian History, Montreal.

Fig. 2. Huron chief and grandson with wampum belt. Frank G. Speck photo, 1910. Courtesy Museum of the American Indian, Heye Foundation.

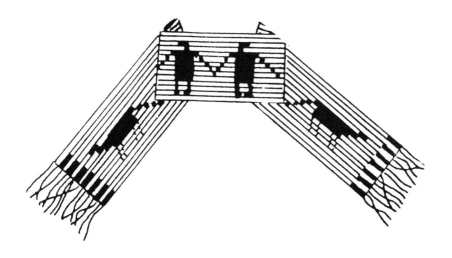

Fig. 3. Logo from Mohawk Council of Akwesasne letterhead.

Fig. 4. Wampum treaty belt. Courtesy Museum of the American Indian, Heye Foundation.

Fig. 5. Wolf Belt. Courtesy New York State Museum.

Fig. 6. Woodlands wampum belt showing arms linked in the "crooked" manner. Courtesy Royal Ontario Museum, Toronto.

Index

More
MAX DANGER
The Continuing Adventures
of an Expat in Tokyo

More MAX DANGER

The Continuing Adventures of an Expat in Tokyo

by
Robert J. Collins

Charles E. Tuttle Company
Rutland, Vermont & Tokyo, Japan

Many of the stories contained in this volume have appeared serially in the *Tokyo Weekender,* which has generously given permission for reprinting.

Published by the Charles E. Tuttle Company, Inc.
of Rutland, Vermont & Tokyo, Japan
with editorial offices at
2–6 Suido 1-chome, Bunkyo-ku, Tokyo 112

Library of Congress Catalog Card No. 88–51066
International Standard Book No. 0–8048–1570–4

First printing, 1989
Sixth printing, 1994

Printed in Japan

FOR JEN
a neat young lady
who understands it all

CONTENTS

7

8

FOREWORD

by Millard (Corky) Alexander

ONE OF THE MORE interesting phenomena in recent publishing history—at least, in the somewhat limited literary sphere of Tokyo and environs—has been the almost instantaneous popularity of one Max Danger, an expatriate American who somehow muddles his way from one baffling episode in the on-going struggle with the "Japanese economic-animal kingdom" to another. And he miraculously stays a half-step ahead in the series of events that has swept him along through the pages of the *Tokyo Weekender* fortnightly for the past 3½ years.

Readers have followed the escapades of Max Danger with amused fascination as he has somehow metamorphosed from a wet-behind-the-ears bumbling neophyte in the mystic ways of Japanese society to a more certain swimmer through the maelstrom of mystery and tradition that keeps Nippon's ways and wisdom perpetually vague to most foreigners seeking their fortune in perhaps the world's most formidable marketplace.

We last saw Max and his wife—the beautiful Gloria, member of three separate PTAs of three different international schools—and their three kids in *Max Danger: The Adventures of an Expat in Tokyo,* which became

9

a runaway best seller for the Charles E. Tuttle Co. and author Robert J. Collins.

Now in its fourth printing, the first volume of Max's adventures has virtually become "must" reading for every newcomer who sets foot in the Tokyo business community, regardless of his nationality, for the imponderables and insufferables that Max confronts on a daily basis are almost invariably based upon truth—at least the peculiar sort of truth that makes simple existence from day to day in surroundings unlike anywhere else on the globe a major accomplishment.

Along the way, Max has learned the ABCs of getting along in the maze of must-dos and musn't-evers that regulate nearly all facets of living in the empire of Japan, both commerically and domestically. For example, he has become a past master at the "drinks after work" syndrome in which the token foreign worker learns to deem it compulsory to meet with the office staff and fellow executives in one, two, or more of the countless bars, saloons, and cabarets that make Tokyo remain the world's major drinking establishment. In fact, Max has even evolved from the hesitant faker of guzzling and the avoider of the *karaoke* microphone into an enthusiastic planner of the after-hours pub-crawling.

Indeed, we readers and Max fanciers are set to wondering about what thoughts might course through the minds of such office staff stalwarts as Serious Hirose and Max's nubile secretary Nipples Akimbo when they ponder the metamorphosis from shy, tentative Tokyo newcomer into the bon-vivant party animal who once found himself donned in a full-feathered chicken suit, leading the fun.

Ah, so! Inscrutable, these foreigners!

10

And yet despite his relative savoir-faire in the byways and inroads of surviving in the international community of Japan, and despite his empathy with confreres, strange things continue to happen to Max Danger, things that in one particular light might seem perfectly explainable, but when involved with Max become arcane adventures in the human conflict and struggle for sanity and continuity of some kind.

For example, who else but Max Danger, through the countless episodes and observations of his fellows, could devise a continuing list of do's and don'ts from "Mister Etiquette"—no one, that's who.

And yet, in the midst of the humorous, dumbfounding notations and never-ending fencing with the unfathomable, Max occasionally—almost inadvertently—stumbles upon Real Truth. As does Gloria. More frequently, the attitudes and previously inexplicable reactions of their Japanese "hosts" become crystal clear to the Dangers, and, in those rare moments of sudden clarity and insight, reveal a shared humanity.

When they meet the ordinary citizens of Tokyo, their new home—the shoe repair man; the lady whose son has suddenly gone bad; the policemen in the corner police box; the youngsters who are nothing but dedicated Yomiuri Giants fans—they realize that these are the *real* people of Japan. In such moments, Bob Collins rises far above the writer who amuses us with tales both imaginary and true and emerges as an authentic chronicler of Real Truth about Japan.

But it's the Max to whom the eerie and the unorthodox occur that people best remember—and whose exploits they will continue to read in the *Weekender* and in this new volume, *More Max Danger*. For anyone who has lived the Japan adventure, these spasms of humor, incredulous occurrences, and Real Truth become the ultimate way to explain it all to those unfortunates who have not yet had the pleasure of enjoying life in Japan.

INTRODUCTION

MY GRANDMOTHER, a wise and wondrous woman, had a handle on Japan. As a college student in the late nineteenth century, she studied all that was known in the West about the Land of the Rising Sun. She understood what there was to understand.

"It's a nation of smallish people," she'd say, "who do clever things with their hands."

My wife's grandmother, a native of old Tokyo, had a handle on non-Japanese. As one of the first of the diplomatic wives to go abroad, she observed the West through the filter of ambassadorial politeness and restraint. She understood what there was to understand.

"They're all big people," she'd say, "who believe their opinions are facts."

As someone involved with the legacy of both these noble ladies, I have long felt a responsibility to set the record straight. I mean, how could old-timers like that—people born years before our parents—have anything but naive and ill-formed opinions about subjects as complex as Japan and the West? And without, as far as I know, the advantage of television.

Max Danger has been inserted in the midst of the commercial and economic empire of today's Japan. As a Westerner, he is not just observing Japan, he is living in and with

13

it. He is also exposing himself to the Japanese, who in turn have the opportunity to relate at various levels with him.

The stories—some true, some almost true, and some that should be true—chronicle the adventures of people on both sides of the issue. It's a random bag, so not every chance encounter, misunderstanding, thrill, or disappointment develops the dramatic potential for a full-blown story.

For example, this morning the superintendent of our building did something he's been doing every day for ninety-one straight days. He rang the doorbell at 7:30 AM and asked if I wanted him to bring the morning newspaper up from downstairs. I did what I've been doing for ninety-one straight days and said "yes." He went away. The fact that he has never returned with the newspaper—not once in ninety-one straight days—probably has something to do with my misunderstanding of certain elements in this ritual, but whatever the story is, there is not enough for Max to sink his teeth into.

The stories do reflect, by design, the type of experiences that relative newcomers to Japan have. (Old-timers have learned to mask their reactions to the mysteries of Dai Nippon, and scholars claim to have "understood things all along.") And the stories present typical Japanese reactions to the often confounding experience of trying to figure out what's going on between the ears of the unpredictable Westerner. All this, in theory, leads to enhanced understanding.

Now, what about the grandmothers? A lot of enhanced understanding has gone on since their days. Max, alone, has been involved in eighty adventures. (Ask for Volume I in your favorite bookstore—my daughter will soon be off to an expensive college.) Is the enhancement sufficiently fine-tuned to challenge the perceptions of old ladies who closed

14

their days writing haiku poetry and playing bridge? Do we know what they saw incompletely or incorrectly? Has naiveté been swept away?

No. And speaking as a Westerner, that's a fact. (But the stories are fun.)

ROBERT J. COLLINS

Tokyo

How Would You *Like to Be Japanese and Work for a Foreigner?*

MAX DANGER often wondered about that. A Japanese salaryman, comfortable in his own country among tens of millions of other salarymen, and with established work habits, business traditions, and common value standards forming basic threads in the fabric of his existence, must find the situation to be more bizarre than most expats realize.

Max's only frames of reference in this regard were the opposite circumstances involving his roommate during their bachelor days in New York. Max's roommate, a Brooklyn native and Music Appreciation Graduate from Oberlin College, got a job with Japan Air Lines in Manhattan. He worked, in New York, for a Japanese boss. (It should be pointed out that the roommate's career interests were directed less toward the airlines industry than they were toward amenable work hours—noon to 8:30 PM. He and Max were out most evenings playing banjos in a Greenwich Village saloon.)

The Japanese boss lived in a house in Westchester County which was considerably beyond the immediate aspirations of Max and his roommate. He had a driver. His maid—a young lady from Puerto Rico—was supporting 176 relatives "back home."

The Japanese boss was continually having visa problems, once drove for three months on an expired driver's license,

17

and never did master the intricacies of his tax status. One of his major concerns was the quality of education in which his son was immersed. The kid was in the third grade and still hadn't been taught to do long division in his head. ("They not use abacus here," he'd complain.)

The behavior causing most comment among his American employees, however, had to do with his "social" activities. He had become a regular at a number of Times Square night spots—in fact, several of his evening female acquaintances took to phoning him during office work hours. (The phone calls were a subject of considerable mirth among his immediate staff. Most of those girls, according to Max's roommate, should not be touched with a pole "less than ten feet in length.")

On top of all that, this Japanese man spoke funny English. The span out of Manhattan was always referred to as the "Broken Bridge." The mayor was someone named "John Rinsei." His meetings were designed for the odd concept of "coming agreement." His lunches in the office, according to the staff, were "Ben Toes." He never uttered his wife's name. Strange guy.

Max and his roommate used to laugh at this man and his peculiar habits. His attempts to get everyone to sing a song at the company New Year's party (company New Year's party?) were the funniest. He actually went up and sang the first song! (His secretary, overwhelmed by the whole thing, sang the only other song. A native of Detroit, she performed all three parts of "Where Did Our Love Go?" by the Supremes.) Max's roommate collapsed in hysterics.

But now in Japan, Max feels a little uncomfortable about the whole thing. A bell is rung, and a chord is struck. If the truth were known, and Max suspects it is, he'd be hard pressed to say "They're not even using computers in the

18

third grade" in Japanese. His defense of the Roppongi "evening ladies" and their phone calls would be even shakier. And as for "coming agreement" meetings, the "let's reach some goddam decision" concept might tend to predominate. (Max once told his Japanese crew not to come back until an agreement was reached. They never came back.)

So here we are with Japanese employees. What must they think? What causes them difficulties? And more to the point, what are *they* laughing at?

Max arrived in Japan in the midst of a Tokyo branch-office reorganization. Not only were bodies being shuffled around, but whole departments were being moved from floor to floor in the building. The seating charts, without which Max could remember nary a single name, became obsolete overnight.

On the third day of this chaos—which was Max's sixth day in Japan—his General Affairs Manager (who was either Shimizu, Watanabe, or Saito, depending on which chart was current) approached Max with the shocking news that someone forgot to designate "rowkas" for the ninth floor. ("Rowkas?" wondered Max.)

"This terrible," said either Shimizu, Watanabe, or Saito.

"You bet your life it is," agreed Max sympathetically.

"What we do?" asked either Shimizu, Watanabe, or Saito.

"We'll manage without it," stated Max emphatically. Being fresh from the Head Office, Max's cost-saving resolve was still unsullied by the realities of life in Dai Nippon.

It wasn't until several union representatives visited Max and the vice president for government affairs made an impassioned plea on the matter "for personal reasons" that Max finally gave in on the "rowkas" issue. He had made, and then rescinded, his first Japan decision. It would not be his last.

The "rowkas" was (were?) scheduled for delivery (installation?) the following Saturday. It (they?) would be ready (operational?) Monday morning. Max asked to be taken to the new machinery. He hadn't the foggiest idea what everyone was talking about—he even admitted as much to the good citizens of the General Affairs Department. ("Danger-san never heard of a 'rowkas,'" new employees are now told. "Heh, heh, *gaijin* [foreigners] are strange." It's become company legend.)

The "rowkas" were, of course, "lockers." Shopping bags have to be put somewhere, and individual space is a basic right of employment. ("I knew all along what they were talking about," Max has later been heard to say.)

On another occasion, Max asked a young kid from the Accounting Department to provide him with some numbers separating gross from net income. The kid, a bright youngster from Keio University, turned pale and bolted from the room. ("Probably should have asked his boss first," thought Max, "or called a meeting with dozens of people.")

The kid did not return to Max's office for several weeks. Max got the numbers elsewhere. One day, however, an appointment was scheduled through Max's secretary. The kid, his section chief, and the Accounting Department Manager showed up. Accompanying them was the General Affairs Department Manager. (It turned out that he was Watanabe-san.)

The kid presented a letter from one of his former professors at Keio University. It attested to the kid's trustworthiness and honesty. (What must have been involved in getting that letter, Max now realizes, makes him shudder.)

The rest of the cast in the meeting provided glowing reviews (written in Japanese but laboriously translated into

English by Watanabe-san) of the kid's eight-month career with the company. Watanabe-san, to cap it all, announced that *his* staff had made a thorough review of the physical plant, and nothing was broken.

"Broken?" asked Max.

"Broken," confirmed Watanabe-san.

"Broken?" asked Max again.

"Broken," confirmed Watanabe-san again.

"Never broken," added the kid.

Max could hear the clock on his desk ticking in the ensuing silence. He looked out the window. Rainy season. It dawned on him what had happened. "Good Lord," he thought, "there must have been dozens of people involved in this." Max had originally asked the kid for a *breakdown* of the figures.

Another situation involving a Japanese staff member must have caused ripples not only within the company, but with parents, friends, relatives, neighbors, and various legal advisors. The results could have been tragic, and all because of communication difficulties centering on the phenomenon of a "foreign boss."

The guy in charge of toting up all corporate costs in Japan was named Yamamoto. Every year for at least ten years Yamamoto would send a report to the New York Head Office. He included in his report all expenses—every single yen—spent by the Japan operation. The expenses included not only payroll, rent, and supplies, but the cost of cleaning office windows and sweeping lobby floors.

Soon after Max's arrival in Japan, he discovered that Yamamoto and the Head Office had two different accounting concepts in mind. The Head Office thought they were getting all those years *incurred* expenses, that is, expenses for which the company was committed, like the cost of a new computer, but was paying for over a period of years. Yamamoto, meanwhile, was merely sending *actual* expenses, or, checks issued during the fiscal year. These things make a big difference to accountants.

When Max revealed the discrepancy to the Head Office, all hell broke loose in the New York accounting and budgeting departments. In the flurry of exchanged telexes, Max found himself defending Yamamoto, since he had been doing what he understood he was supposed to do. The Head Office, meanwhile, referred to Yamamoto as an idiot, fool, incompetent, bonehead, jerk, and even worse. (Max felt obliged to shield Yamamoto from the comments of his peers in New York.)

The last telex in the exchange, from the Head Office to Max, was as follows:

TO: M. DANGER – TOKYO
FROM: W. WYLIE – NEW YORK
RE: YAMAMOTO EXPENSES

TELL THE ABOVE WE WANT CORRECT NUMBERS ON HIS EXPENSES THIS TIME OR ELSE HE'S FINISHED.

WARM REGARDS, W. W.

Max was in Korea when the telex arrived. Max's secretary passed the telex on to Yamamoto. Yamamoto left and did not show up in the office for three days.

When he did come in, Yamamoto was accompanied by a family friend who was also an attorney. They sat on the couch in Max's office; Yamamoto had the look of a man totally shattered by life. (He clutched in his hand, wrinkled and no doubt tearstained, what Max later discovered to be the damning telex.)

Yamamoto couldn't speak. The attorney did the talking. He described "family conferences" during which it was decided that Yamamoto would "resign with honor"—provided the *gaijin* boss allowed it—so as to spare the two daughters who would soon be applying to "good colleges." Not only that, continued the lawyer, Yamamoto was prepared to pay everything back. (With this, Yamamoto began weeping.)

"Pay everything back?" asked Max.

"Yes," said the lawyer, "it's the custom in Japan."

And with that, Yamamoto spilled his guts. For perhaps a year, he had been making monthly visits to a bank on behalf of the company. He had submitted expense vouchers for the taxi rides to and fro. He knew the vouchers for the taxis totaled ¥14,750.

Yamamoto, however, confessed that he had been taking the subway.

The Columnist

"GOOD GOLLY," exclaimed Max's companion as they stepped from the cool darkness of the LaForet Museum into the warm sunlight of a Tokyo autumn afternoon. Max's companion was ecstatic.

"That exhibition of late Edo calligraphy—particularly the demonstrated influence of badger-hair brushes on the evolution of stroke modification—was especially stimulating," continued the companion. He was rocking from toe to heel in excitement.

23

"Yes, it certainly was interesting," confirmed Max. "Let's get a drink."

"Well, I suppose we *do* have time for tea and cakes before the first act at the Kabuki Theater," said Max's companion. "But we don't want to miss the thrilling drum/samisen/ *shakuhachi* overture."

"Plus the clanging things," added Max.

"Particularly the clanging things," stated his companion.

The two gentlemen settled themselves in a cozy little tea-house staffed by ladies in black dresses with white aprons. The aprons served the purpose of distinguishing the wait-resses from the middle-aged clientele.

"Do try the éclairs here," said Max's companion, "they're scrumptious." They, assuming one likes those things, were.

"And now," said the companion, wiping a globlet of whipped cream from the tip of his nose, "there's something I'd like to seriously discuss."

Max sat back in his chair. His companion took the nap-kin from under his chin and re-folded it along the original creases. He laid it carefully next to the *oshibori* (hot towel), which had earlier been rerolled and inserted into its torn plastic bag. A kindly waitress came by and refilled his cup of tea.

"I would like you to consider," said Max's companion, between tiny sips of tea, "writing a column on expat life for my weekly newspaper."

"What?"

"I would like you to consider . . . "

"I *heard* what you said, but I've only been in Japan a short time," said Max.

"The clearer your eye will be for details," rejoined the famous Tokyo editor/publisher.

"But I'm not out and around much," said Max. "I'm always working."

"The more objective you'll be," rejoined the famous editor/publisher.

"All my spare time, what little there is, goes to my wife and children," said Max.

"The more wholesome your opinions for my readership," rejoined the famous editor/publisher.

"I can't write," said Max.

Someone dropped a tray of teacups and saucers in the rear of the restaurant.

"That could be a problem," the famous editor/publisher admitted after a minute or so. He had been making little mountains of sugar on the table and shaping them with his thumb and index finger.

"But," he continued, "if you submit the stories, I'll critique them for quality and then you'll rewrite them."

Max watched his companion playing with the sugar. By dipping his fingers in the tea, he was able to sprinkle little droplets of liquid on the white mountains. Instant erosion, with lakes and rivers.

"So it's a deal then?" asked the famous editor/publisher. He covered the table with his palms as the waitress brought the check.

"It's a deal," confirmed Max, giddy from the éclairs.

They shook hands, and Max spent the rest of the day at Kabuki licking his fingers.

It was a dark and stormy night when Jack Armstrong, President of the American Chamber of Commerce in Japan, savagely murdered his Executive Director and took off for Brazil with the Chamber funds. . . .

"Ah, actually you might want to be a little less specific

when writing about existing institutions," suggested the famous editor/publisher after Max had submitted his first manuscript. "You don't want to write *too* close to home."

It was a dark and stormy night when General Mayhem sent the combined U.S. air, naval, and ground forces on maneuvers in Shimoda without first informing Japan's Self-Defense Forces. . . .

"I know you've never been to Yokota, Yokosuka, *or* Shimoda, but that's not what I meant by not writing 'close to home,' " counseled the famous editor/publisher. "Besides, subtlety plays a role in good writing."

It was a dark and stormy night when Biff Straight, President of the Tokyo American Club, announced that members violating any rules at the Club would be lined up at the edge of the uncovered pool and summarily executed. . . .

"That's better," agreed the famous editor/publisher, "but just a little too dramatic. Think about what you do at work."

It was a dark and stormy night . . .

"Doesn't anything happen to you in the goddam daytime?" queried the famous editor/publisher.

It was a cold and grey afternoon when Bart Holstein, CEO of a major international conglomerate and my boss' boss' boss, arrived in Tokyo and began to chew ass. . . .

"You know Max," advised the famous editor/publisher, "I had in mind something a little different. For your own safety, if nothing else, write about commonplace things."

The day they discovered poisoned meat at National Azabu Supermarket, . . .

"Could we get together again, Max, and discuss this project?" suggested you-know-who. "I'm interested in re-evaluating our editorial thrust."

It was during this second meeting of editor/publisher and prospective writer—a meeting held at the very same tea-house near the LaForet Museum—that the idea struck both men. Such a clever idea it was too, both men agreed. The project began at once.

Since that red-letter day the foreign community in Japan has had the benefit of the type of wisdom readily available in the syndicated newspaper columns and journals back home. A real community service was born in the personification of politeness itself. The beloved Mr. Etiquette made the first of many regular and helpful appearances. And what would we all do without him?

Mr. Etiquette

DISPENSING RULES of etiquette—be they social, sexual, or business—is a bigtime industry. And it has been so for many years.

The leisure class particularly has always been concerned with "proper behavior" and its attendant rules and regulations. (It's one of the few things peasants, sloshing about in the mud, seldom worried about.)

Schools and academies, wherein the study of manners and form comprised the bulk of the curriculum, flourished in seventeenth- and eighteenth-century Europe. Later, Victorian England managed to combine empire-building (and

27

the accompanying new wealth) with heavy doses of "civilized propriety." ("Correctness in manner and speech must follow, *even whilst* in association with local inhabitants and related peoples of colonial jurisdictions."—*Standards,* J.L. B. Clarke, 1885. Author's emphasis.)

Many of the earliest schools in the New World, particularly the New England "women's seminaries," were merely transplanted fabrications of the Old World finishing-school concept. "Hard" academic disciplines were disdained in favor of the "softer" (and therefore more civilized) literature and manners curriculi. Trade-school laborers built the bridges, gentlemen owned them.

The situation in Japan was not much different historically. Traditional pursuits such as flower arranging, the tea ceremony, and brush painting were in the domain of those of leisure. The restraint and control necessary for accomplishment are the precise requirements for evolving rules of polite behavior and standards of etiquette. It's all so civilized.

Things have changed a bit, however. Even the masses now have leisure. They must be instructed. The sheer number of people interested in the rules of etiquette necessarily alters the nature of instruction. Personal guidance, as in the days of yore, can no longer deliver the product. ("Sir Humphrey, one never wears boots to bed," or "Midori-san, you holding teacup upside down *desu*.")

Rules, guidelines, and general information regarding proper behavior are now in the hands of mass media. With that in mind, and with the understanding that not all situations in this respect have been covered in the past, Max Danger offers the following as a service to the expat community in Japan.

1. Never bow from the waist while standing with your back against *shoji*. Hindquarters, in extension, will

rip paper and break wooden slats, thereby dislodging the paper doors from their framework, which in turn will collapse on and about your person. Japanese rarely see this sort of thing, and it therefore detracts from the good impression originally intended by the bow. Plus, one never knows who will be embarrassed by whatever's behind the now-demolished screen.

2. When bowing in close quarters, the *bower* should strategize the manuever so that the head dips to the left of the *bowee*. No one else knows this rule, but common sense dictates the creation of a practical custom so that concussive injuries to the head and shoulders are avoided.

3. Never experiment with the knobs and dials on toilets in modern Japanese homes. Not only might fuses be blown in the immediate neighborhood, but powerful jets of "body-heated" water can lead to an environmental mishap difficult to repair with toilet paper and hand towels. Detailed instructions are necessary for the operation of such space-age toilets, but social gatherings are not the proper occasions for tutelage. Do your business and leave—touching nothing.

4. Never wear toilet slippers back into the living room in a Japanese home. And understand that people dwelling on tatami mats cannot be mollified by attempts at humor. ("Golly, here I go again. I can never remember to change these danged things. Ha, ha, ha.")

5. Do not ask for milk and sugar with your Japanese green tea. It's not done. And it tastes awful.

6. The words "I do not speak English very well" mean

something different, in relative terms, than the words "I do not speak Japanese very well." Under- and over-statements are involved. Therefore, the words "I can't understand these people—they seem so nice but I still don't trust them" should be used with utmost discretion. They've been heard before.

7. Always leave the elevator first if you're a man. If you're a woman, leave last but out of politeness keep your finger on the "close" button as you're exiting until the very moment before your arm is ripped from your shoulder by the closing doors.

8. Always slurp soup. Never slurp sushi. Always eat curried rice with a spoon the size of those your grandmother used when mixing dough for pies. Never stop pouring beer for your drinking companions until the foam erupts and spills all over table and laps. Always feign surprise when this happens.

9. Immediately approach and speak to the Japanese man wearing a wristwatch that: a) fits, and b) is made anywhere but in Japan. He's lonely.

10. All stories involving the following colloquialisms should never be repeated in Japan. The subsequent explanations required will take more time than the story is worth, and subways stop running around midnight.

   a) A horse of a different color.
   b) A pig in a poke.
   c) A snake in the grass.
   d) Birds of a feather.
   e) Raining cats and dogs.
   f) The ease with which a camel goes through the eye of a needle.

g) Made a monkey out of me.

h) He's a complete ass (or a pain therein).

i) Donkey's years.

j) The eye of an eagle.

k) The heart of a lion.

l) The wisdom of an owl.

m) A wolf in sheep's clothing.

n) A bull in a china shop.

o) Crying wolf.

p) Spots on a leopard.

q) The memory of an elephant.

r) A laughing hyena.

s) The day of the jackal.

t) Goose.

u) Bullheaded.

v) I was buffaloed.

w) Chickenshit.

x) Cock.

y) Going ape.

z) Brass monkey.

11. Never wear the hotel *yukata* to a traditional Japanese banquet at a hot-spring resort unless you are: a) a woman, b) wearing tennis shorts underneath, or c) a very small man with short legs. Those things go on for hours.

12. It is unbecoming for a blonde, 5' 7", blue-eyed woman to put hand to mouth and giggle. Don't even consider it.

13. Do not rage at taxi drivers who cannot understand your directions in English. After all, how many New York taxi drivers, or London taxi drivers for that matter, understand English? (Or any Australians?)

14. Do not pull your shirttail out, roll your pants to your knees, wear your suit jacket backwards, and tie your necktie around your head during your performance at a *karaoke* bar. It can only lead to trouble. Particularly if you're driving home. And most especially if your wife thinks you've been working late at the office. And without exception if you're with your Head Office boss. (But always if you're with the local staff.)

Another Dimension

IT HAD BEEN RAINING—a driving, splashing, windswept torrent of water—for twenty-four hours. Muddy rivers cascaded down the mountain roads, engulfing and threatening to submerge the abandoned automobiles scattered randomly in the newly-formed lakes and ponds of the countryside valleys.

It's the "tail of the typhoon," everyone said comfortably, as if knowing *why* the heavens had opened in such spectacular fashion was enough to banish concern.

Nevertheless, Max Danger, feeling for all the world as Noah must have felt, surveyed the situation with considerable concern. (He briefly reviewed his experiences of the last week to make certain he had not overlooked a dream or vision involving cubits and shipbuilding.)

Max and thirty-nine of his company stalwarts were bouncing along the mountainside roads of the Izu Peninsula. It was company travel (trouble) time. Perched on the "*gaijin* seat" in the front of the bus, Max watched the driver negotiate the hairpin curves. Great stretches of the road were under water, thereby blurring the nice little guidelines one considers when navigating in the mountains—ditches and edges of cliffs. In fact, swinging wide on curves created waves of water washing over the edges and onto the tops of tall pine trees growing many meters below. It was truly, and alarmingly, breathtaking.

The driver's head rocked back and forth in an attempt to keep his vision on track with the wipers sweeping across the windshield. Since the windshield was the size of a barn door, the driver nearly left his seat each time the wipers reached the end points in their cycle. Fortunately, he had the steering wheel to hang on to. He had taken off his Mickey Mouse gloves and was gripping the wheel with actual flesh.

The bus hostess had stopped prattling over the intercom at about the same time as the driver doffed his gloves. The relative silence was a blessing, but it also emphasized the drama inherent in the escapade. It did not alleviate Max's feelings of concern to watch her peering intently through the windshield and hear her whisper *hidari* (left) or *migi* (right) to the driver as he wheeled the vehicle around blind corners. She was also doing something unusual for bus hostesses. She was sweating.

Max saw the jumble of stalled automobiles at the same time the driver did. Luckily the wipers were in the middle of their cycle. Max's foot jammed imaginary brakes—the driver hit the real ones. The bus slewed sideways, its rear end clipping the boulders at the very edge of the cliff. Sliding and banging in this fashion, the bus entered the lake formed in a hollow in the roadway. It came to a stop against a red Honda submerged to its windows in water. Eight other automobiles were in the lake, and about a dozen people were standing under trees on the "upside" of the cliff watching the action.

(A question was raised in Max's mind regarding the situation, although the question has nothing to do with this story. For the fun of it, let's take a poll. How many readers—raise your hands—think it's better to: a) stand together under trees on the "upside" of the cliff and watch vehicles plow into each other, or b) send someone, or a group of someones, up the road a few meters to the curve, and signal drivers to stop? Remember, those are *your* vehicles being plowed into.)

In any event, progress ceased. The rain, demonstrating its power, gushed with renewed vehemence. Bubbles of water the size of golf balls bounced from the lake's surface. Serious Hirose, from the mahjong group in the back of the bus, broke the silence. "Why we stop?" he enquired.

Looking back on it now, Max realizes there was never any real danger. One can be stranded far from civilization for days (or months) in other parts of the world, but it's virtually impossible in Japan. Over the next hill or around the next curve there's bound to be a Sony shop or *pachinko* (pinball) parlor.

It did take about an hour to agree upon a plan of action. The bus was capable of sporadic radio communication with its partner containing the other half of Max's company stalwarts. The second bus had encountered a landslide ten or eleven kilometers back, on the same road Max had just traveled, and the thinking was that each group should fend for itself. It was 4:30 in the afternoon.

No, there was no real danger, but there was extreme discomfort. Max's group disembarked from the bus into knee-deep (or waist-deep, depending upon who it was) water. Twenty-two males and eighteen females began a trek on foot

34

down the mountain to a village rumored to be four or five kilometers away.

The wind was blowing uphill, and the trick was to lean forward enough to keep moving, but not enough to fall on your face. Little gaps in the blowing of the wind did send some of the hikers sprawling, particularly the larger people who had to reduce wind resistance by leaning forward at a more radical angle. Max sprawled once, but a heavy girl from the Accounting Department hit the pavement four times.

No part of anyone's body was dry. It would not have been so bad if it had been warmer, but as the sun set, the temperature dropped to below 10 (Centigrade). Head down, water sloshing around his ankles, more of the stuff blowing against his chest, Max began to shiver. The girl in front of him, who was wearing only a thin blouse and short skirt, was actually turning blue. Colds would be inevitable, but Max was worrying about pneumonia.

The inn at the village, which turned out to be about ten kilometers away, had seven rooms and, to no one's surprise, they were all occupied. Space on the lobby floor was available, however, and the old wooden structure became literally a port in the storm. Long lines immediately formed at each of the two toilets in the facility.

Normally a merry lot, no one in Max's company was having fun. A number of people surrounded Mr. Kitagawa, a former Ministry of Finance official and now a senior advisor to the company, and rubbed his arms and legs. He did not look good. One young secretary, pregnant, was wrapped in spare futons and given hot tea. Even Serious Hirose, a tough little character, was having problems. His shivering rattled the *shoji* against which he was sitting.

It was nearly as cold in the building as it was outside. Obviously, it was not the cold of mountain peaks in Nepal;

it was more like the damp and bone-chilling cold of the west of Scotland. Keeping wet clothing on was unthinkable, taking it off was impossible. It was going to be a long evening.

So now, Gentle Reader, you have a picture of the circumstances. With those circumstances in mind, consider the impact the following had on Max and his little group.

The inn was constructed in the third year of the Meiji era (1870). It partially burned down in 1894, but was rebuilt immediately. Because it was against a cliff, but only a few meters from the road, it had suffered from the effects of periodic earthquake-induced landslides which tumbled rocks and mud onto its structure. Parts of the inn had to be repaired every ten or fifteen years.

The inn had its heyday during the first few years of the twentieth century. Located at a strategic point in a mountain pass, it originally serviced walking merchants and peddlers on their way through the territory.

Automobiles damaged business—there were few reasons to stop at that location. The later bussing of tour groups virtually destroyed any thoughts of growth or prosperity. There was no place to park buses, and there was nothing in the area scenic enough to attract tourists. The inn now attracted only locals who came for sentimental reasons, or because it was the only public facility in the general neighborhood. Very few concessions had been made to "modern" amenities.

It did have one thing, however, and that one thing was a godsend to Max's group. It also provided Max with the opportunity to experience something one usually only hears about.

At the rear of the building, connected to the structure and covered by relatively new roofing of plexiglass, was a natural hot-spring bath. It may be stretching things to call the bath a lifesaver, but it sure changed an intolerable situation into something approaching sensual ecstasy.

The pregnant secretary was led to the bath first, followed immediately by Mr. Kitagawa. The blue girl, who had been wearing the flimsy blouse and mini-skirt, had to be carried to the bath. Serious Hirose and Max, the shiverers, joined the next group of a half-dozen people. Within fifteen minutes, all twenty-two males and eighteen females were shoulder-to-shoulder in the hot water. Some wore underwear, some did not.

Max has been wrong before, and will probably be wrong again. Once he had been unable to imagine "an innocent society of folks romping together in rice paddies by day and splashing together in communal baths by night." A lot of laughs had been generated by Max's bumbling into the ladies' bath at a hot-spring resort during the "company trouble" of a year ago.

But lounging in the heat and steam of a countryside bath, rain banging against the plexiglass roof, sensations gradually returning to the extremities, and the blessings of heat penetrating to flesh and bones, Max entered, albeit temporarily, a different and new dimension. Concentration on private pleasures in public circumstances is an accommodation the Japanese have mastered.

"Feels good," stated the tea girl from Keio University, Max's companion on his immediate left.

"Yes, it does," replied Max, eyes closed and a hot towel on his head.

It will never be the same.

The Answer

AN INTERESTING ANAMOLY exists in Japan regarding answers. There aren't any. And to understand this, one must separate "answers" as we know them from statistics.

We are all aware that statistics abound in Dai Nippon. An intriguing exercise in this regard is spending an evening with Japanophiles quoting numbers. ("Do you realize that at this precise moment, 31.84% of all Japanese are sick to their stomachs?" Or, "Did you know that 4,421,309 Japanese traveled abroad during Golden Week, but only 4,421, 303 came back?")

Virtually all government agencies publish statistics on the behavior of the citizenry within the scope of their regulatory concerns. One of the more amazing set of numbers— amazing in the sense of conceptualizing the survey, rather than in terms of practical application—is the study regarding *how early* people arrive on train platforms to catch the Shinkansen (Bullet Train). People in Osaka apparently arrive at the station to catch the Bullet Train to Tokyo a full 60 seconds earlier than people arrive at Tokyo Station to catch the train in the other direction! I mean, it's difficult to take this information standing up.

For those who have wondered, only 68% of the people visiting post offices each day are concerned with mailing something. The remainder are fiddling with their savings accounts, or gossiping.

Of perhaps more relevance is the study which indicates that men spend forty-five seconds cleansing their genitals prior to entering a public bath, whereas women spend less than twenty seconds on the same chore. Extraordinary.

One of the effects of statistically quantifying behavior is demonstrated by the apparent ease of analysis of Japan by outsiders. A scholar, with these numbers displayed before him, can sit in Greenwich, Connecticut (assuming scholarship and Greenwich, Connecticut, are not terms in mutual contradiction), and "figure out" how things work in Japan.

Or can he? While each of us deals in the general sense with Japan as a statistical whole, our day-to-day existence involves individuals doing specific things. With reference to the cleansing of genitals, for example, Max's "tiny stool companion" during his first trip to a Japanese bath was Watanabe-san of the company's General Affairs Department. Watanabe easily spent five minutes, before he entered the bath, at the genital stage, explaining with a comment as specific as it was inane, that he "didn't want to catch disease." Scholars studying mere statistics will miss these little touches.

What happens, when survey numbers in Japan proliferate, is that trends uncovered by the studies become "officially confirmed." The "answers" are already there—in a report somewhere—and individual responsibility for specific replies is obviated.

In this regard, one can imagine Japan as being a vast and integrated baseball team. Everyone knows that people batting .350 are better than people hitting .250. It's as clear as a bell. What is frequently overlooked, however, is the fact that a .350 batter may strike out six out of ten times at the plate. Last year's statistically best pitcher (Kitabeppu) gave up twenty-one home runs. Watanabe-san laboriously scrubs his private bits for more than forty-five seconds.

Max Danger's first real attempt to obtain an answer in Japan had to do with trying to hire somebody. The open job was in the Investment Department, and Max wanted someone with experience. Notwithstanding the fact that every third foreign firm in Tokyo is looking for the same "money man," Max had an advantage because his company enjoyed an acceptable reputation. (In 1985, 46.9% of all university graduates would consider Max's company positively, *if* they were to work for a foreign firm.)

The problem, of course, is that Max wanted an experienced man. This meant trying to hire one away from another company. (Some 85% of all Japanese salarymen are commited for life—or age 58—to the company of their choice after graduation.)

Max settled on one candidate particularly and invited him to lunch. (Japanese salarymen spend an average of forty-seven minutes at lunch.) They ordered steaks. (But 42% of all salarymen regularly eat curried rice at lunch.) Forty-six minutes into the meal, the salaryman automatically began looking at his watch.

Max made his pitch. Challenge, security, money, future, prestige, money, professional responsibility, money, international travel, and money were the keystones. Max entered, with this guy, a level of remuneration that apples to apples exceeded his own. "And we employ," Max added, "people to age sixty." (Only 14% of all major corporations employ people to age sixty.)

The candidate begged for time to make the decision. Fair enough. His commitment, however, could not be made until December. (75% of all resignations occur in June or December—bonus seasons.) His decision would have to be discussed with his wife's parents. (Over 50% of arranged marriages take the prospective husband's employment into account.)

Max kept the pressure on. He sent the candidate annual reports, invited his kids to a baseball game at Korakuen, remembered his wife's birthday with fresh Hokkaido salmon, and sent him a newspaper clipping reporting that only 20% of Japan's employees consider themselves to be "salarymen."

On December 21, five months after the initial contact, the candidate accepted the job. (It was only six months after Max had asked the Japanese directors of his company if they could afford a new investments man. They hadn't answered yet.)

Max and the investments man are now skipping arm-in-arm down the yellow brick road toward the rainbow of corporate profits possible only with intelligent placements, and old-fashioned good timing. It was a match made in statistical heaven.

One night, surrounded by company stalwarts at a *yakitori* (grilled chicken) joint, Max asked the investments man why he finally chose Max's company for employment.

"Nice office?" suggested the genitally pure Watanabe-san.

"Good company trips?" offered Serious Hirose, of company trouble fame.

"Pretty girls?" queried Panda Usukura, the Personnel Director.

"No," responded the investments man. "I realized that over 60% of investments people have changed jobs since 1982, and I wanted to be in the majority. Besides," he continued, chomping on a chicken gizzard, "the company name has the same number of letters as my wife's name. It's good luck."

Visit No. 3

EACH OF THE primary integers—zero through nine—has its own significance in science and lore.

Understanding the concept of zero, for example, led to the development of modern mathematics. The number one represents unique singularity or the very first position in any ordinal progression. Two signifies balance, and is nature's mating number. Three comprises the characteristics of a fundamental geometric structure, the triangle. And so it goes. (Nine is the number of Cubs it takes to lose a game in Chicago.)

The number three, however, has special significance to expat employees. For it is during the *third* trip to Japan that Head Office Visitors begin to demonstrate their expertise. *That's* when the vast fund of knowledge, the in-depth experience, and the enterpreneurial understanding wrought by eight prior working days in Tokyo rear their ugly heads. And *that's* when, for the expat, the problems begin.

Bartholomew ("Call me Bart") Holstein, CEO of a major international conglomerate and Max's boss' boss' boss, arrived in Japan on his third trip. His first two trips involved a swirl of conferences, top-level meetings with ministry officials, and reception-line intimacies with a string of folks named Suzuki. The only in-depth discussion during those trips, as far as Max could tell, was a conversation with a Hotel Okura banquet girl named Noriko about the unfortunate imagery involved with the ice-carved standing bear—a revered corporate symbol—trickling a steady stream of water, from a stalactite forming between its legs, onto the sliced salmon so prettily displayed for the honored guests. Bart and Noriko reviewed the bilingual expressions describing this phenonomen.

But Bart was back—an expert now on all that is Japan. And he was, as he warned in his advance telex, prepared to roll up his sleeves and "get to the bottom of things in Tokyo."

Max, of course, has always been reluctant to criticize the behavior of corporate chieftains. People do not become captains of industry by having heads of bone. The "view from the top," the "breadth of perspective," the "pressures of interacting economic dynamics," and the "awareness of big-picture financial consequences," combine to form points of view undreamed of by the expat drones in the field. (It *must* be something like that, right?)

In any event, Max, without comment, herewith chronicles the behavior patterns exhibited during Bart's first, second, and crucial third visit to Japan. A trend may be discernible.

BREAKFAST AT THE HOTEL OKURA

1st Visit: "Can I possibly get cornflakes and coffee here?"
2nd Visit: "Cornflakes and coffee, please."
3rd Visit: "Don't these people eat anything but corn-flakes and coffee?"

MORNING STAFF MEETING

1st Visit: "It's a pleasure to be here in your country of hard-working people."
2nd Visit: "Your numbers are flat, but I'm certain you'll improve."
3rd Visit: "We cut distribution costs 50% in the last

quarter in the States, I don't see why we can't do the same goddam thing here."

CONFERENCE WITH ENGINEERING DEPTARTMENT
  1st Visit: "I am aware that licenses take time in Japan."
  2nd Visit: "I cleared it with the Ministry—they understand our problem."
  3rd Visit: "Thirteen goddam weeks and you *still* don't have approval?"

INVESTMENT DEPARTMENT GUIDANCE
  1st Visit: "Your expertise is world-renowned."
  2nd Visit: "I think 7.8% sounds kinda low to me."
  3rd Visit: "Production deposits in a wholesaler's bank? Are you out of your goddam minds?"

MARKETING STRATEGY
  1st Visit: "Let's explore going direct. Who's good at this?"
  2nd Visit: " 'Sam' Tanaka at Dentsu Advertising and I have struck a deal. We'll combine the shotgun and rifle approach."
  3rd Visit: "I didn't mean we'd buy the goddam newspapers and television stations. Get 'Sam' on the phone."

SECRETARIAL REFLECTIONS
  1st Visit: "She can actually say English words!"
  2nd Visit: "Is she married?"
  3rd Visit: "Why the hell am I going back to New York via Palau?"

PROFIT DECLARATIONS
  1st Visit: "We're deeply committed to the success of the Japan operation."

44

2nd Visit: "If there's money still in the pipeline, goose it along a little."

3rd Visit: "I'm addressing the New York Securities Dealers' Association the day after tomorrow. If the cash isn't reported by then, this place becomes a rice warehouse."

ENTERTAINMENT REALITIES

1st Visit: "What a cozy little club. Do you come here often?"

2nd Visit: "A bill for $210 seems a little steep, but I guess you know best."

3rd Visit: "Do you know what I can do for $550 in the States, you goddam idiot?"

The third visit is definitely a problem. But now that Bart has gone, Max is beginning to contemplate the fourth visit, since four, or as it's pronounced in Japan, *shi,* can mean "death."

It ain't easy out here in the field.

Public Public Health

THERE IS usually one in every family. Max Danger's eldest son was the one in his family.

Putting vegetation and/or formerly living creatures of this earth into one's month, chewing or grinding the pieces into small mushy bits, and then consigning the small mushy bits via the throat into the stomach, is a process we call "eating."

It is something that has been going on, it appears, for a very long time.

Mankind as a group has not been particularly fussy about *what* makes up the raw material in this routine—it is quite conceivable that *every* imaginable substance has at one time or another gone this route. (Let's stop and think about that. Hmm. Yes, that's right. *Every* imaginable substance.)

Mankind as divided into sub-categories has made refinements, however. Cultural, national, religious, or geographic factors enter the raw-material selection process. One seldom finds Amazonian Indians eating polar bear meat, or Eskimos munching mangos. (It is reported, nevertheless, that people in California *do* eat tofu.)

In Max's family, his son, as if embracing all mankind, has eaten everything in sight all his life. As an infant he ate part of his blanket and one leg of his teddy bear. As a young child he ate an entire banana—peel and all—and half a deck of playing cards. As a pre-teen he ate, on a dare, a tin of Ken-L-Ration mixed with Dog Yummies. In Japan he has eaten, believe this or not, a dish of *natto*.

None of this is to imply that he *digests* everything he eats—his stomach juices are the same as yours or mine. Pizza a la mode or the Kita Burgers across from the American School cause him the same problems as normal people. He has had, in one way or another, his share of the routine "digestive disorders" commonly afflicting all scavengers and birds of prey.

One Sunday evening, as the Dangers were shuffling their way through the Narita Airport routine (the forty-odd-mile trek from the airport into town), Max's eldest made a serious error in judgment. The family had been on a mini-holiday to Guam, courtesy of the Bird with the Proud Tail.

The recorded voice that greets arrivees over and over and over and over and over again with the message about the necessity of reporting upset stomachs to the quarantine officers got to the kid. He mentioned to the nice man with the spiffy uniform that his bowels of late had been less than tight. (He did not mention the details of his recent diet, which included things like bean soup and chocolate ice cream for breakfast, a peanut-butter-and-fish sandwich for lunch, and curried rice garnished with liverwurst sausage for dinner.) The nice man made a note or two, and sent the youngster on his way. No one in the family had been paying much attention.

On the following Wednesday morning—at 7:00 AM, precisely—the sound truck arrived outside the Homat Cornucopia apartment. The racket it made did not fade away. It sounded as if it were parked outside the building.

Well, as a matter of fact it *was* parked outside the building. It carried the two men in white coats who rang the doorbell at 7:01 AM.

Looking back on the episode later, it wasn't the spraying of the Danger apartment that caused the greatest discomfort. It wasn't the special attention paid to the eldest offspring's bedroom—the men in white coats sprayed under the bed, in the closet, and behind the bureau.

It wasn't even the tape put on the windows to keep whatever was being sprayed *inside* the apartment. It was actually rather interesting watching them do that.

It wasn't the fact that the eldest was escorted away for a full day of tests at a clinic over by TCAT (Tokyo City Air Terminal). The teachers at school were understanding, and a classmate brought that day's homework assignment to Homat Cornucopia later that evening.

What caused the greatest discomfort was the discovery of what the sound truck outside the building was doing. It was announcing at the top of its metallic lungs—to neighbors and passers-by alike—that the Dangers should be

47

shunned for the next twenty-four hours. Over and over and over and over again the recorded message reported the simple fact that someone in the house had diarrhea!

Max left for work through the service entrance.

Changes, I

MAX HAS a theory. The theory is that the "Westernization" of Japan is the root cause of all the misunderstanding of Japan by Westerners.

Max's first trip to Japan was not as a corporate businessman with a wife and family, but as an enthusiastic but marginally successful participant in the Tokyo Olympics. That was 1964, and things were different.

In 1964, Japan presented itself to the world as a modern nation, well on the road to recovery from the devastation of war and capable of organizing itself and others along lines compatible with the "big-time" standards of the West.

The Olympics were a showcase, and sure enough Japan performed with the fragile confidence of a debutante at her first ball. Most athletes were housed in Quonset huts in a place called Washington Heights—now a place of grass and trees called Yoyogi Park.

The housing remained from Occupation days and Max discovered, as he's certain a generation of military families before him discovered, that the semi-cylindrical metal structures were marvelous transmitters of sound. Banging track shoes against the wall could wake up close to a hundred people.

48

Food for the athletes from the various countries was provided in accordance with the Japanese understanding of "national dishes." The Americans, for example, were fed, morning, noon, and night, with concoctions like New England baked beans over spaghetti, and Ritz Crackers with Skippy peanut butter and applesauce. A particular treat was chocolate ice cream in grape Kool Aid. (The Germans were the most popular athletes at mealtimes—since they received beer morning, noon, and night. After a week, it was even possible to trade the Ritz Crackers for a beer—with ice cubes in it.)

Max and two French sprinters, in order to avoid the noise and the food, frequently wandered off at night and explored the general area between Yoyogi and Yotsuya. (Les femmes, with some knowledge of English, could occasionally be unearthed around Sophia University.)

During these forays, along the narrow lanes between traditional Japanese houses, Max came to know the Japan of yore. The area is now one of "mansions" and high-rise office buildings, but then it was not. And it was a pure sensual delight.

Very few street lights existed and illumination was provided either by the paper lanterns outside shops, or by the glow of light through the *shoji* of houses.

Most people walking around in the evening wore wooden *geta,* not sneakers, and the clip-clopping of their steps punctuated the calls of vendors issuing unamplified sounds from their actual throats and mouths.

From dusk until about 9:00 PM, the odors of cooking were everywhere. Passing houses, even on what are now main roads, afforded glimpses of life in a distinctly different culture. Once, standing in the shadows, Max and his friends watched a family silently and carefully dressing an old gentleman in a formal kimono: he had obviously died, and his relatives were getting him ready for visits from friends and neighbors.

Another misty night, Max and his friends ducked into a tiny soba shop. It contained a small but lively group of customers. The owner, thrilled about having foreign guests, broke out some very fine saké, which, as far as Max could tell, was "on the house."

A sad-looking young woman with burn scars on her face played the samisen. The owner regaled the group for what seemed like hours with stories in completely incomprehensible Japanese.

Because the mist had turned to a steady drizzle, the samisen lady and the owner's wife escorted Max and his friends with umbrellas—along the dark and mostly unpaved lanes—back to Yoyogi.

They stopped once, at a wooden house belonging to a friend of the samisen lady, and drank hot beer seated on the man's floor. He was wearing knee-length underpants and nothing else—save a towel wrapped around his head. He spoke German, which one of the Frenchmen understood, and explained that the samisen lady had been orphaned during the bombing of Tokyo.

But Tokyo in 1964 was changing. Various hospitality groups treated the athletes to tours of modern Tokyo. One stop was the new structure called Tokyo Tower. Another highlight was dinner in a revolving restaurant atop one of the tallest buildings in Japan—the now old wing of the New Otani Hotel.

Another highlight was a trip to Roppongi, where the Occupation bars and cathouses were still sprinkled among the original fish markets and Chinese restaurants. For a long time, the end of the Hibiya subway line had been in Roppongi, and it was a favorite place for a last drink before catching a cab to the countryside wilds beyond Daikanyama.

There was no doubt in the minds of the three thousand or so athletes participating in the 1964 Olympics that Japan was a foreign country, and was possessed of a rich but remarkably different culture than that of the West.

Of course, the Shuto expressways were under construction, hotels were being slapped up virtually overnight, and a dozen miles of roads were being paved each day. But the people, in their shyness with foreigners, their naive attempts to emulate Western customs, and their willingness to shed real clothing for Western costumes of suits, ties, and leather shoes, were very obviously coming from a different era. The Japanese were not misunderstood. "Westernization" was something that simply had to be done, and the Japanese were trying hard.

Well, "Westernization" is now here. Auto assembly lines outperform the best there is. Japanese bankers control vast chunks of the world's economy. Japanese corporations operate and dominate in all parts of the globe. And now, very few are less understood than the Japanese.

About two months ago, Max and his family stopped for coffee and cakes in the teahouse on the top floor of the Kawai music store in Omote Sando. A spiffy young gent in a tux escorted them to their seats. A young girl in her yellow waitress dress and starched white apron presented the menu. The girl, in command of rather good English, took their orders and crackled off to the patisserie, or wherever the cute little cakes originate. Brahms oozed from hidden speakers.

The people at the table next to the Dangers—a family group of exquisitely dressed Japanese—began to leave. They had obviously been spending a leisurely afternoon shopping and strolling. There were one Issey Miyake and two Hanae Mori bags among the clutter of their parcels. No doubt they were going off to a waiting Mercedes Benz.

Max, not really paying attention, did not realize until the beautiful Gloria tapped his arm that the apparent grandmother of the Japanese group had stopped at his side.

Max looked up. It had just been a little over twenty years, but then again it had been a lifetime.

"Olympia," said the old lady with the scarred face.

Before Max could reply, she turned and walked away.

The Return of Mr. Etiquette

MAX DANGER, as a service to the expat community in Japan, recently offered several examples of proper behavior in the sea of politeness surrounding us all. ("Never bow from the waist while standing with your back against *shoji*," etc.) The response to those bits of wisdom has been overwhelming. Recognizing his debt to loyal readership, and appreciating his own sensitivity to matters of a "civilized" nature, Max herewith replies to the following correspondents with "special" concerns.

Dear Mr. Etiquette: A young lady named Yuki phones me in the office every Tuesday and Thursday morning at 11:30 AM and asks when she'll see me again. She is apparently employed by "Araby Nights—Sex Meetings with Whiskey and Song." I don't know the lady, and I certainly don't know the establishment, unless it's connected with Kentucky Fried Chicken. What should I tell her? Signed: *Perplexed.*

Dear Perplexed: Some terrible person, some absolute

reprobate, has clearly made use of your business card in what can only be called a dastardly scheme to discredit you in the eyes of your friends, relatives, and business associates. Unless you can remember who you gave your cards to since your arrival in Japan—which usually becomes impossible by noon of the day of your arrival—you have no direct recourse. Instead, explain to Yuki that you will "do your best" to make it to her club next Thursday. Don't go, of course—people who phone the office can only mean trouble—but out of curiosity ask for a map. You never know what Head Office Visitors will want to do.

Dear Mr. Etiquette: Does "Come over to my house some Sunday" mean the same if suggested by a Japanese as it does in the States? Signed: *Haven't the Foggiest Idea What Is Expected.*

Dear Haven't the Foggiest: No. Or yes. It depends on the relationship. Common sense dictates behavior. In the States, one clears the nature of the invitation several days in advance. (We'll be in your neighborhood next weekend. We'll drop in with steaks—you find beer somewhere.") In Japan, "clearance" is a matter of months, not days. And bringing food is an insult. Japanese delicacies, supplemented by Chinese dishes and an occasional pizza, will be painstakingly prepared. This takes time. Also, conveniences for everyday living must be moved to the walls (or put in storage) to accommodate the space taken up by foreigners in the house. Parking, for a piece of machinery the size of a Nissan President, must be arranged in the neighborhood. Children, who left to their own devices would probably manage, must nevertheless be instructed on the nuances of Western etiquette. "Dropping in" on Sunday is O.K., but clear it way, way in advance. And don't eat for a day or two before.

53

Dear Mr. Etiquette: Was that the same old lady on the subway who pushed me out of the doorway, elbowed me violently in the ribs, and tripped me with her umbrella, but who earlier in the week conducted the tea ceremony class which my wife and I attended?" Signed: *What's Going On Around Here.*

Dear What's Going On: Yes.

Dear Mr. Etiquette: My teenage son, who now has blue-and-green hair, never returns from his classes at the American School until sometime after midnight. Is there something happening that I don't know about? Signed: *Indecisive In Azabu.*

Dear Indecisive: I can't imagine what you're talking about. The streets at 3:30 PM are full of kids eating junk food, looking at movie posters, and buying cute notebooks and magic pencils. Maybe your son is captain of the wrestling team. Or maybe he's the doorman with blue-and-green hair at "Araby Nights—Sex Meetings with Whiskey and Song." Ask Yuki.

Dear Mr. Etiquette: As a responsible corporate citizen, are there any charities, worthwhile causes, educational programs, and/or social movements around town that I have not heard about? Signed: *The Problem Is Appropriation.*

Dear Problem: No.

Dear Mr. Etiquette: When confronted at a funeral with a pot of burning charcoal, a pile of incense, and a great deal of genuine feeling for a recently departed Japanese colleague, what does one do? Signed: *Spiritual But Not Into Fake Displays.*

Dear Spiritual But Not Into Fake: What *you* know will send the departed's soul straight to heaven—the Twenty-third Psalm and a tender homily by Reverend Smith—doesn't work here. Hum and say those things quietly to yourself. In the meantime, handle the incense routine precisely as the guy in front of you handles it. (He's only watching the guy in front of him.)

Dear Mr. Etiquette: My wife and I have been invited to 57 cocktail parties in the last 30 days. Are there standards for turning down these things? Signed: *On The Fence.*

Dear On The Fence: Not if you wish to risk the real possibility of becoming a social outcast. Accept them all, but develop a repertoire of stories about sick children, Head Office Visitors, bullet wounds, community charity endeavors, business trips to Korea, and get-togethers with the Imperlal Family to cover yourself in the event of your non-appearance. As a point of interest, menstrual cramps and early appointments the next day tend *not* to work in this community. Arriving late from Jakarta does.

Dear Mr. Etiquette: My husband says *"hai"* when he means "yes," *"dozo"* when he means "please," and *"so desu ka"* when he means "no shit." Those are the *only* Japanese words he knows, but he uses them all the time, and quite frankly it's driving me up the wall. Signed: *Up The Wall.*

Dear Up The Wall: Doesn't he know *"domo"?*

Dear Mr. Etiquette: The superintendent of our building has: a) let me into the apartment when I've forgotten my key, b) started my car when the battery was dead, and c) collected my mail and newspapers when I've been out of town. Since tipping in Japan is not an accepted practice, what do I do for him? Signed: *Grateful But Confused.*

Dear Grateful But: Tipping in Japan is *not,* repeat *not,* an acceptable practice. Don't contemplate it. It will ruin it for all of as. However, a fifth of Suntory whiskey at New Year's will get your leaky faucets fixed.

Dear Mr. Etiquette: When all is said and done, aren't the Japanese exactly like us? Signed: *Wondering*.

Dear Wondering: No.

Dear Mr. Etiquette: When all is said and done, aren't the Japanese exactly like us? Signed: *Not Certain*.

Dear Not Certain: Yes.

Gloria's Adventure

GLORIA DANGER, mother of three and PTA member at three different schools, had made the "Tokyo adjustment" remarkably well. In fact, it could be argued that the cultural intercourse she experienced with those in her host country was broader, and in many ways more intense, than that experienced by her husband.

Max, of course, operated primarily in the world of business. Meetings, breakfasts, meetings, lunches, meetings, dinners, meetings, trips to Osaka, meetings, golf, meetings, business entertainment, and meetings certainly develop bicultural breadth. And mistakenly maneuvering a Valued Client into a face-losing business situation—a far worse matter than throwing up on his shoes outside an Akasaka nightspot—approaches the depths of bicultural intensity.

But at least in the business world there are rules, and the rules are not difficult to discern. Not only is behavior controlled—no one sings *karaoke* at lunch or discusses business at dinner—but relationships are maintained within definite and specific guidelines. Section chiefs and corporate vice presidents do not go backpacking together in the hills of Nagano. It's against "the rule." Bicultural encroachment is automatically avoided by the accepted standard operating practices of business.

The beautiful Gloria's world, however, is different. The rules are not easily discernible. What is the protocol for dealing with building superintendents, school bus drivers, the butcher, the ikebana teacher, the lady upstairs, the part-time job agency, the language instructor, the English student, the policemen in the police box, the doctor, his nurse, the amorous joint-venture partner, the tennis pro, the man who picks up the laundry, the three ladies in the bridge group who bid in Japanese, the vegetable vendor, the dressmaker, her husband's secretary, and the landlord's wife? Trial and error develops understanding, and that is broadening. Trial and error can also lead to misunderstanding, and the consequences can be intense.

The beautiful Gloria hired Ikeda-san as a once-a-week cleaning lady early in the Tokyo assignment. Ikeda-san came highly recommended by the previous tenants in the Homat Cornucopia apartment. "She talks a lot, and we're not always certain what she's saying," reported the tenants, "but at least what she says is all in English."

Ikeda-san's "day" was Tuesday. She would arrive carrying a Gucci bag and dressed to kill at 9:30 AM, and stay until 6:30 or 7:00 in the evening. She wore a wig, which she'd doff like a hat upon entering the front door, and would repair immediately to the guest bathroom to don her working clothes. Her working clothes consisted of a Tokyo American Club warm-up jacket and sweat pants, which another client had given her, and a Yomiuri Giants baseball cap which covered her short gray hair.

57

On the second Tuesday of her employment with the Dangers, Ikeda-san confided to Gloria, during a mid-morning tea break, that the other *gaijin* she worked for had terribly messy houses. She cited examples—and Gloria knew three of the four examples cited. Mondays thereafter became the days Gloria would clean the house in preparation for Ikeda-san's Tuesdays.

Wednesdays also became days of activity indirectly involving Ikeda-san. For it was then Gloria would walk around searching for things Ikeda-san had "put in order." In the bathrooms, for example, Ikeda-san had definite ideas about where things should go. All the items normally cluttering the sink area—toothbrushes, toothpaste, razors, eyelash curlers, combs, powder, deodorant, contact lens equipment, aspirin bottles—would be put on the ledge next to the bathtub. Items normally in *that* location—shampoo, hair conditioners, rinses, brushes—would be put in the cupboard under the sink. This practice led to the unfortunate but celebrated incident wherein Max one morning washed his hair with toilet-bowl cleaner.

But Ikeda-san was a good-hearted soul. It was not many months before Gloria and Ikeda-san became buddies. It may have been the special soup concoction Ikeda-san brought to the house when the youngest Danger was sick in bed; it may have been the handmade macramé flowerpot holders presented to Gloria on her birthday; or it may have been Ikeda-san's insistence upon staying late one night and helping to clean up after a dinner party. Whatever it was, Ikeda-san was gradually becoming, at least on Tuesdays, one of the family.

It made Gloria's discovery that Ikeda-san's son (a 47-year-old marginally employed laborer) was regularly beating and generally abusing his mother, all the more difficult to deal with.

Gloria had occasionally noticed that Ikeda-san's movements were decidedly restricted—it would sometimes take several moments for her to get to her feet if she had been kneeling. "Arthur-itis," Ikeda-san would joke. The bruise on the side of her face one morning was explained away as being the result of an accident "on the subway." But the day Ikeda-san showed up with a split lip and cracked tooth in her dentures was too much to ignore.

"He is very frustrated, and drinks too much," Ikeda-san explained.

("*I'm* very frustrated and drink too much," Max reported that evening during the dinner discussion on the subject, "but I don't go around slugging my relatives."

Gloria, nevertheless, insisted that something be done about the problem.

"I agree," said Max, "but I don't think you are the one to do it.")

"You cannot talk to him," Ikeda-san stated on the following Tuesday. "He doesn't come home always, and he doesn't speak English."

Ikeda-san had no other relatives, save an elder cousin in Yamagata. The cousin lived with old neighbors on a farm, and those people were barely able to manage for themselves. Ikeda-san, in fact, was ashamed that *she* was not able to help them more.

Things seemed to stabilize for several weeks. Gloria did not raise the subject, and Ikeda-san appeared to be un-battered. She brought some delicately handmade tree ornaments to the Danger household on the Tuesday before Christmas.

When Ikeda-san arrived on the Tuesday after New Year's with a black eye, Gloria brought the cleaning process to a screeching halt. Her first move was to call the other *gaijin* for whom Ikeda-san worked. No one had noticed anything

59

unusual about Ikeda-san's situation and, for whatever it's worth, no one thought anything could be done about it. Gloria called Max's secretary. Akimbo-san thought the matter should be solved "within the family" and that "foreigners cannot involve with" Japanese family matters.

After a great deal of hesitance and reluctance on Ikeda-san's part, she agreed to show Gloria where she lived. The wig was slapped back on and Gloria helped stuff the American Club warm-up suit into the Gucci bag.

The train ride to the area near the new sumo stadium took almost an hour. Ikeda-san's periodic bouts of sobbing certainly intrigued the passengers observing the old Japanese lady and her tall blonde companion. One wonders what type of dinner conversation *that* encounter produced later in the evening.

Gloria and Ikeda-san sat in Ikeda-san's two-room apartment from noon until 6:00 PM. They drank green tea and reviewed the contents of Ikeda-san's wardrobe. She had six "Western" outfits, all fashionably conceived, and their coordination allowed her to go to each client's house for six months without appearing in the exact same ensemble twice. Ikeda-san subscribed to *Elle* magazine.

Ikeda-san showed Gloria her son's room—he had the larger of the two rooms. None of his clothes were in order; in fact, most of his possessions were piled randomly about the floor. It appeared that he had construction uniforms from at least three or four employers. One poster, a bikini-clad girl on a Kawasaki motorcycle, decorated his walls. A half-consumed bottle of saké stood next to his futon.

The son did not appear, and Gloria had to leave at 6:00. She was not sure *what* she would have done had he appeared. It was clear, however, that something must be done—Ikeda-san seemed even more vulnerable in her own surroundings than in Homat Cornucopia.

Gloria stopped at the police box near Ikeda-san's apartment. Communication was not easy; in fact, the officers had to call in a young policeman from "bicycle duty" in the neighborhood for translations. The explanation of the situation, with corrections, amplifications, reiterations, and requested form-completions, took an hour. The raging heat from the space heater in the box seemed to bother Gloria more than the warmly dressed policemen. Gloria emerged from the ordeal in a sweat, but with a promise that officials would keep an eye on the situation. The Ikedas were known to the police.

Gloria never saw Ikeda-san again. Later, at a cocktail party, Gloria got to talking with another of Ikeda-san's clients. (She had a messy house.) Ikeda-san was still cleaning that house, and the client had not noticed anything unusual about the situation. ("She did fall recently and broke her wrist, however.")

Gloria did speak to Ikeda-san one day on the phone. It was not an agreeable conversation.

"You don't understand," reported Ikeda-san. "Families are important in Japan. And my son," reported the old lady with six Western outfits, "is the only family I have."

Drinks After Work

THERE ARE basic bits of information about doing business in Japan which by now are familiar to everyone contemplating the local market.

If, for example, the Japanese "yes" is still being mistaken for the English-language "yes," then whoever is making the mistake should not be allowed out of the Hotel Okura. (By the same token, if there's a soul alive who does not recognize the significance of introducing new ideas at the appropriate level for "committee review," then that soul has clearly been spending the last decade marooned on a desert isle somewhere.)

Another bit of information about doing business in Japan has to do with "drinks after work." Who doesn't know that the rigid hierarchy within each office restricts the flow of valuable and informative "communication," and that the only way to transcend the barriers inherent in the system is for people of various levels within the hierarchy to get plastered together after work? These things are basic. (An interesting indication of the Japanese attitude toward accountability after drinking is the fact that until a relatively few years ago, intoxication was a *defense* in the event of bodily injury or property damage resulting from automobile accidents.)

"Drinks after work," however, requires the active participation of those within the hierarchy—including foreign management. Understanding the Japanese "yes," or knowing how to introduce new ideas, are mere textbook tactics. Drinking liters of beer, forcing down glass after glass of Scotch and water, and eating chicken on a stick are part of the real world in Japan.

Everyone knows it's important, but proper behavior during these sessions is not described in any text. One must survive and play the events during "drinks after work" as they develop. And that can bring one to a level of cultural and social involvement touching upon core sensibilities. Screwing-up can be politically fatal.

Max Danger suggests that there are basic rules which must

be followed in virtually all situations. Variance will put one at risk, and this author accepts no responsibility for deviance from the following basic precepts.

Never strike a business colleague over the head with a bottle of beer during a "drinks after work" session. Conversation may reach the intense phase, and ideas may be presented which are at odds with carefully developed Head Office programs, but physical mayhem is surprisingly counterproductive. Arm-wrestling over whether or not to establish an export division is also not done. The ground rules are Japanese, and open confrontation on the physical plane is not accepted. (However, pouring beer into the colleague's glass of scotch and water is an effective alternative to a punch in the nose.)

Never laugh out loud when a business colleague (or especially a customer) introduces a pretty young girl as his "administrative assistant." Listen, we're dealing in a different culture here. If a colleague feels that the "drinks after work" session should involve careful note-taking by a twenty-seven-year-old with great legs, who are we to question the maneuver? After all, hierarchical barriers are being transcended, and the legs part may be coincidental. As an aside, it's probably not a good idea to take seriously the random and accidental physical encounters—in the bumping, leaning, and rubbing category—with the administrative assistant over the course of the evening. Remember, notes are being taken.

Never assume that "drinks after work" begins with drinks. Max has eaten most of a pizza, spaghetti with squid, mysterious meat balls, and a whole plate of sweet-and-sour something before the first drinks arrived. Things don't get serious until the plastic glass-like container with ice cubes and the black bottle of whiskey appears. (Watch out for the choco-sticks. Chocolate and whiskey cloud perspective.)

Never plan on the evening being over just because you're standing with eleven people on the sidewalk outside the first "drinks after work" establishment. One person, invariably, will live three hours from Tokyo and must catch a train somewhere. Everyone else will want to go to a second establishment. It may take fifteen or twenty minutes of standing on the sidewalk and shuffling back and forth before a decision is made, but once made, you must attend the second party. After all, everyone else lives two hours away, and you're within a half-hour of Azabu.

Never take the remark that you're a nice guy at face value— it may be stated as a surprising and recently discovered observation in direct contrast with your perceived standard operating procedure in the office. Max once believed he had conquered the hostility he felt emanating from the company union representative. Max was told he was a "nice guy" during one of the "drinks after work" sessions. It had to do with his willingness to sing "My Way" at a sing-along bar. It meant that the union maintained its previous strong position in subsequent negotiations, but now a "nice guy" was unaccountably standing in the way of progress and the fortunes of the laboring class. This only complicated the issue.

Never think that throwing up on the sidewalk outside the last "drinks after work" place changes basic attitudes within the staff. To be around when these things happen is important— whether you are the throwee or thrower—but specific policy implementation will not be immediately affected. One must develop the reputation of handling these things with aplomb over a period of time before substantive results in management effectiveness can be ascertained. It helps if one learns to treat these events not unlike one would treat hiccups in the West.

Never refuse the first taxi that the "drinks after work" staff finds for you. If you do, you'll lose face in the "importance game" we're all playing. Not only that, you may have to walk home from Akasaka.

Never tell your wife you had a "marvelous time" with the crew after work. In the first place, it probably won't be true. In the second place, unless you clobbered a guy over the head with a beer bottle, you'll probably be invited back. Either way, you lose. You may as well keep peace in the family.

It ain't easy out here in the field.

What If?

The "what if" approach to problem analysis is a practical and frequently effective technique in the critical process. ("What if we transfer Employee A to Location B? Will that affect Situation C?")

The "what if" approach to analyzing circumstances *retrospectively* develops insight. "What if William the Conqueror hadn't, and was instead repulsed at Hastings? We would still be saying things like:

Hwæt wē Gār-Dena   in geār-dagum
þēod-cyninga   þrym gefrūnon,
hū ðā æþelingas   ellen fremedon.

And the "what if" approach *applied as a premise to an existing situation* not only develops perspective but creates a scenario in which real issues are easily separated from the smoke.

The exercise today, is to consider Dr. Danger's approach to understanding the U.S./Japan trade problem. What if the balance of trade deficit were the other way around? What if U.S. products were flooding the Japanese market? What if Reagan, hat in hand, had to visit Takeshita with promises that he, too, had no way of delivering?

First of all, consider this market flooded with U.S. goods. Max once reported that the replacement of all Hondas and Toyotas with full-sized Fords and Chevrolets would reduce the Shuto expressways to one lane, diminish parking space in Tokyo by 27.5%, and force all foreigners into hiding during periods of recall. ("All General Motors cars produced this decade must be returned to the dealer as the front wheels have a tendency to fall off at low speeds.")

Uncle Ben's Quick Rice would not have the gelatinous consistency to keep curry from soaking through to the *bottom* of the plate. Real hot dogs, made from ill-defined scraps of pork and beef, would replace the whale-flesh things sold at Japanese baseball games.

And American clothing, designed to fit the 0.07% of the population in Japan over six feet tall, could actually be purchased off the rack by *gaijin*. (Everyone else would have to roll up pant legs and sleeves, stuff newspapers in shoes, and secure the tops of pantyhose over the breast.) Speaking of breasts, imagine the availability here of nothing but American bras. The mind boggles.

The political issues, however, are more intriguing. What if Diet members, after frequent and extensive fact-finding junkets to Washington, returned to their home constituencies convinced that only the economic crutch of protectionism could save Japan? How would the Japanese Chamber of Commerce in America react?

Worse yet, what if the Japanese constituency developed a liking for eating individual grains of American rice with *hashi* (chopsticks)? Or developed a special feeling for the roominess afforded by American bras? What if a complex sub-industry existed to fix the front wheels falling off slow moving automobiles?

More significantly—and Max knows this is difficult to imagine—what if the Japanese consumer had grown accustomed to the competitive price levels resulting from unrestricted free trade? What if things in Japan didn't cost the moon? There could be divisions in the body politic.

Meanwhile, in America, with whom would the President meet to discuss the issue of voluntary export controls? ("Look, Lee, arrange it within your company to reduce auto production by 30%.") How would the unions respond? ("I've told you guys in the shop before, unemployment over in Maebashi is approaching 9%.")

How would anyone in America be nominated for public office? ("If elected, I pledge to cut back the bread-and-butter profits we enjoy as a result of our successful participation in international capitalism. From now on, we Americans must purchase computer chips from people who don't even speak English.")

What if the situation were such that American financial institutions were urged to purchase Japanese treasury notes? ("Japanese treasury notes? Get serious man—the yen's weakening daily and I've got a portfolio to manage.") And what if someone on Wall Street went public with a scheme for the adjustment of the yen/dollar exchange rate in Japan's favor? He'd finish his career teaching art history in the Midwest.

Then there are the Sacred Cows—all countries have them. Imagine telling the American farmers to stop producing corn. ("We are instead opening our markets to *yaki-imo* [roasted sweet potatoes]—complete with the wandering men and their little trucks.") And as for Americans at leisure: picture a lovely Sunday afternoon at the baseball park, whaleburger and cup-saké in hand, watching Ryne Sandberg *ping* one out of Wrigley Field with a section of aluminum pipe.

Ah yes, the issues are complicated. There are solutions, though. One quick way to resolve the current balance of trade problem is to swap countries. With existing real estate prices in Japan being what they are, the exchange of Honshu for most of North America would work in America's favor. Let the Japanese worry about Nicaragua and the Middle East. (They can have Yokota and Zama for military bases, but they'd better not try bringing ships armed with unmentionables into our ports.)

Another solution would be for the good citizens of the United States to wait for a few years, and then when every third bank, store, and manufacturing company in America is Japanese, nationalize them. That kind of thing has happened throughout history, and it can happen again.

Max, meanwhile, takes the simple view. Americans are now getting automobiles, TV sets, computers, wrist watches, and hundreds of other real goods from Japan. In return, Americans are giving the Japanese *pieces of paper!* And the pieces of paper are returning to the U.S. anyway in the form of Japanese investment. What if the Americans are really winning the trade battle?

The Little Pleasures Report

THERE ARE great pleasures in life, and there are little ones. The great pleasures are obvious: you discover that you've been subtracting wrong all these years and that in fact there is an extra ¥11,000,000 in your bank account; the Ministry grants a carte-blanche business license and your employers reward you with a knighthood; or your children receive academic scholarships to the expensive colleges of their choice. These marvelous things require no comment.

It is the little pleasures catalogue which must be maintained and updated. The complexities involved with living as often non-speaking and usually non-reading foreigners in a highly structured society elevate these little pleasures to plateaus unimaginable by those back home. And the sum of the little pleasures can equal the total of the great.

Recognizing something familiar—anything familiar—when lost. One must be very careful around here. There is a terrible sameness about intersections in Japan. All the big ones look alike: a bank on two of the four corners, an appliance store with an up-and-down sign on the third, and on the fourth corner a homemade office building designed by the escaped inmate of a lunatic asylum who went about town posing as an architect until he was finally captured and returned to his cell with walls of padding. And the small intersections are completely identical, save for the alarming inconsistency in the aiming of the round traffic mirrors upon which we rely to prevent serious injury to life and limb.

As an example of the difficulties represented by the above, Max has made seven round trips between Azabu and St. Mary's International School. Initially unaware that one of the Shuto expressways coursed somewhere near wherever St. Mary's School is, Max made the trips on "surface routes." (Ha. That's a good one.) Max has gotten lost, either going or coming, each of the seven times—the last time a spectacular adventure involving the greater Yokohama suburbs and the foothills of Mt. Fuji. The little pleasure involved with spotting the "to Narita" sign was exquisite. One at least and at last knew one was not enroute to Osaka.

The Sudden National Holiday phenomenon. Obviously national holidays are planned in advance—the people who make calendars in Japan have puzzled this all out. But Max's desk diary and pocket date book, made elsewhere, are quite naturally silent on the subject. (One clue as to when these holidays are coming is to look for the days when all your scheduled business appointments are with other foreigners. Those will probably be Japanese holidays.) In any event, the unexpected little pleasure of calling off all meetings and sleeping late is wonderful.

The days when traffic mysteriously vanishes. We all know that traffic is unusually heavy on the last day of the month, on days divisible by five, on paydays, at the end of each calendar quarter, on Fridays, the day after a holiday, when oysters are in season, and if the moon is full. But for some reason, there are also days, two or three times a month, when traffic is extremely light. (The first time this happened, Max mistakenly thought a Sudden National Holiday had

70

struck.) The little pleasure of zipping along to work in half the time is significant. Maybe it's just that there are only two or three days a month which are *not* divisible by five, payday, the end of the quarters, etc., etc.

Discovering a compatible neighborhood joint. The village pub and corner saloon are fabled institutions, as well they should be. Individuals require havens of tranquility in order to escape from the commotion and bustle of life, to engage in inconsequential conversation, or to just stare silently into space. (Sitting at home in a closet is not quite the same. And it might be considered perverse.)

One blowing and rainy evening, while wandering around Minato Ward in a semi-lost condition, Max stumbled upon a place down what turned out to be a dead-end street. Cold and wet, Max entered. A dozen or so "locals" were cozily ensconced about the place—some at a bar, some at four small tables, and some seated in a slightly elevated tatami room at the rear. They were variously and randomly drinking beer, whiskey, tea, or soft drinks, and eating noodles, dried fish, or chicken on a stick. A large-screen TV behind the bar was showing a video-taped U.S. baseball game, on this early December evening, with the volume turned down.

Of course, all sound in the place ceased as Max entered, and, of course, all eyes turned to the intruder. Max was about to form the Japanese words for "Where the hell am I, and how do I get home?" when the joint's owner, whose name turned out to be Suzuki, stated in perfect English: "Maybe you can settle an argument for us. Where did Elston Howard play before he went to the Yankees?"

So Max now has his place, and going there two or three times a month is a superb little pleasure. The TV set plays nothing but old baseball games, the "regulars" are knowledgeable fans, one can either sit silently or chat comforta-

71

bly, Suzuki-san's red-armed wife turns out great yakitori, and Suzuki-san himself has one of the world's largest collections of uncensored back-issue *Playboy* magazines. (And the stories, Max notices the second time around, are actually rather good.)

Getting the smoke in the Homat Cornucopia fireplace to go up the chimney. Not much more can be said about this little pleasure, except that it's only happened once this last winter. Max's living room walls, lampshades, and family members are gradually turning an unpleasant beige-grey.

The joy of raising bilingual children. The Danger offspring negotiate all matters Japanese for the Danger parents. The little pleasure of observing these talents develop is very rewarding—particularly considering that Max's foreign language skills at his children's age were limited to verbalizing Anglo-Saxon expletives.

Cementing Japanese friendships. Hey, we all have Japanese friends, right? Max frequently finds himself doing what many do—referring to acquaintances as "friends." (One does this sort of thing all over the world all of the time.) But the characteristics of real friendship can only be developed by time and effort, by struggling through the good times and bad, and by being "there" whatever the consequences when issues become basic. Friendship implies openness and complete trust. Honest communication is a must. These characteristics are not easily developed even by people growing up as next-door neighbors. Given the difficulties inherent in bicultural intercourse—particularly bicultural intercourse of parties as wildly dissimilar as Japanese and Westerners—the barriers to success are awesome. There is a lot behind all the things we folks do.

Max suspected his first Japanese friendship was forming during his endless discussions with Serious Hirose of his office over the construction details of their jointly owned ski house in Hakuba. At least the communication barrier was being breached. and honesty was being established. "You may be right," stated Serious Hirose after a particularly animated exchange, "but you still shithead." It was a neat little pleasure.

Changes II

ON THE DAY of the Great Kanto Earthquake, September 1, 1923, Masahiro Hata's father had been at his post, making and repairing *geta,* for exactly sixty years. During that period of time, Hata-san's father had watched his neighborhood develop from a waste of swampland to the modern business center of Japan.

He watched the ambitious landfill project conducted by the Mitsubishi Group under the encouragement of the Meiji government. Dirt, stones, and logs were dragged in from the hills of Saitama by round-backed laborers—men and women—pulling handcarts over muddy trails.

He watched the fabulous, two-storied red-brick structures being built along the new stone road, resembling an elevated path through rice fields, which ran parallel to the Emperor's inner moat. He, along with other craftsmen in the immediate vicinity, worried about rumors that the outer moat, over by Nihonbashi, was being permanently closed. Their status as master craftsmen depended to a great extent on their location within that moat and close to the palace. But the increase of commercial activity around what is now Marunouchi gave Masahiro Hata's father and his friends encouragement.

His father, Masahiro Hata's grandfather, had chosen to stay near the palace in Edo days and not join the masses of merchants and laborers over by the Sumida River. To be chosen to repair the footwear of brave samurai—a barracks of sorts existed where the Palace Hotel, Palace Building, AIU, and Nihon Kokan's offices now stand—was indeed an honor. A samurai sword, today a treasured possession, somehow made it into the Hata family at about that time.

Masahiro Hata's father also watched the construction of Tokyo Station. At the time of its completion, it was the most spectacular modern building in all of Asia. It also meant undreamed of prosperity for the maker and repairer of *geta*. People would walk from as far as Saitama to visit the former dirt, stones, and logs, plus marvel at the magnificent new Western structure. Masahiro Hata's father employed as many as seven family members in the business, including the young Masahiro Hata, just to keep up with the demand.

Craftsmen, always a hardy lot, were particularly tough in those days. Once, while cutting wood for his *geta,* Masahiro Hata's father sliced off his thumb. Rather than leave his post, he packed clay around the stump until it hardened and stopped the bleeding. He never saw a doctor as long as he lived.

Several problems faced the Hata family, however. The most severe problem, in the years before 1923, was one of housing. The Hata's lived where they worked. Originally, back in the swampland days, their location was on a dry clump of slightly elevated land next to the muddy road running between the samurai barracks and the Sumida. (That road is today the six-lane street going from the palace out toward the Tokyo City Air Terminal.) Their operation, including the space required to store their lumber, was in the way of progress. Being within the outer moat, but outside the inner moat, made them ineligible for the modest land reforms promulgated by the Taisho government. The Hatas became squatters, and unwelcomed ones at that.

Another problem, oddly enough, had deeper significance. Dutch, French, and English engineers, employed to work on Tokyo Station, went to Masahiro Hata's father to have their leather boots repaired. Working with leather was something the Hatas did not do. Cultural and social barriers separated people who handled the flesh and skin of four-legged mammals. The Hatas were not of that caste.

Nevertheless, business was business, and the times were changing. After what must have been a number of interesting philosophical discussions within the family, Masahiro Hata's father undertook the work. He would deliver the repaired boots of foreigners each evening after dark.

The Great Kanto Earthquake devastated the Hata family business. Their shop, their lumber, and their wood-and-paper house was destroyed by fire. Masahiro Hata's father died the next day, from causes never really explained. Masahiro Hata, a young lad of 24, struck out on his own.

For a while he ran a shoe repair shop in Tsukishima, near the old "downtown" section of Tokyo. He never again touched *geta*. By 1940 he was able to support, in the shop, a wife and two daughters. In fact, in 1940, he claimed he repaired over 6,500 pairs of shoes in one year. That's about eighteen pairs per day.

Again, fire changed the family fortunes. The Tsukishima location was destroyed in the bombing of Tokyo in 1945. Masahiro Hata was then 46. Repatriated from a prison camp in Malaysia, he went back to work. This time, he opened a shoe repair business within several meters of his grandfather and father's original location.

Masahiro Hata bought a new, not used, metal folding chair and set himself up on the southeast corner of what is now the Tokio Marine Insurance Company building in Marunouchi. He fixed the shoes of passers-by until the day he died, at age 88, on May 26, 1987.

Max Danger knew Masahiro Hata, without knowing his name, for a couple years. Shoes, purchased during home-leave trips to the States each July or August, would inevitably wear out sometime during the following spring. Max, stumbling back from lunch at the Tokyo Kaikan, would occasionally stop and sit in that same chair while Hata-san labored over the odd sole or heel. After a while, Max would stop just for a shine. Hata-san knew some English, and had definite opinions about the state of the world economy. No doubt he picked up nuggets of information from other customers passing his way.

On May 25, 1987, Max dropped off at Hata-san's "chair" a pair of black-tassled Florsheim dress shoes, purchased the previous summer in the States for $129.50. They needed new soles and heels, but Max could not wait for their repair. He indicated he'd be back the next day. Hata-san, however, died the next day.

About a month later, after Max had given up all hope for the return of Hata-san and the reappearance of his black Florsheims, another shoe repair person on the same corner—this time a woman—jumped up and grabbed Max's arm as he passed on his way back to the office. She indicated to Max that she wanted his address and/or phone number. He gave her his office address.

Three days later, Mrs. Yuko Toda (née Hata) appeared at his office. A modestly dressed woman, shorter than average, but with a broad, pleasant face, she explained that she was Masahiro Hata's daughter. Her son, an English-speaking manager of a shoe store in the Marunouchi Building—across the street from the former Hata empire—did the translations.

They understood that Max had left shoes for repair at Masahiro Hata's "chair." They confessed that the shoes, in the confusion surrounding Hata-san's death, had disappeared. (The shoes in his possession at the time included those belonging to another man and to three women.) What had happened to those shoes was anybody's guess. "The government," reported Mrs. Toda (née Hata), "has probably taken them."

Three alternatives were offered to Max. The first was a simple payment of the purchase price of the shoes as if they had been new. Mrs. Toda (née Hata) maintained that she would be able to come up with the money within a month.

The second alternative was for Max to select shoes from the store in the Marunouchi Building where her son Masahiro Hata's grandson—worked, and he would arrange to have the cost of those shoes deducted from his paycheck.

The third alternative, offered almost as an afterthought, and with shamefaced reluctance, was Max's choice.

"They were made a long time ago," said Mrs. Toda (née Hata), "and they have some funny carvings on them. But," she added, "they're almost as good as new."

Max chose the wooden *geta* made by Masahiro Hata's father. Somehow they had survived all the fires and family upheavals.

The carvings depict the samurai barracks, with the Imperial Palace in the background, across the rice-field road that is now Hibiya Avenue. And Max won't part with them for all the shoes in Boston.

Author's Note: A sincere thank you is accorded to Mrs. Y. Toda of Tsukiji, who patiently spent hours recounting details of her grandfather's life, as she remembered them from family lore. During the conversation at her house, she proudly displayed the only photograph of her grandfather at his post. Taken around 1880, by a "European," it shows the proud craftsman standing in what appears to be a field. His left thumb is missing.

The Face-Value Hazard

OF COURSE you've wondered why. Many people have wondered why. It would be unnatural *not* to wonder why. But the questions are not always asked.

Living in a different culture broadens one. That's a given. Living in a different culture exposes one to thoughts, ideas, points of view, art forms, social activities, and behavioral patterns undreamed of at home. It's an educational experience. "You can sure learn a lot," as Homer correctly observed, "once you leave Ithaca."

But there is a built-in problem involved with bicultural exposure. It's known as the "Face-Value Hazard." We must continue the struggle to overcome it.

Accepting things at face value is a practical method employed by those abroad to prevent being overwhelmed by the mass of cultural miscellany in which they are suddenly immersed. Accepting things at face value helps preserve sanity by allowing for a screening process whereby the brain has a justified rationale for not mastering all the ramifications of an alien cultural expression. "What the hell, they're *always* dressing up as dragons and marching down Hibiya Dori. Spare me the details."

But, you see, accepting things at face value can become a habit. It often is employed long after the brain has adjusted to the volume of new cultural information bombarding it. In fact, the learning experience can come to a screeching halt after the essentials have been mastered. And the Face-Value Hazard is to blame.

To avoid this common pitfall—to prevent learning-curve dystrophy—one must continually ask why. It's healthy.

Why do you suppose, when you stop and think about it, all females in Japan under the age of twenty-two say "goodbye" to each other in the following fashion: "Bye-bye," "bye-bye." And why are hands waved back and forth against an imaginary plane during this exercise as the train pulls out of the station through the town and over the first mountain? Is this a Zen phenomenon?

Why are so many females under the age of seventeen singing cute songs in cute voices wearing cute dresses with cute arrangements and cute gestures in front of millions on TV instead of being on a platform somewhere saying, "Bye-bye," "bye-bye," "bye-bye," "bye-bye," "bye-bye," "bye-bye," 'bye-bye," "bye-bye," "bye-bye," as the train pulls into the next prefecture?

Why does the Shinkansen, speaking of trains, ban smoking in the *front half* of the Green (First-Class) Cars? For all the good it does, they may as well ban smoking in every other seat. The air will turn blue in a half-hour anyway.

Why is it not possible to order a ham-and-cheese sandwich in the several million places selling ham sandwiches and cheese sandwiches? Putting two things together apparently blows minds. But why?

Why, speaking of restaurants, are waiters unable to remember who ordered what? Max orders things like beef tartar and straight bourbon. The beautiful Gloria likes quiche and iced tea. Do you think these items are ever delivered without the inevitable question? (Or at the same time?)

Why are Japanese men making the male cosmetics industry rich beyond all normal expectations? What are they doing with the stuff once it's purchased? Saving it? And why not take a flyer with a bow tie now and then? Or suspenders? Even striped shirts could be worked in every couple of days.

Why does no one seem to know, or care, what national holiday we are experiencing every few weeks? Are these things sprung by surprise on the general populace?

Why would any otherwise intelligent young man consider joining the national police force and dedicating his life to wearing twentieth-century samurai gear while standing on busy street corners watching himself interrupt the orderly flow of traffic? Life inside those grey buses can't be *that* good.

Why do politicians invariably campaign in white gloves? Gloves serve the dual purpose of providing warmth and protecting against contamination from filth. It's usually warm at election time. Is not the imagery unfortunate?

Why must one guess, assuming one cares, *what* the commercials on TV are selling? A man in white trousers on a chair at the beach with a watch on his wrist and a glass in his hand as the sun goes down (and the tide comes in) listening to Beethoven with stereo headphones accompanied by a dog at his side and a lovely lady in a flowing dress will actually be flogging automobile tires or instant noodles.

(Or tennis rackets.) Have we missed something here? (At least they've more or less removed the lion that walks down the stairs of someone's house and sniffs a piano bench in the burglar-alarm commercial.)

Why, speaking of flogging things, are the voices of U.S. movie stars brought to Japan for commercials dubbed in English? Jet-lag is tough, but can't James Coburn remember "Speak Lark" in his native tongue?

Why can't people around here go home from work until after dark? To put it another way, why are two hours of daylight gone by the time we wake up in the morning?

Why does anyone bother thinking in terms of a "rainy season" with fixed dates for beginning and end. "Rainy season" last year was when the reservoirs went dry. This year it's rained everyday—regardless of the season.

Why televised baseball games begin in the third inning and end at the bottom of the seventh inning has something to do with scheduled programing commitments, and that's understandable. (Not agreeable, but understandable.) But why must the games be conducted in a cacophony of sound created by horns, drums, and chanting voices duly amplified to the very threshold of pain? Can't people strike out around here in silence?

Why do ladies with short little legs, bless their hearts, wear balloon dresses and skirts that fall a few inches from the ankles? Are these fashions adopted unaltered from the apparel gracing the six-foot models of Paris?

Why doesn't the "merge" concept inherent in normal traffic flow (going from two lanes to one) work here? Where is the give-and-take of alternate progression characteristic of other civilizations? Is the influence of the physical law that nature abhors a vacuum particularly dominant on this side of the planet?

And finally, why will many Japanophiles be upset by the

mere asking of the above questions? ("If you don't like Japan, leave.") Are not abstract observations allowed?

When it comes right down to it, the national treasures of Japan are not Nara, Kyoto, or the screens in museums. The treasures are the people. But like treasures everywhere, there are occasional peculiarities. And face-value acceptance is not always advised.

Bye-bye, bye-bye, bye-bye!

Summer Bachelor

WHAT COULD BE better, when you stop and think about it, than temporary bachelorhood during the steamy and exotic days of midsummer Tokyo?

A young, nubile population of office ladies—all with money in the bank and fine clothes on their backs—abound in the coffee shops, pubs, and watering holes each evening after 5:00 PM. An entire generation of females, raised in an environment encouraging at least ostensible subservience to the male ego, roams the byways intersecting the traditional paths trampled by *gaijin* in Dai Nippon. And these girls, with a confidence generated by Golden Week trips abroad, no longer wilt automatically in the presence of men with round eyes.

Ah yes, summer in Tokyo. Billowing skirts and flimsy blouses. A time for exploration, challenge, and conquest. What could be better?

Well, a bad case of hemorrhoids might be better. A poke in the eye with a sharp stick would *not* be better, but root canal work or septic ulcers would certainly be preferable.

One of life's verisimilitudes—one of the core issues in all male/female relationships—seems to involve the female's concern about male behavior when the male is left to his own devices.

Why aren't these matters discussed from the opposite viewpoint? Where are the women going whose husbands remain behind? Are they not returning to friends, neighbors, and former school sweethearts with whom a common language and background at least facilitate the establishment of a "relationship"—assuming one is desired?

And where is it written that females have a lock on the basic question of morality surrounding the circumstances? Are they not of the same gender as the local predators supposedly attacking the defenseless summer bachelors?

It's a heavy issue, and the debate is kept alive by attributing the action of a minority to the intention of a majority.

But it is also an empty issue. Morality notwithstanding, it is not all that easy to "score" in Japan, regardless of whether one is a summer bachelor or not. And if a *gaijin* man *does* develop a "relationship," it's probably attributable to complex factors in his marriage, not to the fact that he's alone for a month or two in July and August.

With reference to "scoring," it takes a rather inflated sense of one's own attractiveness to imagine today's office ladies seriously considering involvement with a foreigner. The Occupation is over, and no one needs rescuing from a dismal existence capped by one bowl of rice a day.

Furthermore, family and social complications brought about by bringing a foreigner home to meet Mom, Dad, and the grandparents tends to deflate the ardor of the most passionate young office lady. There would be enough wind-sucking to deplete the oxygen supply in the immediate neighborhood. Not only that, hooking up with a foreigner might mean being transferred to Cleveland someday.

Max Danger has been a summer bachelor before—in fact, he kept a diary of his escapades. Although this is a family publication, the unabridged contents of that diary are reprinted below. All sexual scenes have been kept intact. People with youngsters may wish to divert their children's attention from this section of the book.

July 1: Took the Beautiful Gloria and kids to the airport. Returned home and realized house keys went with Gloria. Super's aged wife, wearing off-the-shoulder sweatshirt, opened door. Lingering smell of turpentine remained in apartment long after she left.

July 4: Went to American Club party. Danced with wife of Board member. She referred to me, between yawns, as "Mr. Dangerfield." Scratched back of hand on one of her rings.

July 7: Secretary announced, in office, she's approaching motherhood for the second time.

July 8: Trip to Osaka; Japanese dinner served by women dressed up as geisha. Spilled soup in lap, one woman wiped pants with damp cloth. Woman had hit grandmother stage many years before.

July 9: Business finished, returned to Tokyo. Pretty girl carrying tennis racket but wearing high heels in seat opposite on the Bullet Train slept with her mouth open.

July 13: Attended wine-tasting evening at Press Club. The waitress with long hair smiled as she refilled water glass.

July 14: The tan girl with big eyes and a round bottom, an object of vague lust from afar, rose from her chair in the Accounting Department and asked for private audience. It was a "personal matter." She wanted an extra week's vacation—for her honeymoon.

July 19: The damned cat, whose penchant for eating dirt from the flowerpots was increasing, was brought to the vet. Made eye-contact with vet's assistant, a young girl in stained white coat, who announced, "need more exercise please." Not certain to whom this directed.

July 21: Shimizu-san, joint venture partner, offered home-cooked meal at his house. Sat on floor. Mrs. Shimizu, matronly, hovered all evening, bending and serving countless dishes. Mrs. Shimizu wore a brown brassiere.

July 22: Closed favorite hostess bar in company of Head Office visitors. Four hours of giggling and touching. Hostesses disappeared into night before credit-card rigmarole completed.

July 23: Hung around American Club pool. *Gaijin* women bigger, in most respects, than Japanese women.

July 26: Drinks with employees after work. Joined in the activity with several senior typists. Tall girl with too many teeth rubbed my leg with hers under the table. Then she suddenly apologized. "I thought was table leg," she explained. She sat elsewhere upon return from toilet.

July 28: Visited Ari's. A dozen or so other summer bachelors there. Four girls, all over fifty, also there. Had the cheeseburger deluxe.

Aug 2: Fellow *gaijin* and wife asked me to accompany them and visiting unmarried sister-in-law from Pittsburgh to dinner. Unmarried sister-in-law worked in the steel industry—near the furnaces. Told dirty jokes all night.

Aug 3: Made eye contact, for 2.5 to 3 seconds, with pretty girl walking opposite way on sidewalk.

Aug 7: Had drinks after work with two mortgage bankers, a manufacturer's rep, an American Embassy attaché, and an insurance executive at the Old Bar in the Imperial. Watched pretty, sophisticated, cool-looking young women coming and going with escorts. Discussed summer bachelorhood with fellow sufferers. Went to insurance guy's house and played poker until dawn.

Aug 9: Asked girl working at neighborhood liquor store if the guy always lurking in background was brother or boyfriend. Girl blushed. It's her father.

Aug 13: Left Japan to join family on vacation. Nine of twelve stewardesses had grown children.

Well, there you have it. It's not a pretty picture. Raw passion, naked emotion—all crammed into six weeks of bachelorhood. The only consolation is that in the ensuing ten months, Max will have opportunities to redeem himself, and to prepare himself morally and spiritually for future bouts of temporary bachelorhood.

I Feel Vacation

ESCAPING FROM the clutches of Life's Responsibilities—if only for a short time—is more critical to the maintenance of physical and mental health than all the medical potions, vitamin C pills, and Stress Tabs ever made.

The work-play-rest cycle is for most people most of the time a daily occurrence. Additionally, the "work" element in the cycle is seldom sustained for more than five or six days per week. The compilers of the Old Testament had God resting on the seventh day. Creating the universe was apparently taxing even for Him. (Which we can well imagine.)

On an annual basis, humans seem to have tuned into the rhythms of nature, and have developed work-play-rest cycles in accordance with when crops have to be planted or harvested, or when buffaloes are inclined to roam the prairies. (No sense going out to chase the big creatures if they're all wintering in Schenectady.) Festivals, dances, and religious ceremonies were created to fill the void between the periods of real work.

Now then, Home Leave was invented so that modern man would have something to do during the "play" and "rest" elements of the annual work-play-rest cycle. If it weren't for Home Leave, we'd be hanging around the campfire dressed as dragons, or throwing the first beans of the season into the ocean for fertility purposes.

Home Leave, or "vacation" as it's sometimes called, is a good idea. It enables humans to get away from wherever they are—and go someplace else. But, dare it be suggested, the phenomenon requires closer examination.

Max Danger's Home Leave experiences have led to the very real suspicion that the "rest" element has all but disappeared, and the "work" and "play" aspects have merged into a new Life Responsibility—the "godammit, we're supposed to be having fun" syndrome. To put it another way, there have been times when Max secretly craves a return to "work" to catch up on the "rest" and "play" elements so fundamental to human existence. Something is wrong.

87

At first, Home Leave was easy. In Max's case, going to the "Re-Entry Permit" office in Otemachi was a piece of cake. Because of different birthdays, dates of entrance, places of birth, and passport validity periods, Max only had to go five different times on behalf of the beautiful Gloria and the three Danger offspring. And each time, he merely spent a little over half a day mingling in 38°C heat with all the female "entertainers" in Southeast Asia. Simple as pie.

Getting to the airport was equally simple. The fact that Max's business suits were lost somewhere between the Tokyo City Air Terminal and Narita was incidental. There would be at least two hours and forty-five minutes between the time of Max's arrival in New York, and his meeting in the Head Office, to purchase a new executive wardrobe. Easy.

Max's youngest, a lad who does not fly well, performed as expected. He threw up on a fellow executive-class traveler who, coincidentally, was a customer of Max's company. No problem—high-powered corporate animals are a tolerant lot.

The initial meeting in Max's Head Office, attended by none other than his chairman and a crew of serious henchmen, went reasonably well, considering Max was wearing Docksides, a tennis shirt, and khaki trousers dating from his junior year in college. (Those things *should* be refreshing on Wall Street.) Max's planned wardrobe purchases were delayed by the disappearance of his eldest son at JFK Airport. The juices of puberty had begun flowing during the youngster's time in Tokyo, and the milling throng of well-developed American females at the airport had made him, in his own words, "light-headed." (He followed one out to her taxi—"helping with her bags.")

The stay in the New York hotel was pleasant for the

family. Fortunately, none of the Dangers were in their rooms when the burglars arrived and ransacked the premises. Only three cameras were taken, and Japanese cameras are cheaper to purchase in New York anyway.

The visit with the in-laws in Pittsburgh did not go as smoothly as anticipated. The kids love their grandparents, and vice versa, but it is difficult for three growing youngsters to remember to stay at all times on the plastic floor runners protecting the carpets, to remember to wash their hands before touching light switches, or to refrain from eating the fruit "on display" in the living room. The session with Max's daughter, who had climbed a tree in the grandparent's back yard and refused to come down until it was time to leave (three days hence), was unfortunate. The move to a Pittsburgh Holiday Inn solved *that* problem, but the convention of Wild-Assed Common Laborers with Tattoos, or some such group, created new challenges at the motel. ("Look, Daddy, those men and women are swimming in the pool without their clothes.")

It was during the journey from Pittsburgh back to New York, then on to London, that little problems began to crop up. The plane from Pittsburgh, somewhat delayed, arrived at JFK precisely one hour and sixteen minutes *after* the plane to London left U.S. soil. Although it is interesting, hanging around an airport lobby for seven hours is less fun than you might think. The kids, at least, had the opportunity to taste scalded black coffee from a machine for the first time—all shops and restaurants close at night.

Eventually arriving in London brought new little difficulties. A "work slowdown" (i.e., a strike) among baggage handlers compounded the difficulties of luggage retrieval. A "work demonstration" (i.e., a strike) at Customs meant two tweed-clad, pipe-smoking, mutton-headed civil servants were processing the entry of numerous 747s full of visitors arriving every ten minutes. Max and the family made it through the routine in slightly under six hours. A "job action" (i.e., a strike) kept taxis away from the airport, but transportation was sporadically available. It took the Dangers only three hours to go from Heathrow to Belgravia. The "labour protest" (i.e., a strike) of dustmen and garbage collectors did not affect the Danger pursuit of British culture, but the "working demonstration" (i.e., a strike) of hotel porters and lift operators, and the new "employment dispute" (i.e., a strike) of bus drivers, made departure from England to Hawaii more complicated than is really necessary. Max arranged for a hired car to the airport, but a sudden "staff-concern-for-coal-miners-in-Wales" (i.e., a strike) meant no one was available at Heathrow to receive the car. (Max has just been sent a notice from the hired-car company asking for payment of the "first month's leasing charges.")

The plane ride to Honolulu was a breeze. His youngest only threw up once, and no one was seated next to him. His eldest struck up a mildly exotic conversational relationship with one of the stewardesses, and announced he was leaving home and taking up permanent residence in the Ilikai Hotel. The beautiful Gloria, still angry at her daughter for the tree-in-the-backyard-move-to-the-Pittsburgh-Holiday-Inn caper, went to the tourist section of the aircraft and watched *Prizzi's Honor* for the fifth time. Max got two-thirds of the way through a copy of the *New Yorker* before the drunk in the seat behind him made the threatening gestures to the plane's crew which resulted in his forcible restraint and supervision by a federal marshal. Real relaxing stuff.

Hawaii, however, turned out to be a problem. Carefully scheduled reservations on the beach at a fine hotel on the Big Island had unaccountably gone wrong. A "Sorry, Mr.

Danger, we have no record of correspondence" situation developed. Tantrums performed individually and spectacularly did not help. A Japanese tour group had booked the entire place, and since the hotel was owned by Japanese, there really could be no misunderstanding. Hotel employees, Hawaiians, arranged for the Dangers to stay at the Surf Breeze Inn—across a four-lane highway and several acres of moonrock lava from the ocean. Tennis could be scheduled between the hours of noon and 2:00 PM at the fine hotel. Dinner was either provided by Kentucky Fried Chicken or Fern's Fine Foods. The Dangers moved back to Honolulu and stayed at the Royal Hawaiian, blowing the budget for the next two Home Leaves.

The return to Japan was anticlimatic. The loss of three of the Dangers' seven pieces of luggage—Max's bag for the second time—was no problem. The bags would eventually catch up with the people. There was some discomfort, for the beautiful Gloria particularly, when one of the remaining four bags was opened by the diligent customs folks. The necessity of importing a year's supply of Western-sized tampons had to be explained in public, to both the customs officials, and then to the youngest of the Danger children. (The children caught on quicker.) A great deal of wind was sucked over the issue, however.

Back at work, Max relaxed for the first time in a month. For almost a week, correspondence went unanswered, phone calls were unreturned. Max read the papers, chatted with the staff, and went home on time. He scrupulously refrained from telling customers he was back.

And as vacations go, the first week after the return from Home Leave becomes the most important seven-day period in the year. We humans must maintain the work-play-rest cycle, but Home Leave is not necessarily the answer. At this point, Max would love to stay in Tokyo next year, sleep late every day for a month, and fill in the time between with heavy bouts of looking out the window. But sure as hell, an even more complicated vacation schedule will be planned next year. And Max, believe it or not, will probably look forward to it.

Friendship

SERIOUS HIROSE, of "company trouble" fame, became Max's first Japanese friend. It was a relationship that grew slowly—neither Hirose nor Max were looking for new pals at the time.

The seeds of friendship were sown by the business demands of managing the Tokyo branch office. Hirose worked for Max, and it was to Hirose that Max turned for advice and guidance on handling any problems peculiarly Japanese.

The relationship began on a note of vague but mutual distrust. It was obvious that Serious Hirose resented the intrusion of yet another *gaijin* on his local business turf, and Max was disappointed in Hirose's cold and apparently reluctant acceptance of the new and brilliant ideas brought directly from the Head Office.

Eventually Hirose and Max reached the point of at least accepting their relative positions, and agreeing that a considerable amount of compromise was necessary if anything was to be accomplished.

The first "issue" at the compromise stage had to do with employment policy. Max, fresh from the States, knew that a major untapped resource in the business world was represented by one-half the human race—women. He wanted to hire female university graduates for some of the more complex jobs at the time staffed by men. Max deemed the existing talent in these particular jobs, handled by men, to be marginal at best.

Hirose coolly disagreed. "No one in business," he argued, "will follow the leadership of a woman." In addition, Hirose pointed out that the radically new guideline which suggests equal pay, of all things, to women with equal training would destroy the carefully controlled balance of income and expenses. Men should be university graduates, women should be two-year college graduates—or less. It's basic economy.

Hirose and Max compromised. A dozen or so female university graduates were hired for Max, and Hirose continued to stock the typing pools with the usual balloon heads.

The relationship grew to the respect stage when Max discovered that Hirose was quietly defending the "Danger Principle" of excising all dead wood in the distributorship corps. Admittedly, the maneuver was trampling on the time-honored tradition of respect for contributions made three decades ago, but it also saved the company several tens of millions of yen in licensing fees.

Concurrently, Hirose was astonished to learn that Max had recommended to the Personnel Committee that Hirose be given a salary increase significantly above the average for the year. (Hirose and his wife had just had their fourth and, to date, final child.)

The joint effort between the Hirose and Danger families to build a ski-house in Hakuba cemented the relationship. The seven children in the two families got along famously. Communication was never an issue, even under the trying conditions of video game rivalry and skiing competition.

Hirose and Max solved the Japanese toilet issue in the ski-house: Hirose arranged for a new Western toilet. Hirose and Max solved the Japanese tax issue in the ski-house: Max took responsibility under his equalization program.

The beautiful Gloria Danger uttered her first sentence in Japanese—other than the words used for ordering ground beef at National Azabu Supermarket—to Mrs. Hirose during one snowy ski-weekend. (She told Mrs. Hirose that she was "from America, and my fountain pen is brand new.") Mrs. Hirose responded in the first English words she had pronounced since high school. ("I am happy to be here, and your cabbage is excellent.") *All* the kids laughed.

As the months, and then years, went by, Hirose and Max consumed great quantities of beer and *yakitori* together after work with employees, customers, and business rivals. They became a one-two punch in managing the myriad of problems, complaints, and disasters befalling all in the day-to-day activities of international corporations.

Hirose would end up at Max's apartment once or twice a month whenever the "business sessions" after work went beyond the time of the last subway. Max crashed at Hirose's house on two occasions when the sessions took them somewhere out and around the western Tokyo suburbs. Essentially, Hirose and Max formed a solid management team capable of handling most problems. And they became friends along the way.

On the personal side, Hirose was strangely unemotional. He rarely talked about his parents—he never really knew his father, who had been killed in the war. (Hirose does vaguely remember his father coming home once and giving him an American flag he had picked up somewhere in Southeast Asia. Hirose still has the flag and keeps it folded under his bed.)

His mother is a medical doctor in western Japan and has seen only two non-Japanese in her life. She doesn't like foreigners, and is still concerned about Hirose's choice of employers. (She once vetoed a proposed trip to the States, which Hirose had considered when he was in university, because it meant "exposure to barbarians.") Hirose maintains he has outgrown his mother's control, but he never did make it to the States.

One day in late September, a Saturday to be exact, Max received the phone call from home that all expats dread. "Your father is dying," it said. Max made arrangements to catch the first plane out of Tokyo Sunday morning.

Many people, unfortunately, recognize the scenario. The anguish, and sorrow, is close to being overwhelming. Yet the practical considerations of international travel must be handled. Max made it to his father's bedside only hours before he drew his final breath.

The funeral, on Thursday, was an event which for Max was shrouded in fog. Old friends of his parents, indistinctly remembered, hovered about and commiserated. Former classmates, remarkably older and fatter, expressed the appropriate feelings of concern and condolence. A great aunt predictably went into hysterics.

Max, named for his father, listened to the homily delivered by the parish priest with the uncomfortable feeling that the remarks were about *him*. Funerals *are* awful.

It was during the procession to the altar at the end of the service, for the heart-wrenching closing of the casket ceremony, that Max noticed him. But it wasn't until Max was outside the church and into the sunlight that he actually realized who it was.

How Serious Hirose managed to get his first visa to the USA in a matter of days, and how he managed to scrape together the airfare to Chicago has even to this day remained a mystery. But there he was, shambling down the aisle with everyone else, carrying his Buddhist prayer beads, wearing his immaculate black suit and tie, and looking for all the world as if he had just stepped out of Tokyo Station. A black armband was neatly pinned to the sleeve of his coat.

Several hours went by before Max had a chance to speak with Hirose. It was comforting to listen to his detached appraisal of life's joys and iniquities. It was also a relief to think of anything else but the funeral.

They discussed Hirose's impressions during his first 16 hours on American soil. (Each impression had something to do with size.) They discussed mundane matters concerning the office. They chatted in all the agreeable circles of conversation so necessary for easing grief.

Hirose took off early the next morning for Tokyo. He could not be prevailed upon to stay longer. He was scheduled to visit his wicked mother-in-law that Sunday.

If Max hadn't briefly noticed Hirose in the church, but had instead first seen him after the funeral, he might have wondered about Hirose's motives for making the trip. After all, one helluva cost was involved, and the Japanese rules for funeral behavior and attendance do not normally extend internationally.

No, it was clear to Max that Hirose came as a friend. Because in the church, surrounded by strangers all mourning a man unknown to him, Hirose's stoic composure and Oriental inscrutability slipped. The cool customer—the slasher of budgets and scourge of production men—had melted. Serious Hirose had been crying.

Crime and Punishment

RELATIVELY FEW people wear shoes to bed. Mud, caked in the niche between heel and sole, can come loose during the night, spread around on the sheets, stick to the legs, work its way up, and generally cause more trouble than it's worth. Most people don't even *think* about it—they *automatically* take their shoes off before going to bed!

The same might be said about wearing shoes in the bath. Most people don't. The leather gets soaked, it takes a long time to dry, and the shine the next day is never quite right. Besides, imagine washing your feet with shoes on. Difficult, right?

Now, some may have noticed that the Japanese take shoes off in their houses. If one is not living in the mud of mud huts, on the logs of log cabins, or amid stones of a stone castle, there's really no reason to wear shoes indoors. And think of all the unpleasant bits they track about the place. In fact it's a wonder anyone would even *consider* wearing shoes in the house. Some things just make sense.

The police arrived in five minutes—the first on his bicycle from the neighborhood *koban*. (He was, Max noted uncomfortably, the same man he had nearly killed the day before when the bicycle swerved in front of his car.)

"It's over there," Gloria said, pointing across the room. The glass door leading from the patio to the Homat Cornucopia living room was shattered. "It was that way when we came home."

The bicycle policeman remained immobile, staring at the damage so clearly obvious. Broken glass lay strewn about the beige carpet and sparkled in the sunlight streaming through the windows.

The bicycle policeman was interrupted in his studies by the arrival of reinforcements. He quickly said something to the four new investigators, and then all five policemen stood in the doorway and stared at the mess.

As Max was mentally exploring possible Japanese sounds for "Aren't you going to do anything about it?" his level-headed daughter Mona came to the rescue.

"Slippers *desu*," Mona said, indicating to the policemen the little cupboard. The visitors sprang into action, shed their shoes (all of which were identically black and shiny), put on the fluffy rabbit slippers Gloria had purchased in a moment of weakness for the kids, and began the swarming process of police detective work. A crisis—centering on the propriety of footwear in a *gaijin* household with glass on the floor—was deftly diverted.

"Seems got stopped," said the leader of police after walking around for a few minutes. Indeed, it also appeared to Max that the burglar had been interrupted in his work. Several drawers in a living room cabinet had been ransacked, but nothing else in the apartment had been touched. "You scared away," the policeman concluded.

It is a sobering thought to realize that the sound of rattling keys at the door was all that separated the Dangers from confrontation with a thief bent on crime. Max watched the investigators searching for clues. One was studying the stereo hook-up, another was measuring the height of the dining room table. Counting the burglar, a whole lot of strangers had been in the house in the last ten minutes.

The officer wearing Mona's pink rabbit slippers with stiff ears came charging in from the patio. He was jabbering excitedly and pointing to a bag into which he had put something from the garden.

"We have the clue," announced the leader, "and we inform you soon."

With that, the five men rushed for the front door, put on shoes apparently at random, and zoomed off as quickly as they had come. A piece of paper on the mail pile near the door, disturbed by the quick movement of scurrying bodies, floated lazily to the floor.

"Well, I wonder what that was all about?" Max asked the family in general.

"Don't worry, Dad," said Max III, "they have 'the clue.'"

Max lectured the family during the cleaning-up process. "There may be more murders in Detroit or Calcutta on a summer weekend than there are all year in Japan," he pointed out, "but Japan does suffer from the curse of sneak thievery. In fact, the number of 'breaking and entering' crimes is surprisingly large."

"Get a paper bag for this broken glass," observed the beautiful Gloria.

"And the number of sexual assaults," continued Max, "is thought to be considerably higher in Japan than official statistics indicate."

"Where's the broom?" agreed Max's daughter.

Max was into the relative-rates-of-embezzlement-convictions-among-the-industrialized-countries phase of the lecture when the doorbell rang.

It was the police. Again. All five of them. And they had in their midsts a dejected young man in blue jeans and white T-shirt on which was written: "TO LOVE MY HEART IS FOR COOL." (For scholars collecting these things, the caption appeared beneath a cute rendering of copulating penguins.)

"We found him," said the lead policeman simply, "going down hill from here."

Assembling, reorganizing, and suddenly understanding bits and pieces of bilingual explanations enabled all parties to come to what was generally accepted as "an agreement" of what had transpired.

The kid had just broken in and was beginning the business of looting and pillaging when he heard the Dangers approach. He took off like a bat out of hell through the broken door and scaled the patio wall in one mighty bound.

The Dangers confirmed that nothing had been taken— the kid had only dumped the contents of two drawers on the floor.

At the conclusion of these formalities, the police asked the kid to stand at attention. He did. The man on his left whispered something in the kid's ear. With a flicker of the eyes, and an ever so slight hesitation, the kid obeyed. He spent the next minute or so profusely and emotionally apologizing, his upper torso bent parallel to the ground. One of the policemen even asked him to repeat the last few phrases.

"How did you catch him so quickly?" Max asked of the bicycle policeman, as the entourage prepared to depart.

"Easy," replied the worthy man, "we had 'the clue.' "

Apparently the police did little after leaving the Dangers the first time, save drive around the neighborhood in their squad car. After four or five minutes they spotted their man strolling down the hill toward National Azabu Supermarket. Without hesitation, they nabbed him. He was the only one in the crowd walking barefoot.

Japanese don't wear shoes in the house. The thief had left them in his flight where they lay—neatly aligned on the patio stones outside the broken living room door.

Parking Anyone?

THERE IS A "Rube Goldberg" quality to the way things work around here. For those who don't remember, Rube Goldberg was a cartoonist whose specialty was depicting the accomplishment of a simple task through an incredible series of spectacularly complicated events: a candle would burn down through a string releasing a precariously balanced bucket of water onto a sleeping cat who would leap up, scaring a parrot whose cries would start a squirrel running on a treadmill attached with gears to a hatch which, when opened, started a bowling ball rolling down a ramp onto a catapult, triggering its action and flinging a metal ashtray against a gong on the wall, thereby waking the central character in the drama—a man asleep in bed. All in lieu of an alarm clock.

There are good things to be said about these kinds of arrangements, however. Well, at least one good thing—the system guarantees involvement. And involvement means full employment. But adjusting to this three-ring circus of activity takes time. And patience.

Max Danger had the good fortune to witness, and compare, two identical projects as planned and executed in his New York Head Office, and in his Tokyo branch operation. The occasion was the seventy-fifth anniversary of his company's founding, which coincided with the fortieth anniversary of the company's Japan operation.

While on a business trip to New York, Max happened to sit in on a meeting wherein a tiny corner of the Head Office celebration was being planned. The tiny corner of activity involved arranging for complimentary parking in a midtown Manhattan hotel for the guests of the company at a gala reception/cocktail party.

The strategy involved calling in a young dude from somewhere deep in the bowels of the building and telling him to call the hotel and "make arrangements." He said "OK." This aspect of the planning session took between twenty and thirty seconds.

A week or so later, back in Tokyo, Max witnessed the beginning of a series of events in quest of the same goal— complimentary parking for the guests of the Japan branch at a gala reception/cocktail party.

So as to preserve an accurate chronicle of activity— perhaps for future study by management consultants, or for background information to be used in the preparation of doctoral theses—Max is reporting the following on a parallel basis. New York and Tokyo.

NEW YORK, DAY 1   "Call the hotel and arrange for complimentary parking." The young dude says, "OK," and slouches off. Time elapsed: twenty to thirty seconds.

TOKYO, DAY 1   "Call the hotel and arrange for complimentary parking." The seven people from the General Affairs Dept. look at their hands, cigarette lighters, out the window, at the ceiling, at each other— anywhere, in fact, except at Max. Careful questioning reveals that the group is not certain *why* this should be done. Careful explanations follow, with subsequent desultory conversation in Japanese among the group. Finally, consensus is reached. It should be done because it's a good idea. The meeting ends. Time elapsed: forty-seven minutes.

NEW YORK, DAY 2   Nothing.

TOKYO, DAY 2   A meeting is convened during which it is reported that the hotel would like to know the makes and license numbers of the cars of the people attending the party *in advance* so that arrangements can be made. The practicality of this is discussed, but it is concluded—albeit with some heavy wind-sucking—that the "hotel's request" cannot be complied with. The group is charged with the responsibility of effecting an alternate plan—perhaps free parking stickers. The meeting ends. Time elapsed: one hour and nineteen minutes.

NEW YORK, DAY 3   Nothing.

TOKYO, DAY 3   "Do free parking stickers mean free to the drivers but paid for by the hotel or by the company?" The question had merit. A sub-committee is established to analyze the quotation of prices, from the hotel to the company, to determine accountability. Time elapsed: twenty-six minutes.

NEW YORK, DAY 4   Nothing.

TOKYO, DAY 4   Parking must be an extra charge to the

103

company because the ice-carving is being provided at a discount. Would the company consider parking slips, sent with the invitations, instead of stickers? Also, how many attendees will there be? The hotel, a new one, has somewhat limited parking facilities, and arrangements must be made for the cars of regular guests. Answers slowly emerge. Time elapsed: fifty-four minutes.

NEW YORK, DAY 5   Nothing.

TOKYO, DAY 5   "Should the company logo be on the slips, and/or are there special number sequences preferred?" At issue is the question of paying a flat fee for *all* slips mailed out with the invitation, or merely paying for those people who actually attend with cars. Of course—and how can we overlook these things? "And what about overflow?" The meeting group has been expanded by the addition of two serious guys from the Accounting Dept.—the chaps in charge of watching the gala reception/cocktail party budget. Answers sort of emerge. Elapsed time: one hour and thirteen minutes.

NEW YORK, DAY 6   Nothing.

TOKYO, DAY 6   The slips are too big for the invitation envelopes. Should: a) the slips be reprinted, b) the envelopes made bigger, or c) the slips folded? The last alternative is finally selected. Elapsed time: forty-one minutes.

Max is pleased to report, if only for the sake of comparison, that the end result in both places, New York and Tokyo, was precisely the same. Scholars will note, however, that it took the Tokyo operation five hours and twenty minutes to plan for it, whereas it took less than a minute in New York.

Oh yes, the end result was precisely the same. Disgruntled guests in New York lined up in cars for over an hour waiting to pay parking charges on the way out of the hotel. It seems the young dude had resigned from the company within days of receiving his assignment, no one noticed, and nothing had been done about complimentary parking.

In Tokyo, the black cars were backed up to parking level B-3 waiting to pay the fees. It seems that the folding of the parking slips created mysterious technical problems, and if the invitations were to be mailed on time, they had to go out without the slips.

Hey, Rube, why did these things always work in the cartoons?

Author's Note: The Japanese parking slips were eventually mailed, and were received by most guests the day *after* the gala reception/cocktail party.

Changes III

WATANABE-SAN approached the employment-by-foreigners phenomenon in which he was firmly situated with an "expect the worst but hope for the best" attitude.

This is not quite the same attitude as that adopted by sword swallowers and sky divers—"expecting the worst" is presumably not paramount in their minds. It is more like the attitude of lottery ticket purchasers and *pachinko* aficionados—"this could be a waste of time and money, but maybe something good will come of it all."

As Max Danger's General Affairs Department Manager, Watanabe-san was, at age 58, nearing the conclusion of a thirty-five-year career with the Japan branch of a major international conglomerate. Danger-san was only the latest, and most certainly the last, foreign manager in a long string of expats for whom Watanabe-san had toiled. Neither the worst, nor the best, had ever really happened.

"He seems like a nice man," Watanabe-san's wife had said after meeting Max for the first time. Max had been teasing her at a reception about something her husband had either said or done in the office—Danger-san's rapid English was not easy to follow. "And he seems to like you," she added.

"Well, maybe he's more friendly than some of the other *gaijin*," Watanabe-san had admitted, "but he'll be gone someday like all the rest."

Watanabe-san's generation of workers was the last of those with significant memories of prewar Japan. Watanabe-san had been sixteen when the Emperor went on the radio and announced that the war was over and Japan had lost. Until that moment, Watanabe-san had been fully prepared to go wherever he was told and fight the enemy. He had been trained to do that for as long as he could remember. And people like Danger-san were the enemy.

Watanabe-san managed to finish high school, but his priorities in his late teens were more toward feeding a widowed mother and two little sisters than going on with an education. He got a job at a U.S. military base in Chofu running errands for three Occupation officers whose job included compiling up-to-date maps of Japan. Watanabe-san got to travel, learn English, and participate in the machinations and modest profits surrounding the immediate postwar black-market industry. His family ate slightly better than others, but not much.

One of the Occupation officers befriended Watanabe-san, who knew where to procure the young boys the officer preferred to spend time with. When the officer was rotated back to the States, Watanabe-san got a job with an automobile mechanic whose shop was conveniently located across the road from the base. Watanabesan's duties were various. They included everything from going on and off base to drum up business to stealing hubcaps when the need arose. Watanabe-san met a broad range of *gaijin* who were former enemies. And his English improved.

In 1953, Watanabe-san's Occupation boss returned to Japan as a private businessman, and Watanabe-san went to work for him. The small trading company they began was moderately successful. It was bought, merged, and acquired a half-dozen times down through the years. The boss eventually disappeared—he was transferred back to the

States after one of the mergers, and subsequently died of a liver disorder while unemployed in San Francisco. The organization they founded was the genesis of the present conglomerate's Japan branch, and Max was now the "corporate officer" in charge. Watanabe-san was the only one left from the original days.

"Even though he's friendly," concluded Watanabe-san, "he has no idea what we went through."

The current revolt in the office had been simmering for months. Watanabe-san had been given the job of supervising the establishment of a sophisticated electronic data processing system in the operation. Not only did this include the reorganization of physical space, it involved getting to the core of employment relationships—the reassignment of staff. Watanabe-san, who was not a believer in all this "computer machinery business" in the first place, was nevertheless becoming the focal point upon which employee unrest was gradually concentrating. He even began receiving nasty phone calls at home from the college-graduate staff whose lives were being disrupted.

"You will have to figure out a way to handle the problem," Danger-san told him the day Watanabe-san sought advice. "Tell them that increased efficiency means more profit, which means more expansion, which means more jobs."

"What *did* you tell the employees?" Watanabe-san's wife asked that evening.

"I told them," said Watanabe-san, "that the *gaijin* boss ordered the reorganization."

Watanabe-san's "breakdown" occurred not long after that. His wife called Max's secretary one Monday morning and explained that the doctor had told her husband to rest at home for one week. On the following Monday, Watanabe san's wife visited Max in the office with a box of *osembei*

(Japanese-style crackers) and the report that her husband needed one more week of rest.

"He seemed to understand," Mrs. Watanabe reported to her husband that evening. Watanabe-san had been spending his days staring at the television set, which only now and then had been turned on.

Independent inquiries in the office did little to reveal the nature of Watanabe-san's problem—"he became overtired" was about all anyone was willing to say. After the third week, the Personnel Manager suggested that Watanabe-san's assistant should become "acting manager" of the General Affairs Department until further notice. The EDP system was installed, and grudgingly accepted. Danger-san wrote a memo to all employees praising their cooperation. He was not in the office when Mrs. Watanabe visited on the fourth Monday.

"His secretary phoned and said that he's coming to our house tomorrow after work," Mrs. Watanabe reported several days later. Despite the protestations from her husband, Mrs. Watanabe did not call the company back and cancel the visit. She had heard enough stories from her husband in the past about *gaijin* not following convention, and instead doing whatever they felt like doing, to know that a phone call would not stop anything. Besides, her husband was becoming more withdrawn each day and it *was* worrying. She went about cleaning the house, and then organized the shopping expedition for the uninvited foreigner's meal. "Something with meat," she said to herself.

Danger-san arrived promptly at 6:30 PM. He seemed to be familiar with the neighborhood. (It was near the American School.)

The Watanabe abode was adequate for the childless couple, and only slightly cramped when relatives or friends visited. During the past New Year's season the Watanabes had entertained ten people comfortably. The problem of space was never really an issue when their guests were all fellow Japanese.

Danger-san's presence seemed to dwarf the familiar surroundings, however. Bending to unlace his shoes, he tipped over the umbrella stand by the front door. He came within a centimeter or two of smashing his head on the doorway entrance to the living room. He *did* bang his head on the lamp suspended from the ceiling over the low table in the living room. Seated, his legs stretched through the area beneath the table and out the other side. Mrs. Watanabe moved from her accustomed position at the table to the side next to her husband.

"How are you feeling?" Danger-san asked directly, skipping customary small talk. Watanabe-san did not answer. He was concentrating on the foam in the glasses of beer his wife had just poured for the men.

"He feels very tired," Mrs. Watanabe said after a few moments. She poured more beer for Danger-san. He began talking, in his rapid English, about changes in the office. The words were not always clear, but Danger-san repeated "Everything's OK" several times. Watanabe-san, not looking, was listening.

The meal, Mrs. Watanabe was convinced, had been a success. Danger-san ate everything in sight, and made a point of praising every dish. Her husband eventually joined the conversation—pointing out that Danger-san could not possibly like the humble meal so poorly prepared. Rather than being upset, Mrs. Watanabe beamed with pleasure.

The serious phase of the evening began with the whiskey and V.S.O.P. brandy. (The brandy had been a gift from Danger-san after one of his trips back to Japan from the Head Office.) Mrs. Watanabe went to the kitchen with her pots and pans.

"You can't stay away from the office forever," Danger-san said.

"But I am no good to the company any more," Watanabe-san admitted, watching the smoke curl from his cigarette to the area around the overhead lamp. "You have many people like Hirose-kun who are young enough to understand new directions," he said.

Danger-san poured more brandy for both of them. Watanabe-san added water to his.

"When the company began," Watanabe-san said, "I knew everything we were doing. All the people, even the smart ones we hired later, respected me." He put his cigarette out and lit another one. "Now no one can respect a man who is old-fashioned."

Danger-san seemed to be paying attention. He did not appear to be bothered by the noise in the kitchen, but Watanabe-san yelled at his wife for good measure. For some reason, Danger-san smiled at that.

"I can't even *understand* the kinds of things we have to do today." Watanabe-san hoped his voice was even. "This is the end for me."

Danger-san had asked about the early days in the company, and Watanabe-san found himself dwelling on the "growth times"—the times when most of the distributorship contracts existing even today were signed. They were the times before his first *gaijin* boss had disappeared. Danger-san seemed to be the most interested in what everyone thought and did when the first profits were declared and the loans were paid off. It was the time the entire staff—about fifteen people in those days—stayed up all night celebrating in Ginza. "My boss told me then that we could not have succeeded without my help," Watanabe-san reported. "I was a good assistant."

For the next hour or so, Max drank coffee. The beer, saké,

111

brandy, and air in Watanabe-san's house were combining to form the beginnings of a spectacular headache. It was a relief to stand up, sometime around 2:00 AM, and go through the business of getting ready for the long drive back to Azabu.

Standing in the cool night air by his car, Max and Watanabe-san came to an agreement. They shook hands. It would be good to see the old bastard back in the office.

The Shuto Expressway at that hour is all but deserted. Max tried calculating the alcohol-consumed versus time-elapsed formula in the event the orange-stick police patrol nabbed him. He lit a cigar for good measure.

Max also tried calculating the impact Watanabe-san's "promotion" from General Affairs Manager to Personal Assistant would have on the Head Office experts—assuming, of course, they ever found out. Max's chairman, for all he knew, did not even have a "personal assistant."

"Watanabe-san sure seemed relieved with his 'promotion,'" Max thought to himself. "But I wonder why no one ever paid attention to the connection?"

Max then and there decided to bring Watanabe-san with him to his 9:30 meeting in the morning. It was with the president of a major Japanese trading company—a company everyone from Max's chairman to the tea girls were anxious to please. The relationship with that company had developed significant profits for Max's organization down through the years.

The president of the trading company had had *his* difficult times immediately after the war also. He had begun his working career as an automobile mechanic, with a shop across from a U.S. military base. And Watanabe-san had been his very first employee.

A Christmas Story

CHRISTMAS IS a Christian holiday. This point, less obvious as the years go by, must be re-established and confirmed up front.

The birth of Christ is spiritually significant to a major portion of the earth's population—its commemoration is quite properly nurtured and cherished in the hearts and souls of believers everywhere. Furthermore, the starkly simple nativity in a manger began a series of events that has had a profound effect on all humanity, whether or not the events are accepted literally, and whether or not one is a believer. It cannot be argued otherwise.

Now then, what about all the whoop-de-do surrounding this celebration? For those about to spend their first Christmas in Japan, you will find that the Japanese are rapidly becoming world-class leaders in whoop-de-doism. They have discovered the commercial potential, and they are, as we say around here, maximizing market share.

But before a campaign is begun to return things to the basics, think about all the other generally accepted customs which would have to be purged.

Imagine, if you will, what the original Middle-Eastern Christians must have thought when the celebration was transported to Rome and linked with year-ending bacchanalian feasts of decidedly non-religious origin. (And for all we know, Christ was born in June.) It may have been good PR, but it was a quantum leap from the frankincense and myrrh of east Africa.

Europeans contributed significantly to the trappings of the party—fir trees with lights! The music was good, Franz Gruber composed a song on his guitar while marching through snow over hill and dale to his pal's church where rats had eaten the innards of the organ. (Don't ask why no one discovered the rat problem until Christmas Eve.)

Plum pudding and hall-decking with ivy boughs is British. Well done, that.

St. Nicholas, Bishop of Myra and patron saint of Russia, mariners, merchants, and children, is the source of the corrupted name Santa Claus. He was first physically and popularly described by a New York newspaper editor.

Christmas cards, invented by a New Englander, were banned in Boston. (The cards are okay now, but *sending* them should be banned.)

"White Christmas" was written by Irving Berlin, but it has nothing to do with Christianity. Crosby's treatment barely saved the tune from permanent condemnation to the Hall of Banality. Since Herr Gruber plucked out "Silent Night" on his Spanish guitar, only "The Little Drummer Boy" and "Do They Know It's Christmas?" have risen above the mundane. Don't even mention reindeers and roasting chestnuts.

So here we are in Japan. How are *they* supposed to know where the limits begin and end? Tinsel didn't even make it to Tokyo until the end of the war.

Max Danger became involved with planning Japanese Christmas festivities early in the Tokyo assignment. His secretary, Akimbo-san, sought advice on behalf of her brother, a department-store window dresser.

Akimbo-san's brother, a young man of effete and sensitive

114

tastes, walked about a foot above ground. (He had the ability to glide into rooms pelvis first.) A major Ginza emporium "treasured" his work.

Akimbo-san's brother had been given the job of creating the main Christmas display in the showcase window at the store—an assignment earned by reason of the fact that his understanding of things was "international." English words, to the astonishment of his employers, would occasionally pop out of his mouth.

Akimbo-san's brother was striving for realism—"like maker of good movies," he confided during the first meeting in Max's office. He had with him sketches of a manger scene. "I not making mistake of the Christmas problem," he added.

His employers had apparently generated a not inconsiderable amount of notoriety among the *gaijin* world the year before by featuring a semi-nude young lady in red underpants depicted on a massive banner hung from the ninth floor of the store's interior to the main floor level. Folks going up and down the escalators had nine floors to contemplate the caption, "Buy Me Now The Christmas I Love."

Akimbo-san's brother planned to devote one display window to an authentic recreation of the manger scene. He wanted Max's help. All things considered, it was a good idea. And Max agreed to assist in the project.

The first meeting in the department store was held in a basement storage area far from the display windows. Literally thousands of manikins and manikin parts were piled from floor to ceiling in the storage area—all headless. (Heads were kept in round, numbered hatboxes. Heads mustn't be scratched or dirtied.)

The initial job was to assemble a cast of characters for the display. ("What the hell," thought Max, "let them have

115

the three kings, even though they weren't around that night in Bethlehem.")

An interesting problem surfaced regarding the size of the head of the infant Jesus. One of Akimbo-san's brother's "assistants"—a young Japanese boy named Pablo—had with him some art books showing fifteenth- and sixteenth-century Spanish paintings of the nativity scene. Artists in those days frequently made the mistake of painting infants as if they were just little men—all physical parts, including heads, were equally reduced in size. "We cannot find doll with small enough head," reported Pablo. An explanation settled the issue, but Max could not help wondering if others think *gaijin* are born with pinheads.

Another problem had to do with appropriate animals for the scene. European artists were not much help in this regard—they usually painted local barnyard creatures into their rendition of the event. The animals were handy.

Japanese department stores do not stock a wide variety of animalkins. Max drew the line at monkeys and pigs, but gave in on sheep (from a New Zealand wool festival display) and dairy cows (from a Hokkaido milk festival display). Chickens eventually made it to the display, but Max does not remember giving his "permission."

The next, and last, meeting at the store was a revelation. Akimbo-san's brother and his assistants had, over the course of several weeks, put the whole scene together in a cleared area of the basement—a dress rehearsal of sorts. And they had done a good job.

Max did have several suggestions. The bright, yellow halos had to go. Halos can be carried off in paintings, but they look foolish otherwise (unless, one presumes, they're real).

The manikins, as all do in Japan, had blond hair and blue eyes. The debate on the subject gave rise to considerable wind-sucking, but Akimbo-san's brother promised to obtain permission to darken the dummies' classically Nordic features.

And, finally, Max was against the snow. In order for the display to be properly visible to people on the street walking past the store window, the manger scene had to be elevated on a wooden platform. Snow, made of fluffy cotton, served the dual purpose of adding brightness to the display as well as hiding the platform. Akimbo-san's brother was reaching the end of his tether, but he gave in and agreed to great piles of straw instead. ("So much headache," he complained.)

Akimbo-san's brother and Max spoke on the telephone one more time before the December 1st opening of the display. His boss was still concerned about "color," and felt that the scene lacked an eye-catching focal point. Akimbo-san's brother and Max talked about the introduction of a holy star shining over the display and how, with proper lighting, golden rays could be directed to the center of attention—the new born infant wrapped in swaddling clothes. "OK," said Akimbo-san's brother, "but I'm getting exhausted on this one." Judging by the tone of his voice, Max could well imagine.

The Danger family, plus friends visiting from the States, trekked to Ginza during the early evening of December 1st. To be part of an artistic endeavor, particularly one so horrendously public, was rather thrilling.

The display was even better than it first appeared on the floor of the basement storage area. The lighting made a big difference.

The ermine and velvet robes worn by the three kings looked a shade too plush, and a vessel presented by one of the kings to the infant bore a suspicious resemblance to a German beer stein, but the overall effect was positive.

117

The manikin representing Mary was contorted in a surprisingly tender fashion depicting natural motherly concern. Joseph stood proudly removed, with New Zealand
sheep at his side. The staffs of the shepherds were a tad short
—they looked more like canes—but Max knew there was a
technical problem with anchoring them on the platform.
Enough straw was in the room to feed all the donkeys in
Judea.

The Christ-child lay happily in his crib, seemingly aware
of all that was going on around him, his head normal in size
for an infant his age. (He *did* appear to be about a year old,
which made one respect Mary even more for her ability to
remain upright after what must have been a stupendous
pregnancy and delivery.) In all respects, the scene captured
the very essence of the birth of Christianity.

Except that Akimbo-san's brother had obviously lost one
argument with his boss. The argument probably had something to do with "color" or focal points. And knowing
Akimbo-san's brother as he did, Max was certain the poor
man was now approaching a state of nervous collapse.

In the background, but in the very center of the tableaux
as it was composed, was someone else. He brought "color"
to the scene, have no doubt about that. Looking over his
shoulder at the activities before him, smiling benignly from
above as it were, and looking away from his chores of
trimming old *tannenbaum,* was your friend and mine lo
these many years—jolly old Saint Nick.

Well, it was close.

New Year's Resolutions

IT WAS THAT time again. Time for the lists. And time for the resolutions. Max Danger, beginning anew, vowed that the following practises and procedures would be purged from his life (no sacrifice is too small):

1. *Give up returning from Korea in the rain at the conclusion of Golden Week on a Sunday night in the rain at Narita with too many parcels for two people to carry in the rain and catching the expediently first bus to Tokyo Station, which discharges passengers in the rain far from the station, and relaying the parcels in the rain to the taxi ranks and then taking separate cabs in the rain a half-hour apart to Homat Cornucopia with the keys to the apartment in the pocket of the second taxi-taker while the first taxi-taker frets, fumes, and throws a soggy feminine fit at the front door pledging to return to Pittsburgh as soon as the rain stops.* Not only that, Japanese cab drivers do not accept Korean won.

2. *Give up eating food that moves.* It makes no difference how good the damn sauce is.

3. *Give up showing off and reporting absolute knowledge of the whereabouts of the mumble-mumble building in Shibuya when in fact there are 946 buildings in Shibuya and*

119

if one is not certain it can take four days and three nights to narrow the field to those just in the area around the station. Max made it to the wedding as the guests, sporting red faces and white shopping bags, were leaving.

4. *Give up ordering ¥800 steak. Anywhere.* Cows have, inside themselves, exotic parts.

5. *Give up answering the phone with a well-modulated "Moshi moshi."* It's amazing how often that launches folks into rapid-fire Japanese.

6. *Give up presenting name cards with two hands, bowing with exaggerated grace, and mumbling things like "Yurakucho Building" when meeting other* gaijin *for the first time.* It was fun the first eight or nine hundred times, but it's now becoming automatic.

7. *Give up predicting the yen/dollar exchange rate for any period of time beyond the next seven minutes.* And then only if it's a weekend.

8. *Give up keeping track of factional political groups in the LDP.* Max, in truth, wonders why he even tried.

9. *Give up laughing when everyone else is laughing at a story told in Japanese when not one word of the remarks is even vaguely intelligible.* Why do we do that? Displaying camaraderie is one thing, but how do we know what's really being said? ("And the grinning *gaijin* here then put his elbow through the *shoji*.")

10. *Give up hopes of making eye-contact with pretty girls on the street.* Max is working on the theory that there

are in fact moments of true invisibility in life—probably something to do with molecules.

11. *Give up kidding oneself that one drink with the staff after work really means one drink with the staff after work.* Boarding the last train in Kawasaki and discovering it's headed toward Nagoya prompted this resolution.

12. *Give up being over-impressed by the peculiar English that abounds at every turn.* Did you ever try writing the Japanese characters for Ginza?

So as to maintain a balance—an equilibrium of positives and negatives—Max has listed the following worthwhile projects or behavior patterns as goals for the coming year:

A. *Learn the words in Japanese for "Don't take so much off the sides but for God's sake shorten the top."* Max frequents the Surprise Barber Shop in the Palace Hotel, and effective communication has yet to be established.

B. *Try one more time the baked goat cheese on the American Club menu.* It *must* be there for reasons other than comic relief.

C. *Remember to be constantly prepared to pour beer into companions' glasses even though they (the glasses) are only one-third empty.* Incidentally, the way to avoid this social sin of omission is to drink nothing but Campari and soda. No one pours Campari and soda back and forth.

D. *Demand that the stockbroker sells shares much too soon.*

121

This is infinitely better than the alternative—selling shares much too late.

E. *Memorize the words and an approximation of the tune of a lovely Japanese* enka *aria so as to absolutely stun bar hostesses,* karaoke *proprietors, company stalwarts, and goodtime charlies hanging around the late-night "amusement" centers.* Knowing "Jingle Bells" in Japanese has seasonal limitations.

F. *Call in sick three or four times a month at the office.* This is particularly important if one wishes to be "accepted" by the staff.

G. *Stop making lists.*

One-Upmanship

"IN HERE, Danger-san, I hope you can sit on the floor, ha, ha."

"Sitting on the floor is quite all right, sir," said Max. "There are times when I prefer it."

"Prefer it, ha, ha. Take your shoes off there, ha, ha."

Max thanked the kimono-clad waitress who was kneeling at his feet. She was helping with shoe-removal—an activity most people manage on their own at least 365 days a year.

"Watch your head, ha, ha. Japanese doorways very low, ha, ha."

122

Max ducked his way into the tatami room and joined his hosts. A Valued Client and his partner were reciprocating, for a lunch Max had hosted earlier in the month at the American Club, with a dinner at an exclusive Japanese restaurant.

"You sit there, ha, ha, with your feet under the table. Under the table, ha, ha."

The cost already to the Valued Client at the exclusive restaurant—even though the party was just being seated—probably exceeded the charge for the whole meal at the American Club. And the saké hadn't even been poured.

"Here, waitress has special seat for you with back, ha, ha," the Valued Client reported just as Max became comfortably seated. Max stood up again and watched from a great height as a kneeling girl monkeyed around with his pillow and the seat contraption. He did not feel so much like an infant for whom a great fuss of arrangements with high chairs and special cutlery is made in fancy restaurants because he noticed that his Valued Client and other guests *already had* the same "special seats" with a back.

"Foreigners have hard time to sit on floor, ha, ha," the Valued Client stated as Max seated himself again. "Our custom too different."

The dinner party, which included Serious Hirose and Watanabe-san from Max's office, was beginning on a jolly note. The Valued Client, whom Max had only met for the first time at the American Club lunch, was extremely hospitable and extremely Japanese. His concern for Max's well-being was in part nervousness: how was he to know how adaptable this particular *gaijin* was going to be? And it was in part a cultural routine which is mastered by all Japanese businessmen somewhere between the third and fourth grade: "Please accept my humble offering (costing upwards of $1,000 per head), which is sadly unworthy, but I'm doing

123

my best." Being treated as a foreigner is often worse than being a foreigner.

Of course, Max knew the inevitable question was coming. Seated in the elegantly appointed room, separated from other elegantly appointed rooms by either the *shoji* at the sides, or the canal of shoes in the walkway at the front, Max looked forward to the question. It usually came as the kimono-clad waitresses were slithering in and out with the equipment for the meal—the pots, the rubber hoses for the gas fire, the trays of saké, and the exquisitely displayed platters of fish, meat, and vegetables. Max found he had to brace himself for the question, lest in a moment of weakness he'd answer in a fashion which would be personally amusing but which would also kill any and all future business deals with his humble host. The question this evening came as the kneeling girl served the first dish—quivering pink-and-white squares of a substance resembling India-rubber erasers wrapped by ribbons of seaweed and garnished with violet sauce and cute, crispy brown fish with round black eyes. (And, despite the description, actually rather good.)

"Danger-san," asked the Valued Client and host of the evening's festivities, "do you like Japanese food, ha, ha?"

On this particular evening, Max found himself not only enjoying the ambience of the event—and the food was good and well served—but also the challenge of a "one-upmanship" contest which slowly emerged in conversation with the Valued Client.

"My father," reported the Valued Client, "went to Tokyo University and wrote the economic white paper which was adopted by the Japanese government in 1937."

"My father," replied Max ("Christ, this is silly," he thought), "was a Cambridge heterosexual who started an investment bank in London in 1936."

124

"My mother," stated the Valued Client, "studied piano under the great Horigome."

"My mother," Max let slip later in the evening, "wrote the Contract Bridge column in *The Times* for seventeen years."

And so on. The Valued Client's company was the first to import American cigarettes into Japan; Max's company was the first to offer volume discounts to Japanese distributors. The Valued Client's children summered in France; Max's summered (if that's what you call Home Leave) in New York. The Valued Client thought Nixon was a great President; Max believed that Prime Minister Tanaka was only trying to help the poor folk of Niigata. The Valued Client drank eight bottles of beer; Max drank nine. It was the kind of evening designed by circumstances to keep one awake. The Valued Client's partner and Max's two staff members spent a great deal of time nodding in agreement and expressing amazement at the "facts" they had each certainly heard several hundred times before.

And all of this made the evening's conclusion more dramatic.

The restaurant's food and service was exceptional. Max, as the evening wore on, was particularly impressed by the service offered by the young kimono-clad girl in white and blue who made a practice of leaning against him as she poured the beer. (Had it not been for that girl, Max may have lost the beer-drinking contest.)

The Danger/Valued Client party was the last to leave the restaurant. Max was the last to leave the tatami room. (Foreigners *do* have problems standing up after sitting on the floor.)

People sat, or stood, wrestling with their shoes. The kimono-clad girls, assisting with a project which, again, most individuals handle by themselves 365 days a year, got in the way with shoehorns and fingers.

It was finally, and lastly, Max's turn. But his shoes were gone.

"Hoh! Hah! Ara!" everyone ejaculated in astonishment.

"Did you have shoes when you came?" the mama-san asked helpfully.

The Valued Client's eyes widened, fogged over, then widened again.

"Where shoes?" he asked the gathering force of restaurant employees.

No one knew.

Except one lady. She was of the toilet cleaning/room straightening/general maintenance brigade.

A great deal of wind was sucked as she gave her explanation. The Valued Client had to be assisted to a chair.

Max's shoes, somewhat round at the heels and comfortably tattered on top, had been mistaken for a common laborer's shoes—the shoes of the workforce cleaning the restaurant before it opened. (Shoes like that should be removed from sight.) They were locked in the maintenance room—and no one had a key. The Valued Client was mortified.

Standing outside the restaurant, saying "goodnight" and catching cabs, Max was resplendent in his blue pin-striped suit and high-top red sneakers (borrowed from a doorman). The Keds Corporation never had a more enthusiastic fan. The Valued Client's wide white eyes were the last thing Max saw as the man drove off mumbling, into the night.

And the Valued Client is now Max's major customer. Try explaining how that happened to the Head Office.

Life in the Field: A Fable for Our Times

"WILDLIFE RESCUE CENTER officials reported today efforts to free the ducks trapped in the oil spill were generally successful. Volunteers and naturalists from the Center captured and tranquilized the ducks, brought them to the Center and cleansed their feathers by submerging the fowl in solutions of fresh water, baby shampoo, and common kitchen detergent. The ducks were released after their feathers were dried with hair blowers."
—*The Japan Times,* April 26, 1988

"You'll never guess what happened to me today." Dick had just landed back at the nest looking for all the world like something the cat dragged in and someone slammed the door on.

"You look like something the cat dragged in and someone slammed the door on," Dick's spouse said. She had just gotten the three kids to sleep, but his arrival woke them up.

"I know, but you won't believe what happened. It was incredible." Dick's spouse began chewing her tail—a sure sign that her attention was wavering.

"What happened, Dad? What happened, Dad? What happened, Dad?" Dick's kids asked. They had the annoying habit of repeating everything, attributable, perhaps, to the fact that most of their lives had been spent in single file.

"Well, there I was, flying over by the inlet where the green

127

grass grows, minding my own business, and looking for red berries."

"That's not exciting," Dick's spouse interrupted. "I took the kids there yesterday."

"Yes, she did. Yes, she did. Yes, she did," the kids confirmed.

"But listen. I wasn't paying much attention to things and it was only as I was landing that I noticed the water was black."

"Shadows," Dick's spouse noted sagely.

"Not shadows," said Dick. "Sticky stuff. Stinking, greasy, black sticky stuff."

"Dick's spouse stopped chewing her tail and looked closely at Dick. Some of his feathers were whiter than ever, and certainly more than normally fluffy. Other feathers, particularly the ones on his chest and in the middle of his back, were black and pasted to the surface of his skin. Even his green neck-ring was darker than usual.

"Wow, Wow, Wow," said the kids. The family was joined by a half-dozen neighbors who floated over to hear Dick's story.

"Wait. The next part's unbelievable," continued Dick. "You know those hairless creatures who wear the strange costumes?"

"You mean the creatures who once a year hide in the bushes with thundersticks?" asked a neighbor.

"Those are the ones," said Dick, "the ones that are fun to dump on. Well, anyway, one of them comes over and picks me up."

"No!"

"Yes."

"It can't be true," said another neighbor.

"Yes, it is," said Dick. "Not only that, the creature put a hose down my neck and filled me up with water."

"Are you feeling all right?" Dick's spouse asked. "You haven't been sleeping well lately."

"Seriously," said Dick, "this actually happened."

A couple of Dick's neighbors drifted away. Putting up with his stories was sometimes too much.

"What happened next? What happened next? What happened next?" the kids asked asked asked.

"The creature put me in a box, and the next thing I knew I was in a big place with a lot of other creatures and many ducks like us."

"Wait right there," demanded one of the neighbors. "Why didn't you just fly away?"

"It's kinda funny about that," Dick admitted. "In the first place I don't think I could. The black sticky stuff was all over me. But also, for some reason, I didn't really *want* to. I was super-relaxed."

"You didn't *want* to?" Dick's spouse asked incredulously.

"That's right, I didn't want to. I felt like the way we did last year when we ate those green plants with five leaves."

"You mean the ones hidden in the field?" Dick's spouse asked.

"Yeah," said Dick. "Same feeling."

"Then how did you escape?" Dick's neighbor asked. The neighbor, staring at the setting sun, was clearly losing interest.

"Well, when they lifted me from the bubble bath . . . "

"They lifted you from what? They lifted you from what? They lifted you from what?" asked you-know-who.

"A bubble bath . . . "

"Children, your father isn't feeling well and you all should be asleep."

"But . . . But . . . But . . . "

Dick's spouse turned her back on him and settled the kids down. One neighbor remained, but he ducked his head

129

under water as Dick began describing the gadget that made a big noise and blew a warm breeze from its mouth.

The sun was at the waterline on the horizon. Dick lazily swam back and forth, in and out of the sun's reflection streaming across the gentle waves, and pondered the great mysteries of life. He was trailing bubbles. Maybe he would awaken in the morning and realize it was all a dream. Maybe the whole thing, even awakening in the morning, was a dream. One thing was certain though, at least based on past experiences, and that was that he'd probably have quite a headache when next the sun appeared.

Max Danger, Expat, thinks of Dick each time he tries to explain the assignment in Japan to the folks back home.

The Wedding

MAX SUSPECTED something was wrong for almost two hours, but it wasn't until the bride threw up on the people at the head table that he knew for certain.

Iwaki and Wakaki worked for Max. One was a young man, one a young woman. Try as he might, Max could never remember which name applied to which person. (Meeting either of them alone on the elevator, Max would give the Standard *Gaijin* Greeting in Circumstances when Names Are Not Clear: *"hush-a-ma-ki-san."* If mumbled rapidly it covered most situations. Unless the person was named Goto or Ando.)

Iwaki and Wakaki conducted a typical office romance wherein they completely and absolutely ignored each other during the working day, traveled on separate buses during company trips, ridiculed each other in conversations with friends, but always seemed to be the last people to leave the office at night. On the surface, and as a matter of form, they may as well have been on opposite sides of the planet. In reality, everyone in the organization knew the situation was torrid.

Iwaki and Wakaki decided to get married. (Everyone's "surprise" was a delight to behold.) The wedding was scheduled for the second weekend in April. And because the wedding featured the "double whammy" of co-workers merging, the pending ceremony became the highly anticipated company social event of the spring. Hours, which would otherwise be wasted on business, were spent juggling the reception dinner seating arrangements based upon the hierarchical situation of those invited—bosses, former teachers, coworkers, grade-school classmates, and, lastly, parents. Since Iwaki and Wakaki worked for the same company, albeit in different departments, the "bosses" issue took on a special significance. When in doubt, the male's superiors won.

Max, of course, became a key player in the ceremony. As the employer of *both* Iwaki and Wakaki, the "meeting" of the two was considered to have taken place under his auspices. He was therefore chosen to kick off the festivities with a speech describing the work habits of Iwaki and Wakaki, and then delve into their various skills in the leisure arts of skiing, playing tennis, and having funny things happen to them.

Japanese weddings are big business. Enormous buildings are constructed for the sole purpose of hosting such events— some of the more popular halls handle over 100 parties each

131

weekend. Hotels are also attractive venues. Some earn as much as 25% of their annual income from wedding receptions. The sub-industry of providing "ceremony managers" —the people who tell the participants when and where to stand and sit—and the folks who lease wedding costumes and supply gifts for guests, create additional revenue for the business. It is now estimated that the average couple spends something in the neighborhood of ¥4 million for the ceremony and reception—a tidy sum by anyone's standards.

Iwaki and Wakaki selected one of the better-known reception palaces for their event. A determinant in setting the date for the wedding had been the availability of the hall. In a mind-boggling display of culinary organization, the hall was to serve over 8,000 five-course dinners to wedding parties using the facilities on that day alone. And that is amazing by anyone's standards.

Max made his speech before the toast and, by writing "Iwaki—Man, Wakaki—Woman" in the gap between thumb and forefinger of his microphone-holding left hand, was successful in distinguishing the celebrants. The festivities, it seemed, began on a proper note.

It is interesting, thought Max, as he sat through the subsequent speeches delivered between courses of food, how private we humans are about certain things. He thought of this after the salmon paté course, and then again after the soup containing the floating pink-and-white jelly items.

Someone was talking about cute things Iwaki did in grade school as the waiters removed the remains of Max's stuffed lobster. Humans, thought Max, are not reluctant to talk about tennis elbow, gout, astigmatism, or chronic headaches. In fact, Max's neighbor on his left was describing to everyone at the table how sick he was with a cold only weeks before.

Yet one rarely discusses gastric disturbances in polite

company. If bronchitis represents a physical malfunction in the marvelous machine that is our body, and the condition is discussed in public forum, why are sudden gastrointestinal storms suffered in silence? Max thought of this as he excused himself from the table after the sherbet and before the roast beef—while Wakaki's high-school years were being detailed by a classmate—and went off to find the men's room.

Max returned to the table during a speech by Iwaki's college professor, in which Iwaki's penchant for sleeping in class was humorously described. Max was behind on the roast beef course, there having been a line at the men's room. The bride and groom went to change clothes during the fruit and ice-cream course.

The skits and loose-harmony songs performed by friends of both Iwaki and Wakaki were amusing. One girl, a childhood pal of Wakaki's, got up and played the piano with her gloves on. She had a pink bow in her hair. Max spotted the pink bow rushing past him a few minutes later as he and his neighbor with a bad cold stood in line in the corridor waiting to get into the men's room.

Wedding cakes at a Japanese wedding are not the big things looking like wedding cakes at the head table. Those things are plastic. A tiny wedge of real cake is inserted into the back of the plastic thing, and the bride and groom ceremoniously cut the tiny wedge. Real cake, baked in flat pans behind the scenes, is distributed to the guests while the bride and groom change clothes yet again and prepare to re-enter with a flaming sword. The flaming sword is employed to light candles at the guest's tables.

Iwaki and Wakaki's reappearance with the flaming sword took an unusually long time. In the interim, Iwaki's college classmates sang their school song, and one of Wakaki's nephews did a tap dance without music. (The piano-playing

133

girl in the pink bow was nowhere to be found.) One of Iwaki's colleagues in the Accounting Department helped the tap dance by rising and contributing a vigorous chorus of "My Way." Max was able to slip out and find a men's room down on the first floor with a shorter line. The father of the bride was ahead of him in the line.

Finally, the lights dimmed and Iwaki and Wakaki entered with the flaming sword. Wags at Max's table had cut off the wick and created a puddle of water in the indentation on the top of the candle. Iwaki and Wakaki bowed to their parents—minus the senior Mrs. Iwaki who was unaccountably absent at the moment—and began the rounds with the flaming sword. The head wag at Max's table—the guy with the cold—got up suddenly and left the darkened room. He'll miss the results of his little prank, Max thought to himself.

Iwaki and Wakaki approached the next to last table—the table nearest Max's. Iwaki, Max noticed, looked terrified. Presumably that's the look of grooms, but it was more pronounced, it seemed, in Iwaki. His face was there, but his attention appeared to be focused inward. He was nervously swallowing, as if preparing to make a speech.

The candle lit, Iwaki and Wakaki turned to Max's table. Someone, hurrying in the semi-darkness, bumped into Iwaki. The flaming sword sputtered and crackled as the bride and groom tried to light Max's candle. Everyone at the table, except the man across from Max whose head was *on* the table, applauded good-naturedly.

Max looked at Wakaki, now the new Mrs. Iwaki. She seemed to radiate a glow he hadn't noticed before in the office. He caught her eye and smiled, hoping his expression indicated a proper mixture of avuncular concern and genuine happiness as she embarked, in marital seas, upon the most significant voyage of her life. All attention in the

134

room was on Max's table. She parted her lips as if to speak. She was beautiful in the light of the flame. It was then, lurching forward, that she performed the rainbow yawn.

It turned out to be the trigger for perhaps a dozen nearly simultaneous eruptions around the room. And then there were the laggards. The phenomenon spread to the hallways and lines for the toilets—a veritable orgy of regurgitation.

It was the salmon pâté, of course, and all moneys for the weddings that day were refunded. But consider how a little honest conversation at the beginning would have altered events. Or at least made things less messy.

The wedding, however, was memorable.

The Explanation

A BASIC COMPONENT of civilized behavior is "the explanation." One simply cannot show up a day late for a meeting without making some comment or remark about one's recent whereabouts. The explanation becomes the soothing balm for inflammation created by breakdowns in orderly societal intercourse.

Quite obviously, the explanation must match the violation in intensity and detail. One needn't explain at length how the leaping flames, the arrival of firemen, the hacking apart of the house, the hosing of the neighborhood, the rescuing of children, and the pumping of water from the cellar caused delays in the normal *routine de la toilette* if one is only ten minutes late for a dinner party.

By the same reasoning, stating "I missed the bus" will not suffice if one is three months late for one's wedding. Details, in this circumstance, must be provided.

One problem with adulthood is that the range of acceptable explanations narrows as we gain increasing control of our lives. Children, for example, can get away with things like "I was looking at the flowers," or "I couldn't remember my name" when explaining deviant behavior. Only drunks can do that as adults.

Living as foreigners in Japan, however, opens the door to a whole new world of explanation possibilities. With the same control of many of the details of our lives as we had as children, explanations like "I couldn't remember my address" can now be legitimately uttered by adults. And the explanation will be treated with tolerance and understanding.

Max Danger has been collecting explanations since the move to Japan. More specifically, Max has been collecting circumstantial events leading to the explanations. It helps to have lived in Japan to appreciate fully how it is that grown men and women—educated pillars of society and captains of industry—are forced to explain that while driving the car around the block they became helplessly lost. The last time that kind of thing happened to most of us, we were riding tricycles. But the explanation is perfectly understood and accepted. We've probably already been there.

One of Max's favorite circumstantial events requiring an explanation has to do with simply going from Point A to Point B. Visualize, if you will, a map of Tokyo. Point A is Hiroo, Point B is a building across from the Yasukuni Shrine in Kudan. The distance, as those ugly black crows fly, is six kilometers. The Palace is in between, of course, but major surface routes swing around the imperial enclave

136

and course on a fairly direct basis to Kudan. If it were not for traffic, the trip could be made in ten minutes.

A gentleman new to Japan—an educated pillar of society and captain of industry—asked for directions from Hiroo to Kudan. It was suggested to him that driving directly at 3:00 on a business afternoon would not be wise if he planned to make it to Kudan in time for his 3:30 meeting. Instead, it was recommended that he consider taking public transportation.

The subway route from Hiroo to Ebisu—a temporary jaunt going in the opposite direction from Kudan—was described in detail. At Ebisu, the man was told to board the Yamanote train that circles the downtown area and to go past Shibuya to Shinjuku. The man was then told to disembark and take the Toei Shinjuku subway to Kudan-shita.

The effect of this maneuver, again visualizing a map of Tokyo, is to move away from the city center, describe an arc of about 60 degrees on the circle line, and then shoot straight to Kudan from a different angle but more direct train route. All but part of one side of a triangle is encompassed, and about fifteen kilometers are involved, but it can be done in a half-hour.

The man arrived at his meeting in the building across from Yasukuni Shrine in Kudan at 5:45. He could not understand it, he reported. He had followed the directions exactly as described. He had gone to every destination indicated. Faithfully. He did mention, however, that he had felt a little uncomfortable about taking trains. Instead, was "the explanation": he took a taxi!

In another circumstantial event requiring an explanation, the key players were Max and a European lady whose Tokyo experience totaled less than a month. It was, in fact, Max who reconstructed the explanation for the lady after twenty-four hours of hard feelings on both sides.

Max and the lady were strangers. A mutual friend had recommended that the lady contact Max when she arrived in Tokyo. She was to deliver a book to Max from the mutual friend.

They chatted on the phone and agreed that it would be convenient to meet at the American Club. Max told her that cab drivers generally knew the whereabouts of the Club, and that she should either ask for him at the front desk or proceed to the cocktail lounge next to the lobby.

The lady never showed up. And when she rang Max on the phone the next day, she was extremely agitated. "Rudeness," she explained, "was not what she had expected from an associate of their mutual friend—even an American." From her point of view, *Max* had not showed up.

"The people at your club are not polite," she amplified. "When I asked for you at the front desk, they said they had no idea who you were and that they were too busy to try and find you. Furthermore, when I asked for the cocktail lounge, they suggested I leave the premises. It was humiliating."

Max and the lady spoke for a few more minutes. The situation was indeed puzzling. It was, however, the description of her removal from the premises that provided the clue for "the explanation."

"And why," she had asked, "must you use Marine guards to protect your place?"

The cab driver had taken her to the American Embassy.

A final example of circumstantial events requiring an explanation is remembered by Max with some pain. It was the day of the job interview.

Max left the hotel in Nagoya early, got caught in traffic,

and barely made it to the train station in time for the 8:10 Shinkansen express. In fact, he had to run through the station lobby asking directions to the tracks while struggling with an overnight bag and a heavy briefcase.

He caught the train, found his seat in the relatively luxurious "Green Car," and settled back for what turned to be a perfectly delightful two-hour trip. The girls pushing the refreshment carts up and down the aisle were always there at the right time with the right merchandise, no one was sitting in the opposite seats, enabling Max to stretch his legs, and the conductor collecting the tickets was extremely polite as he discussed with Max the procedures for "fare adjustment." All in all, a perfect trip.

The train arrived on schedule to the minute. Max stretched, disembarked, and lugged the heavy bags through the lobby and over to the bank of phones against the wall. He had a luncheon appointment at the Keyaki Grill—one of Tokyo's finest—with a man from a competing corporation who was prepared to heap great sums of money on Max's worthy shoulders in return for employment. "I'd pay anything," he had said in earlier correspondence, "for someone over there in Japan who knows his way around."

Max telephoned the man in his hotel room. He caught him just as he was leaving for the restaurant. It's a shame, Max thought, as he made preliminary small talk, that the man will never understand. Not having been in Japan before, he's never run in panic through the Nagoya train station, never had to make sense of shouted bilingual directions, or never had to try to read *kanji* on the fly. He's probably never ever been on a train for two hours, unless it was broken. To an outsider, "the explanation" sounded so puny.

Max was in Osaka.

A Complete Novel

CHAPTER 1

MAX'S ELDEST, Max III, won a motorbike at an international school food festival. (Scholars, centuries from now, will probably puzzle over that sentence. "We've examined the writing on the ancient manuscript from every angle, and still cannot find a connection between motorbikes, schools, and food.")

The motorbike had a cute little body on cute little wheels. A cute little engine, making cute little noises, propelled the vehicle by means of a cute little chain attached to the aforementioned cute rear wheel. New, it was one of those rare bits of machinery one could cuddle. (Or put on the mantel.) In practice, it was designed for dwarfs.

Max III parked it one day in Shibuya. Someone must have come along, said "My, what a cute little bike," and put it in his pocket, because it was nowhere to be found.

CHAPTER 2

The beautiful Gloria paid the cab driver, gathered her stuff, shot the umbrella out the door, and stepped into teeming rain. It was a rotten day to be out shopping.

It was also a rotten day to lose one's wallet, containing all money, documentation, and house keys. Gloria discovered the loss as she entered the department store. After retracing her steps, sloshing around in the gutter water, and feeling completely ridiculous, she paid a visit to the nice men at the corner police box.

CHAPTER 3

Max Danger stuffed both briefcases with documents, explained to Akimbo-san that he was going into hiding, and left for home. Max knew, as most businessmen know, that the office is the *last* place to be as report deadlines approach.

CHAPTER 4

Max III and his sister were hanging around the house. The Danger children were three in number, and attended three different schools. For reasons fraught with extraordinary complexity, school holidays for all three rarely coincided. The youngest had school, a family trip was out, and it was raining. Max III and his sister, therefore, were hanging around the house.

CHAPTER 5

The beautiful Gloria threw herself upon the mercy of the nice men in the police box. "Yes, I realize I must always carry my Alien Registration Card. But that's part of the problem," Gloria explained in sign language, "I lost it."

CHAPTER 6

Max had reached the B-2 level of the parking garage when he realized his car keys were back upstairs in the office. "Drat!"

CHAPTER 7

"I'll get it," Max III told his sister. The hanging around was being enhanced by a videotaped movie. "Someone must have forgotten their keys."

The unkempt man at the door was a stranger. He spoke not a word, but pointed grimly to the keys in his hand.

They were familiar keys. They were cute keys. They were the keys that came with the cute little bike—and had disappeared with the cute little bike weeks before.

The man motioned to Max III, indicating that he should follow him. He continued to dangle the keys in front of him as he backed away from the front door.

Max III followed the man, at a discreet distance, to the street. There was no cute little bike, but instead a rusty old Toyota. An equally unkempt man was at the wheel of the rusty old Toyota, and he indicated to Max III that he should enter the car.

Being nobody's fool, Max III explained that he was returning to the house for an umbrella. Once inside, he locked the door and related the events to his sister.

"They could be real gangsters," she whispered in awe. "Let's call the police."

The jangling of keys at the front door was actually rather startling.

"My house keys were with the bike keys," Max III reported as he and his sister locked the bedroom door. "We *are* in trouble." They called the police.

CHAPTER 8

The phone rang just as Max was leaving the office for the second time. A whispered voice, which took Max several moments to recognize as that of his son, said something about calling the police. "They're even trying to get in the bedroom door," said the whisper.

Max called the police.

CHAPTER 9

"Someone at home can speak Japanese," Gloria gesticulated. Any of the children would be able to translate

142

Gloria's difficulties to the nice men at the police box. "Let me borrow your phone."

It took several minutes for the message to get through, but when it did, Gloria and the police took off with remarkable dispatch for the Danger abode.

CHAPTER 10

The rattling of the bedroom doorknob was the last straw. "Out the window," Max III whispered to his sister. "You go first."

Squeezing out of the Homat Cornucopia window was no mean achievement. Max III's sister made it rather easily, but he had to struggle. In fact, it was probably when Max III was straddling the sill and working his chest through the opening that good-neighbor Mrs. Tsubota looked his way. Not recognizing him as one of the Danger offspring, she did what any good neighbor would do under the circumstances. She called the police.

CHAPTER 11

"Those two persons outside very extremely angry," reported the spokesman for the fifteen assembled men of the police force. He was addressing the complete Danger family—the youngest had earlier returned home from school and was still wondering why the bedroom door hadn't opened. "You can imagine that they are so angry."

Yes, he could imagine, Max thought to himself. To have four wailing police cars, lights aflashing, descend suddenly upon you and your rusty old Toyota on a quiet rainy afternoon can be unnerving to even the most placid of souls. And to be pulled from your car, whomped against the wall, and searched, is downright unpleasant. It's a wonder, Max reflected, *they* didn't call the police.

143

"We had funny experience with *gaijin* today," unkempt man number one reported to his wife. Unkempt man number two nodded in agreement. They were sitting around an old oil burner which provided both warmth and hot water for tea. The front half of the building, separated from the living quarters, was the vegetable store.

It was because someone had parked the bike in the area on the sidewalk where the vegetables usually go that they had moved it in the first place. And each day, for the last three weeks, they carefully moved the bike aside when they opened in the morning, and carefully moved the bike back when they closed.

For a few days they attached a sign to the bike reading "Whose bike is this?" but when they got no response, they began the ordeal of tracing the owner through the serial number on the cute little engine. It took awhile—tracing the thing from the dealer to the corporate donor to the international school to the prize committee chairman to the Danger household—but they did it. Because the unkempt men were reluctant to move the bike more than the few meters they were moving it each day, they went off in quest of the owner armed only with the keys.

"The boy went back to the house to get an umbrella," said the man. "We waited and waited in the car. Soon a little kid went into the house. And we waited and waited."

"Maybe he misunderstood you," offered the wife.

"He couldn't have misunderstood us," said the second man. "We didn't say anything to him. But it sure was a surprise when the police came."

CHAPTER 13

"The most interesting thing of all," commented Max to the family at dinner, "is how the police strongly urged *us* to apologize to the men. *They* were the ones who roughed them up."

"I think it is more interesting," said Gloria, "that the men made such an attempt to find us."

"But it is too bad," said Max III, "that someone either guessed wrong or mistakenly gave the wrong information during the search."

You see, when matters calmed, issues were explained, and parties to the dispute were introduced—*and* apologies were offered and accepted—the police drove Max III to the vegetable store to pick up the bike. They drove him up and down hills, around corners, and to a section of Shibuya he had never before visited.

The bike, a cute little devil, was not his.

Progress to Date

IT IS IMPORTANT to take oneself from the game occasionally, to sit on the sidelines and quietly reflect upon progress to date. Tiny steps back facilitate great leaps forward.

For an expat scrimmaging with the challenge of adaptation, a basic point to consider in the progress to date examination is the degree to which an awareness of, and a sensitivity to, local cultural patterns and behavioral mores is being developed and appreciated. One lives comfortably only if one knows what's going on.

As a community service, Max Danger offers the following test designed to measure progress to date in the culturalization process. It is suggested that the test be completed in an atmosphere of calm and sober reflection.

1. Japanese intestines are: (a) longer than anybody else's, (b) shorter than anybody else's, (c) wider than anybody else's, (d) nonexistent.

2. Draining the Pacific Ocean and refilling it with American citrus juice would: (a) solve balance-of-trade problems, (b) not be noticed, (c) surprise a lot of fish, (d) lead to the development of trade barriers in the form of dikes and levees around the entire coastline of Japan.

3. Japanese food is: (a) finger lickin' good, (b) an acquired taste, (c) an example of the old axiom that taste and pretty presentation relate in an inverse ratio, (d) designed for special intestines.

4. Most foreigners find that learning to read, write, and speak Japanese is: (a) childishly simple, (b) something that requires at least two hours of study each week, (c) not unlike that task of affixing feathers to the limbs with tar, flapping the arms, and soaring into space to take a good look at the sun, (d) none of the above.

5. Business decisions in Japan are: (a) made with a rapidity that absolutely stuns the senses, (b) made with a deliberation that absolutely numbs the senses, (c) made by committees involving a significant portion of the entire population, (d) made by the Ministry of Finance.

6. The percentage of foreigners exhibiting patience in a traffic jam is: (a) .01, (b) .001, (c) .0001, (d) 0.

7. The percentage of Japanese exhibiting patience in a traffic jam is: (a) 80%, (b) what traffic jam?, (c) my car, my life, (d) only parts of the above.

8. Which is easier: (a) satisfactorily explaining a forgotten Alien Registration Card, or (b) being a rich man *and* getting your camel through the eye of a needle?

9. Daylight Saving Time, a little phenomenon observed over great portions of this globe, cannot exist in Japan because: (a) no one can go home from work 'til dark, (b) sensitive dairy cows in Hokkaido will have their delicate routines disturbed, (c) kids will spend too much time on warm summer evenings playing around outdoors, going to the park, riding bicycles up and down hills, chasing their friends about, getting dirty, and trying to get one more turn at bat before sunset instead of being at home where they belong in front of the TV, (d) it's unwise to tamper with the rising sun.

10. Earthquakes are: (a) worse in concept than in actuality; that is, we're hanging around where tectonic plates the size of continents are colliding beneath our feet, (b) good if they're small and frequent, (c) good if they're large and rare (once every quadrillion years), (d) not particularly pleasant under any circumstances.

11. Golf is: (a) a game wherein a little ball is banged along the ground by a "player" using special sticks collected for the purpose, and with the object being to try and count accurately the number of times the "player" hits the little ball with his sticks before it goes into a hole in the ground; (b) a high-powered performance arena wherein captains of industry test each other's competitiveness and resolve, display athletic prowess and skills unachievable by lesser mortals, and form the sort of "executive relationships" so necessary for the prevention of political and economic collapse; (c) a game played with sticks and a little ball by folks who know it's a whole lot better, since the system supports it anyway, to be out in the fresh air walking through the countryside than wearing a necktie and sitting in the office; (d) no laughing matter in Japan.

12. The Japanese medical profession is world renown for:

147

(a) its diagnostic skills, (b) the interior decor of its spotless clinics and hospitals, (c) its cautious approach to pill dispensation, (d) its neat system of ambulances having nothing to do with hospitals.

13. Sumo wrestlers are: (a) fat people, (b) skilled athletes, (c) in a world of their own, (d) seldom loquacious.

14. Baseball players are: (a) thin people, (b) skilled athletes, (c) in a world of their own, (d) invariably loquacious.

15. The Japanese film industry: (a) panders to a permanent market of thirteen-year-olds, (b) does an outstanding job dramatizing for the world the trauma of Japan's internal conflicts and adjustments on the way to super-power-dom, (c) loves the Rainy Season, (d) is located primarily in Tokyo; however, some production units are based in Osaka and there is quite a bit of traveling back and forth going on at almost any given time, as you would imagine.

16. Mastery of the language: (a) makes it easier, (b) makes it more difficult, (c) all of the above, (d) all and none of the above.

Answers

A = 2.5 points, B = 8 points, C = 0.9 points, D = either 6 or 7 points. Total your score and divide by the square root of today's yen/dollar exchange rate, then add the number of times you've been lost during the last four weeks. A score of 80–100 means you're Japanese and shouldn't have been taking this test in the first place. A score of 60–80 means you've arrived in Japan during the last six months and your perspective remains unclouded. A score of 40–60 is an embarrassment and means you're a Japan veteran. A score of 20–40 means you're Japanese and shouldn't have been taking this test in the first place.

Marital Tension

"Explaining some things upon arrival at home in the wee hours is far easier than explaining other things."
—Rabelais (*c.* 1490–1553)

EXPLAINING THE FACT that one is wearing a chicken costume at 4:30 AM is one of the things that is *not* easy. It would be far easier, far easier indeed, explaining the 4:30 AM hour if dressed in a normal suit and tie. ("You see, the train jumped the rails and went several miles inland before anyone noticed.")

For example, one early morning Max was standing in the dark at the bedroom closet door very quietly taking off his necktie. The beautiful Gloria stirred ever so slightly in her well-deserved slumbers.

"What time is it?" she gently inquired. "And where the hell have you been?"

With but the barest pause, Max responded with the air of a martyr about to earn his title.

"I didn't want to wake you," he said, putting the necktie he had just taken off back around his neck, "but I have an early morning breakfast meeting and must leave the house soon." (He was able to grab an hour's nap on the couch in the living room before leaving for the "breakfast meeting.")

Chicken costumes, however, complicate the issue.

The evening began simply, as many do, with "drinks with the staff after work." Max, of course, was wearing a suit and tie. The occasion was nothing in particular—it had to do with a guy in Serious Hirose's department passing an examination for some kind of license. The timing was important, however. It had been almost two months since the last drinks-with-the-staff-after-work session.

The first stop in the adventure was a beer hall under the train tracks near Tokyo Station. The word "cozy" is perhaps overworked as a descriptive adjective, so instead picture a low-ceilinged room designed for fifteen or twenty people but crammed with sixty or seventy people seated on tiny benches and hunched over low tables, walls yellowed by decades of smoke, beer-breath humidity steaming the window, air pungent with the aroma of chicken on sticks, and trains roaring a few meters overhead every thirty seconds, then supply your own adjective. "Intimate" perhaps.

A discussion developed within Max's group about the rowdy behavior of folks participating in Chinese New Year celebrations.

"One year," Serious Hirose explained, "we went to a Chinese restaurant for a party. One of my friends put a package of firecrackers in my back pocket."

Hirose leaned back and looked at the metal ceiling of the beer hall tucked beneath the tracks near Tokyo Station. He had the smiling, far away look of all men recalling the good old days of Japanese university studenthood.

"No one was more surprised than me," said Hirose returning to the present, "when someone lit them."

It was enough to swing the mood of Max's group, and plans were immediately made to jump on one of the overhead trains and roar down to the Chinatown section of Yokohama. There would still be plenty of time to catch the

150

tail-end of a dragon dance or the remnants of a sumptuous banquet.

"There is nothing," all agreed, "like a good Chinese New Year's party."

Leaving the noise, chaos, smoke, smells, and crowds of the beer hall beneath the train tracks near Tokyo Station, Max was not yet aware that he had just spent the quietest moments of his evening. There is *really* nothing like a good Chinese New Year's party—in Japan.

Try as he might, Max could not remember when it was during the evening that the idea of changing from his suit into the chicken costume began to seem like the reasonable thing to do. The following day sheds light on the facts of behavior only—the motives remain buried with the songs, dances, food, wine, gusto, and laughter of the night before.

The Chinatown section of Yokohama was crowded. It was not the kind of crowd that crushes or impedes movement. Instead, people strolled, ran, bumped into each other, got in the way in doorways, sometimes shuffled, but always moved.

Kids threw firecrackers. Shills shouted. Chinese songs joined the cacophony of sound blaring from most storefronts—the best of rock and roll, and country and western.

Under a flashing red sign, Max and his group bought fried noodles from a sidewalk vendor whose wok was the size of a satellite dish. They elbowed up to the beer and Chinese whiskey booths and got involved in a game which called for finishing a drink before chanters and clappers stopped chanting and clapping.

It was during the walk to an area where a dragon dance was forming that Max spotted the chicken costume. The store, selling food, stationery, children's toys, wristwatches, and cigarettes, was crowded. But there, hanging behind the lady at the cash box, was the costume—in all its yellow glory. Max bought it.

The dragon dance and swirl of activity around it was actually becoming a bit wild for Max and his hardy crew. It is difficult abandoning oneself to the emotion of the moment wearing a suit, tie, and carrying a briefcase and shopping bag full of chicken costume parts. The affliction of thirst was gripping the adventurers as well.

Hirose found a family restaurant/saloon/hostess bar/ salaryman meeting place/coffee shop/game center establishment about the size of the average Homat apartment. People were singing, laughing, drinking, and setting off firecrackers.

It was about this time that Max, his friends, and their new friends locked arms in a circle and hopped to a folk dance, that he began to think of the chicken costume and how it might contribute to the evening's gaiety. Max, and the shopping bag, slipped into the men's room.

Of course, a six-foot chicken is *de facto* unusual. That's a given. People don't see that every day, but it is interesting to note that on this particular evening a six-foot chicken was no more unusual than a six-foot dragon, a guy in a horse's head, or girls dressed up as concubines—all of whom were there.

Oh boy, was it fun. Hirose upheld the honor of Max's group—in the group silliness contest—by wrapping a tablecloth around his shoulders and over his head, then performing an amusing pantomime in rhythm of an old lady scooping fish (or rice or seashells or something). The chicken discovered two brands of beer he had never heard of before, and more than one young lady approached and played with his feathers. Oh boy.

The decision to move to a different "club" was as sudden and apparently undirected as the shifts in movement of whole flocks of birds in the sky. One moment the group was singing a drinking song, the next moment everyone was grabbing brief cases and shopping bags for a quick visit to an establishment boasting prettier girls. "Just down the street," said those who knew.

Max saw no good reason to change back into street clothes for so short a journey. Indeed, amid the chaos of flashing fireworks displays, dancers snaking through the throngs of revellers, and the noisy camaraderie of people having fun, the chicken costume blended right in. Max danced briefly in the street with two guys wearing dragon heads with long streamers. Someone even handed him a tall bottle of saké. Oh boy.

It was as Max's group was readying for the long trek back to Tokyo—a trip involving taxis since trains had stopped running hours before—that the little problem was discovered. The club with prettier girls had a large and spacious men's room. Max brought the shopping bag containing his street clothes to the room to change. The bag, however, contained women's underwear, a blouse, tweed skirt, and a purse belonging to one Yuko Ogawa. It did not contain his suit and tie. The wrong bag had been grabbed at the previous establishment, and that joint had closed over an hour ago. Was that ever hilarious.

"Well, Mr. Chicken, you were probably working late at the office." Gloria's voice was muffled by the bedclothes pulled over the lower half of her face.

"Uh, actually, I was with the guys from the office," Max explained, not certain what more there was to say.

"Did you have a good time, Mr. Chicken?" Gloria asked.

"Well, in a way there were amusing moments, but . . . "

"Tell me, Mr. Chicken, did you lay any eggs?" Gloria inquired.

"Heh, heh, in a way I did," replied Max, relieved that Gloria was apparently taking this thing rather well.

"That's good," said Gloria, rolling over in bed and turning off the light on the nightstand. "Because that'll be the last laying you'll do for a very long time."

The Absolute Last of Mr. Etiquette

DEAR MR. ETIQUETTE: My husband came home at 4:30 this morning wearing a yellow chicken costume and carrying the underwear and personal belongings of a Ms. Yuko Ogawa of Yokohama. My question is this: Why is it that for some reason I can imagine a perfectly acceptable and rational explanation for it all? Signed: *This Better Be Good, Buster*

Dear Better Be Good: Well madam, ahem, I think you'll find that the demands of business in Japan include participation in all kinds of late night semi-intoxicated tomfoolery—the type of behavior which certainly would not appeal to you and me as mature adults—and which, if the truth were known, is actually about as enjoyable as shin splints. The rigidity of corporate hierarchies in Japan, however, creates a desperate need for both the safety-valve factor afforded by drinks-with-the-staff-after-work sessions and the opening of communication channels which during the day are choked by form and protocol. If I were you, I'd pin a medal on your husband's sensitive breast, and congratulate him on his mastery of top-executive mores and behavior patterns. He probably had a difficult evening.

P.S. It's funny you should mention a chicken costume. The other evening I attended a Chinese New Year's celebration in Yokohama, and there *was* this guy in a chicken costume turning cartwheels down the street while some girl was running after him with his suit and tie in her arms. He beat her to the taxi, and she stood on the sidewalk and burst into tears. Now *he* was having fun.

Dear Mr. Etiquette: I called my doctor and told him that my foot was swollen and painful. He said to rest it and call him the next day. I called the next day and told him that although I rested it, the foot was even more swollen and painful. He asked if it hurt more when I moved it, and I said yes. He said, "Don't move it then," and directed me to call him again the following day. When I called and told him that my foot was so swollen that I couldn't wear a normal shoe and the pain was becoming more than just unpleasant, he agreed to an appointment. When I showed him my foot, he examined it from every angle and carefully measured its size as compared to my other foot. He prescribed pills and presented a bill for ¥21,000. When asked for a diagnosis, he reported that my foot "was swollen." Did I get ripped off? Signed: *A Reformed Jogger*

Dear Reformed: No. (And consider yourself lucky the foot wasn't amputated when you weren't looking.)

Dear Mr. Etiquette: Isn't it impolite to use your own chopsticks to pick food from a communal plate. After all, those things have been in our mouths. Signed: *Not Certain Whether One Is Being Overly Fastidious Or Not*

Dear Overly Fastidious: One may poke, prod, and pick

155

anything one desires with chopsticks. Think of them as extensions of your fingers. One may not, however, clean them in your hair or wipe them under your arms.

Dear Mr. Etiquette: Why is it that after all the time I've spent in Japan. I have never observed Japanese talking to each other with the same barely-controlled passion and ill-disguised hostility that characters on televised dramas seem to employ? *Signed: Wondering If There Might Not Be A Certain Element Of Play Acting And Exaggeration Built Into Popular Cultural Offerings Which Serve As A Vicarious Release For The General Populace At Large*
   Dear Vicarious Release: Beats me.

Dear Mr. Etiquette: Exactly what day was it you visited Yokohama and saw a guy in a chicken costume cavorting about shamelessly in public? Signed: *This Really Better Be Good*
   Dear This Really: Last Friday, as I recall. Why?

Dear Mr. Etiquette: How can I break the unpleasant habit of bowing to everyone and everything I come across during the course of a day—even voices on the other end of a telephone? Signed: *With Deep Respect, Wondering*
   Dear Respect, Wondering: Move to Spain.

Dear Mr. Etiquette: Is jealousy a factor in the attitude shared by many *gaijin* toward the special successes of a small group of "foreign talents" on local television? Signed: *What Good Was Taking Latin in High School?*
   Dear Latin In High School: No.

Dear Mr. Etiquette: I am a fourth-generation Japanese-American, born and raised near the beach at Malibu, a graduate of UCLA, and a holder of a Ph.D. in TESL granted by the University of Chicago. When stationed with my husband in England, I guest-lectured at Oxford on the influence of Norman-French on the language spoken by Anglo-Saxon serfs in the twelfth century. My hobby at the time was teaching deaf and dumb children to recite the complete works of James Joyce and to repeat Danny Kaye monologues in appropriate dialects. Why can't I get a job teaching English now that I live in Japan? Signed: *Etsuko Swanson*

Dear Mrs. Swanson: Don't be silly. (Heh, heh. I can never tell whether or not people are putting me on with these naive questions.) Take a peek at yourself in the mirror. Do "native English speakers" ever look like that?

Dear Mr. Etiquette: Why do most of your questions have nothing to do with etiquette? Signed: *Smells A Rat*

Dear Smells: That question is not polite.

Dear Mr. Etiquette: Was the girl chasing the guy in the chicken costume clutching a handful of feathers? Signed: *A Lot Depends On Your Answer*

Dear A Lot: Since the time of our last correspondence, an old buddy of mine and I got together at lunch and discussed The Meaning of Life and all its ramifications. It's a good thing too. I now remember that it was a *Thursday* I was in Yokohama, the guy was wearing a *giraffe* suit, and he was *praying in a temple*. I can't imagine what got into me.

157

Dislocation

"YOU WILL EITHER be transferred sometime this summer, or not. If not, it will either be by the end of the year, or late next spring. Unless, of course . . . "

There is nothing like the crystal clear, unequivocal career-path guidance that expats receive while laboring abroad for love of country and company.

"If things clear up in Beirut, your name's at the top of the list. You may, however, wish to brush up on your Spanish—Madrid and Miami are opening soon."

Residency overseas, with families and schooling involved, calls for especially sensitive career counseling and advice.

"Let's see, did you come from Aerospace or the Food and Industrial Paint division?"

It is comforting to know that one is not merely a pin on the corporate headquarters map of worldwide activities.

"Why not send in your résumé and we'll see if we can find something for you in either Toledo or Birmingham."

And it is important for expats to able to exchange views regarding new assignments with people whose fingers firmly clutch the corporate pulse.

"You're right, the damned thing came up from Personnel and I just assumed it was Birmingham, Alabama. I *do* know the Toledo job's in Sweden."

Yes, the specter of relocation looms larger with each passing month on assignment. And it has been thus since the dawn of commerce. "Oog, you come back to cave on our side of mountain. We discover brontosaurus now extinct."

You would think, however, that the experience accumulated down through the eons would have contributed to a standard model of performance in handling the cares and concerns of the overseas warrior as he's shifted from battlefield to battlefield. Why must the process still be one not unlike the invention of the wheel? (And imagine if we still had to do *that* each day—no one would ever get to work until noon.)

One of Max's business colleagues was a young man named Powell. He had been transferred from the Head Office to Japan several years before Max. Powell was sailing blithely along in Tokyo, feeling, as he put it, "somewhat cocooned" from the trials and tribulations normally dished up by the Head Office. His name was disappearing from mailing lists.

During a visit to Tokyo, the vice president of Powell's division suddenly looked up from his papers and notes, stared at Powell, and then asked him what he was doing in Japan.

"Attending this meeting," Powell replied with feeling.

"I mean, what the hell are you doing *in Japan* attending this meeting?" he asked.

"It only seemed," said Powell, "the proper thing to do."

Well, it appears that a decision had been made at "corporate levels" regarding Powell's career, but the execution of that decision left something to be desired. A different Powell in Hong Kong (which as we all know is close to Tokyo) was mistakenly notified of the transfer and had relocated with his family, months before, to Manila. The muddle was solved, with all the wisdom the corporation could muster, by transferring *both* Powells to London. There, at least, the company could keep an eye on them.

Consider the adventures of Ted K. and his family. They

were transferred to Tokyo one fine spring day and moved into Homat Cornucopia next to the Danger apartment. The fact that the move occurred in the middle of the school year did not dampen the enthusiasm felt by the family for the Japan odyssey. Mrs. Ted K., by making several round-trip expeditions to the States and back, managed to corral the three children and organize their entry into the Tokyo international school system.

The Ted K. furniture trickled in all spring, and by June the family was settled. (The Ted K. grand piano even made the trip—it was positioned next to the one wall shared in common with the Dangers.)

Because of an articulate report initiated by the Head Office Human Resources Department and run through the expense-control sub-section of the Accounting Department—both groups famous for possessing the business acumen of nuns in a cloister—a Delivery System/Staff Services Study was organized for Senior Management. Senior Management, its attention as diverted by Zen considerations of flower petals on a pond as influenced by currency exchange rates, bought the scheme. Ted K. and his family were shipped back to the States in the middle of the following school year, never having gone through one cherry blossom viewing season.

Nothing is particularly remarkable about the above—people sharing the experiences of Ted K. and his family are legion. What is interesting is that Ted K. and his family were sent *back* to Japan thirteen months later. "It is not my position to second-guess the wonderful folks in Human Resources," reported Ted, "but the maneuver cost the old corporation one year and a million dollars." Ted K. was explaining this at the same Homat Cornucopia apartment he had rented before—120% more precious than it was the first time around—and he was explaining it with the attitude of one called upon to describe the underlying rationality in the behavior of chimpanzees zonked on cocaine. He had been in Japan, this second time, twenty-one months. The party at his apartment was his sayonara bash—the Ted K. family was yet again being transferred to the States.

"Nice country you all got here," Ted K. told one and sundry, "but I ain't coming back."

Max was even beginning to sense the Grim Reaper's shadow flitting about on the edges of his own career path. Cleverly disguised questions such as "Can you speak Portuguese?" or "Have you ever considered living in the southern hemisphere?" were popping up more and more. One particularly subtle inquiry began with the "just out of curiosity" phrase. "Do you still have a house in the States," Max was asked, just out of curiosity, "that you could move into in a hurry?"

It was during this period, as Max was wrestling with his thoughts and slowly formulating in his mind a response to the inevitable relocation question, that the letter came.

"Don't be silly," said the beautiful Gloria, "you'll have to open the letter sometime." It had remained untouched on the dining room table all evening. "It *might* say we've been rejected."

The letter has become, for many expats, a powerful indication that the end is near. It usually arrives two-and-a-half to three years after the relocation to Japan, and its appearance heralds a pending transfer as surely as robins herald spring.

The letter stimulates debate within the family, it forces people to soberly ponder goals and ambitions, and it brings into the open the pro and con specifics of life in old Edo.

Max opened the letter. In his category of employment,

161

three out of four expats are history six months after its arrival. "And come to think of it," Max mused, "Tokyo isn't such a bad place after all."

Max and Gloria each read the letter silently. They decided not to tell the children for a few days—it was not even certain between the two of them if being one of the three-fourths who leave or the one-fourth who stay would be better at this time in their lives. But the odds were that the relocation issue would have to be dealt with soon. The Dangers had reached the top of the waiting list.

The letter was an invitation to join the Tokyo Lawn Tennis Club.

The Great Bicycle Race

TOKYO, WITH some twelve million souls, is the world's largest functioning and services-integrated city. Of course, there are larger masses of people in other countries huddled around metropolitan centers—and those "cities" may number more bodies—but there is nothing like Tokyo.

With a coordinated communication system, running water and sewers, paved streets and roads, and comprehensive public transportation, the capital of Japan is organized as no other city in history. And, by and large, Tokyo works.

One feature of the public transportation system is a circular train line, running on elevated tracks, which serves as a connecting link between suburban transportation arriving on its rim and urban rapid transit shooting as spokes to the hub of central Tokyo. To dwell within the Yamanote

Line was once considered to be the ultimate in city living. However, changing patterns of land use and burgeoning population growth have blurred the original distinction between inside and outside the line. In some parts of the city, the distinctly urban characteristics of skyscrapers, entertainment centers, and huge shopping malls have burst the Yamanote boundary. In other parts of the city, the elevated train runs through the city-villages and local communities more reminiscent of the days of yore. A circuit of the line is a tour of Tokyo of the last half century.

"Wouldn't it be a good idea," someone mentioned in Max's poker group, "to get up early tomorrow morning and ride our bicycles around Tokyo? "The suggestion was not received enthusiastically. It was 1:30 AM.

But the idea did have merit. And within a month, a "tour" was organized. The man with the original idea, upon sober reflection in the cold light of day, backed out of the project. "Too many hills, come to think of it," was his assessment.

Max, meanwhile, pulled together four other people from the poker group, they in turn pulled together random children and an occasional wife. As word of the project leaked, co-workers, neighbors, and various idle adventurers joined the team.

About the only characteristic shared in common by the explorers was the complete absence of an ability to read any signs written in Japanese. Native Tokyoites, when asked to join the expedition, sagely pointed out that one could ride in relative comfort on trains around the circle line in an hour. Riding on bicycles could take all day. ("And that's why we built the circle line in the first place.")

Nevertheless, the hardy adventurers assembled at 7:00 AM one fine Sunday morning at Ebisu Station, one of the twenty-nine stops on the Yamanote Line. There were eleven businessmen—three of whom had not ridden a bicycle since their teens. There were also three schoolteachers, three housewives, and seven children ranging in age from eight to seventeen.

Equipment ranged from sleek eighteen-speed machines that looked like they could coast uphill all the way down to a fat, midget bicycle with which the poor eight-year-old was saddled. The physical condition of the troopers ranged from pretty close to perfect (the eight-year-old) down to typical middle-age spread brought about by exercise limited to climbing on and off bar stools.

The first dispute of the day occured at 7:01 AM. If the group proceeded clockwise from Ebisu Station, the hilliest section of the ride would come at the end of the day. Going counter-clockwise would mean getting the hills out of the way early, but then everyone would be tired for the remainder of the trip.

"We are nothing," Max suggested, "if not democratic." A vote was taken. Then another. And another. The 12–12 deadlock was finally broken by the eight-year-old exercising his first independence on matters that counted. The group headed for the hills. The Great Bicycle Race—a race against the sun—was on.

The initial stop of any significance, other than brief pauses to put chains back on sprockets and to figure out where the hell the overhead tracks had gone, occurred at Shimbashi. Located at the edge of Ginza, the area offered the first signs of civilization in the form of places to get a drink and go to the toilet. The previous two hours had been spent first in the hilly residential areas of Gotanda and Shinagawa and then in the flatlands and old landfill territory around Hamamatsucho. A whole lot of pedaling had gone on, but the group had only traveled about one-fourth of the circuit.

A celebration was in order, however. "Another round of beers," ordered the accountant, one of those who hadn't cycled since his teens. "We don't accomplish this sort of thing every day."

The tiny restaurant had probably never served a *gaijin* before, let alone twenty-four of them. The lady in charge of the establishment had to send a youngster around the corner to obtain more beverages—it is not every Sunday morning that there's a call for sixteen cokes, five orange drinks, and twenty-four beers. Particularly in a tea and cake shop.

"Well, we won't stop at every station," Max concluded as the group pulled itself together and prepared to leave, "but we may as well sample the local fare as we go along." And that, for better or worse, became the theme for the rest of the trip.

The adventurers had sashimi at the next stop, which was in Ueno—beyond the "downtown" business section and into the native "downtown" area of Tokyo. A little-league baseball team of nine-year-old boys, each wearing uniforms and all on bicycles, led the group through the tricky side streets between Nippori and Nishi Nippori. The overhead train tracks rarely ran parallel to major roads, and the maze of alleyways and paths through the old residential areas could easily have swallowed Max's group forever.

At Sugamo, which was considered to be the approximate midpoint in the journey, the lady in the fried eel shop not only plied the adventurers with more of her wares than most people see (or eat) in a lifetime, but also insisted that her husband lead the group on his motorbike to the next station. He knew, she reported, more shortcuts than anyone in the neighborhood. And indeed, traveling with them down a road the approximate width of a bicycle's handlebars, he proved that he did.

165

At Otsuka, the group had tea. It was 4:00 in the afternoon, and it was estimated that there was but a mere three hours to go before the return to the Ebisu starting point. Three hours, if enraptured by drama or passion, might seem to be remarkably short. Three hours, if pedaling through miles and miles (or kilometers and kilometers) of urban sprawl, could last a lifetime.

After another round of cokes, orange drinks, and beer, it was concluded that safety precautions—taken earlier to protect the children—were neither necessary nor advisable. The original concept had been that adults would lead *and* bring up the rear. The kids would be encapsuled by a battalion of maturity.

In fact, the adult stragglers at the rear were often so far behind that the kids would have to be sent back to look for them. Additionally, the eight-year-old, on his fat little bike, was particularly good at ferreting out proposed routes and determining if the street went through or was just another "goddam dead end." "Another goddam dead end," he'd report three out of four times. (It was later calculated that he covered twice as much ground as anyone else.)

The new order for the closing stretch involved two teens at the rear whipping encouragement into the breasts of one schoolteacher, two housewives, and the accountant. The other wife and two teachers pedaled in the middle, secure in the knowledge that over the hill or around the next bend there'd be yet another place with a restroom to be visited. Leading the pack were the men and the other kids—a key participant being the eight-year-old.

Leaving the simple structures of wood and concrete typical of the northern reaches of the city and entering the steel and glass of Shinjuku skyscrapers can be breathtaking. Not only is the four or five kilometer approach uphill, the pace and intensity of vehicular and pedestrian traffic increases spectacularly upon nearing the station. Gone were the bucolic neighborhoods and small shops and stores with helpful proprieters willing to provide directions for lost adventurers. Shinjuku, with crowds of two to three million people milling around in the streets on Sunday afternoons, is big-time stuff. Max and the group walked their bicycles through the hordes, and all agreed that *that* was the most difficult part of the trip.

The race with the sun was, at least figuratively, downhill after that. The last rest stop took place in Yoyogi—an area of town that was at least recognizable to most members of the group. One of the teachers and the accountant lived a few minutes from Yoyogi, but all agreed it would be a shame to drop out at this stage. Fueled by cokes, orange drinks, beer, and chicken on sticks, the adventurers pushed off for Ebisu.

Sunset officially occurred at 7:35 PM on this fine Sunday. There was no way of seeing it behind the neon lights of honky-tonks and restaurants in the Ebisu area, but the adventurers were acutely aware of it as they approached the station. The leaders reached the race's starting point at 7:31 and the stragglers made it within a minute or two of 7:35. Friends and relatives, assembled for the purpose of joining the victory celebration, cheered as each cyclist collapsed in the open area facing the station. Japanese travelers even paused in their scurrying to watch the spectacle of twenty-four *gaijin* lolling in exhaustion on the curb, against poles, and in the arms of loved ones. The race, such as it was, had finished. And everyone had won.

Some Observations

1. The red glow of saddle sores and associated chafing is, for some reason, not visible through shorts and trousers.

2. The number of rest stops during a journey of this sort bears a direct relationship to the number of beers consumed. One kid went to the toilet only twice all day. Max remembers at least eleven instances in his own case.

3. Eighteen-speed racing bicycles do not coast uphill.

4. Some housewives are in remarkably good shape; some schoolteachers are not. One teacher finished the race in tears.

5. Eight-year-old kids on fat little bicycles do not have the sense to appreciate how tired they must be. The one in Max's group wanted to ride his bicycle home from Ebisu.

6. Japanese people are much nicer in small groups and humble neighborhoods. Everyone there was warm and helpful. The sophisticated crowds in Shinjuku, meanwhile, are awful.

7. Sightseeing on a bicycle is impossible going uphill. Max only saw half of Tokyo—the downhill parts.

8. The sausage that people consume in the Mejiro area has the type of taste that lingers. The last four rest stops included in their purpose attempts to eradicate that taste.

9. Excuses given the following day at the office can be surprisingly creative. Max phoned the other ten businessmen, and of the eight who were not at work that day, the excuses ranged from "working on a special project at home" to "he's had a flare-up of an old athletic injury" to "he caught something that has temporarily paralyzed him."

10. Doing it once, as they say about climbing Mt. Fuji, is a truly exciting activity. But only a raving lunatic would even *consider* leading a disparate group of folks around the center of the world's largest city on bicycles *twice*.

Max is prepared to clobber the next person to raise the subject at poker.

Chicken Inouye

CHICKEN INOUYE weighed 100 pounds soaking wet. Of that amount, at least 20 pounds were brains. His principal occupation was walking around in the wake of Max and other company big shots explaining, repairing, correcting, and adjusting the pronouncements of his leaders.

Inouye-san did not pick up his nickname because of a lack of moral or physical fortitude. He was as tough an hombre as ever trod the corridors of corporate power.

He became Chicken Inouye in his school days because, despite a powerful and analytical mind, he concluded that life for him would be simpler if he could settle on one item of agreeable food—and stick to it. The feathery fowl won his approval, and for over twenty years Inouye rarely put anything into his mouth unless it was, or came from, a chicken. Some people are like that.

Max first observed Inouye's mental wizardry during a meeting he and Serious Hirose had with visiting clients from Germany. Inouye was one of the troopers brought to the meeting to fill the chairs at the end of the table, and to nod in agreement whenever his side made a point. (Support personnel at big meetings in Japan fill an important role. And *they* are the ones who end up doing the work.)

The meeting was conducted in English—a tongue with which only Max was comfortable as a medium of communication. Pronouncements would be made, and then there'd be long periods of translation so that the staff of both sides would be apprised of the thrust of the arguments. The German/Japanese translations took the longest.

Chicken Inouye sat calmly at his end of the table suggesting, during the periods of translation, points that Max may wish to confirm (or nail down) in the discussion with the clients. Max did, and the meeting, from his perspective, went very well.

Afterwards, during the inevitable review in the office, Inouye announced that he had known all along what strategies the clients were employing.

"My German," he said, "is not as good as my French or Spanish, but it's better than my Korean." Chicken Inouye made several tens of millions of yen for the company that day.

On another occasion, Inouye was dragged from his charts and graphs and brought to a meeting involving a long-term investment scheme presented by a Japanese securities firm. While everyone else wrote down numbers and played with their pocket calculators, Chicken Inouye gazed at the ceiling. For all anyone knew he was visualizing a barnyard of plump and defenseless hens.

"It's no good," he told Serious Hirose later. "There is an error in their assumptions and the mathematics won't work." When this was confirmed after one solid hour of arithmetic, Chicken Inouye was taken by the staff to a *yakitori* establishment near Tokyo Station. He drank two beers and ate sixteen wings—a record even for him.

Chicken Inouye was a bachelor. One could imagine him being born a bachelor, going through his middle life as a bachelor, and finally meeting his Maker as a bachelor.

Inouye did bachelor things. He would now and then show up at the office at 5:00 in the morning because he "happened to wake up early." He'd sometimes stay in the office for two days and nights in a row working on a project, then disappear for a day or two. He once mistakenly went to the office on Sunday. ("I *thought* traffic was unusually light," he remarked later.)

Girls in the office were called upon, by the other guys, to keep Inouye's clothing in order. He would wear things until they fell apart if it weren't for someone paying attention to his wardrobe. He once showed up wearing two different types of shoes. "But they're the same color," he stated when this was pointed out to him.

It is difficult to determine who was more astonished—the people in the office, or Chicken Inouye himself—when his engagement to be married was announced. Amano-san, one of the sweetest girls in creation, and Inouye's clerk for many years, was the lucky bride-to-be.

Once the news was out it became immediately obvious that the match was made in heaven. Who but Amano-san would understand Inouye's little oddities and pecularities? He had called her "Miss Amamiya" for the first three years she worked for him. And she had sewn, by her own count, 450 buttons on his clothing over the course of a decade.

The wedding ceremony and reception was small, dignified, and without high-school teachers or grade-school classmates. A marriage at age forty need not have the whiz-bangery of a wedding at twenty-eight.

Max learned of the little stunt planned by co-workers at the buffet dinner after the ceremony. The stunt, in Max's opinion, was not in keeping with the mature and civilized nature of the occasion—at least to an individual as mature and civilized as Max. (Come to think of it, it was Inouye who talked Max into buying and wearing the chicken costume in Yokohama.)

Nevertheless, the stunt was too far along in organization

to do anything about it. Quite simply, Inouye's buddies in the office had arranged for a crate of live chickens to be delivered to the honeymoon suite at the Fujiyama Hotel in Atami. The delivery was to be made at midnight, and there were to be no less than six chickens in the crate. All before-and-after expenses were to be borne by the buddies, but a bill for the chickens was contrived to be delivered to the happy couple in the morning. What cut ups, Max's staff.

The new Mrs. Inouye was actually the first person to return to the office after the honeymoon. She had already retired from the company, so her visit was unofficial. There was another day to go in Inouye's vacation.

Mrs. Inouye was in the office to pick up her new husband's underwear. It seems that Chicken Inouye had developed the habit over the bachelor years of having his laundry done somewhere between his apartment and the office. It had been as convenient for him to change things in the office as it was at home, so the bottom right drawer of his desk contained clean underwear, the bottom left drawer had the dirty stuff.

The girls and Mrs. Inouye chatted and giggled and talked about the new marriage. It seems that Inouye had lectured the hotel proprietor on efficiencies in management, and had convinced the poor man to cut prices in half on weekdays and double them on weekends.

The buddies hovered in the background, waiting for word on the crate of chickens.

"Oh, that," said the new Mrs. Inouye, when the discussion turned that way. "I really wish you hadn't done that."

Apparently, the chickens had been delivered at the scheduled time, there were eight in two crates, and their arrival had been both disruptive and amusing. Inouye had studied them for awhile, and then around 1:30 AM had let them loose in the hills behind the hotel.

172

"You cannot imagine how expensive this is going to be for us," said Mrs. Inouye.

It seems that Chicken Inouye had concluded that chickens were dirty. He had never had the chance to observe them up close before, but now his mind was made up.

"From that night on, explained Mrs. Inouye, one of the sweetest girls in creation, "he only eats sashimi."

Sayonara, Part I

IT HAD TO happen sooner or later. And with a jarring and sobering suddeness, it did.

"We are creating a new position in the Head Office," Max's boss explained during the 3:00 AM (Tokyo time) phone call, "and it's right up your alley."

"But . . . "

"I knew you'd be pleased," continued the boss. "We've decided to liaise on an organized basis with our Japanese clients in the States."

"But . . . "

"Don't thank me," said the boss. "A lot of other people were involved in the decision too."

"But . . . "

"I know you probably have a lot of questions about the transfer, but they can wait. I just wanted you to hear the good news from me," the boss explained.

"But . . . "

"And by the way," added the boss, "you'll be working for the Senior Vice President of the Major Accounts Division."

"But . . ."

"You'll like him. His name is Moriarty."

And with that, the die was cast.

The reaction in the Danger family tended to polarize rather than unite the individual members. The eldest offspring, Max III, stated simply that he was remaining in Japan.

"I only have three-and-a-half years of high school left," he declared, "and I'll support myself delivering Mr. Guido's Pizza."

The youngest child, who rarely noticed where he was anyway, was prepared to leave Japan the next day. To him, going to the States was Home Leave—hotels and Disneyland.

Mona, Max's level-headed middle child, had perhaps the most balanced approach.

"I'll go back with you if you insist," she conceded, "but I'm returning to Japan when I'm old enough." Mona, at nine, nearly was.

Max and the beautiful Gloria found themselves swinging back and forth on the issue. Unfortunately, their moods did not at first coincide. While Max was speculating on his new career opportunities, Gloria was visualizing the transportation service she'd be running with the kids in a station wagon, and the breathtaking excitement of watching weeds grow in the flower garden.

When Max began talking about putting his Japan expertise to work with another employer in Tokyo. Gloria was in the it'll-be-a-bloody-damn-relief-to-speak-to-shopkeepers/-repairmen/-folks-on-the-street/-and-random-strangers-in-complete-sentences stage.

It was a few weeks before they both got around to agreeing, concurrently, on the general concept of going home to refresh perspectives while holding open the option of returning to Japan sometime in the future. It was a sensible conclusion, but one reached by a linear logic that Japan had taught is not the exclusive form. Be that as it may, the Dangers were about to become history.

"We'll have to make a trip to Korea," Gloria announced one morning at breakfast. "It may be our last chance to buy Japanese antiques."

Most expat families acquire a considerable amount of furniture and knick-knacks in the Orient—*tansu* chests, Imari bowls, and hibachi grills tend to head the list.

In the four decades since the war, a great number of expats have come and gone, and *tansu* chests, Imari bowls, and hibachi grills have gone with them. There are more of these things now in Greenwich, Connecticut, St. Louis, Missouri, and London than there ever were in Japan.

For twenty years there has been a flourishing business in Korea keeping up with the demand—a cottage industry of carpenters who tear down old sheds and barns, "distress" the wood even further, build chests and charcoal grills, then arrange the sale of these "antiques" to people returning someday to New Jersey. And in New Jersey, who cares (or knows) how genuine the article may be.

"And we'll have to schedule a sayonara party for our friends," added Gloria, "to use up all the booze."

The Dangers had accumulated, during the Japan assignment, more bottles of liqueurs, whiskey, wine, and spirits than most liquor shops carry in inventory. Well-meaning (and well-received) gifts from overseas visitors, returning Japanese, and party-goers on the circuit had swollen the Homat Cornucopia pantry to the point where Campbell's soup cans, spaghetti packages, and Ritz Cracker boxes were now being stored in Max's clothes closet. One should never throw out half-consumed bottles of brandy—even if there are thirteen of them.

175

"But before we do all that," said Max, "I'll be very busy, night and day, introducing my replacement throughout the company and to all our clients."

The very idea made Max shudder. Granted, it had only been a few years ago that someone had taken Max around. He had been introduced throughout the company and to all the clients. What made him shudder was not the work involved in the project—in fact, it would be a pleasure to visit old friends and accept congratulations on a promotion—but it would also mean reliving certain scenes which in retrospect were embarrassingly vivid examples of naiveté in action.

When introduced to a prospective client, Max had lectured him on how much more influential his company and its connections would be than the source presently used by the client—an outfit called Mitsubishi Heavy Industries.

On another occasion during the introductory rounds, Max described his company's banking relationships and presented the idea that Crocker Bank offered an international stability and permanence which the Bank of Tokyo could never achieve. (In the same vein, Max had, at the beginning, directed his General Affairs Department to switch the company insurance program from a fly-by-night carrier named Yasuda Fire and Marine to a substantial international insurer called American International Assurance. AIA no longer exists in Japan.)

But more to the core of the matter, Max dreaded the private confrontations with his own staff regarding their initial impressions of his replacement. The Japanese have a burning desire to categorize people. ("Hiromi Katayami, age 47, housewife, Toyama," say the letters to the editors.)

If Max had been asked once, he had been asked a thousand times if he were "a typical American." He would always answer in the affirmative, brushing from his mind the millions of blacks, Euro-Americans, New World Hispanic-Americans, American Indians, Middle and Far Eastern-Americans, Illegal-Americans, and the twenty-seven Americans from Madagascar who make up the fabric of the U.S. of A. To a nation of folks who still refer to the great grandchildren of people who emigrated from Inchon to Osaka as "Koreans," pinning down "typical" is crucial.

Max's replacement was an American whose parents came from Havana. The man's grandfather escaped from Lithuania and went to Cuba, where he married a black woman. A graduate of the Harvard B. School, the replacement's name was Eduardo Misevich. His previous assignment had been in Denmark. Try quantifying the wind to be sucked over that.

"Of the five moves we've made in the past," Max told Gloria in bed late one night, "and of all the hassles we've experienced in adjusting to Japan," he continued, "I am really going to miss this place."

Gloria turned from her back to her stomach, and said nothing for almost a minute. An Azabu Fire Department siren wailed in the distance—probably another cat in a tree or a harmlessly drunk salaryman sprawled on the sidewalk.

"I'm coming back," said the beautiful Gloria. "I'm not finished here yet."

Sayonara, Part II

THE FINAL PARTY took place on the last night in a bare Homat Cornucopia apartment—an open house in an empty house. The movers had packed and gone, the Dangers were packed and going.

About a hundred friends and acquaintances had dropped in over the course of a rainy Saturday evening and the atmosphere was relaxed and informal, though tinged with a touch of melancholy. Relationships that are perhaps more intense and interdependent than they would be under different circumstances are nevertheless difficult to sever. And it is an unfortunate fact of expat life that in most cases the severance is permanent.

The smaller group hanging on at the end exchanged stories and joked with the Dangers about adventures they had shared and problems they had endured. Delivering a baby on Mt. Fuji, the contrived parties for visiting firemen, the mindless antics on employee outings, getting lost, and countless errors in communication were all reviewed.

Max nearly died in Japan; his best friend did. The beautiful Gloria had never been as active as she was in Tokyo. The youngest Danger started school in Japan, the eldest got his first part-time job. And Mona had fallen in love with Prince Hiro. The family had grown in all but the numerical sense.

"Here are the last of the new address cards," said Max. "If you're ever in Reichenbach Falls, look us up."

"If I'm ever in Reichenbach Falls," replied Max's upstairs neighbor, the Wag, "it's because I'm lost."

"We'll be there next week," contributed the downstairs neighbor, who seldom joked.

It was a good evening.

The Dangers arrived at the airport early the next day. Max's senior employees and closest co-workers had arranged a private "hospitality" room, and it was there the final speeches were made and gifts exchanged.

The girls in the office presented Gloria with a bouquet of

178

flowers and supplied the children with cookies and candies for the trip. Serious Hirose, memorializing the Western-toilet-at-floor-level-in-the-ski-house-at-Hakuba affair, presented Max with a no-nonsense "plumber's helper" which would have to go on the plane as carry-on luggage. No one, until the very end, mentioned the chicken-costume caper.

After the final handshakes and hugs, the Dangers and Max's business colleagues and allies began the shambling stroll out the room and down to the departure area. It was the time for final private words and confidences—the time to express special feelings of appreciation.

They really were a good group of people. Despite language difficulties and cultural differences, Max had never been so close to co-workers as he was to his Japanese company staff. He had sure spent a lot of time with them, in and out of the office, and he would miss their collective stability and support.

It was Akimbo-san, Max's secretary, who heard it first. The group was milling about outside the customs control area saying the final sayonaras. Not a few tears were being shed.

"Red courtesy phone you have to go," said Akimbo-san in her special syntax. "The announcement voice is calling you."

The group waited with the Dangers while Max went to the phone. He was gone quite a while. There began to be concern about the timing of things—the Danger flight was approaching the "last call" stage. As Gloria was toying with the idea of taking the family to the gate, Max's head appeared in the distance bobbing above the sea of black surrounding him. He had the stunned look of one who had just witnessed a terrifying cataclysm.

"Who was it?" asked Gloria, as Max came with in earshot.

"Moriarty, my new boss," answered Max, shaking his head in shock and disbelief.

"What's the matter, Daddy?" asked Mona, a youngster particularly sensitive to the currents of emotion and mood. "Are you okay?"

"I can't believe it," said Max," still shaking his head. "I can't believe it."

"Believe what?" asked Gloria.

"Well, you won't believe it," said Max as he regained his composure, "but listen to this."

And it *did* take a long time before anyone else believed it.